*Family Therapy
of Drug and
Alcohol Abuse*

SECOND EDITION

Family Therapy of Drug and Alcohol Abuse

EDWARD KAUFMAN, M.D.
University of California, Irvine

PAULINE KAUFMANN, L.C.S.W.
Phoenix House, New York City

ALLYN AND BACON
Boston London Toronto Sydney Tokyo Singapore

Executive Editor: Susan Badger
Senior Editorial Assistant: Dana Lamothe
Cover Administrator: Pat Torelli
Composition Buyer: Superscript Associates
Manufacturing Buyer: Megan Cochran
Production Coordinator: Superscript Associates
Editorial-Production Service: TKM Productions
Cover Design: Mike Fender

Copyright © 1992, 1979 by Allyn and Bacon
A Division of Simon & Schuster, Inc.
160 Gould Street
Needham Heights, Massachusetts 02194

Library of Congress Cataloging-in-Publication Data

Family therapy of drug and alcohol abuse / [edited by] Edward Kaufman,
Pauline Kaufmann. — 2nd ed.
     p.   cm.
    Includes bibliographical references and index.
    ISBN 0-205-13430-0
    1. Drug abuse—Treatment. 2. Alcoholism—Treatment. 3. Family
psychotherapy. I. Kaufman, Edward. II. Kaufmann, Pauline.
    [DNLM: 1. Alcoholism—therapy. 2. Family Therapy. 3. Substance
Abuse—therapy. WM 270 F198]
RC564.F36 1992
616.86'0651—dc20
DNLM/DLC
for Library of Congress   91-33192
                                                    CIP

Printed in the United States of America

10 9 8 7 6 5 4 3 2 1   96 95 94 93 92 91

*To the families we came from
and the new families we are creating.*

Contents

Preface

The Family Therapy of Drug and Alcohol Abuse had its roots in the mid-1970s. The book was conceptualized at a time when family therapy was fighting for a place in substance-abuse treatment. Shortly after it was published, family therapy became established as an essential aspect of substance-abuse treatment. This overall acceptance of the importance of the family in chemical dependency helped to make "Kaufman and Kaufmann," as it grew to be called, a very successful handbook for professionals and paraprofessionals in the field. Some 15 years later, it is certainly time for an update of this seminal volume; hence, we introduce this second edition.

This book is about families—families of origin and nuclear families, second-chance families, and therapeutic families. The coeditors, in the process of their work with families and colleagues, have become deeply and closely related. The families we have worked in and with have taught us the pain and love of intimacy, the longing for and fulfillment of closeness, as well as the need for individuation and distance.

Our work in therapeutic communities has shown us the need in families for rational authority, competence, and mutual respect based on performance, not assigned titles or academic degrees. Much of what we have learned we owe to our nonacademic colleagues, whose rich albeit painful experiences have become integrated and "professionalized," as they have worked in the therapeutic communities.

In the solution of common treatment problems, distance marked by academic titles has disappeared. Therapeutic treatment families have developed and continued to monitor themselves as they worked and grew. We have been part of this experience, and we invite you to share this with us.

At the time of this book's inception, we were aware that families were being excluded from treatment for two major reasons: the lack of knowledge of workable family therapy techniques and the therapist's own unresolved anger toward his or her own family of origin. Presently, there are several workable systems of family therapy for substance abusers, which will be presented in this book, as well as more willingness on the part of therapists to examine their own family issues.

With growing availability of drugs and billions of dollars involved in the legal and illegal marketing of drugs, more and more young people coming from every level of society have become involved with drugs. Currently, almost every adolescent who requires residential care is problematically involved with the abuse of drugs and/or alcohol.

Similarly, adult heroin addicts did not commit violent crimes in the early 1950s. They were schooled in such nonviolent activities as shoplifting, con games, and pickpocketing, and used these skills to earn the money for their drugs. The available heroin at that time was sufficient to absorb their aggressive energies. Presently, heroin addicts are much more violent and therefore are, more likely to be apprehended and institutionalized. When they are in institutions, their families become more available for treatment. Optimally, this treatment should take place in community-based residential settings rather than correctional institutions.

Treating the family of a substance abuser is a complicated process. Treatment takes place simultaneously on many levels. In meeting the needs of the family as an entity, the spouse subsystem, the sibling subsystem, and the individual needs of each person in the family must be considered. These three areas must interlock and work in harmony. Teaching and demonstrating effective parenting is an important aspect of treatment. Encouraging families to form positive social networks aids in the total treatment. Part of family therapy is the problem-solving process that occurs. Hopefully, these techniques become internalized so that the family maintains them throughout its lifetime. Although family therapy and change in family structure is not a societal panacea, it can help family members to have a rich life and have a positive impact on their offspring as well as the communities of which they are a part.

In order to ensure effectiveness of the family in the community, the therapist may have to enter the community network as a facilitator. He or she may have to involve vocational guidance or educational specialists, intervene with the school or employer directly, or deal with other members in the individual's extended network. In some cases, a new network may be provided through multiple family therapy. In other words, we do not believe that we can solve all problems through family therapy. In many cases, family therapy alone is not enough; in some cases it is a valuable or essential adjunct to other modalities. However, the wider therapy ranges into an individual's network in an adaptive way, the more likely the treatment will succeed.

In the original volume, most of the chapters on drug abusers dealt with families of origin and most of the chapters on alcoholics dealt with nuclear families. The major reason for this is that alcoholics tend to be older than drug abusers. However, these differentiations have become more and more blurred of late, as alcoholics and drug abusers have become progressively similar in every way, including age. Certainly, in our work with the families of younger alcoholics (and many of these individuals abuse other drugs as well), we have seen no differences between their families and the families of drug abusers.

We will not comment or explain why certain chapters from the first volume are not repeated in this second edition. Generally, dated chapters were excluded so that newer family issues and techniques could be included.

Chapter One is the only chapter in this book that is not specifically directed toward substance abusers. We have included it because Salvador Minuchin's way of looking at a family and his therapeutic techniques remain a cornerstone of successful therapy with drug abusers. Our selection of contributing authors have worked as family therapists for many years with substance abusers and provide a variety of approaches. We asked them to utilize a format that clearly states what the family patterns are and/or what to do to change them. We emphasized that the authors present the specifics of how to use their therapeutic modality in such a way as to be available to the reader for testing and incorporating to his or her own treatment system.

As we enter the 1990s, the newest system of family therapy are *integrated* and thus borrow from several techniques, melding them into a workable multimodel system. Interestingly, this integration was predicted in our first edition. To this end, two chapters have been added, Chapter Eight by Harvey Joanning and Chapter Ten by Howard A. Little, Gayle A. Dakof, and Guy Diamond. They espouse different by new integration of modalities. Both of these approaches evolved from five-year family therapy treatment grants awarded by the National Institute on Drug Abuse (NIDA). Behavioral treatment, a vital aspect of most integrated approaches, is well described by Barbara S. McCrady in Chapter Twelve.

Our recently acquired body of knowledge on stepfamilies necessitated a chapter (Chapter Eleven) by Judith Zucker Anderson since so many substance-abusing families have unresolved stepfamily issues. Although most chapters address the issue of combined drug and alcohol abuse, several chapters deal exclusively with alcoholics or drug abusers. Chapter Fifteen, by Marion L. Usher, not only deals with alcoholics but emphasizes a pscyhoeducational approach that is so helpful, particularly in the first months of therapy, with these families.

The past decades have been marked by the growth of the 12-step movement beyond alcoholics and their spouses. This growth has been spearheaded by Cocaine Anonymous and Adult Children of Alcoholics 12-step groups. In Chapter Thirteen, Timmen L. Cermak, a leader in the latter field, provides us with a therapeutic framework for dealing with adult children of alcoholics in any setting—individual, group, or family.

This second edition of *Family Therapy of Drug and Alcohol Abuse* contains even more valuable therapeutic methods than the first. Still, these techniques cannot easily be mastered from a book, particularly without a great deal of practice. We expect the reader will evaluate them and try out those that seem to fit. Obviously, in some cases, consultation and evaluation will be helpful or necessary before techniques can be used successfully. We welcome you as a reader of these chapters and hope that you can learn as much from reading them as we have from writing them. It is our hope that "Kaufman and Kaufmann II" will be read by a new generation of family therapists as well as reread by those whose careers "Kaufman and Kaufmann I" helped to shape.

Acknowledgment

We wish to express our appreciation to Laura Lowe for coordinating the details necessary to get this book published.

List of Contributors

Judith Zucker Anderson
Department of Psychiatry and
  Human Behavior
University of California, Irvine
15615 Alton Parkway, Suite 220
Irvine, CA 92668

David Berenson
215 Main Street, Apt. 207
Sausalito, CA

David W. and Judith S. Brook
New York Medical College
Department of Psychiatry and
  Behavioral Science
Valhalla, NY 10595

Timmen L. Cermak
Genesis
1325 Columbus Avenue
San Francisco, CA 94133

Gayle A. Dakof
Department of Counseling
  Psychology
Temple University
249 Weiss Hall
Philadelphia, PA 19122

Guy Diamond
Philadelphia Child Guidance Center
34th and Civic Center Blvd.
Philadelphia, PA 19104

Debby G.

Harvey Joanning
Department of Family
  Environment
Iowa State University
Ames, Iowa 50011

Edward Kaufman, M.D.
Department of Psychiatry and
  Human Behavior
University of California Medical
  Center
101 City Drive, South
Building 53, Route 81
Orange, CA 92668

Pauline Kaufmann
Director of Family Therapy
  Phoenix House
100 West 78th Street
New York, NY 10024

Howard A. Liddle
Temple University
249 Weiss Hall
Philadelphia, PA 19122

Barbara S. McCrady
Center for Alcohol Studies
Smithers Hall
Piscataway, NJ 08855

Salvador Minuchin, M.D.
Family Studies, Inc.
P.O. Box 1035, Cooper Station
New York, NY 10276

Dennis M. Reilly
Southeast Nassau Guidance Center
3375 Park Avenue
Wantagh, Long Island, NY 11738

Alvin A. Rosenfeld
Jewish Child Care Association
575 Lexington Avenue
New York, NY 10022

M. Duncan Stanton
Department of Psychiatry
University of Rochester
300 Crittendon Blvd.
Rochester, NY 14642

Thomas C. Todd
Forest Hospital
555 Wilson Lane
Des Plaines, IL 60016

Marion L. Usher
2021 Hillyer Place, NW
Washington, D.C. 20009

CHAPTER ONE

Constructing a Therapeutic Reality

SALVADOR MINUCHIN, M.D.
Director, Family Studies, Inc., New York

Psychotherapy has been handicapped by the nineteenth-century concept of man as a hero. Individual psychotherapy emphasizes psychological constructs inside the individual and elaborates contrapuntal relationships between the individual and his or her context. This concept of the patient as a carrier of his or her psyche surrounded by the boundary of skin required in complimentation the figure of therapist as objective observer. The relationship between the therapist and the patient is organized according to rules that maintain both the therapist and the patient in parallel orbits while developing in fantasy transferential intimacy.

Pathology inside the patient is related to fixation or dysfunctional learning at some point in early life. In all therapies there is the assumption that it is essential to correct the early dysfunctional learning in order to produce growth and change.

This has created an orientation in therapy that involves the search for psychopathological dynamics. We have created a generation of sleuths who are looking for psychodynamic clues to an emotional crime. A generation of psychopathologists has been schooled in the search for the weakness in people's experience. This group of experts is objective, benevolent, and optimistic. They understand that they are only explorers of subterraneous rivers that exist, that they are not adding to or subtracting from life; therefore, they are not responsible for change, only for discovery.

Family therapy operates on the theoretical assumption that man is part of his context and that individual changes require a change in the reciprocal relationship of man in his context. Family therapy searches for pathology in the loop between the individual and his or her social network.

The therapist joins the family in the therapeutic system and becomes part of the circumstances of the family members; as such, the therapist intervenes, modifying the family members' experience and organizing and constructing their own reality.

This concept is troublesome because it means that a family's reality in therapy is a therapeutic construct. We have detoured comfortably around it in theoretical analysis of therapy by adhering to the concept of insight, so a therapist's task can be seen as merely exploration of the truth. The concept of therapeutic reality puts a heavy responsibility on therapists. They must recognize that their input organizes the field of intervention and changes the family's reality and their own. The freedom of a therapist as a constructor of reality is limited by the finite reality of family structures, in general, and by the idiosyncratic way in which they are manifested in the patient's family.

With this conceptualization of therapy, it is essential to make explicit our map of normal family functioning as well as our ideas of therapeutic change.

Concepts of the Family

The Matrix of Identity

Family therapy is a product of the twentieth-century philosophies that approach human beings as members of social groups that govern their behavior. This is a departure from the body of thought that has handicapped individual dynamic therapy by putting the whole of the individual's life inside him or her, as though humans remained constant in spite of their circumstances. In fact, family therapy has gone too close to the opposite pole, sometimes approaching the human being as a mere respondent to field pressures.

Effective therapeutic techniques depend on a broad view of the human experience. Although it is certainly correct to locate people's behavior in the feedback loops of social group processes, it is also important to recognize that the individual has a range of responses to these processes. Within the family transactions, each family member has a number of choices. The wider the range of choice, the greater his or her experience of freedom within the system. This experience of freedom, or autonomy, is essential for the individual. Equally important is a sense of belonging — of coming from a certain reference group. Indeed, the individual's sense of well-being depends on the proportioning of these two ingredients. Dependency and autonomy are complementary, not conflicting, characteristics of the human condition. Their proportioning is negotiated in the development of the system and crystallized by the current social context.

Families mold and program a child's sense of identity early in the socialization process. The sense of belonging comes with the child's accommodation to the groups within the family and his or her assumption of the transactional patterns that form the family structure. The sense of autonomy occurs through participation in different family subsystems in different contexts, as well as through participation in extrafamilial groups. A psychological and transactional territory is carved out for each person, determined by the contrapuntal relationships of individual and system.

The family, then, is the matrix of its members' sense of identity of belonging and of being different. Its chief task is to foster their psychosocial growth and well-being throughout their life in common. This is the first element of a therapist's schema of a family.

The family also forms the smallest social unit that transmits a society's demands and values, thus preserving them. Therefore, the family therapist must see the family as the link between the individual and larger social units. The family must adapt to society's needs as it fosters its members' growth, all the while maintaining enough continuity to fulfill its function as the individual's reference group.

The Family as a System

The family therapist must also recognize that the human family is a social system that operates through transactional patterns. These are repeated interactions that establish patterns of how, when, and to whom to relate. When a mother tells her child to drink his juice and he obeys, this interaction defines who they are in relation to one another in that context and at that time. Repeated operations build patterns, and these patterns underpin the family system. The patterns that evolve become familiar and preferred. The system maintains itself within a preferred range, and deviations that pass the system's threshold of tolerance usually elicit counter-deviation mechanisms, which reestablish the accustomed range.

The System Develops Over Time

In the early development within the family context, a child develops certain parts of his or her biopsychological potential, and this is what the child becomes familiar with as being himself or herself. In the measure in which the child encounters other social groups and develops in another context new areas of competence and interpersonal skill, certain aspects of the child's personality are activated in his or her complementary relationship with significant people. The potential of the individual is developed and restricted at the same time as certain types of transactions become more available and familiar. These responses tend to be identified as *self,* while other aspects of self remain potentially available, and some hardly available because of disuse.

A reciprocal interplay develops by which the individual determines the range of his or her responses. Certain aspects of personality are confirmed more frequently by significant people as self, and that reinforces the continuous use of certain alternative behavior and modalities of being.

When people marry, they must develop a number of common transactional patterns. Each spouse has his or her own behavior patterns and value system, including expectations of how people should and will relate to him or her. These patterns clash and mesh in the small events of daily life, and each spouse changes in accommodation to the other.

Areas of autonomy and complementarity are defined. The range of choices narrows, and after some period of life together, the range is reduced to the preferred patterns. The spouses become predictable to each other. In areas of narrowed experiential range, the spouses develop implicit or explicit contracts, with value overtones. Even dysfunctional patterns can become preferred, and the couple will maintain them as long as possible. If the patterns are violated, each spouse may feel betrayed, though neither may remember the origin of the pattern.

But family circumstances change through time, and the family must be able to change. Other transactional patterns are activated, and new structures develop in a balanced process of morphostasis and morphogenesis. Alternative transactional patterns always exist within a system, though these are hidden from the observer by the dominant preferred patterns. But when change becomes necessary, the functional family activates the alternative patterns of the system.

The Differentiation of the System

Family systems are differentiated; they carry out tasks through subsystems. Individuals are subsystems within a family, as are dyads such as husband and wife, and larger subgroupings formed by generation, gender, or task. People accommodate kaleidoscopically in different subsystems to achieve the mutuality necessary for human intercourse. A child has to act like a son so his father can act like a father, but he may take on executive powers when he is alone with his younger brother.

The rules defining who participates within a subsystem, and how, are the subsystem boundaries. The functioning of these boundaries is an important key to the system's viability. They must be defined well enough to allow the subsystem members to carry out their functions, but they must not isolate the subsystem from the rest of the system.

The nuclear family has at least three subsystems: spousal, parental, and sibling. These subsystems are units with differentiated functions. They offer and demand the exercise of specific social skills in different contexts. For example, in the parental or executive subsystem, parents and children negotiate decisions from positions of unequal power. In the sibling subsystem, children interact more as peers, negotiating issues of competition, defeat, accommodation, cooperation, and protection. The spousal subsystem is an arena of complementarity, of learning how to give without feeling that one has given up.

Each subsystem must keep negotiating boundaries that protect it from interference so it can fulfill its functions and resolve its problems. But the boundaries' selective permeability does not preclude the possibility of summoning other family members to resolve specific subsystem problems.

The family is a differentiated social unit structured by transactional patterns. In some areas, the system is quite flexible, offering a broad range of choices. In other areas, preferred patterns are tightly maintained. Alternative patterns exist but are not used. The family is constantly subjected to demands for change, sparked by developmental changes in its own members and by extrafamilial pressures. Responding to these demands from within and without requires transformation. The positions of family members toward each other and the external world change, as they must. But the system must also maintain the continuity to protect its members' sense of belonging.

Stresses are inherent. All families are subject to crises when a member enters a new developmental stage, a new member joins, a former member leaves, when the family is making contact with social institutions, and so on. In general, families respond to these periods of existential crisis by marshalling their resources. If necessary, alternative transactional patterns are mobilized and new ways of responding to changes in circumstance are evolved.

Family Pathology

Sometimes families respond to demands for change by increasing the rigidity of their preferred transactional patterns. The range of choices narrows, and family members develop stereotyped responses to each other and to the extrafamilial environment. The family becomes a closed system, and family members experience themselves as controlled and impotent. At this point, a family comes to therapy. The stereotyping process often leads to labeling one family member the deviant. Or the family may enter therapy because of "lack of communication" or "inability to cope."

Difficulties in a family are not an indicator for therapeutic restructuring. The difficulties of performing a family's tasks in modern society are real and intense, and stress in a family system is anything but abnormal. Family therapists may minimize the real problems inherent in the processes of adapting while maintaining continuity, just as individual dynamic thera-pists have minimized the difficulties in the individual's social context. A family in transition should not be labeled pathological. That label should be reserved for families who increase the rigidity of their transactional patterns in the face of stress, avoiding or resisting any exploration of alternatives.

> A couple in therapy began to contemplate divorce seriously when the hus-band's union was engaged in a bitter strike. The husband's position was, "You refuse to take my needs into consideration. You have always exploited me because of my sense of responsibility and duty. I will not give in to you any longer. I have begun to realize that I have rights, and my dignity as a human being is paramount." The wife's position was, "You are selfish. You have stopped considering the family's needs and are only concerned with your own. You are so wrapped up in yourself that you don't see me. If you want to leave, you can go now instead of asking me to do things for you like a typical male chauvinist." The therapist read the decision to consider divorce as the effect of massive intrusion from an extrafamilial context into a spousal conflict, result-ing in increased stereotyping. He strongly advised them not to come to any decisions until the strike was over, and he pointed out to the couple how much the husband's position resembled his union's stance in the strike negotiations, and how much the wife sounded like the management. Two weeks after the settlement of the strike the couple wanted to stay together and work on the problems of the family.

The Family in Therapy

The family therapist's definition of a pathogenic family, then, is a family whose adaptive and coping mechanisms have been exhausted. Family mem-bers are chronically trapped in stereotyped patterns of interaction that are severely limiting their range of choices, but no alternatives seem possible. In this time of heightened rigidity of transactional patterns, conflict over-shadows large areas of normal functioning. Often one family member is the identified patient, and the other family members see themselves as accom-modating his or her illness. The family has gone through a reification process that gives priority to dysfunctional areas.

It is not essential to explore the development of these dysfunctional patterns in most cases. The family's history is manifest in the present, and change can only be achieved in the present. It is possible to explore any family member's past or open up alternative modalities of being with the family of origin, but it is not necessary. The exploration of the "hows" of our previous relationships can be significant in understanding how we became what we are, but it is usually not necessary for changing the present family context. The therapeutic process will be that of changing family members' psychosocial positions vis-à-vis each other. The therapist may or may not try to help his patients understand their narrowed reality. But he will always address himself to the actualization of possible change. The therapist may tell a family member that he or she is dependent, angry, or depressed. But she will know that this focus can reinforce the already crystallized interactions. The therapist may or may not explore the family members' feelings, but he will always explore the system of complementarity that elicits those feelings. This approach emphasizes the transactional nature of experience and simultaneously suggests the possibilities of change.

Of course, any description of therapeutic technique presupposes that the therapist has begun to join the family in such a way that family members trust the therapist, even if they do not agree with him or her. The therapist must know how to affiliate with the family and support it through the sense of dislocation its members will experience as change develops.

Challenging the Patients' Reality

The first step in the process of change is a challenge to family members' self-perception and experience of reality. Challenging reality is a prerequisite for change common to all therapeutic processes. In psychoanalysis, the analyst challenges the patient's experience of reality on the basis of an expanded self. The patient is taught that the psychological life is larger than the conscious experience, and learns to free-associate in order to block the usual screening processes with which he or she organizes reality. The analyst organizes the data the patient presents according to psychoanalytic constructions.

In family therapy, the challenge is based on the axiom that family members have alternative ways of transacting. The family therapist does not challenge patients, only their patterns of interaction. What we call "reality" is the reality of the most preferred or available experiences. The purpose of therapy is to activate certain aspects of the individual and the system that render available new modalities of transaction. For example, in a family where the husband was overly central, the therapist paid special attention to the wife's feeble efforts to communicate, conveying the impression that her inputs were more meaningful than her husband's. In a family whose identified patient was a college dropout who had been diagnosed as schizophrenic, the therapist supported the mother, who was willing to consider her son lazy, and snubbed the father, a very competent physician who preferred a crazy son to a failure. In other words, the therapist joins the family in ways that make it possible to activate the alternatives whose presence he or she postulates.

A family with an identified patient has gone through a reification process that overfocuses on one member. The therapist reverses this process. He or she enters and joins the family by paying attention to the family-evolved reality—the symptoms of the identified patient. The therapist expands his or her focus to the symptom bearer, and then abandons the symptom bearer to move toward family interaction. This sequence may occur in the first session, or it may develop over a number of sessions.

> In a family with a bright 17-year-old boy who was failing in school, the parents and a younger sibling spent much of the first session discussing the identified patient's school performance. He remained silent, acting uncomfortable when attacked, but for the most part was lost in his own thoughts. The mother said to the father that if the boy went to a private school where he could be challenged, his performance might improve. The father said this was unrealistic, for it would involve great financial sacrifice for the whole family. He added that the mother was blind to the boy's laziness. Finally, he said that if the boy did go to private school, it would have to be her responsibility, but if she wanted to deprive the whole family, he would consent.
>
> The therapist talked with the identified patient about his school, his friends, his areas of difficulty and interest, his teachers, and his plans for next year. He challenged him for letting his parents make such an important decision for him. He suggested that the boy was acting like an 11-year-old; only thus was it appropriate for his younger brother to discuss him with his parents while he remained silent. He also pointed out that the boy was manipulating his parents to control him by acting younger than he was. Then the therapist challenged the parents for taking decision-making power away from the boy. He then moved away from the identified patient to the parents, and explored the coalition between mother and son that left father feeling excluded. The mother's plight then came into focus: how the family made her the center for decisions, overburdening her, and how her own orientation toward serving her family facilitated this overcentralization.
>
> The third session was held with husband and wife alone. Then the focus went back to the older boy's problems in school, but now the utilization of these problems in the family was very much part of the picture.

The speed of the movement from symptom to patient to family will depend on the nature and intensity of the symptom, the flexibility of family interaction, and the therapist's style. When a symptom is serious, the family system is extremely rigid. In such a case, the therapist must stay with the symptom of the identified patient for a while. Moving away from it will increase the pressure within the system, increasing the symptom's intensity until the therapist responds to the family's reality. When the identified patient's symptoms are milder, the therapist can move faster.

Psychotherapy as an Experimental Field

How does the therapist become acquainted with a family's range of possible interactions, challenge the present reality, create the possibilities for alternative interactions, and still support family members while maintaining a position of expert leadership? This is the artistry of therapy, no doubt, but it is buttressed by the therapist's map of goals and by the planned flexibility of the experimenter.

The therapist meets a field of stabilized family interactions. He or she becomes involved with the family members upon observing how they interact. He or she tracks the content of their communications and the ways they communicate, and tests the limits of family flexibility, requesting the family members to interact in a different way.

The therapist lets himself or herself be organized by the family's response to inputs. This way, his or her inputs can challenge family interactions without going beyond the thresholds the system can tolerate. When he or she suggests a modification of the way family members interact, the therapist is introducing an experimental probe. The responses will provide information about unmapped areas and directions for the next intervention. Some discussions of therapeutic strategies make it seem that the therapist's strategies are organized regardless of the family's feedback. In the reality of therapy, however, family responses modify the therapist's behavior, and the therapist must be alert to these responses to confirm hunches or change strategies.

> A newly married couple with a 12-year-old child from the wife's previous marriage came to therapy because of the child's crippling asthma. He had asthma since the age of 2, and had always slept with his mother. With the mother's remarriage, his asthmatic attacks had increased, especially at night. He now had his own room, but usually his mother or stepfather slept in his room to allay his fear and monitor his wheezing. The therapist directed the parents to shut the door of their bedroom, not to go to the child's bedroom unless it was absolutely necessary, and never to sleep with him. He explained that the family was in a transitional situation, and everyone would have to adapt to the new circumstances. The task was unsuccessful. The mother was convinced of the necessity for change, but she was unable to ignore her son's calling her for fear of precipitating a serious attack. The therapist learned that this route to change was closed.
>
> In the next session, he asked the boy for the names of two close friends at school. The boy, a loner, took almost three minutes to give two names. The mother tried hard to attract his attention so she could prompt him, but the boy, acting on a suggestion the therapist had made earlier, did not look at her. The therapist got up from his chair to give the boy a handshake. He labeled the three minutes' thinking for himself a triumph of autonomy, and discussed how difficult the task was for the mother. He further discussed, with the boy and the stepfather, what kinds of things they could do to respectfully block mother's unnecessary interventions. An exploratory task had indicated a closed pathway. Another had indicated a new and promising direction.

Constructing the Therapeutic Reality

A therapist never deals with a family's whole reality. He or she never knows the dynamics of the total situation, and the therapeutic challenge is begun before a great deal has been learned about the family. The only purpose of the beginning interventions is to shake the ridigity of the field. If the alternatives that the therapist indicates feel right to the family members, the process of change has begun. But even when the therapist and family are well into the therapeutic process, he or she is operating in terms of "partial constructs." The therapist's position in the therapeutic system allows the therapist to organize his or her own reality and program his or her experience of the patients' reality. The therapist will dismiss many elements of the family's life as "not part of the therapeutic reality." In effect, the therapist selects partial constructs to be the reality of therapy, in accordance with goals.

To change the reality of a patient, we need to change the reality of the relationship between the patient and his or her context. The therapist is in the position of a "constrained changer." The family has the capacity to control the therapist by determining his or her complimentary responses. The family may also activate the therapist's rescue fantasy and induce him or her to supplement a system's needs. The therapist, then, is in and out of a system that needs to change. He or she can operate as an active participant transacting with family members, as part of a dyad or triad, or as a creator and director of family scenarios. In both situations he or she will facilitate the experiencing of alternative reality. In every situation he or she has the limitation of his or her own life experience, value system, and esthetic sense; nonetheless and paradoxically, the more real the therapist's involvement, the more objective and experimental he or she becomes.

Sometimes the therapist is simply picking one point in a circle and calling it the beginning. For example, a man and woman who have been married for 20 years are discussing their sex life. For as long as they can remember, they have agreed that the wife should close the door when she wants sex. The husband is unhappy about this, because he feels he should initiate the act. The wife claims he does initiate: she closes the door when she sees that he wants sex. The husband says that she initiates it: whenever the wife looks at him in ways that indicate she is wondering if he wants sex, he indicates that he does. The feedback process can be elaborated further and further back. The therapist picks any point of entry that seems promising.

The following examples show how a therapeutic construct can also be a new causal linking for the family, one which allows them to reorient their positions in relation to one another. In one session a younger girl attacked her 13-year-old sister, the identified patient, by deriding her for letting their stepfather bathe her. The therapist challenged the mother for "allowing her daughter to tattle about family situations." The actual event was that the younger daughter talked and the mother was silent. The therapist's construction, "you allowed her to talk," connected two events in a statement of causality that shifted the mother's anger, which for the first time was directed at the younger daughter instead of the older girl.

A young husband described a situation in which he had been very depressed. He said that his wife suggested that she return to her parents in order to protect him in this situation. The wife had transformed an event in her husband's life to an interspouse problem. The therapist went one step further and challenged the ease of the wife's move from wife to daughter, including the extended family in a therapeutic construct.

The father of a 14-year-old educable retarded child picked up a ball the boy had dropped and put it in the boy's lap. Later in the session, the boy dropped the ball again, and this time the therapist put in the boy's lap. Clearly the therapist had been induced by the family's organization around the boy, which had rendered the child almost helpless. If the therapist had instead challenged the parents for immobilizing the boy, the slender event could have generated sufficient emotional intensity to further therapeutic change.

The first session with a family with an anorexic daughter finished with the whole family experiencing the child as protecting her mother from loneliness of her relationship with her busy, aloof husband. The anorexia at the center of the family's life receded, to be replaced by the therapeutic highlighting of the distance between the spouses.

A Family Therapy Grammar

With this view of family therapy as a construction of reality, it is useful to derive certain ad hoc rules that form an intermediate step between the basic steps of therapy and the therapeutic reality. Rules can help an inexperienced therapist operate with some level of competence; they can also direct an experienced therapist through the beginning stages of therapy with a family he or she does not know.

The rules discussed below are instructions the author finds himself repeating to different therapists who are treating families. They have a certain universality because the spring from generic ideas about the family and the therapeutic process, but they are rules only in the sense of something that is repeated. They will probably be correct about 60 percent of the time—that is, they are better than chance. But their usefulness diminishes as the idoisyncracies of each therapeutic system appear.

Creating the Therapeutic System

The therapist must establish himself or herself as the leader of the therapeutic unit; this is a sine qua non of therapy. To assume leadership, the therapist must join the family and accommodate himself or herself to its transactional patterns. This process of joining is essential before and at the time that the therapist introduces restructuring maneuvers.

Restructuring interventions are directed toward making alternative transactions available. The therapist directs the family to explore these alternatives by entering into alliances and coalitions with different family members. In these processes the therapist moves from a position of proximity in which he or she interacts with other members of the therapeutic system, to a disengaged position from which he or she directs family members to enact certain transactions, creating interpersonal scenarios that become the experiential field of the family member.

Some family therapists suggest that the therapist must be indirect in his or her goals because family members will resist direct leadership. Although this position is sometimes correct, it is frequently unnecessary. When properly joined by the therapist, family member cooperate with him or her in the therapeutic process. When the therapist is enabling, his or her inputs will not be resisted.

The therapist organizes the process in terms of what is possible. If a diagnosis creates a solution that does not help, the "beginning of the circle" can be set at another point. The therapist will construct the truths of therapy technique or strategy is measured only insofar as it is goal related. These strategies are good or bad because of how they work. Being correct has nothing to do with relevance. The therapist must learn to focus on that which is relevant. "Truth" needs to be relevant.

Supporting the Family's Functions

Other middle-range concepts of therapy can be derived from concepts of normal family dynamics. The family system supports individuation and differentiation. It also supports a sense of belonging. The therapist will support both.

Rules That Support Individuation.   Family members should speak for themselves. They should tell their own story. Family members should not tell what other members think or feel, though they should be encouraged to ask the speaker questions. Two members should not discuss a third who is present without his or her participation. Family members should be discouraged from asking each other for data they should know, or from consistently checking, verbally or nonverbally, for approval of statements or actions. Competent acts should be signaled whenever they occur and family members should be encouraged to transact competently.

Dealing with an identified patient, the therapist should avoid crystallizing the symptoms by discussing other positive and negative aspects of the symptom bearer and of other family members. Broadening the focus to the complementary underpinnings of the symptom—who elicits it, what its function is—is also helpful. If two members of the family have labeled a third the deviant, the therapist should not address the identified patient immediately. He or she should go to another family member to try to elicit different data, so the identified patient does not experience the therapist as joining in the process of labeling. However, the therapist will usually avoid joining with the scapegoated family member against the other family members because of the danger that the more powerful members will attack the therapist through his or her vulnerable ally and intensify the scapegoating. The therapist determines the success of tasks because success is defined by the therapist's punctuation. The end of a transaction can be longer or shorter depending on the therapeutic goal.

Rules That Support System Functioning. The therapist will often work to clarify or reinforce functional subsystem boundaries. For example, he or she will almost automatically support the boundaries that define the executive subsystem. If the spouses elicit a child's support when discussing a husband-wife issue, this will be blocked. When spouses and therapist discuss a couple's sexual life, other family members should be asked to leave the room. It is preferable, if the identified patient is a child, not to enter the conflicts of husband and wife before the therapeutic system is established well enough for the family members to know that they can depend on the therapist. Spouse conflicts, in such cases, may appear early in therapy, but the therapist does not explore the area until it is known that the family trusts him or her to defend them.

The functions of each subsystem will be rewarded. For example, if a member of a family is doing well, the therapist can praise the other person's role in facilitating the change in behavior (e.g., parents may be complimented when a child improves).

When members of a subsystem are defined as unequal, the therapist may relabel the definition of power (for instance, by saying to a supposedly weak spouse, "How do you get your wife to organize your actions?"). The exploration of complementarity moves members away from accusation and stereotyping.

When working with a subsystem, the therapist may ask members who do not belong to that subsystem to leave the room or move their chairs back to define their noninvolvement.

The therapist can use subsystems to define problems or change moods. If the adolescents of a large family are experiencing difficulty negotiating issues of independence, separate sessions can be held with the parents and adolescents, with the younger children excluded. When working in a hostile atmosphere between spouses, the therapist can promote mood change by bringing in the children, moving the spouse subsystem to the parental subsystem.

These are ad hoc rules, to be discarded as each therapeutic system develops and its elements become clear.

Family therapy has come to a point of development at which it may be profitable for its practitioners to make their philosophies explicit; this chapter has been written in this spirit. In conclusion, it should be pointed out that family therapy is not a tool for humanistic revolution; in fact, it is often the opposite. One of the family's tasks is to provide continuity with a society that the family therapist, in his or her own value system, may consider restrictive. Family therapy is the active process of changing dysfunctional patterns of transaction and eliciting available alternative patterns. It is a process in which therapist and family members, working together, search for and enact an alternative reality that expands the possibilities for the family and its members.

CHAPTER TWO

Family Processes Associated with Alcohol and Drug Use and Abuse

DAVID W. BROOK, M.D.
New York Medical College
Valhalla, New York
Director of Group Psychotherapy
City Hospital Center
Elmhurst, New York

JUDITH S. BROOK, ED.D.
New York Medical College
Valhalla, New York

Since the publication of the first edition of this book in 1979, there has been an ever-increasing interest in research into intrafamilial interactions in alcohol and drug use and abuse, and the literature in the field has grown rapidly (Brook & Brook, 1985). The roles of family members have been more clearly delineated, and a number of studies have looked at risk and protective interactive factors involved in alcohol and drug use and abuse. Operating within a developmental theoretical framework, we have called our own approach to this problem *Family Interactional Theory* (Brook, Whiteman, Gordon, Brook, & Cohen, 1990). We believe such a theoretical view, resting finally on data analyzed and interpreted using appropriate statistical techniques, offers the most useful way to integrate material from

The preparation of this chapter was supported by Research Grants DA03188 and DA02390 from the National Institute on Drug Abuse, and in part by Research Scientist Development Award, Level II, DA00094 from the National Institute on Drug Abuse to Judith S. Brook. The authors would like to acknowledge Susan Karaban for her assistance in the preparation of this article. Correspondence concerning this article should be addressed to Judith S. Brook, Department of Psychiatry, New York Medical College, Valhalla, New York 10595.

15

sociocultural, environmental, biological, interpersonal, and intrapersonal spheres of knowledge.

According to Magnusson (1988), up to the present little has been done to integrate theories, methods, and analyses, and to weave a useful and understandable whole from the patchwork of prior research using an interactional view. The complexities of multiple reciprocal interactions on the individual must be emphasized. Interactions encompass all influences that impinge on the individual from within and without, changing as the individual changes. The hypotheses upon which we have based our research have taken these complexities into account, focusing on the integrated, reciprocal, dynamic interactions occurring during development, in order to view the individual's complete functioning as much as possible, using a holistic, longitudinal perspective.

The limitations of our theory depend on the limitations of our data and our statistical analyses. Many investigators have contributed to our understanding of the family processes involved in adolescent substance use and abuse, and we are grateful to them all. However, some investigators' research efforts have been of particular importance to us in formulating a longitudinal, interactional, developmental approach to research design and theoretical integration. Thus, only an incomplete review is given here.

Family Interactional Theory and Psychosocial Etiology

The psychosocial theory of problem behavior proposed by Jessor and Jessor (1977) viewed drug use as part of a constellation of "problem behaviors," including sexual promiscuity and delinquency, which occurred during, and as a part of, the adolescent transitional period between childhood and adulthood. Problem behavior was so designated because it presented difficulties for the adolescent, for the family and parents or parental surrogates, and for society as a whole. Personality attributes associated with problem behavior included greater tolerance of deviance, less religiosity, greater emphasis on independence, lower achievement values, and more social criticism. Such adolescents relied less on parents for support, responded less well to parental control, were more influenced by peers, and relied more on peers for modeling and approval of drug use. These adolescents were less conventional, were more sensation seeking, and showed lower school achievement, and attended church less often than adolescents who did not show problem behaviors.

In recent years, Bentler, Newcomb, and colleagues, operating within an interactional developmental theory of drug use, developed a domain model. This model (Stein, Newcomb, & Bentler, 1987) has incorporated biological, interpersonal, intrapersonal, and sociocultural domains to explain drug-taking behavior. These researchers have made increasingly important contributions to our understanding of the etiology and consequences of drug use.

Another researcher in the field has been Kandel (1975), who identified four stages in adolescent drug use that form a sequence from the use of legal drugs to the use of illegal drugs: (1) beer or wine; (2) cigarettes or hard liquor; (3) marijuana; and (4) other illicit drugs, such as cocaine, heroin, PCP, amphetamines, and other opiates. Kandel was able to identify adolescents who were likely to move from one stage to the next. Delinquency, parental drinking, and peer sociability predicted initiation into the use of hard liquor. Drug-using peers and the adolescents' own beliefs and attributes predicted the onset of marijuana use. Psychological distress, peer modeling, and a poor parent-child relationship predicted the use of other illicit drugs (Kandel, Kessler, & Margulies, 1978).

The relationship between frequency of use and stage of drug use has been studied by Brook and colleagues, who found that peer and personality factors related to different stages and frequency of use, whereas family factors were more related to stage than to frequency (Brook, Whiteman, & Gordon, 1982). Stage of drug use was independently affected by personality, peer, and family factors, but frequency of drug use was indirectly affected by family and personality factors mediated by the characteristics of the peer group. In other words, family and personality factors influenced whether the adolescent would use a particular drug, whereas peers were more influential on the occasions and timing of drug use.

The interconnections and interactions of family relationships, personality characteristics, and peer influences on adolescent marijuana use have been investigated (Brook, Whiteman, & Gordon, 1983) by using a psychosocial developmental approach, focusing on domains of causal influences and their interactions. According to this view, which is a part of Family Interactional Theory, the parents serve as bearers of societal values through introjection related to a warm, relatively conflict-free, parent-adolescent mutual attachment relationship, which results in greater adolescent identification with the parent. The result of this kind of attachment is increased identification with the parents, and introjection of their conventional values and behavior, which is manifested in the adolescent's own conventional behavior and attitudes. Increased adolescent conventionality and, to a lesser extent, psychological well-being shield the adolescent from associating with drug-using peers, and decrease the influence of peers in general compared to that of parents.

This attention to an interactional model is viewed in a different context by Cooper, Grotevant, and Condon (1983), who use a family systems approach. In a study of intrafamilial communications and adolescent psychosocial development, both individuality and connectedness are important in developing identity and role-taking skills during adolescence. Self-assertion, separateness, permeability, and mutuality involve different aspects of interactions within the family, reflecting multidimensional ongoing intrafamilial processes. These researchers emphasize the importance for development and autonomy of "individuated family relationships, characterized by separateness, which gives the adolescent permission to develop his or her own point of view, in the context of connectedness, which provides a secure base from which the adolescent can explore worlds outside the family."

Other important theorists who have examined interactional approaches include Magnusson (1988); Labouvie and colleagues at Rutgers (Labouvie & McGill (1986), and of course Bentler, Newcomb, Huba, and Wingard at UCLA. The latter investigators have used causal modeling in a further exploration of the behavioral latent variables affecting drug use and their interactions, and have identified important complex causal influences involved in drug use (Stein, Newcomb, & Bentler, 1987; Newcomb & Bentler, 1988). Also at UCLA, Coombs and Paulson (1988) have confirmed the utility of an interactional approach to the study of familial effects on adolescent substance abuse.

Siblings also have an influence on adolescent drug use, both as suppliers of drugs and as models for use (Brook, Whiteman, Gordon, & Brook, 1987). Several other mechanisms have been suggested to account for sibling effects on drug use, such as sibling rivalry and differential parent effects. In addition, recent work has confirmed the importance of interactions between siblings and parents in adolescent drug use (Brook, Whiteman, Brook, & Gordon, 1988), as well as in child and adolescent development in general (Dunn, Plomin, & Daniels, 1986). For example, Patterson (1982) found that siblings played a catalytic role in the occurrence and continuance of intrafamilial aggression.

Another aspect of this interaction was noted by Montemayor (1984), who found that males, but not females, argued more with mothers and siblings when the mothers worked than when they did not work. Family risk factors for adolescent drug use such as paternal drug use or parental divorce have also been studied by Needle, McCubbin, Wilson, Reineck, Lazar, and Mederer (1986). Drug-abusing siblings can supply drugs for each other, help each other use drugs, and betray each other's drug use. Kaufman and Borders (1988) have elucidated the role of ethnicity in familial interactions in drug use, with an eye to clarifying the importance of ethnic understanding in treatment. Coombs and Coombs (1988) have noted the ways in which a drug user manipulates his or her family, which comes to "fulfill instrumental rather than expressive functions," especially during the maintenance stage of drug use.

In a large-scale study of brothers (Brook, Whiteman, Brook, & Gordon, 1988), three pathways of sibling influence leading to drug use were identified. The first pathway deals with the causal link between the influences of the older brother's personality on the younger brother's personality; we have termed the hypothesized mechanism through which the two are linked the *personality influence mechanism.* According to the personality influence mechanism hypothesis, the older brother's personality has an influence on the younger brother's personality through identification and modeling. This identification is likely to lead to common values, attitudes, and behavioral orientation. The older brother's tolerance of deviance, and deviance itself, were associated with deviant orientations and behavior in the younger brother.

A second pathway between the older and younger brothers' personalities is what we have termed the *genetic temperamental connection.* According to the genetic temperamental connection hypothesis, genetic factors may partially explain the close similarities in structure and behavior in the two brothers, via the inheritance of similar temperamental or psychophysiological characteristics or reaction patterns. It is likely that both the personality influence mechanism and genetic temperamental connection act together, so that the younger brother's personality is influenced both by the older brother's personality through the personality influence mechanism, as well as by the common genetic heritage (genetic temperamental connection) both brothers share.

In regard to the third pathway, the younger brother's personality also serves as a mediator for the sibling relationship. The mechanism through which the sibling relationship is linked with the younger brother's personality, which we have called the *environmental reactive mechanism,* serves to connect the two brothers via another, more indirect, route. A difficult sibling environment, marked by a troubled relationship between the brothers, leads to increased intrapsychic distress manifested as a lack of responsibility in the younger brother. One might speculate that the reaction to a difficult sibling relationship is disengagement, which is manifested in (1) behavioral withdrawal from responsibility or (2) internal pressures shown as intrapsychic distress. In contrast, a sibling relationship characterized by less conflict, as manifested by less jealousy, and by a mutual attachment characterized by greater nurturance, admiration, satisfaction, and sibling identification, was related to less inner-conflict and less intrapsychic distress in the younger brother.

Overall, then, a close and nonconflictual mutual attachment between the siblings characterized by greater mutual identification was related to more conventional attitudes and behavior, and less intrapsychic distress, greater responsibility, and less drug use in the younger brother. It seems clear that the mutual influences and interactions of both parents affect the sibling relationships, perhaps with the occurrence of feedback loops, which affect adolescent drug use, although parental child-rearing techniques and parent-child interactions also have direct independent effects on adolescent drug use (Brook et al., 1987).

The complex integrated developmental model based on the work of Brook and colleagues (1990) studying the interrelationships of behavioral "domains" in adolescent drug use is shown in Figure 2.1. This model also includes a depiction of the influences of childhood factors on adolescent drug use. As can be seen in the figure, the model emphasizes relationships between domains of behavior, each of which contains a number of component personality/behavioral attributes arrived at either through an examination of the intercorrelations of measures for such attributes or, in some cases, through factor analytic techniques. Linkages between pathways were arrived at through the use of multiple hierarchical regression analyses. Other investigators have used similar analytic techniques to look at interrelationships, but methods that should be pointed out as coming into increasingly widespread application are the use of LISREL or EQS programs, frequently used by Bentler, Newcomb, and associates at UCLA (Bentler & Newcomb, 1986; Newcomb, 1988).

Psychosocial factors may be further examined by an in-depth look at the integrated developmental model in Figure 2.1, which offers a fuller explanation of the direct and indirect relationships involved in adolescent drug use. For example, the parental trait of conventionality is associated with mutual parent-child attachment and internalization of parental values, which are associated with greater adolescent conventionality. Greater adolescent conventionality is linked with less friend drug use and ultimately less drug use on the part of the adolescent. During the past two decades, we have done considerable research studying children and adolescents who have been raised in environments conducive to drug use who have refrained from drug use. In our cross-sectional and longitudinal studies, we have focused on protective factors that may offset the effects of negative environmental stimuli in the socialization process. Such protective personality factors refer to traits of conventionality such as lack of rebelliousness, responsibility, and high achievement.

In our theoretical conception, the parent-child relationship involves mutual influences. It is important that we not view the child as an amorphous blob being molded by the parents. Our evidence, based on both cross-sectional and longitudinal analyses, indicates that the child's characteristics affect the mother-adolescent relationship; that is, the characteristics affect the mother's relationship to the child, which impacts later on the adolescent and on the relationship with the mother. For example, childhood aggression predicts lack of mutual parent-adolescent attachment, which in turn is related to adolescent unconventionality and ultimately to drug use.

These findings of the reciprocal relationship of parent and child traits have been confirmed by other investigators, who also reported that children's differing characteristics elicit different behaviors from the parents.

Reciprocal influences are not only present in the mother-child relationship but in the father-child relationship and the sibling relationship as well. In a study of 75 families of heroin-abusing and heroin-dependent youths, Kaufman and Kaufmann (1977) found that most of "the mothers were emotionally enmeshed with their drug-abusing children (mainly sons)," and that almost half the fathers were as well. In these families, parental feelings depended on the drug-abusing children's behaviors and on parental closeness with them (Kaufman, 1985).

As previously noted, the family is a complex system and encompasses a network of relationships. When examining a relationship, care is needed when ascribing measures of behavior to one member of the dyad or the other, as every measure may be influenced by both of them. Also, the behavior of one family member to another is influenced by the relationships of the other family members with each other. A case in point is the youngster whose parents manifest marital discord. In our studies, we find that if the adolescent has a secure attachment with at least one of his or her parents, this is sufficient to offset the impact of marital discord on adolescent drug use. In a related vein, our results suggest that even if the adolescent has a disturbed relationship with one parent, the effects on drug use are small if the child has a good relationship with the other parent.

Family influences include not only parent-child relations but sibling relations as well. Sibling risk factors that predispose to drug use, such as jealousy or lack of affection, can be offset by a secure parent-child bond. Different risk and protective factors also interact with other factors from the various domains, giving an end result of more or less drug use. The risk of adolescent drug use as a consequence of older sibling drug use (a risk factor), is diminished if the peers do not use drugs (a protective factor). High parental affection leading to high mutual affection and identification with the parent (a protective factor) can serve as a buffer for low marital harmony (a risk factor).

Although not specifically aimed at studying drug use, the work of Cooper, Grotevant, and Condon (1983) and their colleagues has provided observational data concerning the connection between family interactions and adolescent identity formation. Such observational work, particularly focusing on intrafamilial patterns of communication, in future research on family interactions and drug use, may provide further confirmation of the impact of risk/protective interactions in the family on adolescent drug use.

Because little is known about genetic influences on family interactions, and hence on drug use, the topic will not be explored here, other than to point out the necessity of not confusing family interactions with underly-

FIGURE 2-1 • *Hypothesized Developmental Integrated Model*

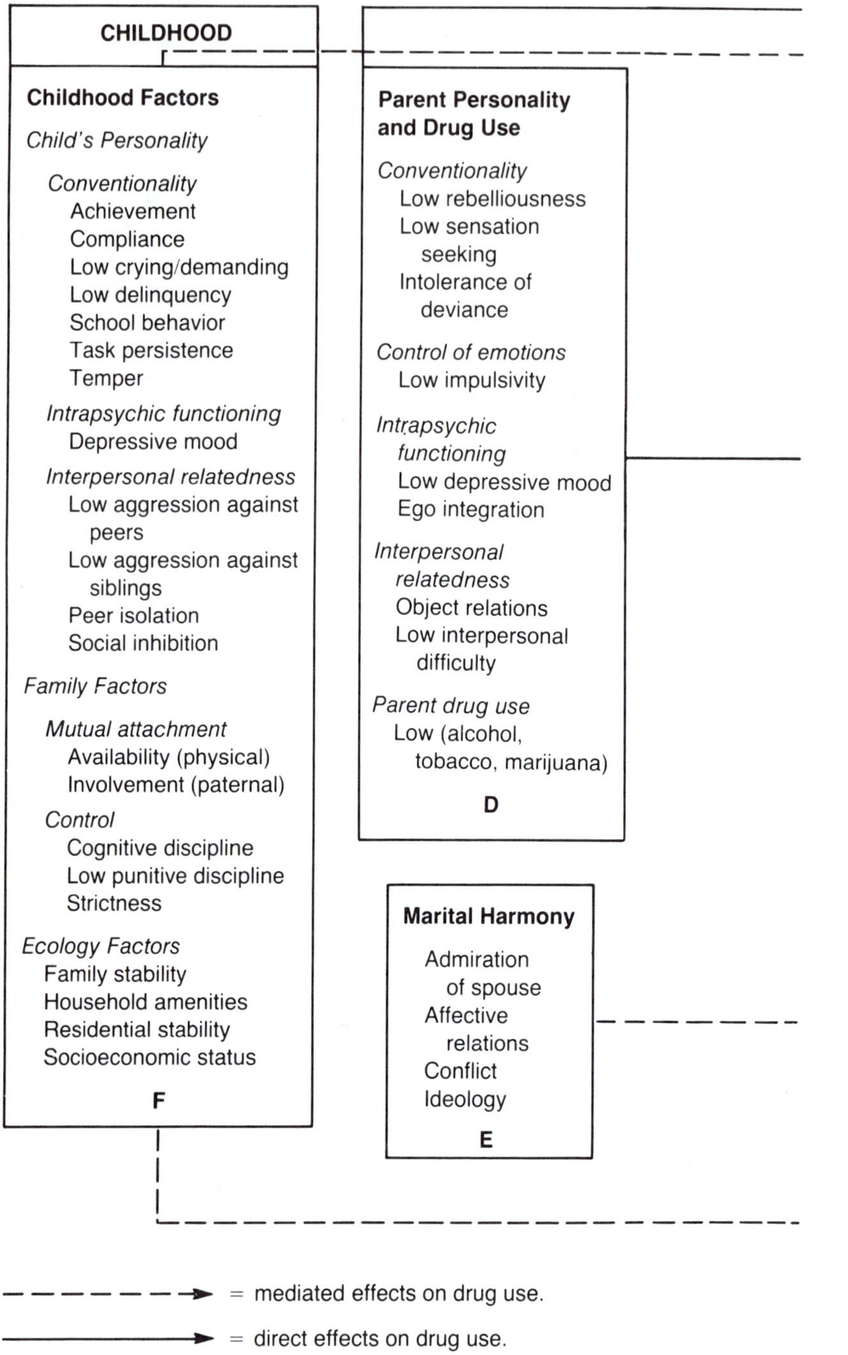

CHILDHOOD

Childhood Factors

Child's Personality

Conventionality
Achievement
Compliance
Low crying/demanding
Low delinquency
School behavior
Task persistence
Temper

Intrapsychic functioning
Depressive mood

Interpersonal relatedness
Low aggression against
peers
Low aggression against
siblings
Peer isolation
Social inhibition

Family Factors

Mutual attachment
Availability (physical)
Involvement (paternal)

Control
Cognitive discipline
Low punitive discipline
Strictness

Ecology Factors
Family stability
Household amenities
Residential stability
Socioeconomic status

F

Parent Personality and Drug Use

Conventionality
Low rebelliousness
Low sensation
seeking
Intolerance of
deviance

Control of emotions
Low impulsivity

*Intrapsychic
functioning*
Low depressive mood
Ego integration

*Interpersonal
relatedness*
Object relations
Low interpersonal
difficulty

Parent drug use
Low (alcohol,
tobacco, marijuana)

D

Marital Harmony

Admiration
of spouse
Affective
relations
Conflict
Ideology

E

– – – – – –▶ = mediated effects on drug use.

───────────▶ = direct effects on drug use.

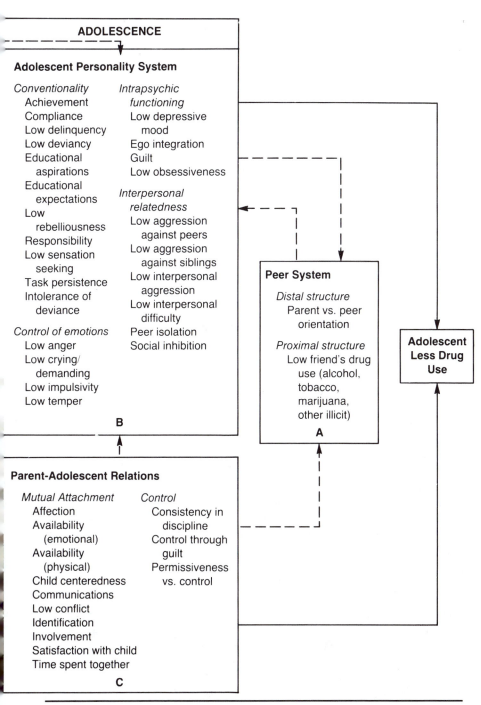

ADOLESCENCE

Adolescent Personality System

Conventionality
Achievement
Compliance
Low delinquency
Low deviancy
Educational
  aspirations
Educational
  expectations
Low
  rebelliousness
Responsibility
Low sensation
  seeking
Task persistence
Intolerance of
  deviance

Control of emotions
Low anger
Low crying/
  demanding
Low impulsivity
Low temper

*Intrapsychic
functioning*
Low depressive
  mood
Ego integration
Guilt
Low obsessiveness

*Interpersonal
relatedness*
Low aggression
  against peers
Low aggression
  against siblings
Low interpersonal
  aggression
Low interpersonal
  difficulty
Peer isolation
Social inhibition

B

Peer System

Distal structure
Parent vs. peer
  orientation

Proximal structure
Low friend's drug
  use (alcohol,
  tobacco,
  marijuana,
  other illicit)

A

**Adolescent
Less Drug
Use**

Parent-Adolescent Relations

Mutual Attachment
Affection
Availability
  (emotional)
Availability
  (physical)
Child centeredness
Communications
Low conflict
Identification
Involvement
Satisfaction with child
Time spent together

Control
Consistency in
  discipline
Control through
  guilt
Permissiveness
  vs. control

C

Note: Domains A–E were assessed during adolescence in both the Father and Mother Studies. Domain F was assessed during childhood in our Mother Study only (Brook et al., 1990).

ing genetic influences, if this is possible. This field, the biology of family behavior, or behavioral genetics, is very new but promises exciting findings in the future. The issue mentioned here is not to confuse the biological predisposition with the resultant behavior (Scarr & McCartney, 1983).

This is a separate issue from that of direct genetic influences on substance use (see Goodwin, 1979). Adoption studies have revealed that alcoholism occurs with increased prevalence among adults who were adopted in childhood if the biological parents were problem drinkers over that seen in people with no alcoholic history in the biological family. Alcoholism or heavy drinking in the adoptive parents was of little importance in this regard (Cloninger, Bohman, & Sigvardsson, 1981).

It is likely that a risk-diathesis interactional model explains these and similar findings. That is, a genetically transmitted predisposition (probably based on disturbances in metabolic or neuroreceptor functioning) provides a vulnerability to alcoholism, which depends for its phenotypic expression on complex interactions with the various psychosocial risk factors discussed in this chapter. The relative importance of individual risk factors versus genetic diatheses probably varies from factor to factor and from one population cohort to the next. As noted by Kaufman (1985), alcoholism is not an individual, marital, or nonfamilial disorder, but "may reflect larger alcoholism-generating family systems." Evidence regarding whether the same model is applicable to all drug use and abuse and, indeed, to a wide range of psychiatric disorders is greatly needed to buttress this theoretical model in many areas of human behavior.

A word should be mentioned about the modifying effects of environmental or contextual factors. Based on our recent work in related areas, it appears that such variables can have significant risk-protective effects on familial processes. Such variables as crime, neighborhood poverty and decay, or a lack of support structures in the community are related to and impact on the familial factors with which this chapter primarily deals. Further research along these lines will most likely yield useful knowledge about the important biopsychosocial interactions leading to drug use and abuse.

Clinical Implications

The clinical implications of these family findings are complex. To begin, it seems clear that adolescent substance use and abuse must be considered in the light of an adolescent's interactions and relationships with family and peers who are not substance users; a strong adolescent attachment and identification has protective effects against adolescent substance use, as does association with nonsubstance-using peers. In addition, all of the causal factors listed in Figure 2.1 have been found to play a role in adolescent substance use. The causally linked chain of events indicated that parental traditionality and conventionality were linked with an affectionate and nonconflictual parent-adolescent relationship, which led to increased identification of the child with the parents, which in turn was associated with increased conventionality in the adolescent. Conventionality in the adolescent was correlated with associating with nondrug-using peers, which led to nonuse of drugs in the adolescent.

These findings suggest possible points for therapeutic or preventive intervention. At least four points of intervention are suggested by the model. Points of intervention, using various techniques, include those directed at the parent alone, both the parent and the adolescent, the adolescent alone, and the peer group. If one wishes to intervene early in the causal chain of events, the point of intervention should take place at the family level. Interventions aimed at altering the parents' personalities in the direction of greater conventionality and psychological adjustment should lead to a more enduring and affectionate parent-child bond.

A slightly later point of intervention involves working with one or both parents and the child, although not necessarily together, on disturbances in their attachment relationship. If both parent and adolescent are not available together, one would still wish to work with either one separately in developing a stronger and more affectionate parent-child bond. Changes in the attachment relationship should lead to changes in the adolescent's personality characteristics. The data showed that an affectionate mutual attachment between parent and child was linked with the development of responsible, nonrebellious, and conventional attitudes toward societal norms.

Perhaps a strong parent-child bond leads to strong internalization of parental values, behavior, and attitudes. A strong parent-child attachment may also provide children with the feeling that they can control what happens to them, and that they can and will acquire the problem-solving skills to enable them to do so. A secure attachment may also result in increased adolescent maturity and self-esteem, which would further enable them to develop in an optimal manner. If parents are emotionally unavailable and their ways of relating to their children are extremely disturbed and at the same time ingrained, one might attempt to alter parental personality traits.

A later point of possible intervention might be directed at altering the adolescent's personality in the direction of greater conventionality, which is likely to lead to less drug use and to affiliating with drug-resistant peer groups. For clinicians working with adolescents, knowledge of the parent-adolescent relationship should throw light on its disturbances and causation, as well as providing the potential for intervention if one cannot directly effect changes in the adolescent's conventionality. Finally, one can also intervene at the level of the peer group. Placing an individual at risk in prosocial peer groups should decrease the risk of the adolescent's using drugs. The use of group psychotherapy for this purpose can also be helpful.

The importance of early childhood personality and environmental precursors in foretelling drug use has been highlighted in the ongoing classic study of Block, Block, and Keyes (1988). In their study, ego undercontrol influenced values and susceptibilities associated with drug use.

Our research findings (Brook, Whiteman, Gordon, & Cohen, 1986; Brook, Whiteman, Nomura, Gordon, & Cohen, 1988) also provide a dramatic demonstration of the effect of childhood personality and early family influences on the adolescent's personality and the parent-adolescent relationship. The findings indicate that childhood drug-prone personality traits, such as aggression, and adverse childhood experiences (i.e., parental sociopathy), determine to some extent drug-prone personality traits in the adolescent and a weak bond between parent and child. Since the indirect effects of adverse childhood personality traits and experiences are long-lasting, logic dictates that one try to break the chain early in the child's development. Certainly, clinical experiences suggests that it is often easier to work with children than adolescents since their personalities are less formed, more flexible, and easier to modify, and symptoms are often less fixed and more amenable to change. Since poor achievement, poor control of behavior, and greater aggression are frequently present in children at risk for drug use, it should be possible to identify children who would benefit from treatment.

Intervention with children and adolescents who are at risk might alter their developmental paths so that they will develop drug-resistant personality traits. Thus, an implication of our developmental integrated model is that during development there are several temporal points and distinct psychological domains at which interventions to ameliorate drug use and drug-prone personality traits and experiences are possible.

These findings also indicate that the treating clinician should not consider the substance-using or substance-abusing adolescent apart from the influences of and relationships with family, peers, and environmental factors, and their interactions as well as the nature and effects of these influences and interactions during childhood. The reestablishment and maintenance of the interacting effects of the protective and warmly supportive system of relationships noted above is of primary importance for preventing or terminating adolescent drug use. Probably the use of family-based therapeutic interventions is most effective for these purposes, given the presence of such a complex network of etiological and associated factors. As noted, it is also important to try to change the presence, intensity, or influence of risk factors, either through family-based interventions or through the use of environmental interventions combined with family and/or individual therapy. Of course in any individual child or adolescent some risk factors cannot be changed (see the list below). In that case, it is particularly important to try to increase the presence, intensity, and influence of the ameliorating protective factors noted elsewhere in the chapter.

Although these goals may seem to be difficult or impossible to reach in many cases, it is important for the clinician to make attempts to achieve them. In many cases partial successes may be achieved initially, which may gradually lead over time to more promising, healthier, and less destructive sets of interactions.

A possible route for interventions that should not be overlooked is through the influence of siblings. In our recent work with siblings and their influences on adolescent drug use (Brook et al., 1987), we found that a mutual attachment between siblings characterized by nurturance, mutual identification, and a lack of conflict protected adolescent boys against drug use, particularly the influences of older brothers on younger brothers. It may be that in certain cases, especially those resistant to more direct interventions, focusing on the sibling relationship could provide a pathway for successful familial therapeutic intervention. Cicirelli (1985) has stated that sibling relationships must be viewed in "the context of the larger family system and cultural milieu" in which they can play an important role supporting or opposing adolescent drug use.

To summarize, family factors correlated with adolescent drug use, not necessarily in order of importance, include:

1. Relative lack of parental supervision, less involvement and control, and low familial goal-directed behavior
2. A weak parent-child mutual attachment
3. Conflictual parent-child relationship
4. Intrafamilial tension and conflicts in adolescence
5. Parental and sibling tolerance of deviant, illegal, or unconventional behavior
6. Parental and sibling deviant, legal or illegal drug behavior
7. Parental and sibling unconventionality, aggression, or social isolation
8. Parental psychopathology or poverty
9. Parental divorce, death, or abandonment

It should be remembered that peer drug use and peer support for drug use and deviant behavior are among the most important predictors of adolescent drug use.

The presence of any of these familial factors indicate places for therapeutic interventions, which probably are more effective when made in an intrafamilial context. Because of the increasingly important role of peers throughout adolescence, and especially in late adolescence, the earliest family-based interventions possible are likely to be the most effective, perhaps using interlocking group psychotherapy as suggested by Kaufman and Pattison (1981). Early interventions, even in childhood, can preempt possible noxious influences, then or later, of the peer group, and mitigate against other risk factors more effectively than later interventions.

The interaction of familial factors with environmental or context factors also has important clinical implications. Clinically, it is very difficult, if not impossible, to successfully intervene therapeutically if the family and the adolescent live in a neighborhood in which there are physically deteriorating buildings, piles of uncollected garbage, crack houses, constant physical dangers, violent crimes, great poverty, and easy availability of drugs. All of these environmental factors can probably contribute to the likelihood of drug abuse, and must be considered in relation to the familial factors noted earlier.

A high rate of social problems and few available neighborhood or community supportive structures, therefore, impinges to a large extent against successful therapeutic interventions for drug abuse. Thus, concerted community and civic action undertaken by dedicated leaders working to improve the environment in which children and adolescents live may be regarded as a necessary first or concomitant step to family-based intervention procedures. Some progress in some areas may be possible in the absence of community environmental action, but the latter will be of great help in instituting successful family-based interventions against drug abuse. Conversely, family involvement can stimulate greater community action and contribute to the establishment of useful environmental and contextual support systems. Although there have been few studies of the interactive effects of efforts at intervention at multiple levels using a risk-protective model, this approach appears promising, based on our work and that of others in related areas.

It should be kept in mind that although abstinence is the ideally desired goal in the treatment of drug abusers, drug abuse can in some cases become a recurrent, chronic, refractory disorder. In those cases, relapse into drug abuse can occur even after a long period of abstinence has been achieved. If this happens, the clinician should not lose hope or become too discouraged prognostically. Rather, a renewed effort at involving family members and environmental supports, as mentioned above, often can direct the adolescent back onto the abstinence track.

Important therapeutic efforts can be made by involving the adolescent and the family in a variety of community-based self-help groups, ranging from AA to local groups such as those described by Macdonald (1984). These groups offer useful support for both the adolescent and his or her family, often by strengthening and offering support for drug-free peer group activities, and by organizing community standards of limit setting for adolescent groups and increased school and legal involvement in the prevention and cessation of drug use. Additionally "social network intervention," as described by Callan, Garrison, and Zerger (1975), offers large group interventions as a part of a therapeutic community program. Such large groups can involve relatives, friends, or other members of the extended psychosocial environment. In such cases, the leader should be an "outsider" who is unattached to the people involved.

Perhaps the most important point to be kept in mind concerning familial interventions and treatment approaches is that the cyclic behavior of the family must be addressed. Family processes and interactions around drug use and abuse must be changed. Brief intervention aimed only at helping the addict achieve abstinence for a short time is not enough for successful treatment. Long-term, more encompassing, family treatment of the intrafamilial (and, if possible, extrafamilial) disturbance and malfunctioning is most helpful. Such treatment is also most likely to prevent or mitigate both recurrence and the future drug use and abuse of siblings or other family members. Of course, as noted above, adolescents in families in which there is drug use or abuse are proportionately more at risk themselves, depending on the risk-protective factors discussed earlier. It is our belief that whichever intervention methods are used, bringing about changes in the risk factors and interactions noted earlier remains an essential focus of any treatment program. This recommendation is based on our long-term research into family interactions.

Special mention should be made of the particular difficulties involved in understanding the family processes involved in dual diagnosis cases, in which there is both a psychiatric disorder and substance abuse. A review of research in this field concerning etiology and therapeutic intervention in such cases is beyond the scope of this chapter, but a high correlation has been found between the occurrence of certain psychiatric disorders, such as affective disorders and antisocial personality disorders, and substance abuse (Meyer & Hesselbrock, 1984).

Of particular interest in this regard is the persistent denial by pediatricians and mental health professionals, including psychiatrists and psychologists, of the possibility of drug abuse in many of their patients, especially those who are regarded as "higher-functioning" or "more intact." Although too little research has been done on intrafamilial contributions to dual diagnostic cases, clearly identification of such patients and their families is of great importance. Every patient seen, including those with pediatric, medical, and psychiatric problems, should be asked about substance use, both by themselves and in their families, in a factful but direct manner. Often enough, cases of either substance abuse or psychiatric disorder that seem intractable and resistant to treatment will turn out to reveal dual diagnosis somewhere in the family.

AIDS and Drug Abuse in Families

Special attention should also be called to the growing AIDS epidemic and its connection to IV drug use, which is now the most important risk factor for the deadly viral disease. The spread of the disease and its significance for adolescents is underlined by recent surveys that reveal an incidence of 1 in 300 college students infected with the AIDS virus. Family risk factors relating particularly to IV drug use are relevant here, since needle sharing or sexual relations with an infected needle user are increasingly significant in the spread of the disease. In addition, many AIDS victims are abandoned by family members because of the stigma of the disease or because of fears of contagion.

According to Stanton and Todd (1982), a cyclic pathological triadic system in the families of drug abusers exists in which the adolescent drug abuser interrupts or is overinvolved with or involved in conflicts between the parents or between two other adult family members. A similar system exists in single-parent families, with different adults playing the role of the absent parent. For those addicts who marry during adolescence, a strong parental influence remains that can interfere with marital success, with most addicts maintaining strong, if dysfunctional, family ties. Stanton and others have emphasized the importance of loss or separation in drug addicts' families, as well as an intense fear of separation.

Clinically, it is well recognized that IV drug users come from disturbed or disruptive families, with poor intrafamilial relationships concurrent with low self-esteem among family members (Jaffe, 1986). Other drug or alcohol abuse among family members is common, as is neglect, abuse, or abandonment. The continuation of risk-taking behavior, including needle sharing and unsafe sexual practices, among IV drug users even after they know about the risks of hepatitis and AIDS is well known clinically. Indeed, the *preference* of IV drug users to share needles over the individual use of separate needles is a clinically well-known phenomenon, which may interfere with implementation of public health officials' plans to distribute free sterile needles to interdict viral transmission.

Our group at Mount Sinai and at the City Hospital Center at Elmhurst, Mount Sinai Services, is currently conducting research designed to elicit a greater understanding of those interactive factors, both intra- and extrafamilial, that contribute to the continuation of such self-destructive risk-taking behavior. We are also looking at ways in which HIV-infected people cope with their illnesses, and attempting to understand those psychosocial factors that can lead to more effective coping among victims of this dread disease. Such studies may help to enhance the prevention of HIV transmission and the quality of life of those infected until a definitive medical cure is found, and may help to contribute to compliance and proper, compassionate treatment after such a cure is found.

Conclusion

This chapter has included a description of ongoing research into familial processes associated with substance use and abuse. Research using hypotheses based on Family Interactional Theory has shown the importance of evaluating the roles of risk and protective interactions in the onset and maintenance of substance use and abuse in adolescence. Many different interactions play a complex set of roles, and therapeutic interventions must take into account these research findings in order to have maximum beneficial effects. Dual diagnoses and AIDS present special problems in looking at intrafamilial interactions and in using this knowledge to intervene therapeutically. Our findings buttress a number of the clinical and theoretical observations concerning intrafamilial interactions of families of adolescent drug abusers made by Kaufman and Kaufmann (1979) in the first edition of this book.

References

Bentler, P. M., & Newcomb, M. D. (1986). Personality, sexual behavior, and drug use revealed through latent variable methods. *Clinical Psychology Review, 6,* 363–385.

Block, J., Block, J. H., & Keyes, S. (1988). Longitudinally foretelling drug usage in adolescence: Early childhood personality and environmental precursors. *Child Development, 59,* 336–355.

Brook, D. W., & Brook, J. S. (1985). Adolescent alcohol use. *Alcohol & Alcoholism, 20*(3), 259–262.

Brook, J. S., Whiteman, M., Brook, D., & Gordon, A. S. (1988). *Sibling influences on adolescent drug abuse: Older brothers on younger brothers.* Unpublished manuscript.

Brook, J. S., Whiteman, M., & Gordon, A. S. (1982). Qualitative and quantitative aspects of adolescent drug use: Interplay of personality, family and peer correlates. *Psychological Reports, 51,* 1151–1163.

Brook, J. S., Whiteman, M., & Gordon, A. S. (1983). Stages of drug use in adolescence: Personality, peer, and family correlates. *Developmental Psychology, 19,* 269–277.

Brook, J. S., Whiteman, M., Gordon, A. S., & Brook, D. W. (1987). *The role of older brothers in younger brother's drug use: Modeling and drug advocacy effects.* Unpublished manuscript.

Brook, J. S., Whiteman, M., Gordon, A. S., Brook, D. W., & Cohen, P. (1990, May). The psychosocial etiology of adolescent drug use: A family interactional approach. *Genetic, Social & General Psychology Monographs, 116*(2).

Brook, J. S., Whiteman, M., Gordon, A. S., & Cohen, P. (1986). Dynamics of childhood and adolescent personality traits and adolescent drug use. *Developmental Psychology, 22,* 403–414.

Brook, J. S., Whiteman, M., Nomura, C., Gordon, A. S., & Cohen, P. (1988). Personality, family, and ecological influences on adolescent drug use: A developmental analysis. *Journal of Chemical Dependency Treatment, 1,* 123–161.

Callan, D., Garrison, J., & Zerger, F. (1975). Working with the families and social networks of drug abusers. *Journal of Psychedelic Drugs, 7*(1), 19–25.

Cicirelli, V. G. (1985). Sibling relationships throughout the life cycle. In L. L'Abate (Ed.), *The handbook of family psychology and therapy, Vol. I* (pp. 177–214). Homewood, IL: Dorsey Press.

Cloninger, C., Bohman, M., & Sigvardsson, S. (1981). Inheritance of alcohol abuse: Cross-fostering analysis of adult men. *Archives of General Psychiatry, 38,* 861–868.

Coombs, R. H., & Coombs, K. (1988). Developmental stages in drug use: Changing family involvements. *Journal of Chemical Dependency Treatment, 1,* 73–98.

Coombs, R. H., & Paulson, M. J. (1988). Contrasting family patterns of adolescent drug users and nonusers. *Journal of Chemical Dependency Treatment, 1,* 59–72.

Cooper, C. R., Grotevant, H. D., & Condon, S. M. (1983). Individuality and connectedness in the family as a context for adolescent identity formation and role-taking skills. In H. D. Grotevant & C. R. Cooper (Eds.), *Adolescent development in the family* (pp. 43–59). San Francisco: Jossey-Bass.

Dunn, J. F., Plomin, R., & Daniels, D. (1986). Consistency and change in mother's behavior toward young siblings. *Child Development, 57,* 348–356.

Goodwin, D. W. (1979). Alcoholism and heredity: A review and hypothesis. *Archives of General Psychiatry, 36,* 57–61.

Jaffe, J. H. (1986). Opioids. In A. J. Frances & R. E. Hales (Eds.), *American Psychiatric Association annual review—Vol. 5* (pp. 137–159). Fairfield, PA: Fairfield Graphics.

Jessor, R., & Jessor, S. L. (1977). *Problem behavior and psychosocial development.* New York: Academic Press.

Kandel, D. B. (1976). Stages in adolescent involvement in drug use. *Science, 190,* 912–914.

Kandel, D. B., Kessler, R. C., & Margulies, R. Z. (1978). Antecedents of adolescent initiation into stages of drug use: A developmental analysis. In D. B. Kandel (Ed.), *Longitudinal research on drug use: Empirical findings and methodological issues* (pp. 73–99). New York: Halsted.

Kaufman, E. (1985). *Substance abuse and family therapy.* Orlando, FL: Grune & Stratton.

Kaufman, E., & Borders, L. (1988). Ethnic family differences in adolescent substance use. *Journal of Chemical Dependency Treatment, 1,* 99–121.

Kaufman, E., & Kaufmann, P. (1977). Multiple family therapy: A new direction in the treatment of drug abusers. *American Journal of Drug & Alcohol Abuse, 4*(4), 467–478.

Kaufman, E., & Kaufmann, P. (Eds.) (1979). *Family therapy of drug and alcohol abuse.* New York: Gardner Press.

Kaufman, E., & Pattison, E. M. (1981). Differential methods of family therapy in the treatment of alcoholism. *Journal of Studies on Alcohol, 42,* 951–971.

Labouvie, E. W., & McGill, C. R. (1986). Relation of personality to alcohol and drug use in adolescence. *Journal of Consulting and Clinical Psychology, 54,* 289–293.

Macdonald, D. I. (1984). *Drugs, drinking, and adolescents.* Chicago: Year Book Medical Publishers.

Magnusson, D. (1988). *Individual development from an interactional perspective: A longitudinal study.* Hillsdale, NJ: Lawrence Erlbaum.

Meyer, R. E., & Hesselbrock, M. N. (1984). Psychopathology and addictive disorders revisited. In S. M. Mirin (Ed.), *Substance abuse and psychopathology* (pp. 2–17). Washington, DC: American Psychiatric Press.

Montemayor, R. (1984). Maternal employment and adolescents' relations with parents, siblings, and peers. *Journal of Youth & Adolescence, 13,* 543–557.

Needle, R., McCubbin, H., Wilson, M., Reineck, R., Lazar, A., & Mederer, H. (1986). Interpersonal influences in adolescent drug use: The role of older siblings, parents and peers. *International Journal of the Addictions, 21,* 739–766.

Newcomb, M. D. (1988). *Drug use in the workplace: Risk factors for disruptive substance use among young adults.* Dover, MA: Auburn House Publishing Company.

Newcomb, M. D., & Bentler, P. M. (1988). *Consequences of adolescent drug use: Impact on psychosocial development and young adult role responsibility.* Newbury Park, CA: Sage.

Patterson, G. R. (1982). *Coercive family process.* Eugene, OR: Castalia Press.

Scarr, S., & McCartney, R. (1983). How people make their own environments: A theory of genotype environment effects. *Child Development, 54,* 424–435.

Stanton, M. D., & Todd, T. C. (1982). *The family therapy of drug abuse and addiction.* New York: Guilford Press.

Stein, J. A., Newcomb, M. D., & Bentler, P. M. (1987). An eight-year study of multiple influences on drug use and drug use consequences. *Journal of Personality & Social Psychology, 53,* 1094–1105.

CHAPTER THREE

From Psychodynamic to Structural to Integrated Family Treatment of Chemical Dependency

EDWARD KAUFMAN, M.D.
Professor of Psychiatry
University of California, Irvine

PAULINE KAUFMANN,
M.S.W.
Director of Family Therapy
Phoenix Foundation

Drug abuse and dependence do not occur in isolation; they afflict a particular member of a specific family living in a community that is part of a larger society. If drug abuse is seen from the vantage point of these four concentric circles, intervention tends to be ecological, sociological, familial, and psychological. An individual psychodynamic approach can not stand alone, or can any approach that ignores one or more of these circles.

The growing number of addicts[1] in the last 10 years is a result of many interwoven determinants. It is frequently difficult to find which factor is primary. However, the most important causes over the past decade are societal, involving community and familial dysfunction.

A survey was made of 20 young women who were residents in a drug-free therapeutic community. By means of in-depth interviews, it was revealed that 18 of them had been sexually abused before the age of 11 by their father, father-surrogate, or older brother. Although it was tempting to come to certain conclusions based on this information, further questioning revealed that all of these young women came from inner-city families where bedrooms and beds were shared by two or three other members of the family, and sleep space was allocated on the principle of first-come, first-served. It was not unusual for sisters and brothers to share a bed, and sometimes children and one or other of the parents did so.

We have a "chicken and egg" dilemma here. Which came first, the socioeconomic or the psychodynamic factors? The following two sets of observations deal with the addict and his or her family. They are the result of over 30 years of therapeutic work with addicts of varied ethnic and socioeconomic origin, and have proved valid regardless of the social class, race, sex, or drug of choice. Other observations that differ according to these variables will be described later in the chapter.

Common Features of the Addict

1. Drugs are used to facilitate or obliterate concern with sexual performance, communication, and assertion. In neurotics they are used to alleviate symptoms and in psychotics to provide an internal homeostasis (Kaufman, 1974, 1976).
2. Social factors are important in all classes and ethnic groups. In ghettos and other areas where poverty is concentrated, drugs may be the only available means to an exciting and seemingly fulfilling life. In the middle and upper classes, use of drugs represents an attempt to deal with a lack of meaning in one's life, emotional sterility, and the absence of intimate relationships (Kaufman, 1974, 1976).
3. The more out of keeping from an individual's social background and cultural norms a pattern of drug abuse is, the more likely it is that the user is suffering from severe underlying mental illness (Kaufman, 1974, 1976).
4. There is no orderly progression from dependence to independence, and pseudoadult stances are common.
5. Identification with quasi-parenting older delinquents, peers, and siblings is common.
6. Addicts are deficient in self-care with impaired self-regulation, self-soothing, and self-regulation.

Common Features of the Family with an Addict Member

1. The drug addict is often the symptom carrier of the family dysfunction.
2. The addict helps to maintain family homeostasis.
3. The addicted member reinforces the parental need to control and continue parenting, yet finds such parenting inadequate for his or her needs.
4. The addict provides a displaced battlefield so that implicit and explicit parental strife can continue to be denied.
5. Parental drug and alcohol abuse is common and is directly transmitted to the addict or results in inadequate parenting.

6. The addict forms cross-generational alliances that separate parents from each other. The closest alliance is between mother and precedes the addiction.
7. Parental death, divorce, or abandonment is common in the addict's early years (before drug use). Early sibling and paternal grandparent death is quite common.
8. Generational boundaries are diffuse—there is frequent competition between parents. Frequently the crisis created by the drug-dependent member is the only way the family gets together and attempts some problem solving, or is the only opportunity for a "dead" family to experience emotions.
9. Addicts form unstable pseudofamilies of procreation.

The histories of hundreds of addicts with whom these writers have worked are characterized by circularity and replication. The nuclear families of addicts tend to replicate the pattern of the family of origin. Therapeutic communities have seen two and three generations of families with addict members. When family therapy becomes part of the treatment of the adult addict or part of the addict's reentry process, new family patterns are learned, and the cycle of dysfunction that produced an addict member in the family is interrupted. In Kaufman's early work (1974) with addicts, families were presented by the patient through fantasies, distortions, and, in some cases, accurate reportage, but the families themselves were most often not included in the diagnostic or therapeutic process. More recently, psychodynamic factors have been integrated into family treatment.

It is only with a knowledge of the structure of the total family unit that the family can be understood and its potential therapeutically developed. Although our knowledge of the family structures of addicts has developed over 30 years of working in the field, we did not approach the formal study of family structures until recently. Presented below is a quantitative study of family structures based on Kaufman's (1979) work with 61 families of former heroin-dependent individuals housed in Su Casa, a residential treatment setting located in the ethnically diverse lower east side of Manhattan, and with 14 families of heroin addicts at the Awakening Family, a synanon-derived program in Los Angeles County.

Studies of addicts from one social class or ethnic group, and generalized to all addicts, account for many of the differences cited in the literature about the family structure of addicts. Kaufman's previous work (1976) has emphasized the vast differences between addicts from different ethnic, social, and cultural groups. The multiplicity of ethnic groups at Su Casa and the Awakening Family permit some generalizations about addict families, as well as hypotheses about ethnic-specific patterns. However, selection of these populations had also contained some biases that prohibit us from making sweeping generalizations about all addict families. The families evaluated constituted less than one-fourth of the families of clients who entered residential treatment. Thus, families who were geographically distant or emotionally disengaged tended not to participate and were not a part of the sample. This led to a strong bias toward involved and perhaps enmeshed families. The dynamic patterns were derived mainly from observations in multiple family therapy rather than from individual family interviews. This setting may provide further bias through overidentification, as families too readily recognize patterns in themselves that they see in others.

The ethnoracial breakdown of the 78 patients[2] in this study is shown in Table 3-1.

Italian and Jewish families of origin tended to be involved in family therapy in a high proportion of cases. The spouses of Hispanic residents attended more readily than the families of origin. Blacks, who constituted a third of the residents, did not become involved despite the constant presence of a black cotherapist at Su Casa. Of the 78 patients, 62 (79 percent) were males, and 16 (21 percent) were females. The average age of both patient groups was 25 years.

Of the 75 families, 8 (10 percent) families consisted of mate only, 67 (86 percent) of the families contained at least one member of the family of origin. There were 12 mates of residents whose family of origin also attended that were part of the group, so there were 20 mates (26 percent) in all.

The author observed that the 14 families at the Awakening Family were sufficiently similar to those at Su Casa to warrant combining the two samples. Although the Mexican-American California group had some similarities to New York City Puerto Ricans, there were also marked differences.

TABLE 3–1 • *Patient Ethnoracial Breakdown*

	Number	*Percent*
Hispanic		
(two Mexican-American)	18	23
Italian	15	19
White Anglo-Saxon Protestant	14	18
Jewish	10	13
Black	8	10
Irish	7	9
Greek	1	1
Mixtures		
(two with one Italian parent each)	5	6

Structural Patterns

The basic patterns of familial interaction were analyzed structurally using the concepts of Minuchin (1975). Thus, parent-child relationships were designated as enmeshed, clear, or disengaged, terms that will be defined later. Most families were observed for over six months. In addition to postgroup discussions of patterns, verbatim transcripts of all sessions were recorded and later analyzed to confirm initial impressions. Several months' of sessions were recorded on videotape and presented to several experienced family therapists who reviewed the structural patterns with the therapists. Nevertheless, all of the observations were quite subjective.

Some 56 of 64 (88 percent) mother-child relationships were considered enmeshed, as were 23 of 57 (40 percent) father-child relationships.[3] Two mothers were disengaged, as were 24 fathers (42 percent). Seven fathers and one mother died at a time that was crucial to the onset of drug abuse. Many parental divorces also occurred at the onset of drug abuse and appeared causally related. No relationship between an addict and his or her parent was designated as having clear boundaries. However, in the case of 6 mothers and 13 fathers, their relationship to their addict child was equivocal or varying, or insufficient information was available to classify these relationships as either enmeshed or disengaged. The mother or stepmother was present in all but one of the families of origin who participated. A total of 23 fathers did not participate in the family therapy, but 16 of these were classified by hearsay mainly as disengaged.

Of the 17 mates of male addicts, 11 (65 percent) women and 1 homosexual mate were quite passive and submissive. Three female mates were dominant and two relationships were too egalitarian to be so classified. All three male mates who attended were former addicts receiving methadone treatment who were quite dominant. One male mate who was talked about extensively in therapy had died traumatically shortly before his wife entered treatment. Although the woman to whom he was married was quite a strong person, their relationship was apparently balanced.

Siblings tended to fall equally into two basic categories: one group was composed of fellow addicts whose drug dependence was inextricably fused with that of the resident, and the other consisted of older siblings who were either the parental child who assumed an authoritarian role when the father was disengaged, and/or were themselves highly successful. Some of these successful siblings had individuated from the family, but many were still enmeshed. A third, smaller group of siblings was quite passive and not involved with substance abuse. Enmeshed addicted siblings buy drugs for each other, inject the other, set the other up to be arrested, or pimp for one another. At times a large family may show sibling relationships of all these types. When addict siblings vary widely in age, their drug abuse may not be enmeshed but is rather a product of similar parental and societal factors. Three addict sibling pairs were treated simultaneously in residence and, in the two cases where the families attended regularly, with beneficial structural shifts. One sibling who was not in residence, but who attended multiple family therapy regularly, showed great progress, as did the resident. Many successful siblings were quite prominent in their fields, and in these cases the addict sibling withdrew from any vocational achievement rather than compete.

Mothers tended to be enmeshed with addict children in all ethnic groups. The study showed that 6 of 10 Jewish and 7 of 13 Italian father-child pairs were enmeshed. Puerto Rican, black, and white Protestant fathers tended to be disengaged or absent from the therapy. The black and Greek samples were too small for generalization. However, most of the black families had strong, involved mothers, and the Greek family consisted of three totally enmeshed generations.

According to Minuchin (1975), enmeshment and disengagement refer to a preference for a type of transactional interaction. *Enmeshed* family subsystems are frequently handicapped in that a heightened sense of belonging requires a major yielding of autonomy. Thus, stresses in one family member cross over to the other (Minuchin, 1975). *Disengaged* systems tolerate a wide range of individual variation but lack a feeling of loyalty, belonging, or the ability to request support when needed (Minuchin, 1975). Narcotic addiction in a family member places such a great stress on the family that secondary enmeshment or disengagement can be expected. However, the authors' impressions are that these patterns, particularly mother-child enmeshment, antedated—and indeed led to—abuse of and dependence on narcotics.

The most frequent pattern observed was that of a male addict enmeshed with his mother, thereby separating her from her spouse, who retaliated with either brutality to the addict and/or disengagement from the family. The extent of what was considered pathologic enmeshment was quite variable. Extremely enmeshed mothers may become psychotic or suicidal when their sons act out or individuate themselves. In one case, a mother who was chronically psychotic and who had repeated psychiatric hospitalizations was symbiotically tied to her addict son during her psychotic episodes. Early in their family therapy the addict helped provoke an overt psychotic episode in his mother in order to reestablish their symbiotic tie. When this pattern was demonstrated in the family sessions, the cycle was interrupted. After the mother emerged from her psychosis, she poignantly told her son in the group, "I will not hold you to me any more." Another extremely enmeshed mother made a suicide attempt when her son left the program. Enmeshed mothers think, act, and feel for everyone in the family, but more so for their addict child. Several mothers regularly ingested prescribed minor tranquilizers or narcotics that were shared overtly or covertly with their sons. Many mothers suffered an agitated depression whenever their son or daughter "acted out" in destructive ways. Mothers who received prescription tranquilizers or abused alcohol frequently increased their intake whenever the addict acted out. The mother's psychosomatic symptoms are frequently blamed on the addict. In a Puerto Rican family, the addict's brothers told him that if their mother died from asthma, they would kill him.

The relationship between mothers and daughters tended to be extremely hostile, competitive, and at times chaotic. Half the mother-daughter relationships were also severely enmeshed. When her mother committed suicide, a daughter also made a serious suicide attempt. One father committed suicide after his wife ordered him out of the house for his brutality. The son assumed a parental-child role and did not use heroin until shortly after his mother remarried (to a man with addicted twin sons). A third of the fathers were alcoholic, though all but four of these had abandoned their families or died from alcoholism and were not a part of treatment. The one father who had himself been a heroin addict raised five of his six children as addicts. In the majority of Italian and Jewish families the entire family was quite enmeshed. Frequently both parents collaborated with the addict to keep him or her "infantilized" under the guise of protecting the addict from arrest or other danger. The pattern of father-son brutality was quite common, although it was seen in fathers who were enmeshed as well as disengaged. With disengaged fathers, brutality was frequently their only contact with their children. However, enmeshed fathers do beat their sons, thereby pushing the sons into strong coalitions with the mother against the father. Harsh physical discipline was common between Italian fathers and their sons. However, this was a multigenerational problem that was a part of enmeshed intimacy. In these Italian families, physical beatings did not seem to be traumatic in and of themselves. It is much easier for a father to hit a child once or twice than enforce a discipline over hours and days. In a Mexican-American family, the father was described as disengaged by his son before the father was seen in therapy. However, he attended every family session and after a while his machismo relaxed so that he could tell his son that he frequently worried about him so much that it impaired his functioning at work. Although the mother was the family "switchboard" through whom all communications went, the father was the family spokesperson who made the final decisions and stated them, a common pattern in Mexican-American families. This particular father was "too equivocal" to be classified as enmeshed or disengaged.

Overt incest was reported in only one father-daughter pair but was suspected or experienced covertly in many parent-child and sibling pairs. This is a much lower incidence of incest than is reported in most recent studies of female addicts, including the survey quoted earlier in this chapter.

It may be a function of the predominant use of a group setting, which did not condone discussion of this sensitive issue.

The addict acts as a barometer of family functioning, even when in treatment, so that his or her disruptive behavior is a symptom of familial dysfunction. There may be an extended period of familial difficulty during which the addict's abuse of drugs is denied by the entire family. Alternately, the addict is the scapegoat upon whom all intrafamilial problems are focused. Often the family's basic interactional pattern is dull and lifeless and only becomes alive when mobilized to deal with the crisis of drug abuse (Reilly, 1976). Guilt is frequently used to manipulate and may be induced by the addict to coerce the family into supporting the maintenance of a habit or by parents to curb individuation. Many mothers had severe psychosomatic symptoms that were blamed on the addict, thereby reinforcing the pattern of guilt and mutual manipulation. Mothers' drug and alcohol abuse and suicide attempts were also blamed on the addict.

Most of the fathers who were present in the therapy were very hard workers who had become supervisors, and who set very high performance standards for their sons, which were not met or even approached. Many sons, particularly Italians, worked directly for their fathers, frequently in the construction field. They were protected in this way from having to meet the usual demands of employment. Several fathers suffered disabling physical injuries after the onset of their son's drug dependence that prevented them from continuing to work.

Physical expressions of love and affection are generally either absent or used to deny and obliterate individuation or conflict. Anger about interpersonal conflicts is not expressed directly unless it erupts in explosive violence. Anger about drug use and the denial of its expression is seen quite frequently and is almost always counterproductive. All joy has disappeared in these families, as lives are totally taken up with the sufferings and entanglements of having an addict child. However, in many cases, the joylessness preceded the addiction. As Reilly (1976) noted, communication is most frequently negative, and there is no appropriate praise for good behavior. There is a lack of consistent limit setting by parents, and deviance may be punished or rewarded at different times (Reilly, 1976). This may even occur when there is no splitting of the parental alliance as described earlier. As in delinquent behavior related to drug abuse, there is vicarious parental gratification derived from the "risqué" aspects of the addict's life.

Discussion

The basic structural pattern in the families we have observed in this group is compatible with observations about other families of drug abusers, as well as those of alcoholics and schizophrenics (Alexander & Dibb, 1975; Klagsbrun & Davis, 1977; Noone & Reddig, 1976; Reilly, 1976). That is, the mother and son are symbiotically tied to each other prior to the onset of drug abuse, and the father is excluded and reacts with disengagement and/ or brutality. However, several of our observations concern other factors that have not been sufficiently developed in the literature.

The family patterns of narcotic addicts vary in different ethnic groups. The father may be disengaged in white Protestant and black families but enmeshed in Italian and Jewish families. Larger samples of families from each ethnic group must be studied, and more rigorously, to clearly delineate these patterns. In addition, there should be a study of "normal" families in each ethnic group to determine what if any differences there are from addict families in these ethnic groups. Our preliminary observations on the relationship of the female addict to her family must also be documented by further studies. The communication patterns of these families are less distorted than those of schizophrenics. Double binds are clearer and more overt, but frequently the adolescent's only escape route is through drugs.

Siblings are of crucial importance either through their own addiction, which is enmeshed with that of the identified patient, or in their role as a parental, authoritarian child or as an extreme success with which the potential addict cannot compete. Addicts may themselves have been parental children who have no way of asking for relief from responsibilities except through drugs. More commonly, an addict is the youngest child, and addiction maintains his or her status as the baby. Addict spouse pairs frequently duplicate roles with each other that they have developed in their families of origin and that may not be correctable unless work is done with the original family as well as the newly created nuclear family.

It is of interest that several, but not all, of the hypotheses about the families of addicts based on our earlier work with individuals has been supported by more recent work with families. The conclusions made in 1970 based on these psychoanalytic interviews were:

> *The fathers of these addicts were reported as intelligent, accomplished, cold, distant, sadistic, sexually and aggressively competitive with their sons and seductive with their daughters. Mothers were perceived as either distant or overtly seductive. There were many mothers who were psychotic and several who were themselves drug and alcohol abusers. Repeated masturbatory fantasies about mother as well as overt sexual attraction to her were common in male patients. Several siblings were also opiate dependents and in most of these cases there was a symbiotic tie between the addict siblings. (Kaufman, 1974)*

Thus siblings and fathers were seen quite similarly to their counterparts in the family studies. However, many alternative roles were not revealed. The importance of mothers was grossly underestimated as described in these psychoanalytic interviews.

Families who do not participate voluntarily in treatment must also be studied to determine their role, if any, in the etiology of drug abuse in the identified patient. Alexander and Dibb (1975) have stated that "a minority of opiate addicts maintain close emotional and financial relationships with their parents." However, this statement was based on a retrospective study of records of patients in methadone treatment in British Columbia. Methoadone-maintenance patients, in the authors' experience, tend to insulate their families from therapy more than addicts involved in any other form of treatment. In the 18 families studied (Alexander & Dibb, 1975) they noted that the father was dominant when present, as he was in 11 of the cases. However, their treatment sample was limited to Caucasians. Noone and Reddig (1976) found that a majority of drug abusers and addicts maintain close ties with their families of origin. They observed that such families frequently undergo "mock separations" through overdoses or institutionalization that ultimately strengthen loyalty bonds. In a study of 85 addicts, Stanton (1977) noted that of addicts with living parents, 82 percent saw their mothers and 58 percent saw their fathers at least weekly, and 66 percent either lived with their parents or saw their mothers daily. Vaillant (1966) reported that 72 percent of addicts still lived with their mothers at age 22, and 47 percent continued to live with a female blood relative after age 30. Interestingly, Vaillant also noted that of the 30 abstinent addicts in his follow-up study, virtually all were living independently from their parents. This may be evidence of how strong an enemy the family is if it is not made an ally through treatment. That only one-fourth of the residents at Su Casa and the Awakening Family were involved in family treatment is as much a reflection of limited outreach and treatment resources as it is a true indication of family involvement. Since multiple family groups frequently were composed of over 40 individuals, further outreach would have been counterproductive.

The symbiotic tie between mothers and sons has been consistently noted in the literature. Fort (1954) noted that such mothers were "overprotective, controlling and indulgent" and resembled the mothers of alcoholics and schizophrenics. "They were willing to do anything for their sons, except let them alone." In a comparison of mothers of drug addicts, schizophrenics, and normal adolescents, the mother's symbiotic need for the child was highest in the mothers of drug abusers (Attardo, 1965). Fort (1954), in a group comprised mainly of ghetto addicts, noted the "frequent virtual absence of a father figure" and that in the rare instances where there was prominent father figure, "he was most frequently a severe dominating person" who demanded that his son "grow up" but who desired to keep him an infant so that he would not be threatened by him. More recent studies of middle-class families have noted the presence of a strong father (Alexander & Dibb, 1975). Kirschenbaum, Leonoff, and Matiano (1974) noted that "the father's position as strong leader of the family seemed to be a fiction . . . needed and nourished by the mother as the 'real head of the family.' " Schwartzman (1975) also noted that fathers were either "strawman" authoritarian figures or distant but clearly "secondary to the mother in terms of power."

Several authors have noted that drug use is essential to maintaining an interactional family equilibrium that resolves a disorganization of the family system that existed prior to drug taking (Minuchin, 1975; Noone & Reddig, 1976). The "addictor" in the system may be the parent(s) or the spouse, as noted by Pearson and Little (1975). Wellisch, Gay and McEntee (1970) noted that one partner, usually the male, is supported or taken care of by the other and so becomes an "easy rider" throughout the relationship. Our experience is that the male addict dominates either the addicted or nonaddicted spouse to take care of him in much the same way he related to his mother. This pattern was particularly clear in Puerto Rican addicts.

We hope this material will stimulate further family work and the development of precise research instruments so that these ideas and hypotheses can be validated. The dynamics and structural sets described in this chapter should certainly be looked for by anyone who works with addicts and their families. It is hoped that the therapist will seek out these maladaptive sets, validate them, and begin to change them in addict families, for it is only when these changes occur that addicts returning to their families are not drawn back into patterns that inevitably lead to readdiction.

Endnotes

1. After a brief crusade to change the term *addict* to *drug dependents* or *drug-dependent individuals,* the authors frequently resort to the former term because it is clearer. *Addict* means someone who has been dependent on drugs for a substantial period of time—in this sample, generally for over six years.

2. There were 3 sibling pairs in residence, thus 78 patients and 75 families.

3. Parents of the sibling pairs were considered separately here because relationships differed.

References

Alexander, B. K., & Dibb, G. S. (1975). Opiate addicts and their parents. *Family Process, 14,* 499–514.

Attardo, N. (1965). Psychodynamic factors in the mother-child relationship in adolescent drug addiction: A comparison of mothers of schizophrenics and mothers of normal adolescent sons. *Psychotherapeutic Psychosomatic, 13,* 249–252.

Fort, J. P. (1954). Heroin addiction among young men. *Psychiatry, 17,* 251–259.

Kaufman, E. (1974). The psychodynamics of opiate dependence: A new look. *Am. J. Drug & Alcohol Abuse, 1,* 349–370.

Kaufman, E. (1976). The abuse of multiple drugs: Psychological hypotheses, treatment considerations. *Am. J. Drug & Alcohol Abuse 3,* 293-304.

Kaufman, E. (1979). The therapeutic community and methadone: A way of achieving abstinence. *Intern'l J. Addictions, 14.*

Kirschenbaum, M., Leonoff, G., & Maliano, A. (1974). Characteristic patterns in drug abuse families. *Family Therapy, 1,* 43-62.

Klagsbrun, M., & Davis, D. Substance abuse and family interaction. *Family Process, 16,* 194-174.

Minuchin, S. (1975). *Families and family therapy.* Cambridge, MA: Harvard University Press.

Noone, R. J., & Reddig, R. L. (1976). Case studies on the family treatment of drug abuse. *Family Process, 15,* 325-332.

Pearson, M. M., & Little, R. B. (1975). Treatment of drug addiction: Private practice experience with 84 addicts. *Am. J. Psychiatry, 122,* 164-169.

Reilly, D. M. (1976). Family factors in the etiology and treatment of youthful drug abuse. *Family Therapy, 2,* 149-171.

Schwartzman, J. (1975). The addict, abstinence and the family. *Am. J. Psychiatry, 132,* 154-157.

Stanton, M. D. (1977). Some outcome results and aspects of structural family therapy with drug addicts. National Drug Abuse Conference, San Francisco, May 5-9.

Vaillant, G. (1966). A 12-year follow-up of New York narcotic addicts. *Arch. General Psychiatry, 15,* 599-609.

Wellisch, D. K., Gay, G. R., & McEntee, R. (1970). The Easy Rider Syndrome: A pattern of hetero- and homosexual relationships in a heroin addict population. *Family Process, 9,* 425-430.

CHAPTER FOUR

Structural-Strategic Family Therapy with Drug Addicts

M. DUNCAN STANTON,
PH.D.
University of Rochester
School of Medicine

THOMAS C. TODD, PH.D.
Forest Health Systems
Des Plaines, Illinois

Although there is a body of literature on the nature and importance of family factors in drug addiction (Glynn, 1984; Harbin & Maziar, 1975; Klagsbrun & Davis, 1977; Seldin, 1972; Stanton 1979a, 1985), less has been written on the actual methods for family *treatment* of addiction (Heath & Atkinson, 1988; Heath & Stanton, 1991; Stanton, 1979b, 1988). Thus, family-oriented therapists were left to their own resources if they wanted to progress from an "understanding" of addict families to the adventure of bringing about change. It is the purpose of this chapter to present some strategies and techniques that we hope will not lessen the adventurous nature of the trip but will help therapists keep from getting lost or discouraged while sailing these waters.

Funding for this work was provided through grants from the National Institute on Drug Abuse (DA 1119) and the Attorney General of Pennsylvania's Public Health Trust Fund (56772). It was conducted at the Philadelphia Child Guidance Clinic. Research and clinical support was provided by the Philadelphia V.A. Hospital Drug Dependence Treatment Program and the University of Pennsylvania.

Other project staff, who contributed substantially to the development of this treatment approach, included Henry Berger, M.D., Gary Lande, M.D. (therapy supervisors), Gerald Hawthorne, David Heard, Ph.D., Sam Kirschner, Ph.D., Jerry Kleiman, Ph.D., David Mowatt, Ed.D., Paul Riley, Alexander Scott, M.S.W., Samuel M. Scott, Peter Urquhart (therapists), Esther Carr, John M. Van Deusen (research associates), Elton Hargrove, Charles P. O'Brien, M.D., and George Woody, M.D. (Philadelphia V.A. Hospital Drug Dependence Treatment Program).

Our experience has primarily evolved within the context of a research program on the effectiveness of family therapy with drug addicts (Stanton, 1978; Stanton, Todd, and Associates, 1982). It gained impetus in 1972, when we undertook a survey of family contacts of 85 addicts at the Philadelphia Veterans Administration Drug Dependence Treatment Center (DDTC). Results showed that of those with living parents, 82 percent saw their mothers and 59 percent saw their fathers at least weekly; 66 percent either lived with their parents or saw their mothers daily. The figures become more striking when one realizes that the average age of these men was 28 years and all of them had previously been separated from home and in the military for at least several months. The data also corroborate other studies (reviewed in Stanton, Todd, and Associates [1982]), such as Vaillant's (1966) follow-up study of New York addicts in which he found that 72 percent of the total sample, or 90 percent of those with living mothers, still resided with their mothers at age 22.

This made us recognize how intensively involved the addict is with his or her family of origin. At this point, we have seen these close entanglements so often that we are skeptical when any addict, especially one under age 35, tells us that he or she does not see his or her parents regularly. Such knowledge has helped us to insist that the parents be involved in treatment, even when the addict tries to persuade us that the "real problems" are with the spouse or girlfriend or boyfriend.

The therapeutic aspects described in this chapter are based primarily on more than 60 families seen in family treatment within the research program, although we also had less systematic experience with drug-using families prior to the project. Much of the work in the early stages was exploratory, and part of our goal here is to help others to learn from our mistakes. The families were followed up 12 months after treatment, and the results are dramatically better than for a matched group of clients in the DDTC methadone/individual counseling program (Stanton, Todd, and Associates, 1982). Of the family therapy cases who were provided with incentives so they would attend sessions, two-thirds could be considered "good" outcomes—a rate that was double that for the comparison group of motivated methadone patients who did not receive family treatment.

The family therapy model employed in the project had two major influences. Many of the treatment concepts derive from the work of Minuchin (1974) and colleagues of the Philadelphia Child Guidance Clinic, particularly a psychosomatic research project, in which one of us participated.[1] Since structural family therapy is described at length in the present volume, only the highlights will be presented in this chapter. Structural therapy has been shown to be effective with a variety of problems and different kinds of therapists. A case in point is one of the major outcome studies to date with this approach (Rosman et al., 1976), in which 50 cases were seen by 16 therapists with widely ranging levels of experience and who came from 4 different disciplines. Our own work with addicts has involved 9 different therapists from 4 professions, most of whom had modest clinical credentials; 3 of them were paraprofessionals and did not have academic degrees.

Structural family therapy typically focuses on patterns of family interaction and communication within the session and attempts to influence these patterns directly and actively. Tasks or "homework" are assigned to consolidate changes made during the sessions. In this approach, past history and insight are deemphasized, with the major stress placed on changing current interaction. The therapist usually attempts to set boundaries and restructure the family, often by reinforcing generational boundaries between parents and offspring.

From this earlier work, we have evolved a treatment model that incorporates both structural and strategic practices, in addition to introducing some distinctive features of its own. We call is *structural-strategic therapy* (Stanton, 1981a, 1981b; Stanton, Todd, and Associates, 1982). The general thrust is strategic, but many of the moment-to-moment, or *micromoves,* within sessions are of a more structural nature, combined with the regular use throughout of "noble ascriptions" (see below). Specifically, the procedure is to (1) apply Minuchin's structural theory as a guiding paradigm; (2) work structurally within sessions through the actual enactment of new patterns, and the application of structural techniques such as joining, accommodating, testing boundaries, restructuring, and so forth; and (3) apply Haley's strategic model in terms of its emphasis on a specific plan, extrasession events, change in the symptom, collaboration among treatment systems, and the like. A more detailed breakdown as to these clinical operations is presented in Stanton, Todd, and Associates (1982).

A second major source of our ideas has been Jay Haley, who served as a major consultant to our project. Haley introduced ideas originally worked out with families of schizophrenics, first in Palo Alto, California, later at the Philadelphia Child Guidance Clinic,[2] and more recently at the Family Therapy Institute of Washington, DC with Cloe Madanes. In addition to having helped develop structural family therapy, Haley contributed many ideas to the project that are uniquely his own. These can be found in Haley (1973, 1976, 1980). A summary of his therapy approach with this problem will be offered in the section entitled Course of Therapy.

Clinical Context

The major part of our work has been done with patients who initially enrolled for methadone treatment at the Veterans Administration DDTC. Most of them were male, under age 35, and had been addicted to opiates for at least two years. Half were black and half were white. To be selected for our project, patients usually had to have contact weekly with one parent or parent-substitute (e.g., stepmother, mother's boyfriend) and at least monthly with the other. The majority of the patients had been treated previously for drug addiction.

Upon admission, patients' eligibility for our program was determined. If a treatment opening existed, eligible clients were then assigned to a family therapist. If not, they went the regular methadone treatment route and were assigned to a drug counselor for individual counseling and monitoring of medications. The family therapist served as the client's drug counselor for those in family treatment. It was the therapist's responsibility to meet with the client and discuss bringing his or her family into treatment (Van Deusen, Scott, Stanton, & Todd, 1980; Stanton, Todd, and Associates, 1982). This often led to a lengthy process in which the therapist contacted the parents and other family members and encouraged their participation (Stanton & Todd, 1981; Stanton, Todd, and Associates, 1982). It usually necessitated a number of telephone calls and, in a few instances, home visits. In 71 percent of the cases, the family was successfully brought into treatment.

Family therapy proceeded as an adjunct to the DDTC program and was accompanied by at least weekly urine testing (randomly scheduled) and other administrative linkages. In general, however, family therapy evolved into the major mode of treatment for those who participated in it.

Family Characteristics

Families in our project exhibit many of the patterns described in the earlier literature (Alexander & Dibb, 1975; Harbin & Maziar, 1975; Klagsbrun & Davis, 1977; Reilly, 1976; Schwartzman, 1975; Seldin, 1972; Stanton, 1979a, 1985). For example, there is a very close, dependent, mother-son relationship paired with a distant, excluded father (although in several of our cases the roles were reversed and the father was the parent closest to the children). Approximately 50 percent had a parent with a drinking problem. Furthermore, in most cases the fathers were observed to be most upset by their son's addiction, as the mothers tended to minimize it. This differs from typical child or adolescent problems, where the mother is more likely to voice the complaint.

There is usually a lack of constructive pressure for change in these families. The addict is discounted as a person, the family feels powerless, or the family blames outside causes (peers, neighborhood) for the addict's problem. In some families, the addict's drug problem is the focus for all family problems. Further, the addict is often overprotected by the family and treated as a helpless and incompetent person. In these families, drugs are viewed as an all-powerful force that cannot be resisted.

The special role that the addict plays within the family is particularly important. His or her actions help to maintain family stability — largely at his or her own expense.[3] Thus the addict serves a "noble," sacrificial purpose (Stanton, 1977).

Course of Therapy

In the remainder of the chapter, we will present basic principles drawn from our work with the families of addicts.[4] Obviously, not all apply equally well to all families, nor do all families move through these stages with equal speed. Our usual length of treatment is 10 to 12 sessions, but some families have required fewer, and several have needed as many as 18.

Before discussing the treatment in more detail, its general approach can be understood by a summary, written by Haley for this chapter, which is expanded on in his book on therapy with problem young people (Haley, 1980).

There are certain assumptions that improve the chance of success with young adults who exhibit mad and bizarre behavior, or continually take illegal drugs, or who waste their lives and cause community concern. For therapy, it is best to assume that the problem is not the young person but a problem of a family and young person disengaging from one another. Ordinarily, an offspring leaves home by succeeding in work or school and forming intimate relationships outside the family. In some families, when a son or daughter begins to leave home, the family becomes unstable and in distress. If at that point the young person fails by becoming incapacitated, the family stabilizes as if the offspring has not left home. This can happen even if the young person is living away from home, as long as he or she regularly lets the family know that failure continues. It can also exist even if the family is angry at the offspring and appears to have rejected him. Family stability continues as long as the young person is involved with the family by behaving in some abnormal way.

A therapist should assume that, if the family organization does not change, the young person will continue to fail year after year, despite therapy efforts. The unit with the problem is not the young person, but at least two other people: these might be two parents, or a mother and boyfriend or sibling, or a mother and grandmother. It is assumed that two adults in a family communicate with each other by way of the young person and they enter severe conflict if the young person is not available to be that communication vehicle. The therapy goal is to free the young adult from that triangle so that he or she lives like other normal young people and the family is stable without the problem child.

This therapy and its premises has no relation to a therapy based on the theory of repression where an individual is the problem. Therefore, there is no concern with insight or awareness and there is no encouragement of people to express their feelings with the idea that this will cause change. Therapists accustomed to experiential groups or psychodynamic therapy have difficulty with this approach.

The therapy should occur in the following stages:

1. *When the young person comes to community attention, the experts must organize themselves in such a way that one therapist takes responsibility for the case. It is better not to have a team or a number of separate therapists or modes of therapy. The one therapist must be in charge of whether the young person is to be in or out of an institution and what medication is to be given, and when. Only if the therapist is in charge of the case can he put the parents in charge within the family.*

2. *The therapist needs to gather the family for a first interview. If the young person is living separately, even with a wife, he should be brought together with the family of origin so that everyone significant to him is there. The goal is to move the young person to more independence, either alone or with a wife, but the first step to that end is to take him back to his family.*

   There should be no blame of the parents, but instead, the parents (or parent and grandmother, or whomever it might be) should be put in charge of solving the problem of the young person. They must be persuaded that they are really the best therapists for the problem offspring (despite past failures in trying to help him). It is assumed that the members of the family are in conflict and the problem offspring is expressing that. By requiring the family to take charge and set the rules for the young person, they are communicating about the young person, as usual, but in a positive way. Certain issues need to be clear:

   a. *The focus should be on the problem person and his behavior, not on a discussion of family relations. If the offspring is an addict, the family should focus on what is to happen if he ever takes drugs again. If mad and misbehaving, what they will do if he acts bizarrely in the way that got him in the hospital before. If anorexic, how much weight she is to gain per day, and how that is to be accomplished.*

   b. *The past, and past causes of the problem, are ignored and not explored. The focus is what to do now.*

   c. *The therapist should join the parents against the problem young person, even if this seems to be depriving him of individual choices and rights, and even if he seems too old to be made that dependent. After the person is behaving normally, his rights can be considered. It is assumed that the hierarchy of the family is in confusion. Should the therapist step down from his status as expert and join the problem young person against the parents, there will be worse confusion and the therapy will fail.*

   d. *Conflicts between the parents or other family members are ignored and minimized even if they bring them up, until the young person is back to normal. If the parents say they have problems and need help too, the therapist should say the first problem is the son, and their problems can be dealt with after the son is back to normal.*

e. *Everyone should expect the problem person to become normal, with no suggestion that the goal is a handicapped person. Therefore, the young person should not be in a halfway house, a day hospital, kept on medication or on maintenance methadone. Normal work or school should be expected immediately, not later. Work should be self-supporting and real, not volunteer.*

3. *As the problem young person becomes normal (by achieving self-support, or successfully going to school, or by making close friends) the family will become unstable. This is an important stage in the therapy and the reason for pushing the young person toward normality. The parents will threaten separation or divorce or one or both will be disturbed. At that point, a relapse of the young person is part of the usual pattern, since that will stabilize the family. If the therapist has sided with the parents earlier, they will lean upon him at this stage and the young adult will not need to relapse to save them. The therapist must either resolve the parental conflict, or move the problem young person out of it while it continues more directly. At that point, the young person can continue to be normal.*

4. *The therapy should be an intense involvement and a rapid disengagement, not regular interviews over years. As soon as positive change occurs, the therapist can begin to recess and plan termination. The task is not to resolve all family problems but the ones around the problem young person, unless the family wants to make a new contract for other problems.*

5. *Regular follow-ups should be done to ensure that positive change continues.*

Our approach to the families of heroin addicts is based on the above principles and, as previously mentioned, shows considerable evidence of success. While other family therapy approaches may yield insightful observations about these families, we are interested in what *works* rather than what is interesting or "true" at some level of interpretation. This statement may seem obvious, but we have seen others become so enamored of family dynamics that the means for effecting change escape them. Furthermore, it has not been characteristic for most other programs to evaluate their degree of success in any objective fashion. We have made an effort to monitor our own effectiveness in order to develop further our techniques.

Initial Phase

Given the general approach, a more detailed description can be offered of the steps in the therapy. The initial contact with the addict and family (to get them into treatment) may demand considerable time and effort by the therapist (Stanton & Todd, 1981; Stanton, Todd and Associates, 1982; Van Deusen et al., 1980). Our research design required that we get at least the addict and both parents or parent-substitutes together before proceeding.

When we encounter resistance from the addict, particularly protestations of independence from parents, we generally stress our need for the perspective that only parents can provide. Once we are given permission to contact the parents, we stress the need for help from everyone and studiously avoid any implications of blame. We also emphasize that this program differs in one significant way from programs that have failed in the past: we involve the parents actively, rather than excluding them (Stanton & Todd, 1981; Stanton, Todd, and Associates, 1982; Van Deusen et al., 1980).

It is necessary to emphasize the importance of a *nonblaming stance* in this treatment. We find that the confrontative techniques that may be useful in group therapy with drug abusers generally do not work with these families. Instead, such approaches tend to foster massive family resistance and counterattack. This is not to say that we do not challenge families, but that we try to express our points in nonpejorative ways. We typically *ascribe noble intentions* to the behaviors we observe in the families ("He's defending the family like any good son would." "You are trying your best to be a good mother."). This serves to lessen overt resistance, and allows therapy to proceed more smoothly and rapidly. We call these techniques *noble ascriptions*.

Early sessions typically focus on setting common goals for treatment. At this stage all goals should relate directly to helping the index patient stay off drugs. If the family brings up other issues, their relevance should be questioned—the family should have to justify them as pertinent to the primary goal. To keep therapy focused and productive, it is often appropriate to establish a date for detoxification and then to help the family prepare for it. At all times the therapist should avoid a power struggle with the parents or the addict, for he or she will always lose in the end and treatment will falter.

The major goal of the therapist in the early stages is to form an alliance with both parents, so that they can take an effective stance toward the addict. It is critical that the therapist keep the parents working *together* in the early stages. He or she should not allow them to get into their own marital difficulties, as this will divide and deter them from the task at hand. One way of facilitating this in cases where the addict and mother are overinvolved is to get the father to take charge of his son or daughter.

Usually the experience of father and son or daughter relating must first come about in the session before it can be generalized to the home situation. It may be possible to get them engaged in discussing some common interest such as work or a hobby. The mother should be present during this exchange and may need the therapist's subtle support while her husband and child are engaged.

Other tactics may also be used, depending on the specific clinical situation. When it appears that the mother endorses the drug behavior of the addict, with the father consistently more punitive, it may be possible to force the mother to deal with the negative behavior of the addict, thus breaking the alliance with him or her. Alternatively, the therapist may meet only with the parents to formulate a strategy to which both parents will adhere.

Middle Phases and Crises

As change starts to occur and the addict stops or curtails taking drugs, a family crisis can be expected. It normally happens three or four weeks into treatment. Most commonly it will revolve around the parents' marital relationship, with them talking about, or taking steps toward, separation or divorce. This puts tremendous pressure on the addict to become "dirty" again in order to reunite the family. At such times, the therapist will need to devote considerable time and energy to resolving the crisis. He or she will have to be accessible and perhaps constantly on call. The therapists's goal is to get the parents to hold together in relation to the addict and not let them separate, at least until this storm is weathered. If the transition is handled skillfully, treatment is usually on the way to a successful outcome, for succeeding crises will be easier for the family to cope with; a previously recurrent pattern has been broken and real change has occurred.

After an initial improvement, it is not uncommon for other problems to crop up in family sessions. The therapist must beware of getting thrown off the track by these difficulties, as they sometimes are introduced to avoid the primary goal of treatment. One approach the therapist can use is to deal with such problems only if the family can justify their relevance to drug taking (e.g., "He can't get off drugs if he doesn't first have a job to replace them"). Should the therapist become lost as a result of these side issues, he or she can always reorient the therapy by returning to the primary symptom. It is important for the therapist to raise the question, "How does this relate to his or her drug problem?" before the family does.

Data from the Addicts and Families Project confirmed that major crises and their management are a critical factor in working with addicts and their families. In 36 out of 39 families, a major crisis emerged involving the addict (Mowatt, Heard, Steier, Stanton, & Todd, 1982). The therapists worked with family members to get them to resolve the crisis in a way that changed the usual pattern of family interaction. In 26 of the 36 cases, the crisis was successfully resolved; in 7 of the remaining cases, the crisis was unresolved; and the other 3 cases involved multiple crises. When the degree of successful outcome was examined, as indicated by freedom from opiate use, the expected relationship was found between occurrence and resolution of crises and successful outcome of therapy.

In instances where drug taking by the addict has recurred, the question of responsibility arises. Who is responsible for the individual's drug use? Often there is a good deal of squirming in response to this question. Conventional drug treatment programs get around it by either taking responsibility themselves or thrusting it on the index patient. However, when seen in a context where addiction serves a clear family function, the conventional view has shortcomings. It should be remembered that the addicted individual was raised by, and in most cases is still being maintained by, his or her family of origin. It is thus with the family that responsibility rests, and the therapist should help the family either to accept it or to *effectively* disengage from the addict so that the addict must accept it on his or her own.

At the suggestion of Jay Haley, we have also explored a variation on the responsibility theme, in which the family takes charge of the detoxification process in the home (Stanton, Todd, and Associates, 1982; Stanton, Steier, Cook, & Todd, 1984). Our aim is to have the family help the addict detoxify "cold turkey." It might be done over a weekend, and preparation with the family is required to anticipate such problems as the addict getting out of the house, a sibling or friend bringing him or her drugs, parents relaxing their vigilance, and so on. "On call" medical and therapeutic backup are available to the family throughout. It appears wise to negotiate a contract beforehand to undertake the process a second time, in case the first attempt fails; if the family members know they might have to go through it twice, they are more likely to succeed the first time. Normally detoxification takes place at the drug treatment center, so if it fails, the family does not feel responsible. However, if family members are themselves involved in the process, they are not going to take subsequent drug use by the addict so lightly. They will be angry with the addict and may in this way be able to establish appropriate distance from him or her. In addition, the therapist can use either success or failure of the first attempt to his or her (and the family's) advantage. Obviously, a successful home detox has the family doing just what it should do, and getting credit for it, as well. Conversely, failure can serve a disengaging function.

Final Phase

It should be remembered that we are dealing here with a brief-therapy model. One advantage of this model is that it catalyzes and compresses into a time span of three to five months a process that may otherwise be prolonged with a questionable increase in effectiveness. The short-term, contractual arrangement forces more rapid change. If the therapist can maintain the family as an ally in this process, it can be quite effective.

Treatment may evolve toward other issues if freedom from drug taking has been maintained for a month or more. Two topics that often arise are gainful employment or schooling and, where appropriate, getting the addict out of the home. Underlying both topics are issues of separation: either physical separation or separation through increased competence and the resulting independence of functioning.

There are a number of ways of dealing with these issues. They can sometimes be approached through the assignment of small, unchallengable tasks, such as having the addict look up two jobs or two apartments in the classified section of the newspaper. It is ideal for the parents to participate in these tasks, so that they feel some sense of participation in the addict's eventual success. Another approach is to shift the roles of the parents, to, for example, either those of grandparents (rather than overinvolved parents) or of parents to any younger children they might have (e.g., "You can let her go because you have these other kids to worry about"). Further, if the parents are retired or near retirement, the therapist may want to work with them on planning this stage of their lives.

Another subject that may emerge in later stages is the parents' marriage. If the index patient is stabilized and clean, it may be possible to deal with this. It is crucial to keep the addict from getting involved in the parents' problems once they start to deal with marital issues. In fact, it is rather common for the addict to attempt to reenter their relationship after he or she has been clean for a while, so the therapist must be prepared to help the parents resist the addict. If the therapist can orchestrate treatment so that the parents vocally tell their child to stay out of their marital discussion, a reasonable outcome can probably be expected.

Termination difficulties will not generally arise if adequate change has occurred and been maintained long enough for the family to feel a sense of real accomplishment. Otherwise, the family will be fearful and may generate crises or other problems in order to keep the therapist involved. In any case, it is probably advisable to space final sessions further apart and perhaps to tentatively arrange for a kind of innoculatory follow-up session two to four months after termination.

Special Issues

There are certain aspects of this treatment that deserve additional discussion. Most of them pervade the total treatment process and have been arrived at through the pain of experience. Although the bulk of this material deals with heroin addicts, we do not feel that the principles are necessarily limited only to this group. Heroin addicts are perhaps the most intractable of drug abusers, but our feeling is that if a therapist can be successful with *these* cases, others will be comparatively easy.

Administrative Support and Flexibility

Without clear commitment and support from the administrative arm of the overall drug treatment program, this treatment will flounder and probably fail. It is a truism to say that drug addicts are manipulative, and we have found that changes in administrative procedures are often necessary to plug loopholes and adapt to particular family situations. For example, we encountered instances in which the index patient approached the DDTC medical director to get him to talk to his or her parents about treatment; this "flanking move" would have succeeded had the medical director not contacted and allowed the family therapist to take charge of the issue. In another case, the therapist put the father in charge of his son's methadone, so that all raises or decreases were to be cleared with father. Without administrative support, this process could have been undercut and the father's authority nullified.

A similar issue is the amount of control the therapist has over management of the index patient's overall program. When we started our research program, each client had both a drug counselor and a family therapist. With such an arrangement the addict's interpersonal skills surfaced, and he or she could often succeed in getting these two helpers to struggle over treatment and their respective turfs; he or she played them off against each other. We changed this by having the therapist wear both hats—family therapist and drug counselor—thus eliminating the triangulation. It also gave the therapist control over medications by making all changes go through him or her. This eliminated a lot of undermining and also allowed the therapist to deal with crises more effectively. We do not think this treatment will succeed unless the therapist has such control.[5]

A practice that we would advocate, and that exists in a number of drug treatment programs across the country (Coleman & Stanton, 1978), is that of *requiring* the family to come in either at, or immediately after, intake and before any treatment whatsoever begins. In situations where this is practiced, it engenders only a slight increase in dropouts and saves much of the effort expended in recruiting families. If clients know there is no other way to get treatment or methadone without bringing their families in, they can usually find a way to do it.

Urinalysis Results

The results of weekly urine test have been quite helpful in our family treatment. They give a tangible indication of progress and do not allow family members (or the therapist) to sidestep this issue. They can also serve as aids in getting the family to take responsibility and put pressure on the index patient to remain clean. It usually helps to negotiate the ground rules for failure with the family at the outset of treatment. The idea is to get advance agreement that they will believe the urine tests. If the addict protests that someone has switched or will switch urine samples, the therapist should get the family to agree on the number of times they will accept this story before they can finally trust the urinalysis results.

Parental-Addict Triad

It has become clear to us that family treatment must first deal with the triad composed of addict and both parents before proceeding further. If this step is skipped, therapy will falter and possibly fail. In some cases with married addicts, we started with the marital pair and found that it only served to strain or dissolve the marriage; thus, the addict would end up back with his or her parents. However, families will differ on the rapidity with which the transition from family of origin to family of procreation can be made. In some cases, the parents can be eased out of the picture within a few sessions, whereas in others they have to be involved throughout treatment. The key is to start with the parental-addict triad and to move away from it in accordance with parents' readiness to release the addict.

We attempt to include all siblings living at home or in the immediate vicinity. Again, the rule of thumb is to see how family members interact before concluding that any member is not needed in the sessions. Siblings may serve a number of functions in the sessions. They may act as allies to the addict and help to get the addict to assert himself or herself more appropriately. Often they provide a useful alternative focus and prevent exclusive attention from being given to the addict. It is not unusual to find siblings who are also addicted or have problems as severe as those of the addict. Finally, siblings always provide additional data on family interactions, which the therapist may use to advantage.

Other Systems

It would not be accurate to view our treatment approach as always limited just to the addict and immediate family. This may be the primary system involved, but other interpersonal systems are also engaged as appropriate. We deal with them if they are particularly relevant to the case and can serve to facilitate or hinder therapeutic progress. Such systems might include friends, vocational counselors, employers, school or legal authorities, and, of course, the staff of the drug treatment program itself.

Subsequent to the work described above, the first author (MDS) has shifted to an increased emphasis on the inclusion of grandparents, great-grandparents, and other important relatives in therapy with substance abusers — often using a network approach (Landau-Stanton & Stanton, 1985; Stanton, 1992; Stanton and Landau-Stanton, 1990). The determination that, for instance, grandparents and parents are often in competition for the loyalties of the identified patient has led Stanton to predominantly treat the extended family. Such experiences have also tended to highlight the importance of death-related dynamics and unresolved grief in these families (Coleman & Stanton, 1978; Stanton, 1977; Stanton & Coleman, 1980) requiring that such issues be dealt with therapeutically (Landau-Stanton & Stanton, 1985; Stanton & Landau-Stanton, 1990).

It would not be accurate to view our treatment approach as being limited to the addict and family members. Although this may be the primary system involved, other interpersonal systems are engaged as needed. In some situations, the primary "customer" for therapy is another professional helper rather than a family member. The second author (TCT) has worked extensively in Sweden, where the treatment context often includes multiple helpers who must be involved in family treatment for it to be successful. (See Todd, 1991, for further discussion of these issues.)

The second author has also been engaged with his colleague, Matthew Selekman, in developing innovative methods of involving the drug abuser's peer group. Rather than the peer group being regarded as the enemy, these peers can prove to be important resources even if they are not abstinent themselves (see Todd & Selekman, 1991; Selekman, 1991).

Single-Parent Families

Because of the restrictions of our research design, most of our work has been with families in which two adults of different sex were involved, either as parents or in quasi-parental roles. In cases where only one parent is available — usually the mother — the process differs somewhat. Here, the therapist may have to at least temporarily fill a parental role toward the addict, and at other times, must assume an almost spouselike role toward the parent. Often the latter is a way of substituting for a role that has been played by the addict. The next step is to develop alternative structures and supports for the parent through inclusion of relatives, friends, and so on — in other words, to establish or build on the natural support system. In this way the parent will be less dependent on the addict and able to move toward greater disengagement. When applicable, another approach is to help the parent get a job or develop more outside activities. Still another, stated earlier, is to transfer some of the attention from the addict to any younger siblings remaining in the family. Again, joining with the parent is a crucial part of the process, and under no conditions should the therapist become engaged in a direct power struggle with the parent over separation of him or her from the index patient.

Female Addicts

We have worked with only a few families in which the index patient was female. Our impression is that the dynamics are similar in many ways to those for males, as are the therapeutic strategies. However, this is an area that needs further exploration.

Therapists

As a closing note, let us mention some qualities and behaviors in therapists that appear to contribute to successful treatment. The ability to be active is important and is a cornerstone of structural-strategic therapy in general. Passive, reflective styles usually do not work well. On the other hand, the therapist must be able to be supportive, concerned, accessible, and enthusiastic. Flexibility is also essential, as drug addicts' families are very skillful and will "trip up" an inflexible therapist. Finally, since these families can be very demanding and draining — especially in a brief-therapy context — we would not recommend that a therapist carry more than three or four such cases at a time, particularly while learning these techniques.

Endnotes

1. Psychosomatic project staff, besides Minuchin and Todd, included Lester Baker, M.D., Ronald Liebman, M.D., Leroy Milman, M.D., and Bernice Rosman, Ph.D.

2. Members of the PCGC schizophrenia project were Charles Billings, M.D., Harold Cohn, M.D., H. Charles Fishman, M.D., Paul Gross, M.D., David B. Heard, Ph.D., David Hunt, M.D., Gary Lande, M.D., Lawrence Miller, M.D., David T. Mowatt, Ed.D., Lee Petty, M.D., Alberto Rish, M.D., Meyer Rothbart, M.D., and Frances Ziegler, M.S.W.

3. The role of the addict in family homeostasis is elaborated on in a paper and book from our project (Stanton, Todd, Heard, Kirschner, Kleiman, Mowatt, Riley, Scott, & Van Deusen, 1978; Stanton, Todd, and Associates, 1982).

4. A more detailed presentation, including specific cases, is given in our book, *The Family Therapy of Drug Abuse and Addiction* (Stanton, Todd, and Associates, 1982).

5. Haley has emphasized similar issues in his work with severely disturbed young people, and makes it a general rule only to work with therapists who have overall control of the case.

References

Alexander, B. K., & Dibb, G. S. (1975). Opiate addicts and their parents. *Family Process, 14,* 499–514.

Coleman, S. B., & Stanton, M. D. (1978). An index for measuring agency involvement in family therapy. *Family Process, 17,* 479–483.

Coleman, S. B., & Stanton, M. D. (1978). The role of death in the addict family. *Journal of Marriage and Family Counseling, 4,* 79–91.

Glynn, T. J. (1984). Adolescent drug use and the family environment: A review. *Journal of Drug Issues, 2,* 271–295.

Haley, J. (1973). *Uncommon therapy.* New York: Norton.

Haley, J. (1976). *Problem-solving therapy.* San Francisco: Jossey-Bass.

Haley, J. (1980). *Leaving home.* New York: McGraw-Hill.

Harbin, H. T., & Maziar, H. M. (1975). The families of drug abusers: A literature review. *Family Process, 14,* 411–431.

Heath, A. W., & Atkinson, B. J. (1988). Systemic treatment of substance abuse: A graduate course. *Journal of Marital and Family Therapy, 14,* 411–418.

Heath, A. W., & Stanton, M. D. (1991). Family therapy. In R. J. Frances & S. I. Miller (Eds.), *Clinical textbook of addictive disorders* (pp. 406–430). New York: Guilford.

Klagsbrun, M., & Davis, D. I. (1977). Substance abuse and family interaction. *Family Process, 16,* 149–173.

Landau-Stanton, J., & Stanton, M. D. (1985). Treating suicidal adolescents and their families. In M. P. Mirkin & S. L. Koman (Eds.), *Handbook of adolescents and family therapy* (pp. 309–328). New York: Gardner Press.

Minuchin, S. (1974). *Families and family therapy.* Cambridge, MA: Harvard University Press.

Mowatt, D. T., Heard, D. B., Steier, F., Stanton, M. D., & Todd, T. C. (1982). Crisis resolution and the addiction cycle. In M. D. Stanton, T. C. Todd & Associates, *The family therapy of drug abuse and addiction.* New York: Guilford.

Reilly, D. M. (1976). Family factors in the etiology and treatment of youthful drug abuse. *Family Therapy, 2,* 149–171.

Rosman, B. L., Minuchin, S., Liebman, R., & Baker, L. (1976). Input and outcome of family therapy in anorexia. In J. L. Claghorn (Ed.), *Successful psychotherapy.* New York: Brunner-Mazel.

Schwartzman, J. (1975). The addict, abstinence and the family. *American Journal of Psychiatry, 132,* 154–157.

Seldin, N. E. (1972). The family of the addict: A review of the literature. *International Journal of the Addictions, 7,* 79–107.

Selekman, M. D. (1991). "With a little help from my friends": The use of peers in the family therapy of adolescent substance abusers. *Family Dynamics of Addiction Quarterly, 1*(1), 69–77.

Stanton, M. D. (1977). The addict as savior: Heroin, death and the family. *Family Process, 16,* 191–197.

Stanton, M. D. (1978). Some outcome results and aspects of structural family therapy with drug addicts. In D. Smith, S. Anderson, M. Buxton, T. Chung, N. Gottlieb, & W. Harvey (Eds.), *A multicultural view of drug abuse: The selected proceedings of The National Drug Abuse Conference—1977.* Cambridge, MA: Hall/Schenkman.

Stanton, M. D. (1979a). Drugs and the family: A review of the literature. *Marriage and Family Review, 2*(1):1–10.

Stanton, M. D. (1979b). Family treatment approaches to drug abuse problems: A review. *Family Process, 18*(3), 251–280.

Stanton, M. D. (1981a). An integrated structural/strategic approach to family therapy. *Journal of Marital and Family Therapy,7,* 427–439.

Stanton, M. D. (1981b). Marital therapy from a structural/strategic viewpoint. In G. P. Sholevar (Ed.), *Handbook of marriage and marital therapy* (pp. 303–334). Jamaica, NY: S. P. Medical and Scientific Books.

Stanton, M. D. (1985). The family and drug abuse: Concepts and rationale. In T. Bratter & G. Forrest (Eds.), *Alcoholism and substance abuse: Strategies for clinical intervention* (pp. 398–430). New York: Free Press.

Stanton, M. D. (1988). Coursework and self-study in the family treatment of alcohol and drug abuse: Expanding Heath and Atkinson's curriculum. *Journal of Marital and Family Therapy, 14,* 419–427.

Stanton, M. D. (1992). The time line and the "Why now?" question: A technique and rationale for therapy, training, organizational consultation and research. *Journal of Marital and Family Therapy, 18,* in press.

Stanton, M. D., & Coleman, S. B. (1980). The participatory aspects of indirect self-destructive behavior: The addict family as a model. In N. L. Farberow (Ed.), *The many faces of suicide* (pp. 187–203). New York: McGraw-Hill.

Stanton, M. D., & Landau-Stanton, J. (1990). Therapy with families of adolescent substance abusers. In H. B. Milkman & L. I. Sederer (Eds.), *Treatment choices for alcoholism and substance abuse* (pp. 329–339).

Stanton, M. D., Steier, F., Cook, L., & Todd, T. C. (1984). *Narcotic detoxification in a family and home context: Final report 1980–1983.* Report prepared for the Treatment Research Branch, National Institute on Drug Abuse (Grant No. RO1 DA 03097).

Stanton, M. D., & Todd, T. C. (1981). Engaging "resistant" families in treatment: II & III. *Family Process, 20,* 261–293.

Stanton, M. D., & Todd, T. C. (1982). The therapy model. In M. D. Stanton, T. C. Todd and Associates, *The family therapy of drug abuse and addiction* (pp. 109–153). New York: Guilford.

Stanton, M. D., Todd, T. C., and Associates (1982). *The family therapy of drug abuse and addiction.* New York: Guilford.

Stanton, M. D., Toss, T. C., Heard, D. B., Kirschner, S., Kleiman, J. I., Mowatt, D. T., Riley, P., Scott, S. M., & Van Deusen, J. M. Heroin addiction as a family phenomenon: A new conceptual model. *American Journal of Drug & Alcohol Abuse, 5,* 125–150.

Todd, T. C. (1991). The evolution of family therapy approaches to substance abuse: Personal reflections and thoughts on integration. *Contemporary Family Therapy, 13*(5), 471–495.

Todd, T. C., & Selekman, M. D. (1991). Beyond structural-strategic family therapy. In T. C. Todd & M. D. Selekman (Eds.), *Family therapy approaches with adolescent substance abusers.* Boston: Allyn and Bacon.

Vaillant, G. E. (1966). A 12-year follow-up of New York narcotic addicts: III. Some social and psychiatric characteristics. *Archives of General Psychiatry, 15,* 599–609.

Van Deusen, J. M., Scott, S. M., Stanton, M. D., & Todd, T. C. (1980). Engaging "resistant" families in therapy: I. Getting the drug addict to recruit his family members. *International Journal of the Addictions, 15,* 1069–1089.

Van Deusen, J. M., Stanton, M. D., Scott, S. M., & Todd, T. C. (1980). Engaging "resistant" families in treatment: I. Getting the drug addict to recruit his family members. *International Journal of the Addictions, 15,* 1069–1089.

CHAPTER FIVE

Family Therapy with Adolescent Substance Abusers

PAULINE KAUFMANN, M.S.W.
Director of Family Therapy
Phoenix Foundation

The very title of this chapter is antithetical to a basic assumption about adolescence. From the more conventional point of view, family therapy for adolescents is contraindicated. If we assume that adolescence should be the beginning of separation from the family of origin as part of establishing one's identity, then family therapy runs the risk of antithetically bringing the family closer together.

It is difficult, if not impossible, to separate ourselves from something we have not experienced. For many of the adolescents who have had or are having problems with substance abuse, living in the family has not been a nurturing experience. If we assume that fixation at an early stage of development occurs because of deprivation on the one hand or indulgence on the other, we can understand that many of these adolescents are stuck. They are literally hanging around, mouths open, waiting to be fed. If they are not fed by human means within the context of a familial setting, they will frequently resort to the use of chemicals to give them the illusion that their needs are being met pharmacologically.

It is not surprising that separating these adolescents from their families and placing them in a conventional therapeutic community has not met with much success. The family has demonstrated graphically its problem in dealing with an adolescent's drug abuse and acting out. It is apparent that rehabilitation is not a spontaneous growth process. It is our experience that many adolescents and their families work out their problems and free the adolescent for the completion of his or her growth tasks when family therapy is an intrinsic part of the total treatment.

Rationale for Family Treatment

Within the structure of a 9:00 A.M.-to-5:00 P.M. therapeutic community, we see family therapy as the primary treatment modality. New York City, like many large metropolitan areas, has a growing population of young people between the ages of 12 and 18 who are multiple substance abusers. Many of the families they come from have been bombarded by poverty, inadequate housing, disease, unemployment, and the problems of one-parent families. The adolescent is not only a product of his or her family's difficulties but frequently of the curriculum of poverty. Part of that curriculum in the inner-city consists of early experimentation with drugs and alcohol in an attempt to have some illusion of joy. The family's precarious homeostasis involves every member of the family. The adolescent is frequently scapegoated when he or she attempts to act out and in any way upset the balance. When these adolescents are admitted to a therapeutic community for drug addicts, they replicate their problems and roles in their family of origin. They find themselves in the role of scapegoat in the therapeutic community, of being isolated and eventually ejected. They go home, and once more the cycle is started. The home is not able to contain them. They often land in the courts, training schools, and holding institutions. At best, they complete this cycle and are out on the streets again, at around the age of 18, surviving in a way that is destructive to themselves and to the society in which they live.

To have an impact on this problem, we had to have a treatment design that included the total family. This design not only had to take care of the needs of the adolescent within the family but of the total family within the community. We saw the tasks of the adolescent as being these: attending school, dating, establishing peer relations, forming trial vocational plans, defining roles and generation boundaries, beginning gradual individuation, and forming new dyadic and triadic relationships within the immediate community. In order for the adolescent to achieve this, we saw the need to restructure the total family, so that recidivism would be curtailed. For the adults in the family, we have to be immediately useful if we were to enlist their aid: we had to provide them with a support system. This was even more mandatory when there was a one-parent family. This support system included various community agencies where they could get adequate housing, monetary assistance, daycare for children of working mothers, employment training, and other services. We had certain levers that were extremely useful. The family invariably came to us at a point of crisis. This would be through a court referral when the adolescent had broken the law, from school personnel who found the adolescent "uneducable," or from the family when the acting out of the adolescent had so disrupted family functioning that general anarchy prevailed.

We offered the family an alternate school that was part of the Board of Education school system and where their adolescent could be between 9:00 A.M. and 5:00 P.M., six days a week. The family had to agree to be involved in therapy a minimum of once a week, with the total family attending. They also had to agree to be available by telephone in case of emergency or to come in for additional sessions if and when they were indicated. Most families, because of the crisis, were very willing to go along with any of the demands or any part of the contract that we articulated. We had difficulty in some cases when the crisis had abated in getting families to keep their part of the contract. Some of the usual problems were parents competing with the setting, fear of losing control over the adolescent, some fear — especially in one-parent families — of abandonment by the children, and some need to indicate that their failure was not their fault and that the new setting had to fail also. We undercut much of this by being of continuing usefulness to the parents.

When there was a dramatic change in an adolescent's behavior — for instance, if he or she had been doing well in school and suddenly there was a series of failures — we arbitrarily made the assumption that something was happening at home that was interfering with our student's success. We would call the home and invite the entire family in. Frequently, it took a great deal of planning and support to get the family to come. Without exception, we found our assumption was correct, with a family crisis reflected in the failure of the adolescent or in his or her acting out within the 9-to-5 environment. We would then institute a series of intensive family sessions. Sometimes we worked with the adults in the family alone, particularly if there were a mother and a father or father-surrogate. If the crisis were such that the adolescent was invariably pulled into the difficulty and could not free himself or herself, we would offer to have the adolescent live in for a short period of time so that the parents would have time to work out their problems. They would have to agree to come at least three times a week until the crisis was resolved. With few exceptions, the family experienced this as giving and helpful, and as evidence of our concern for the parents in the family, as well as the adolescent. We would have the entire family meet before the adolescent was returned to it. Aside from dealing with the particular crisis, much time was spent with parents to help them understand the necessity for restructuring the family. They were supported while they tried out new ways of relating to each other, and helped to set appropriate boundaries between themselves and their children.

Marcie and Her Family

A typical family who came to us for help consisted of Debby Marks,[1] age 45, divorced with husband's whereabouts unknown; Carl, her oldest son, age 23; Sam, age 18; and Marcie, the identified patient, age 15. Debby Marks applied to have Marcie admitted to our day treatment program at the point where Marcie had been expelled from her second residential treatment home. Marcie had been considered untreatable by these two residential centers and unmanageable by two foster homes. She had been brought back to court by the social agency and faced the possibility of being sent to a training school. Debby, the mother, was in a state of acute anxiety. She was given an appointment and came in with Marcie. The mother did all the talking. She presented the history of Marcie's stay at various places and kept finding fault with her, alternately crying and yelling. Marcie smoked incessantly during all this, looked at no one, and answered questions belligerently and monosyllabically. The first contact with these two members of the family involved presenting Marcie with her choices and making it clear that the day center was a possibility but had certain basic regulations that she would have to accept as part of the contract. We also made it very clear to Debby that the total family would have to be involved. We took Marcie off the hook by stating that Marcie's behavior was very difficult but the problem was that the entire family was in trouble, and we saw Marcie as only one aspect of that problem. Marcie tried to intervene and use what had been said to fault her mother and her brothers. We suggested very strongly that we end the session and that we have another one the next day with the entire family present.

When the family arrived for the second session, they seated themselves in a manner that was a graphic representation of the relationships and the structure of the family. Mrs. Marks and Carl, age 23, sat together and immediately talked with each other while waiting for the director of the center to join the family therapist and the family. Marcie sat by herself and Sam was the furthest away from the center of the circle that the group formed. Carl tried immediately to take the session over by criticizing Marcie in terms of how much misery she caused her mother. This was interrupted, and we directed ourselves to the mother as the executive of the family. We asked her to tell us how she experienced life at home with her three children. She informed us immediately that Sam was an alcoholic and she needed some help in finding placement for him. Marcie was responsible for her mother's ulcers, she said. She was forever worried about Marcie and could have no life of her own. Marcie had not only been thrown out of every place Debby had taken her but she had also had an abortion and played around with drugs and alcohol. She smoked incessantly. Carl added that she smoked marijuana most of the time. According to Debby, Carl never gave her a moment of trouble. He ran the house, supervised Marcie when the mother wasn't around, and attended college. Further questioning elicited the information that he was taking one course at a community college and was unemployed. He depended on his mother for whatever money he had. Carl did not date, had no friends, and spent his time looking at television and doing a few tasks around the house. He was obviously a depressed, passive young man.

The Treatment Process

In a subsequent session we obtained the additional information that Sam was on probation, having been brought to court because he participated in a mugging and stealing in his neighborhood. He had been in a hospital for a short period of time to "dry out." However, he denied being an alcoholic and would not voluntarily become part of any program to deal with his drinking. We felt, and the mother agreed, that Sam needed to be placed in a structured environment where liquor would not be obtainable and where he would have an opportunity to find some satisfaction in living other than drinking.

In these two sessions we had addressed most of our questions to the mother. We were careful to demonstrate that we saw her as the adult in the family who was responsible for making decisions about her two younger children. We addressed Carl directly when it came to his own plans. We had very little success in getting him to look at his life. He obviously saw himself as a parent, and was unwilling to consider playing any other role. In the third session, with the entire family present we began the restructuring that we thought should take place. As a result of our previous work and the discussion in the third session, the family agreed that Marcie would attend the day center from 9 to 5, and go home each night. Sam would be put in a residential treatment house of the same program in a different area so that he would have a chance to deal with his drinking and begin to establish some goals for himself. We posited the idea of a parenting team. At home, Debby was responsible for what happened. In the day center, the team would be responsible for Marcie from 9 to 5, and would be in communication with Mrs. Marks so that both the home and the day center would have similar limits and goals for Marcie. We would be available to Debby by telephone and by personal contact. The parenting team would consist of Mrs. Marks, the family therapist, the director of the daycare center, and the director of the residential treatment center where Sam would be staying.

Defining Roles

The treatment team agreed that during the next week Sam would be placed in one of the residential treatment centers of the program, that Marcie would be admitted to the daycare program, and that several sessions would be held with the mother alone in an attempt to get her to create workable boundaries between her and Carl so that he could be freed to look for a job or attend school and could begin to form appropriate peer relationships. In the next few weeks the entire family had three stormy sessions around Carl's relationship with his mother and his abuse of his parenting role within the family. The family was helped to restructure its operations. With our help, the mother limited Carl's role in the family. He was seen as having more time than the others and so was given certain duties around the house. He was limited and prevented from acting as a surrogate parent with Marcie and also as the conveyor of information from the siblings to his mother. Mrs. Marks was encouraged and helped to form direct relationships with all of her children, and not to go through Carl when she had something to say to them.

Growing Resistance and Recidivism

In the ensuing three weeks, the reports from the school on Marcie were very positive, and her interaction within the day center was appropriate. Sam had settled in, had not had a drink and seemed to be working well. Carl still stayed home most of the day and would occasionally try to direct Marcie's activities in the evening. The mother intervened with this and seemed to have a degree of success. At the end of the third week, Carl called to say that his mother was sick with the flu and that the family could not come in. This was checked with Marcie, who said that her mother was indeed sick and that Carl was running the house once more.

During the next week, Marcie's behavior underwent a dramatic change. She slept during classes, was extremely irritable, fought with her peers in the residence, and was late four out of five mornings in getting to school. Sam seemed not to show any effects from his mother's illness. At the beginning of the fifth week, Mrs. Marks called, in tears. She felt that everything had fallen apart. Marcie and Carl had had a fist fight and had broken furniture. She had been unable to intervene effectively and was becoming desperate. We scheduled a meeting of the total family for the next day. When they arrived, the old seating arrangement was resumed, with Marcie and Sam on the outside and the mother and Carl together; Debby looked quite ill. She cried during the entire session. She felt that things had been better before and that she just couldn't handle what was happening with Marcie. Carl had been very helpful to her while she was sick and Marcie was back to her old behavior.

We pointed out that when Debby became sick, Carl went back to the role that he had played before, and this was impossible for Marcie to accept. We suggested that Marcie move into the residence on a 24-hour basis for a limited time until Mrs. Marks felt better. Marcie used this as a way of striking out at her mother and saying that she never wanted to live at home anyway. Thus started again the cycle of mutual faulting, crying, and withdrawal. Once more the therapist intervened and suggested that Marcie do this for herself, that it was important that she continue with the gains that she had made. In the meantime, her mother would have to agree to come in for two sessions by herself and one with Carl. The family agreed. During these sessions, boundaries between the mother and Carl were established once more. Debby agreed to make certain demands on Carl. She also suggested that perhaps it would be better if he went to stay with his maternal grandparents for a while. They wanted him to live with them, and the grandfather was very anxious to have him work in the family construction business. We pursued this further, and Mrs. Marks stated that she had a friend whom Carl objected to her dating and she felt it would be a relief if Carl were out of the house for a while. We encouraged her in this and asked her if she would bring this up and discuss it with Carl when both of the other children were present. She seemed much relieved at this suggestion and said she really wanted to do this.

At the final session held with Carl, Marcie, Sam, and their mother, they agreed that Carl would stay with his grandparents and begin to work in the grandfather's business until he was making enough money to live on his own. Marcie would stay in the daycare center but would come home each night, and Sam would stay in the residential treatment center. Mrs. Marks brought up her dating. Marcie liked the whole idea, liked the man and thought it was "neat." Sam said it was all right with him. Carl thought it was ridiculous that a woman his mother's age should date. He got very little support from anyone, including the therapist, who suggested that perhaps it would be important for Carl to start his own dating life and that what his mother did would be something that she herself decided. With this support, Mrs. Marks became very definite, saying she had every intention of dating, that it was her own business and that she was very glad that Marcie liked the man she was seeing.

Marcie returned home after a two-week stay in the residence. The family had been in treatment for six months. The two children, Sam and Marcie, continue to use the facilities. Carl is slowly beginning to move away from home and Debby is still seeing the same man. The mother and Marcie are developing an appropriate relationship. They seem to be enjoying each other, and conflicts that arise are generally able to be resolved through some discussion—if not at the time that they occur, then at least several hours later.

In the treatment of the adolescent substance abuser within the context of the family, we have found certain techniques effective and useful. We have helped the family and the staff to see the therapeutic community as an extension of the home and the home as an extension of the therapeutic community. Thus, any possible manipulation by the adolescent is undercut. This approach is experienced as supportive by the parent or parents. During crises when the acting out of the adolescent overloads the family structure, the adolescent is invited to live in at the residence, thus giving the total family a chance to heal and restructure itself. During this period the entire family and/or individuals within the family are seen on an intensive basis. When the crisis is resolved, the adolescent is returned home.

We have found that if we are to be successful, our help to the family must be concrete and immediate. Our efforts frequently concern the economics of the family, housing, schooling, clothing, and other circumstances or problems of everyday living. Our overall goal is to restructure the family in such a way that each individual has a chance for optimal development within the family. Thus, boundaries between family members are made clear and consistent. Children are helped to have direct access to the adults in the family. Spouse transactions are helped to be clear and unambiguous. Where there is a parenting child, his or her duties are limited and clarified. Coalitions within the family are open and flexible. Boundaries around a marital pair or the heterosexual dating pair are made consistent and delineated. Where there is an extended family, the role and authority of the generations are clarified.

Frequently family therapy ends with a focus on the therapy of the marital pair or the heterosexual pair who are living together or planning to do so.

The Role of the Therapeutic Community

The family we have presented is part of a daycare program started 3 years ago entitled Step One of the Phoenix Programs of New York City.[2] One of the project's most dramatic results is the greatly improved educational functioning of the adolescents who are in this program. Some 90 percent of the adolescents who come to Step One have a history of school failure. They have been labeled uneducable, emotionally disturbed, delinquent, and truant. Over 70 percent are sent to the courts for delinquent behavior, and the majority of these children come from one-parent families in which the mother is generally present. There are two teachers supplied by the Board of Education for 40 children in two classrooms. The teachers report that they have less than 10 percent truancy and 10 percent lateness. Approximately 90 percent of the students' skills have improved sufficiently so that they will be able to graduate from high school before they reach age 18. This is a dramatic contrast with the general achievement of this group within the public school system.

There is a growing number of reports of the failure of large urban school centers in dealing with the inner-city adolescent. Step One, and our experience in this daycare setting, may well be a model for a more successful way of educating the troubled adolescent in the large cities. Certainly such a plan, characterized by the following, is economically feasible: having smaller institutions instead of large, expensive, impersonal buildings; 20 children in a class; a school that is open from 9:00 A.M. to 6:00 P.M. with hours when teachers are not there occupied by group activities related to the facility within which the children spend most of their time; a rich recreation program; and evening sessions in which parents and children are together in family therapy and family educational sessions.

Family and community stresses on the family are frequently reflected in the behavior of adolescents who are striving for some identity. They are programmed for failure by the very community in which they live, and frequently their only escape is into a world of fantasy aided by drugs and alcohol. The Phoenix Program, although it is limited, has had a degree of success that augurs well for replication within the larger school system.

Endnotes

1. All names have been changed to preserve anonymity.
2. This project operates under NIMH grant #1 H80 MH 01049.

References

Kaplen, S. L. (1977). Structural family therapy for children of divorce: Case reports. *Family Process, 16,* 75–83.

Minuchin, S. (1974). *Families and family therapy.* Cambridge, MA: Harvard University Press.

Minuchin, S., Montalvo, B., Guerney, B. G., Jr., Rosman, B. L., & Chumer, F. (1967). *Families of the slums* (pp. 352–378). New York: Basic Books.

Narceso, J., & Burkett, D. (1975). *Declare yourself: Discovering the me in relationships.* Englewood Cliffs, NJ: Prentice-Hall.

Sager, C. J. (1976). *Marriage contracts and couple therapy.* New York: Brunner/Mazel.

Sager, C. J., & Kaplan, H. (1972). *Progress in group and family therapy.* New York: Brunner/Mazel.

Wairond-Skinner, S. (1976). *Family therapy: The treatment of natural systems.* London: Henley and Boston.

CHAPTER SIX

Multiple Family Therapy with Drug Abusers

EDWARD KAUFMAN, M.D.
Professor of Psychiatry
University of California, Irvine

PAULINE KAUFMANN,
M.S.W.
Director of Family Therapy
Phoenix Foundation

Multiple family therapy (MFT) is a technique that is particularly useful and applicable to drug abusers and their families. This type of therapy can be used in any treatment setting for drug abusers, but is most successful in residential settings where the family is more available and accessible. MFT was initiated as a modality by Laqueur, La Burt, and Morong (1971) in an inpatient unit of a state hospital but, as used by the authors, it has many other roots. These include social network intervention (Speck & Attneave, 1971), multiple impact therapy (Ritchie, 1971), the ward or town meeting concept of both the psychiatric and Synanon modes of the therapeutic community, and a host of group and family therapy techniques. Group techniques run the gamut from psychoanalytic through psychodramatic, existential, gestalt, and encounter. Family techniques include sculpting or choreography (Papp, 1973), structural (Minuchin, 1974), and systems (Fogarty, 1974). All of these are described in detail in other chapters of this book.

Group Composition and Environment

The greater the motivation and involvement of the patient, the easier it is to initiate the family into therapy, particularly in MFT. Thus, it is extremely difficult to generate MFT in low-intervention programs such as most meth-

This chapter is based on material included in "Multiple Family Therapy: A New Direction in the Treatment of Drug Abusers," *American Journal of Drug and Alcohol Abuse, 4*(4), 467–478 and the 1974, 1975, 1976, 1977, 1978 National Drug Abuse Conferences.

adone maintenance programs or outpatient psychotherapy clinics. It becomes progressively easier to do so in day programs and inpatient settings. However, the setting that most readily lends itself to the establishment and continuance of a successful MFT group is a residential therapeutic community (TC). One reason that families come to groups in this setting is that they may be required to do so if they are to visit the resident. Also, since the identified patient (IP) is now drug free for the first time in years, he or she can be related to without chaos and with trust and warmth. It is best to have the IP invite the family to come in, but the therapist may send a form letter or call. The last may be necessary in order to involve a reluctant family or family member.

One of the authors finished four years' work with a patient in a methadone maintenance program (MMTP). Therapy was unsuccessful despite the use of an ancillary mental health clinic and several group psychotherapy experiences. During this time the patient consistently refused to have his mother or any family member involved in treatment, although he lived with his mother throughout the treatment. Federal guidelines about confidentiality, particularly as they are applied to MMTP, and a noncoercive attitude on the part of the New York City agency sponsoring the treatment, prohibited insisting that the family be involved. Finally, after several drug overdoses and detoxifications, the patient agreed to enter a therapeutic community. After two weeks in residence, the patient and his family appeared at the first MFT to which they were invited. The mother's crucial role in treatment was immediately apparent. However, two involved aunts and an older brother, none of whom had ever been mentioned previously, attended regularly. This extended family was found to be necessary for restructuring the family system and changing this difficult patient.

In a residence the group may be composed of all of the families in the TC or separated into several groups of three or four closely matched families. Our experience is with the former, partly because there is a lack of primary therapists, as well as because we view the group of families as one community.

There are generally as many as 40 to 50 individuals in the weekly multiple family group, including 10 to 15 families. The group includes identified patients and their immediate families as well as any relatives who have an impact on the family. Friends and lovers are included if they are an important part of the addict's network and are drug free. If they are abusing drugs or alcohol, they are excluded from the group until they can control this symptom, which is disruptive or destructive to the group. When there are no rigid guidelines about excluding family members and friends, a good deal of meaningful material is produced. One client's drug-abusing boyfriend arrived with his "only drug-free friend," who happened to be the client's former husband. Although she was able to ask them to leave before the group began, the feelings that were stirred up between her and her ex-husband re-created old unresolved problems that were dealt with in MFT.

Families should be oriented and interviewed prior to entering the group. A genogram can be made and a family map begun during the initial evaluation. Once it becomes apparent in the group that a troubled family requires them, individual family sessions are provided. Some family secrets may have to stay within the family, but generally participants are encouraged to bring the content of these individual sessions into the multiple family group, as this remains the primary modality of family therapy. An experienced family therapist works with counselors in the program as cotherapists. The total group frequently functions as adjunctive family therapists. Usually family members take their cues from primary therapists and will be appropriately confronting, reassuring, and supportive. At times the family's own needs prevent this, and their anger at their child or their possessiveness will spill over to all the former addicts in the group. Families share experiences and offer help by acting as extended families both to each other and to the residents outside the time they spend together in therapy. Residents who accompany each other on visits serve as supports in the home and behavioral reporters in MFT groups. Supporting residents may help the IPs with their family "homework" on visits as well as in the MFT.

The group is seated in a large circle with cotherapists distributed at equal distances to provide observation of the total group. We do not use a "fish bowl" with the primary family in the center of the group because this discourages the participation and identification of the other families. Families sit together, and their seating arrangements are carefully observed, as they usually follow structural patterns. They may be asked to separate if there is a great deal of whispering or disruption. The group begins with everyone introducing themselves, giving name and role. A group member will describe the purpose of the group, generally stressing the need for families to communicate honestly and to express their feelings openly. At times this description emphasizes the importance of understanding and changing the familial forces that have led to drug abuse. The first family is frequently worked with for about an hour.

The conflicts focused on set the emotional tone and influence the topics discussed in the entire group. Many other families will identify with these conflicts, express feelings, offer support, and work on similar conflicts. Generally three or four families are worked with intensively in a night. Almost all families participate verbally, and usually all families are emotionally involved.

The informal contacts that take place before and after group are crucial. Therapists should mingle and interact during these pre- and post-group sessions. Many presession contacts are excellent grist for the therapeutic mill. Postgroup interaction may either confirm insights and validate feelings or undermine therapeutic work if it is not monitored. Families of "splittees" (patients who leave the program) are encouraged to continue to attend to maintain their structural shifts and to facilitate the IP's return to treatment.

The Therapeutic Team

A prerequisite for the therapeutic team is a primary therapist who is experienced in group and family therapy and comfortable in large groups. There must also be several cotherapists who are an integral part of the treatment program and can provide feedback from the group to the program and input from the program to the group. The group should be used to train counselors in the dynamics of families and the techniques of family therapy. All too frequently, younger counselors in TCs tend to overidentify with their clients' hostility to parents because of their own conflicts. Similarly, counselors who are themselves parents may overidentify with the parental system. Thus, counselors should have supplementary training experiences that focus on their own family of origin. Counselors should also have supplementary didactic courses and assigned readings, particularly if they are to become primary therapists. Cotherapists should work together as a team that agrees to disagree so that there is a unity that allows room for individual differences. This provides a role model for a parental system that is unified but not rigid.

Speck and Attneave (1971) cited qualities of a good network leader, which are also important in an MFT primary therapist: "A sense of timing, empathy with emotional high-points, a sense of group moods and undercurrents and some charismatic presence . . . along with the ability to dominate, the leader must have the confidence that comes with considerable experience . . . the ability to efface himself, to delegate and diffuse responsibility . . . rather than collect it for himself." The role of the MFT therapist, like the network leader, is similar to that of the good theatrical director, but with a greater concern for the therapeutic than the dramatic. Interestingly, Papp (1973) also emphasizes the therapeutic aspects of theatricality in MFT, particularly as seen in sculpting: "True theatre strips away superficiality to the bare bones of meaning, reveals a hidden truth, shares a universal experience." Minuchin (1974b) also notes that the therapist functions "like the director of a play, setting the stage, creating a scenario, assigning a task and requiring the family members to function within the new sets that he has imposed."

MFT is a stimulating and rejuvenating experience for the therapist and treatment program as well as the family. The therapist becomes the paternal and/or maternal figure for a host of families who become a single family network and, in many ways, a single family. The therapist assumes temporary parental control of all of these families at the same time as he or she is the child of all of them. Thus, the therapist gives and takes in a multitude of parental and childlike roles. At the same time, the therapist must step away from this emotional entanglement and be objective. A therapist may even say to his or her cotherapists and the group, "I am going to join this family system to experience it. Pull me out if I'm getting too involved." The primary therapist must always keep in mind that one of his or her primary functions is to be considered a supportive ally by every member of the group. He or she must also feel capable of and correct in interrupting any communication that is destructive or disruptive.

Family Dynamics and Techniques

These will be discussed in detail in other chapters of this book. Only those dynamics and techniques that are most applicable to MFT will be discussed here. Generally those techniques that are most familiar to the treatment system are most readily used in MFT. Thus, in MFTs and TCs confrontation and encounter are used in the service of structural changes. The therapist must join the treatment system as a whole as well as each family. New techniques can be gradually introduced to MFT and then to the overall program, or vice versa.

In the early phases of treatment, the families support each other by expressing the pain they have experienced in having a drug abuser in the family. The family's sense of loneliness and isolation in dealing with this major crisis is greatly attenuated by sharing the burden with other families. The means by which the family has been manipulated are quite similar and form the beginning of a common bond. The addict son or daughter has lied to and stolen from his or her family. Many families have given the addict money for drugs to keep him or her from stealing and risking incarceration. Group members express commiseration for the family's suffering. The family is strongly encouraged not to repeat this pattern. The family learns to see its covert hostile aspects rather than its apparent benevolent ones.

Many addicts who have difficulty with the demands of a TC will try to convince their families to take them back once again and protect them from its "evils," just as the families had protected them from jail. Intervening in this system helps prevent many from quitting the group early on. We call this "closing the back door." Many families are able to do this merely through group support. Others must learn to recognize and reduce the addict's ways of provoking guilt and enmeshing them in the addict's problems before they can close the door to the cycle of symbiotic reinvolvement. An initial period of ventilation of anger and resentment may be necessary before strategies for change can be introduced. An atmosphere is created in which all families are encouraged to be open and express everything about everyone. This does not give the family permission to hurt sadistically under the guise of honesty.

Giving food may be utilized as an important family transaction. Food may also be limited gifts to the entire group. This helps create a sense of the group as one family. It may also alleviate the families' guilt and permit them to gratify their need to give without "infantilizing" the IP.

As the therapy progresses, the role of the family in producing and perpetuating the addict's abuse of drugs is identified. Patterns of mutual manipulation, extraction, and coercion are identified and negated. The family's need to perpetuate the addict's dependent behavior through scape-goating, distancing, protection, or infantilization is discouraged, and new methods of relating are tried and encouraged. Families tend to feel guilty when the addict confronts them with their role in the addiction cycle. This has occurred in the home and recurs in the early phases of multiple family therapy. If the therapist does not intervene, the family will retaliate by inducing guilt or undermining growth, and may ultimately pull the addict out of treatment.

Drug dependence is viewed as a family problem in which there can be no scapegoats. Parents must be given a great deal of support in family sessions because of their own guilt and the tendency of patients and even counselors to attack them. For some parents, even the admission in public that there is a family problem leads to shame and reactive hostility. Such parents require individual family therapy sessions where they can receive individual support. When they can overcome their embarrassment about expressing feelings in "the public" of the group, they have taken a valuable step toward the overt expression of feelings in general. Counselors in the program and families frequently lead the group away from working with the family system to the IP and his or her problems in the TC. When this occurs, the group must be refocused on the family program. Counselors will often similarly focus on other individual drug-abusing family members and should be helped in redirecting the focus to the family system. Frequently material is revealed in MFT that could lead to severe setbacks and punish-ments for residents. It is important that the family therapist have input into the program's use of such disciplines so that they do not undermine the family therapy or re-create destructive family patterns within the program.

Multiple family therapy groups help residents actualize insights about their family that they have achieved in their own therapy. Many families learn to express love and anger directly for the first time in these groups. Deep emotional pain is expressed when appropriate, and other family members are encouraged to give support to such expressions rather than nullify or deny them. Frequently the entire group is in tears or applauds appreciatively. Kissing, hugging, and rocking are ways that families tend to obliterate pain under the guise of giving comfort. In situations where families are emotionally isolated, encouraging the mutual exchange of physical affection is helpful.

The identified patient acts as the barometer of the functioning of the total family. When his or her behavior becomes maladaptive or disruptive, it is assumed that the family is under increased stress and may be reverting to former destructive patterns. This is particularly true in adolescent day programs when there is frequent parental contact. The identified patient's behavior is viewed as part of the family stress at the same time as it is handled as his or her individual responsibility by peers in encounter groups within the TC. As an extension of the TC, peers can be quite supportive of each other yet hold each other responsible and challenge each other more effectively than can adults. Therapeutic homework is frequently assigned to reinforce the family's structural changes. Not only are family tasks assigned but different family roles are also allotted in restructuring the family. Weak ties between family members are strengthened by either suggesting joint activities that build closeness and/or identifying the fears and patterns that have led to weak ties. Strengthening such ties will diminish other enmeshed ones. Overwhelming family members may be asked not to attend sessions for several weeks to strengthen other ties. The family pain at having an addicted member can be used to motivate overinvolved family members to begin to separate.

Any number of other therapeutic strategies may be useful in restructuring the family. Much will depend on the individual therapist's style. We consistently focus on dysfunctional communications. We delineate individual boundaries by not permitting family members to speak or feel for each other. We point out nonverbal coercive communications that tend to overwhelm family members, inhibit expressiveness, or produce double binds. We ask that messages be stated clearly with underlying meanings made explicit. We also assign tasks to family members to promote individuation. It is most important for mothers who are single parents to find pleasure in their own lives and for couples to learn or relearn to enjoy each other. Frequently grandparents must be brought in and intergenerational patterns demonstrated before parents can change. Interpretations that simultaneously focus on the responsibility of both parties are effective and diminish guilt provocation and scapegoating. They also help maintain the therapist's position as an ally of every family member.

We have found that psychodramas dealing with negotiation and resolution of disagreements, formation of positive subgroups, changing communication styles, and teaching verbalization of anger, affection, or friendship are all helpful in changing the dysfunctional system. The "empty chair" technique can be used to tap deep feelings—generally anger at the withdrawal of the member or anguish at loss—about family members who are not present. Family sculpture (Papp, 1973) is a technique that is very valuable in MFT with drug abusers. Its use with alcoholics is described in detail elsewhere in this book.

In the latter phases of MFT, families express intense repressed mourning responses, which are essential to a healthy family adaptation. Feelings about a sibling who has died from an overdose come out most easily. In still later phases, a lost parent can be mourned. Family secrets and myths are also revealed in the later phases of MFT. When anxiety stirred up by early shifts has been resolved, more advanced tasks can be assigned. In the final phases, the family and IP are separated from the group.

A knowledge of the specific dynamics of a family permits further "family" therapy with the individual alone and also provides crucial material for individual and group therapy. Frequently we learn of the resident's overwhelming anger toward a parent. At times it is obvious that this anger is too destructive to be expressed in the presence of the parent, even in a moderate way. The resident is then encouraged to express the anger in his or her own therapy before expressing it to his or her family.

Videotape can also be used to confront family members with emotions that are denied. By repeated replays it is possible to have family members recognize such patterns as guilt induction and infantilization through enmeshing affection and denigration. Videotapes of MFT are excellent teaching devices and are available from the author.

As noted earlier, families in MFT act as supports for each other outside the session, and may continue to do so after therapy has been terminated. These families frequently replace the entire network of the addict with a new, therapeutic one.

Sample Group

We would like to describe a typical multiple family therapy session to illustrate these family dynamics and therapy techniques.

> The 10 families and three therapists were grouped in a circle that included over 40 individuals. The group began with everyone introducing themselves by stating their name and role in the group. A group member was asked to describe the purpose of the group. He emphasized communication and confrontation of feelings. In this group, four families were worked with intensively, but the remaining families identified strongly with them.
>
> The first family consisted of the identified patient (IP), a 27-year-old Italian male, his older brother, mother, father, and wife. The mother dominated the family and their communications. The father was crippled and

unable to work, so the mother had assumed the financial support of the family. It emerged that the father did not take care of his physical health because of his worry over his addict son. The group then pressured the father to make a dental appointment, and when he was vague, they exerted pressure on him to make a commitment, which he did. The son experienced his guilt and began to cry, stating that he still needed his father. His mother cried in response to her son's tears and the three of them embraced. We learned that the IP, his wife, and son ate most of their meals at the mother's house prior to treatment. They were continuing this pattern on weekend passes and the wife and child were eating their meals there during the week. The wife and child were given the task of eating most meals at home during the week and the nuclear family was asked to eat in its own home three out of four weekends. The mother and father readily agreed to reinforce this individuation. The IP and his wife embraced, bringing tears to the eyes of most group members.

The next family on which we focused consisted of a 23-year-old resident, his mother, and his father. This family was also Italian, as were two others. (One cotherapist was Sicilian.) We worked with them to consolidate an insight from a previous session. They had devastatingly insulted their son and denied doing so. They had been shown the sequence on videotape to break through their denial. They accepted that they had devastated him and in getting in touch with their anger at him, they were able to refrain from putting him down in this session. The group also pressured them to involve their drug-abusing daughter in therapy.

The third family consisted of the identified patient, a 34-year-old Irish male, a younger sister, and a brother. The mother had been quite active in MFT but did not attend this session because the family had moved away. The father had never been present but was frequently discussed because of his pattern of severe withdrawal. The father had not left his bedroom in three years and never came out when his son visited. In this session the son realized how much he had identified with his father's emotional isolation, even to a point of duplicating his posture. He was helped to recognize and experience this rigid control system. His anger toward his father would be a subject for future group work. He also realized how he had attempted to be a father to his younger siblings to the point of neglecting his own needs. The sister reached out to him and partially broke through his isolation with her poignant plea. Another resident who was attending the group with his mother identified heavily and sobbed about not being closer to his own sister. He was asked to talk to the first resident's sister as if she were his own. In doing so, he reached a deep level of yearning and anguish. His mother reached out to him and began to rock him. To diminish the infantilization, the therapist asked the mother not to rock him. Freed from his mother, he was able to sob heavily about missing his sister and his guilt in pushing her away. We returned to the Irish family, but were still unable to break through the IP's emotional isolation. It was pointed out that it was difficult for him to express feelings because of his identification with his father and his need to stay the big brother who had no weaknesses.

Discussion

We would like to summarize the literature on MFT which has influenced our work, and discuss it in the context of our experience. Laqueur, La Burt, and Morong's (1971) objectives with schizophrenics are identical to our own with drug abusers (i.e., "improvement of communication between all members of the family and achievement of better understanding of the reasons for their disturbing behavior toward each other"). Laqueur and colleagues remind us that MFT "affords the families an opportunity to learn from each other indirectly, through analogy, indirect interpretation, mimicking and identification"; thus "the resources of all family members tend to be exploited more successfully when several families are treated together in one group than when each family is treated as a separate entity." The researchers point out that schizophrenics (like drug addicts) are helped to transfer the energies of early symbiotic relationships to external objects in such groups. Laqueur and colleagues emphasize how important it is for the therapist not to be caught up in the multiple double binds set up by patients and parents in order to demonstrate that emotional distance from these patterns can be developed; thus, the therapist is a role model for individuation. Likewise, the IP may identify with another individuating family member and separate with much less anxiety than is usually associated with such learning.

Leichter and Schulman (1974) conduct MFT in an outpatient setting and, like Laqueur, choose three to four families in a manner that creates a homogeneous yet balanced group. They insist that the entire nuclear family be included, and have at times expanded the group to include the extended kinship where relevant (i.e., grandparents or divorced spouses). They cite types of families for whom MFT is preferable to working with one family. Such families include those who are isolated or whose system is circulatory and rigidified, especially when symbiotic. MFT is also helpful when there is a missing parent (usually the father), since the group provides parental substitutes.

Leichter and Schulman (1974) also have found that particular dynamics lend themselves to resolution in MFT. Reality testing is strengthened as distortions within a family are readily apparent to other group members, who point them out in a manner that is readily accepted. In turn, others can correct the reality of their own family. Likewise, transferences to nonfamily members in the group can be traced to the person's own family. The degree of distortion can be quickly pointed out as the person who has caused overreaction is present in the group in his or her own reality. Another goal in these groups is to bridge intergenerational alienation and isolation through experiencing the universality of human needs and emotions. Adults can provide conflict-free parenting to the children of others in MFT, and parents and children alike can gratify their own need to be parented. The unreality of the "good" child in the family can be pointed out, as can the price such a child pays for this position in the family. At times even the addict can be the "good child." In general, it is easy for one family to perceive another family's malfunctioning, learn to think in such terms, and then apply new thinking to his or her own family. Leichter and Schulman (1974) note that MFT provides a particularly fertile ground for the emergence of "spontaneous and unexpected attitudes and insights" that occur almost as a "byproduct" of ongoing processes.

Papp (1974) has learned that "hopeless" families do better in groups. After six months of trying to match families, she assembled a group composed of the last three families on a waiting list. Thus, she "learned by default that there are no barriers of race, religion, culture, education, psychiatric diagnosis, politics or prejudice which cannot be transcended in a group and used to therapeutic advantage." Papp's pioneering use of sculpting has been very helpful to these authors and is quite useful in MFT. Family sculpting, or choreography as she later termed it, can transform a group from an inhibited, intellectualized, or anxious rambling body into an "active, alive, highly involved, purposely focused entity."

The literature on the specific use of MFT with drug abusers is quite sparse. A very early paper was written by Hirsch (1961), which discussed a therapy group composed of parents of adolescent drug abusers at the Riverside Hospital in 1958. This group did not include complete families, but these parents were encouraged to share their mutual difficulties. Since 1958, parent groups that excluded the addicted child have not been uncommon, particularly in therapeutic communities. We have not found that including the total family in any way reinforces unwholesome defenses or leads to a deterioration of communication. However, these parent groups have been more educational than therapeutic and have not dealt with resolutions of underlying conflicts.

Berger (1973) and Bartlett (1975) have led MFTs with addict families. Berger's groups met only monthly in association with the therapeutic community of the Quaker Committee on Social Rehabilitation in New York City. His groups has a code in which they sought to elicit truth in order to examine the past and present without blaming or provoking guilt. They focused on patterns that contribute to self-hate and hurting oneself by hurting one's parents. Another emphasis is on those nonverbal behaviors of members who are not initially aware. They become conscious of them through the observations, interpretations, and reactions of others. Berger also uniquely focuses on "crisis creators," "help rejecting complainers," preachers, and placaters. A small family group within the larger group is used, with two residents assigned as advocates of the "truth," one for the family and one for the resident.

Bartlett (1975) writes of an MFT on a detoxification ward; this group is of necessity short term. In the first session or two, the family denies underlying problems. By the third session, the therapist confronts the family with its behavior and underlying dynamics and structure, particularly stressing the family members as "pusher" and the addict roles as scapegoat, interpreter, go-between, and emotion-supplier. In the fourth through sixth sessions, ti is decided that a treatment plan will be implemented. This is obviously not a simple decision, and underlying issues such as assertions of parental authority and the addict's power to maintain anxiety in others must be dealt with. The therapist supports the parents' capacity to exert change in their own home and accept the hypothesis "that change is possible."

Bartlett (1975) reports a follow-up study of a group of seven families treated by Kaufman in which five patients remained drug free a year after termination, and no siblings became addicted. A later study by Kaufmann showed that of a group of 45 adolescent substance abusers at Phoenix House, the rate of recidivism after 12 to 18 months of treatment was over 50 percent. When the entire family had been part of treatment in another group of 45, the recidivism rate dropped to 20 percent. Recidivism was evaluated by a one-hour in-depth interview with the family in addition to a cross-check with school and/or employment. Hendricks (1971) compared a group of male narcotic addicts who received multifamily counseling with a control group who did not. He found that one year after release, 41 percent of the treatment group remained in outpatient status compared to 21 percent of all male outpatients.

Our belief is that drug addiction is a symptom of family stress exacerbated by societal stress. We are primarily involved with the forces in the family that produce and maintain the symptom, as well as those forces within the therapeutic community that serve to maintain these symptoms. The staff and residents constitute their own family system. These also can be dealt with in ways that are similar to those used to deal with family dysfunction. The MFT group frequently acts as a barometer that reveals the overall functioning of the TC and underlines problems or cohesion in the TC family.

Middle-class families, particularly Italian, Greek, Irish, and Jewish, tend to be quite enmeshed. Puerto Rican and black mothers tend to be overinvolved with sons who are drug addicts. These family structures are described in detail in Chapter 3. Enmeshed families tend to be the ones that come regularly to therapy, and distanced families come rarely, if ever. Thus, in MFT is appears that most, if not all, families of addicts are enmeshed. The multitude of cultures and languages in our families is frequently bridged by the universal aspects of the problems, but it also presents many difficulties despite the use of therapists from several ethnic groups.

In some cases, distance between family members is a necessary goal. In many families the goal is a restoration of the family homeostasis. Certainly an intact family of origin with appropriate mutuality is curative and can prevent drug abuse. Similarly, so is a healthy nuclear family composed of the addict, nondrug-abusing spouse, and their own children.

Multiple family therapy is unique in contemporary society in that families expose themselves to one another and try to have a significant effect on each other's way of life. MFT enriches and stimulates the totality of any therapeutic program that utilizes this technique.

In our experience, MFT reduces the incidence of premature dropouts, acts as a preventive measure for other family members, builds a subculture that acts as an extended "good family," and creates and supports structural family changes that interdict the return of drug abuse.

References

Bartlett, D. (1975). The use of multiple family therapy groups with adolescent drug addicts. In M. Sugar (Ed.), *The adolescent in group and family therapy* (pp. 262–282). New York: Bruner/Mazel.

Berger, M. M. (1973). Multifamily psychosocial group treatment with addicts and their families. *Group Process, 5,* 31–45.

Fogarty, T. (1974). Evolution of a systems thinker. *The Family, 1,* 26–43.

Hendricks, W. J. (1971). Use of multifamily counseling groups in treatment of male narcotic addicts. *Intern'l. J. Group Psychotherapy, 21,* 34–90.

Hirsch, R. (1961). Group therapy with parents of adolescent drug addicts. *Psychiatric Quarterly, 35,* 702–710.

Laqueur, H. P., La Burt, H. A., & Morong, E. (1971). Multiple family therapy: Further developments. In J. Haley (Ed.), *Changing families* (pp. 82–95). New York: Grune & Stratton.

Leichter, E., & Schulman, G. L. (1974). Multi-family group therapy: A multidimensional approach. *Family Process, 13,* 95–110.

Minuchin, S. (1974). *Families and family therapy.* Cambridge, MA: Harvard University Press.

Minuchin, S. (1974b). Structural family therapy. In S. Arieti (Ed.), *American handbook of psychiatry* (Vol. 2) (pp. 178–192). New York: Basic Books.

Papp, P. (1973). Sculpting the family. *The Family, 1,* 44–48.

Papp, P. (1974). Multiple ways of multiple family therapists. *The Family, 1,* 25.

Ritchie, A. (1971). Multiple impact therapy: An experiment. In J. Haley (Ed.), *Changing Families* (pp. 36–44). New York: Grune & Stratton.

Speck, R. V., & Attneave, C. L. (1971). Social network intervention. In J. Haley (Ed.), *Changing families* (pp. 312–332). New York: Grune & Stratton.

CHAPTER SEVEN

From Multiple Family Therapy to Couples Therapy

EDWARD KAUFMAN, M.D.
Professor of Psychiatry
University of California, Irvine

PAULINE KAUFMANN,
M.S.W.
Director of Family Therapy
Phoenix Foundation

The literature of family therapy is replete with stereotyped assumptions that lose their usefulness when they become dogma. For example:

1. The identified patient is the symptom carrier for the total family. (Why not the family as the symptom deliverer?)
2. The identified patient helps maintain the family homeostasis. (Destructive at best, so why maintain it?)
3. The identified patient must solve his or her problems within the family context.

We have found that the health of the family is directly related to the quality of the relationship between the authoritative adults in the family.

Our experience has been in a daycare treatment center for adolescent drug abusers[1] and in two residential settings for adults.[2] Our interest is in the health of the entire family and the return of the previously addicted client to his or her family and community.

Couples who were part of our multiple family therapy groups began to ask for couples sessions. The frequently stated rationale was that they had problems that related only to the couple and could not be resolved with adolescents present. A number of couples had difficulty assuming responsibility for the family's dysfunction with the children present.

With the adult addicts, a primary focus was frequently on the couple relationship between the addict and spouse or potential spouse.

Su Casa and the Awakening Family have been described elsewhere in this book. The Phoenix Foundation's House Center has a population of 45 adolescents ranging in age from 11 to 17. The center operates six days a week from 9:00 A.M. to 5:00 P.M. A school program manned by the New York City Board of Education is an integral part of the daycare program. Approximately 2/3 of the population is male. Some 60 percent are black, 25 percent are Hispanic, and 15 percent are white. Many of the adolescents are on probation and sent by the court. They are referred because of truancy, petty theft, and possession of narcotics. Frequently they come under a Petition for Persons in Need of Supervision. A smaller number of adolescents are brought by their parents after they have been expelled from school because of violence in the classroom, gross infractions of rules, and possession of dangerous weapons.

Contact is generally initiated by the mother's telephone call. At the time of the initial contact, the parents are usually in a state of crisis. They feel they have nowhere to turn and are ready to accept any kind of help that is offered. We make it clear that the first appointment must be attended by both parents or parental surrogates as well as all the siblings living in the house. If there is a grandparent or relative living in the house, we insist that he or she come, too. In this first interview, the family is encouraged to talk about the problem of the identified patient, and his or her abuse of drugs and subsequent delinquent behavior. No other information is deemed important.

The operation of the daycenter is explained. It is made very clear that the identified patient will not be accepted unless the parents are an integral part of treatment. They be available by telephone and they must contact the center when regulations at home or school are broken. Also, the parents must attend multiple family therapy once a week at the center with their other children as well as the identified patient. School attendance is stressed, with the parents held responsible for getting their child to school on time. The school notifies parents whenever a student is late or does not come to school. It is the parents' job to see that the school is notified in case of illness or any other problem that may keep the identified patient from attending school.

The therapists are supportive and reassuring to the family. Parents are told that as long as they are involved in the program, take responsibility for coming to all the family therapy groups, and see that their son or daughter attends school, there is usually no recurrence of ongoing destructive behavior. Most parents, perhaps because of the crisis they have been through, agree to participate actively in the program. Generally, their enthusiasm tends to diminish as their son or daughter begins to fit into the program. At this point, a family meeting is called and once more the terms of the contract are reinforced. It is made quite clear that the program cannot help the child unless the parents participate actively. Usually it takes one or two such reminders. On rare occasions, the student is expelled until he or she can come back with parents. This has been done when there was no other way of getting the parents to attend family therapy sessions.

These sessions are open-ended multiple family therapy groups. Parents are assigned to one of the two existing groups as their child is accepted into the program. The new family introduces itself to the group and states its reason for being there. Within a very short time, group members who have been in family therapy for a while orient the new parents. An entire social network is created by the group. It is used for socializing and support, as well as sharing sources of information with the new members. In the beginning, all discussion is related to the problem of the drug-abusing identified patient (IP). Thus, the spouse system is looked at from the IP's vantage point, as is the sibling subsystem; generational boundaries, as well as alliances within the family, are examined from this same focus.

It is not unusual to have a student do very well in the first two or three months and then lose all interest in the program and begin to be late and cut classes. When this happens, the therapist assumes that something has gone awry in the family and calls the parents in for an individual session. Generally, it is discovered that there has been a crisis in the relationship of the marital pair or the parental surrogates, and the identified patient has been used as the battlefield. If this is the case, the therapist will suggest that the student become a 24-hour resident for a week or two, at most, and that the parents receive intensive couple therapy until the crisis is resolved. When the parents think they are ready, a final session is held with all the siblings and the resident, and once more the terms of the initial contract are restated. By taking the student out of the house, the parents become available for working on their relationship, thus treatment of the total family can continue.

As the family continues to attend the multiple family sessions, the parents and the children become assistant therapists for the new families coming in. This is generally the point at which drug abuse is no longer the problem for the identified patient, and other siblings in the family are doing well. Up until this point, the group has been concerned with the problem of drug abuse. When other matters have been introduced, they have been related to the central problem. When the presenting problems of drug abuse and school attendance have been resolved, the content of multiple family therapy sessions concerns marital problems. It is at this point that parents are invited to the couples group and leave the multiple family therapy group. In the couples, group procedures are reversed. Couples may not speak about their children; they must focus on the relationship between themselves. If material is brought up about the children, it is allowed only if it is relevant to the problems the couple are having. Invariably, three issues are discussed: money, sex, and intimacy.

Generally money, particularly its use as a power ploy, is the first problem to be discussed. It is the easiest issue on which to focus. Many of these couples have had little or no experience in the lover-spouse role. Their courting rarely lasts very long; sometimes it never existed at all. It is not unusual to see people who have been married 20 years or longer evince a great deal of shyness in the group. They are encouraged by other group members to touch, hold hands, and set up "dates" when they go out together. Much of this is a learning situation, and couples frequently are uncomfortable during this phase.

In a number of cases, the husband or the lover, when he has become angry and frustrated, has beaten his mate. This is noted, but not specifically examined. Instead, the group helps the couple "exhume" tender feelings that may have existed but have been buried in the family strife. Couples are taught how to fight creatively in the present rather than relive past conflicts, and how to go about resolving problems. The more experienced group members encourage the others to talk about their sexual life. For many couples, sex has become an abortive experience and a source of pain rather than pleasure.

A number of divorced parents have attended the couples group with their new husband, wife, or lover. When this occurs, the divorce becomes a reality during the group experience, and both parents are free to make a more lasting commitment to their new partners. As the couples begin to get pleasure from their own relationship, the use of the children as a battlefield diminishes. The couples are able to solve their problems between themselves. The generational boundaries between them and their children become appropriate and realistic. The parents begin to be able to separate themselves from their own families of origin. Crises are dealt with by all members of the family in a problem-solving manner. Couples attend the couples group for 10 to 25 sessions. When they leave, they know that the center is available to them for consultation. Couples are asked to come back after a three-month period for a "checkup" on a one-time basis. By this time, their children, who have been attending the daycare center, have graduated and are back in the community, either in a community school or in a job, and are living at home. An informal survey of some 100 families two years after having been in multiple family therapy and couple therapy indicates that approximately 75 percent of the families are doing well. There is no recurrence of a drug problem, and the parents are apparently enjoying each other.

The movement from multiple family therapy to couples therapy was a natural evolution in this setting. If an adolescent who had been doing well in the daycare center started cutting school or experimenting with drugs and was having trouble at home, the parents were called in for a couple session.[3] Thus, couples therapy was incorporated into the program's design. By removing the identified patient from the home, the recurrence of the old dysfunctional pattern was prevented. Parents had to resolve their couple problems, for the identified patient could no longer be used as the battlefield if he or she was not there. In the few sessions of intensive couple therapy with the children not present, one began to see that the couple, as they resolved their own problems, took responsibility for the identified patient and asked for his or her return.

It was from these crisis experiences that therapists began to understand the need for seeing couples without their children. As couples talked about themselves in the couples group, the pronoun *we* began to be used more and more. The couple experienced their "we-ness" when they dealt with the children in the family. They expressed some amazement at how easy it seemed to be when they were in agreement. From this, they developed ways of talking to each other about the children and the problems they presented. Couples spoke about generational boundaries in terms of their many different ideas about distance and closeness. Occasionally, a mother wanted to see herself as her daughter's friend, or a father wanted to be a pal to his son. Other members of the couples group talked about parenting and the distance between the generations that was necessary and good. As the partners began to invest more in each other rather than in the identified patient, the child had fewer crises. Members of the couples group made each other aware whenever a couple would form a covert alliance with the identified patient or one of the siblings. The members of the couples group became increasingly aware that the parenting people were the center around which the family revolved. Sibling problems were minimal when these two felt good about themselves and each other. In the group sessions, the couples monitored each other and shared experiences. They also alerted each other to "slippage." Sexual problems that could not be discussed in the multiple family therapy group were the subject of many couples sessions.

The identified patient and other siblings are rarely mentioned in couples group. If a couple are asked about a particular child, the answer is usually short, and they frequently say, "When we're doing fine together, the kids have no problems." Occasionally they will add with some amazement that they are really having fun with their kids. The couples group reinforces the fact that parents are the foundation for the structure of the family, with much of the family dependent on the parents' stability.

After the final session in the couples group, the entire family has its last session with the family therapist. In this last session, gains are noted and fears expressed. There is frequently an easy kind of affection among the family members, as well as some anxiety about how the family will function when it is not coming to the daycare center. At this point, the therapist informs the family of an appointment in three months for a checkup, and that its members are free to call the daycare center at any time. Things are not ended, they are just being changed. This movement from multiple family therapy to couples therapy is growth inducing. Parents report that they feel they can begin to take responsibility for their children as a couple.

One other interesting development occurred in the couples group: The members formed a social network, and many of them saw each other on weekends, went to movies or dances together, and frequently visited each other's homes. They exchanged services and babysat for each other or had the older children come to the house of a mother who was not working on a particular day. On the whole, they found each other helpful and supportive. Many of the couples continue to use the daycare center as a resource for problem solving, not only for the family but for neighbors and relatives. They not only share problems but also celebrations such as marriages, births and birthdays.

Another type of couples group evolved with the adult addicts. This group is composed of addicts and their spouses, and includes in-house couples. The MFT group is used as a screening device to evaluate the viability and therapeutic potential of the relationship between the addict and spouse. If no member of the family of origin is available and the addict-spouse dyad is felt to be such that it would be conducive to a drug-free, healthy state, then the patient is added to the couples group after 4 to 10 sessions in MFT. When the family of origin is available, then a great deal of work is done with the addict in that system before or concurrent with the couples group. (Unfortunately, at Su Casa, the MFT and couples group met at the same time. At the Awakening Family, this was not the case.) Therapists never work directly with the spouse's parents, though in some cases, she or he was coached in how to deal with her or his family of origin. If there is ample trained staff, then direct work should certainly be done with the spouse and his or her own family.

Another issue that can be dealt with in the MFT prior to couples group is the parenting function of the addict. MFT is an excellent opportunity to help the addict to become a parent again as well as to develop a united parental subsystem with his or her spouse. Thus, a couple works together in MFT to control their disruptive eight-year-old. Likewise, a divorced father whose teenage sons attend the MFT achieves a level of self-esteem that permits him to ask his drug-free children not to smoke (cigarettes) as a step toward establishing himself as a loving, limit-setting father.

In the couples group, many of the principles described in this book are applicable, although many others are not. This is because in groups with residential clients, present drug abuse is not as much of a problem as the spouse's attitude toward drug intake, and if the spouse's behavior contributes to or provokes drug abuse, this behavior is identified and shifted. In most cases, the couples who reach the stage of couple therapy have a relationship that is evaluated as potentially constructive. Thus, the spouse is not encouraged to detach emotionally or physically, but the major purpose of the group is to establish a mutual, loving relationship between partners.

Couples groups are an excellent way to deal with newly established in-house couples or the ex-addict's relationships as he or she moves out into society. At the Awakening Family, any in-house couple who wants to build a relationship is asked to meet with the cotherapists of the couples group to evaluate their relationship and its potential suitability for work in that group.

Many of the techniques described in this book are used with couples, particularly structural, communication, and systems approaches. Some techniques, such as examining and shifting triangulation, are particularly suited to a couples group. The therapist must be aware that couples will such him or her into a triangle, replacing issues such as children, money, power, drugs, alcohol, and affairs with their relationship to the therapist. An important technique with couples is to examine their hidden agendas and rule-governed behavior (Haley, 1976). One rule to remember is that partners tend to balance each other and that balancing may be more important than what the couples feel is a fixed attitude on their parts. The stereotype of female spendthrift and male tightwad is frequently reversed in couples where there is a male addict. However, if he gives up spending money on drugs, he rapidly becomes the tightwad, which may push the spouse into becoming a spendthrift. Another rule (Haley, 1976) is that spouses tend to provoke each other into escalating quarrels that can be abated only by pulling in a third party (in-law, child, therapist). In the addict-spouse pair, there is frequently competition over who is the sickest and most needy. They may be a source of many quarrels and continues when the addict is drug free.

Spouses tend to communicate through a third person (Haley, 1976). This can be dealt with even if that person is not a member of the group, as couples who are used to this pattern will find someone in the group to communicate through. Frequently the problem a couple presents is not the real problem at all. The presenting problem may be a protective device that keeps the marriage going, such as an affair to provide needed distance, tapping anger to alleviate depression, or provoking substance abuse (Haley, 1976). Substance abuse may be provoked or supported in the potential addict because of the spouse's need for self-punishment, to control someone who is weak, to have someone to punish, or out of a need for love that is so desperate that the love object must be rendered so helpless that he or she is incapable of leaving (Whalen, 1953).

The therapist must take great pains to ensure that he or she is not unknowingly the object of the couple's triangulation. Likewise, the therapist must not join one side; otherwise, he or she becomes part of the problem rather than its solution (Haley, 1976). The therapist must also realize that despite similarities, all couples are different and, in particular, different from his or her own coupling relationships (Haley, 1976).

A critical period in every relationship occurs when one partner gives up substance misuse, for the nonusing partner must find an entirely different way of relating. There are totally new expectations and demands, and for the first time there is communication — an art that neither may have ever learned. Thus, couples must support each other in learning the basic tools of communication. Sex has been used for exploitation and as a means for asking total forgiveness to the extent that it becomes nonexistent. This too must be slowly redeveloped; in many cases the ex-substance abuser has sex "on the natch" (off drugs) for the first time in her or his life. Difficulties also arise because the recovering abuser has given up the most precious thing in his or her life (drugs or alcohol) and expects immediate rewards. The spouse has been "burned" too many times and is not willing to give rewards that the substance abuser feels he or she deserves. Spouses are encouraged to begin to trust and reward at the same time and ex-abusers are asked to reevaluate their expectations. The ex-substance abuser may go through a period of mourning for months or years after giving up the previous substance-love object. This depression should be alleviated. If it is not, it can lead to a homeostasis that is dependent on it and as crippling for the couple as substance abuse. When and if the depression lifts, it also causes new conflicts that must be resolved.

In-house couples are in a situation much like summer camp. There are a limited number of partners available in a closed environment, and if any of them make the slightest move toward each other, they are designated as a couple by the entire house. A couples group should permit them some distance and give them permission to separate if they choose. An advanced couple who has worked out many of their problems can be an excellent role model for newer relationships. At the Awakening Family, any couple who develops a relationship is asked to write a paper on what a relationship is, which they read to the entire house. This provides a model for mutual relationships.

Cotherapist pairs should be a man and a woman who are able to disagree within the group to establish a model for health conflict resolution. This type of balance in the cotherapy team also helps prevent unhealthy coalitions and triangulation. Couples groups in either an adult or adolescent program provide a natural means for structural shift and subsystem support. It is critical that the shift not be made simply because such groups exist, but with the full knowledge that such a group will support certain systems and weaken others. If this is always kept in mind, then such specialized couples groups can be extremely helpful and, in some cases, essential.

Endnotes

1. Day Care Center of the Phoenix Foundation funded by NIDA Grant No. 1 H80 MH01049
2. Su Casa, New York, New York, and The Awakening Family, Norwalk, California
3. In single-parent homes, the authority couple could be a mother and grandmother, a mother and older sibling, a relative, or anyone functioning as an ongoing authority figure in the family.

References

Framo, J. L. (1965). Rationale and techniques of intensive family therapy. In I. Boszormenyi-Nagy & J. L. Framo (Eds.), *Intensive family therapy*. New York: Hoeber.

Haley, J. (1963). Marriage therapy. *Arch. Gen. Psychiatry, 8*, 213–234.

Haley, J. (1976). *Problem solving therapy*. San Francisco: Jossey-Bass.

Laqueur, H. P. (1968). General systems theory and multiple family therapy. In J. H. Massermass (Ed.), *Current psychiatric therapies* (Vol. VIII). New York: Grune & Stratton.

Minuchin, S. (1974). *Families and family therapy*. Cambridge, MA: Harvard University Press.

Minuchin, S., Montalvo, B., Guerney, B. G., Rosman, B. L., & Schumer, F. (1967). *Families of the slums*. New York: Basic Books.

Whalen, T. (1953). Wives of alcoholics: Four types observed in a family service agency. *Quarterly J. of Studies on Alcohol, 14*, 632–641.

CHAPTER EIGHT

Integrating Cybernetics and Constructivism into Structural-Strategic Family Therapy for Drug Abusers

HARVEY JOANNING
Iowa State University

The late 1940s was a time when a number of psychotherapists increasingly expressed their dissatisfaction with individually oriented psychotherapy. These same people began to work with entire families as an adjunct to individual patients. Out of these early efforts has grown the field of applied human systems theory, commonly known as *family therapy.*

Family therapy represents a shift in how human problems of living are conceptualized and treated. The focus of theory and treatment is on the social network in which people live. Problems are seen as emergent in social contexts. Simple cause-and-effect explanations of human behavior are discarded in preference to cyclical or systemic descriptions of social interaction patterns that contain problem behavior as but a partial arc of a more

This chapter is based in part on a grant from the National Institute on Drug Abuse that was completed at Texas Tech University and in part on work presently being conducted at Iowa State University. The author would like to acknowledge the following individuals who make up the generic "we" used throughout this text: Charles Cole, David Brown, Linda Enders, Tom Henrich, Greg Howard, Melody Justice, Bruce Kuehl, Julia Malia, Laura Mutchler, Neal Newfield, William Quinn, and Frank Thomas.

Requests for additional information should be addressed to Dr. Harvey Joanning, Associate Professor and Director, Family Therapy Doctoral Program, Department of Family Environment, Iowa State University, Ames, Iowa, 50011.

encompassing recursive cycle of social behavior. The addition of cybernetic theory in the 1950s and constructivist theory in the 1960s has helped family therapy become a unique approach to therapy that rejects positivist notions of an ultimate reality and a corresponding "correct" way to do therapy. Family therapy theorists recognized that *reality* and *treatment* are cognitive constructions that emerge as families and therapists interact (Maturana, 1980).

The approach to drug-abuse treatment described here is an extension of the theoretical and pragmatic changes that have been the hallmark of the family therapy movement. We have attempted to build an overall treatment model that is guided by systems theory; that is, all people involved in dealing with adolescent drug abuse are interconnected. Consequently, we use a "treatment team" that can include family therapists, school officials, legal authorities, or any qualified professional who is attempting to limit drug abuse in a community (Joanning, Gawinski, Morris, & Quinn, 1986). We also believe that family therapy is a "coevolutionary" process; that is, the family being treated influences the treatment team as much as the team influences the family.

In our approach to family systems therapy, the family is seen on a regular basis by a treatment team. The team consists of a therapist who interviews the family in one room while two or three colleagues observe through a one-way mirror from another room. At times a member of the community, such as a teacher, social worker, or clergy, may join the team or sit in a session with the family. The therapist typically interviews the family for 10 to 15 minutes at the beginning of a session to explore "what happened during the week." He or she then takes a break to consult with colleagues behind the mirror while the family is asked to discuss some point or issue they have raised during the first part of the session. The interviewer then joins the team behind the mirror to discuss the information just received and to plan the rest of the session. The interviewer typically rejoins the family for approximately 30 minutes to gather additional information and to interact with the family in a manner suggested by the team. The interviewer then again takes a break and visits with the team to plan a final intervention or "homework" designed to use the information provided by the family to "push" or "bump" the family toward change. "Information" includes what the family said about themselves and how they interacted with each other and the interviewer during the session. The terms *push* and *bump* are used to imply that we cannot directly change the family but merely perturb or influence them.

The perturbation or "bump" we attempt to give the family deserves further elaboration. We do not see ourselves telling the family what to do to overcome their problems, but rather we attempt to establish a context for change. We believe that families ultimately change themselves, that they already possess what they need to make a change, and that the nature of any change is difficult or impossible to predict. Our job as therapists is to listen carefully to what the family says their problem is, how each family member believes the problem has come to exist, what each member sees as an appropriate solution to the problem, and what the family has already done to try to get rid of the problem. Interestingly, the family may not see drug abuse as the problem. It is not unusual for the referring agency or school to see drug abuse as the problem, whereas the parents in the family may complain about their child's disobedience and the adolescent may lament that his or her parents "are always on my case for no reason." How the family and the referral source define the problem is very much a "construction" that must be carefully woven into creating a therapeutic context (Joanning, Newfield, & Quinn, 1988).

Our early sessions with families involve asking questions and promoting family dialogue around the issues identified in the preceding paragraph. We use the information gained to form an initial intervention, or sometimes simply asking the questions will lead the family to spontaneous change. For example, when one family was asked how they thought the problem of their son's drug abuse came to be, an older daughter timidly said she thought her brother was just emulating her father who she described as a drunk. Apparently this was the first time any of the three children in the family had ever acknowledged and challenged their father's behavior. When asked why she had made her comment, she responded that the therapy session was a safe place to speak up and that the opportunity had never presented itself before. Clearly the therapy session provided a context for change, at least for the daughter in this family.

In another example, the team took a much more active role in providing a context for family change. A 15-year-old son was staying out late each night, failing in school, and using a variety of drugs. Although the parents worried and complained verbally to the therapist, they said little to their son. When the therapist verbally "pushed" them to take a firm stand with their son, they deferred to one another, neither parent willing to confront the son. Upon further probing, it became apparent that the parenting subsystem in this "blended" family had not emerged as a team. Each partner attempted to parent his or her own biological children but did not "intrude" on the other partner's children. The treatment team "bumped" the family by commenting that the wayward 15-year-old was not as dumb as the parents thought. He was taking full advantage of the fact that his mother and stepfather had not agreed on the "game plan" for how this new family was to be "coached and managed." The therapist further commented that the team behind the one-way mirror was wagering among themselves as to whether the son or the parents would eventually "win the game." The introduction of this sports metaphor especially engaged the athletically minded father who, during the following week, convinced his wife that they had to "coach together."

The parents returned to the next session and announced to the therapist and their children that from then on both parents had to be consulted simultaneously regarding requests from the children. Further, they insisted that the 15-year-old son would be in the house by 7:00 P.M. each evening and had to raise his grades to a C average or would not be allowed to participate in football, an important part of the boy's life. This change in the family was not predicted by the treatment team. In an ethnographic interview (described later in this chapter), the family told an anthropologist that the team "wagering on who would win the game pushed us over the edge." The parents decided they had to work together in parenting all the children, not just their own.

This vignette is an example of perturbing or "bumping" a family toward change, that is, providing a context in which change is more likely to occur without specifically telling the family what to do. Our experience has been that "telling" a family what to do is rarely as effective as building a situation in which the family attempts something different for themselves.

We cannot predict what the family will do in reaction to our perturbation. We must wait until the next session to hear and see what the family did, if anything. If the family made a change following our intervention (e.g., task, comment, ritual), we use that information to plan our next perturbation. If the family did nothing significantly different, we are informed that the perturbation we introduced was meaningless noise to the family and we change our approach (e.g., pursue a different line of questioning, introduce a new semantic frame). Consequently, our next session begins with a review of "what happened during the week," and the therapeutic process cycles back on itself. Each cycle is considered a recursion in that the family and team have both changed at least slightly during the week as each of these two social systems attempt to accommodate to the process of mutual influence triggered in the prior session. Overall, the team and family constitute a therapeutic system that is made up of two interacting subsystems that coevolve through a process of mutual influence.

From Structures to Constructions

The models of therapy that initially most influenced our work were structural (Minuchin, 1974; Minuchin & Fishman, 1981), strategic (Haley, 1976, 1980), and systemic (Palazzoli, Boscolo, Cecchin, & Prata, 1978). We have also borrowed heavily from earlier research using family therapy to treat drug addiction (Stanton & Todd, 1982) and have more recently been influenced by the epistemological shift discussed by leading family therapy theorists (Dell, 1982; Keeney, 1983). Overall, our approach to therapy can be classified as structural/strategic family systems therapy, although we have done considerable work to integrate this hybrid model with a constructivist epistemological stance when dealing with adolescent drug abusers and their families. More specifically, we now approach therapy as constructivists but draw ideas for intervening from structural, strategic, and systemic models of family therapy as well as our own imagination. Furthermore, we have come to believe that therapy is essentially a dialogue among human beings and that reality exists only in dialogue, not independent of people engaged in dialogue.

Traditionally, structural and strategic family therapists have not taken a constructivist approach to therapy. Rather, they have worked from a model of how families should be structured so as to optimize their functioning. Families who vary from this idealized model are encouraged to change their structure to approach the ideal. If families are reluctant or unable to move toward the model, they are worked with strategically (e.g., through the use of metaphor, paradox, ritual) to initiate desired change. Constructivists do not adopt a model-specific view of the world. Each individual (or family) is seen to have his or her own "world view" or epistemological stance. Therapists must become aware of that world view and integrate it into their perturbations (interventions) in order to establish a therapeutic context in which the family will evolve to a different way of organizing itself to deal with a problem. This evolution is commonly perceived by a therapist as "change."

Because our team of therapists views the structural/strategic model as a useful model, but only one of an infinite number of possible models of how a family could be organized, we have moved from a traditional structural/strategic approach to therapy. However, we do start from the structural/strategic model because it has proven to be useful when thinking about families. The key is to remember that it is only one model. It helps us to plan interventions, but it may not be how a family views itself or how a family should organize itself to be optimally structured.

As the name implies, structural family therapy is concerned with the structure, or organization, of families seen in treatment. Structural problems have been evident in the families we have seen in a controlled outcome study designed to treat drug abuse among adolescents (Joanning, Quinn, Arrendondo, & Fischer, 1984). Of 28 families who completed structural/strategic family systems therapy in this study, 16 exhibited behavioral interaction patterns in which one or more major structural "problem" was perceived by the treatment team, that is, the team constructed or invented descriptions of the problem in structural terms. The structural model postulates that the parents or "executives" in a family must work closely and agree as to how to parent their children. If such agreement is lacking, consistency in parenting will not emerge. Inconsistency in parenting is seen as providing the potential for inappropriate adolescent behavior.

Furthermore, covert marital problems may either contribute to inconsistent parenting or compel an adolescent to misbehave to divert parental attention from their marriage and to the child. In this situation, the child's misbehavior can be viewed as part of a three-person triangle in which the child serves to moderate stress in a marriage. As the adolescent begins to gain independence from the family by becoming more involved with peers and activities outside the home, marital stress "heats up" and the child misbehaves in some way in reaction to the stress (e.g., takes drugs to escape emotionally the stress at home). As the parents become aware of and grow concerned about their child's drug use, they focus on him or her and their marital stress "cools down." This cyclical process becomes evident as the therapy team observes the family interact and/or tell their story of how life is in their family. Although other responses may emerge to calibrate family interaction, the pattern just outlined is one we constructed to describe family interaction that occurred frequently in our research.

One of these patterns, parental inconsistency, has manifested itself as one parent "ruling with an iron fist" and the other "wearing a felt glove." The more authoritarian parent will argue that the other parent is "too soft"; that is, permissive and lax. The more supportive parent will counterargue that the other parent is "too hard"; that is, arbitrary and irrational. This disagreement about how to parent can be seen as isomorphic to the marital situation; that is, the marital partners have some long-standing disagreement about how they relate to one another and this disagreement is mirrored in their argument over parenting style or philosophy. The goal of therapy, if this situation emerges, is to "heat up marital intensity" and bring this covert disagreement out into the open where it can be dealt with and resolved. If this happens, it has been our experience that adolescent drug use will diminish because stress will be lowered in the home and/or the parents will be able to work together to set limits around their child's behavior.

Strategic family therapy shares many of the conceptual and therapeutic maneuvers of the structural model and is therefore often combined with it (Frazier, 1982). The strategic model adds flexibility often needed when dealing with families struggling with problems that are not primarily structural. In our team's perception, 12 of the 28 families in our study presented patterns built around problems or contextual events that demanded interventions tailored to the unique situations faced by these families (e.g., unresolved grief due to death of a family member, adolescents who persisted in rebellious behavior in the face of united parents).

Taken together, structural and strategic models of therapy supply a theoretical system useful in conceptualizing cases as well as providing guidelines for building interventions. Our research has developed this structural/strategic model even further by borrowing procedures and concepts from systemic family therapy.

Systemic family therapy is noted for its use of teams and its emphasis on working cybernetically. The therapy team is seen to be interacting recursively with a family; that is, the team says something to the family through the interviewer and then watches and listens to what happens. Likewise, the family says or does something in the presence of the interviewer and the observing team and then listens to the team's comments as relayed by the interviewer. In turn, the family says or does something and the team again responds with their comments. A process of interaction evolves as each recursion of the cycle occurs. Consequently, the specific process of therapy involving each family and their team is not predetermined but rather emerges as therapy proceeds. Furthermore, the "reality" that evolves during this process may very well be different for the team and the family. To ensure that our treatment team is aware of the reality emerging for the family being served, our research has added one additional element to the cybernetic process just described.

Ethnographic Interviews

We have trained our therapists in anthropological field techniques, especially ethnomethodology, and have used this interviewing strategy to assist us in gathering information about the families' perceptions of therapy. These professionals have interviewed families between interviews and following the completion of therapy to record and analyze the families' stories "of how you would describe your experience to a friend." These interviews have proven invaluable in helping us understand how the team and the process of therapy is perceived by the family. Consequently, we are now using interviewers trained in ethnographic interviewing techniques to interview families after every third or fourth therapy session as well as following the completion of treatment. This allows us to know how we are doing as we work, as well as to hear how the families perceive treatment after they complete therapy. These interviews feed information back into the process of therapy to "inform" our work. Because we are attempting to work cybernetically, we are trying to maximize information feedback loops between the team and the family. It is our belief that such cycles of information will increase the likelihood that both families and teams will change in useful ways.

Ethnographic interviewing is new to family therapy and bears further description. We recommend that such interviews begin following the third or fourth treatment session—far enough into therapy so the family has something to comment on but early enough so the treatment team can adjust their approach to dealing with the family in response to what the family says during the interview. The purpose of these interviews is to provide information to the treatment team or therapist about how the family is experiencing the process of therapy. These ethnographic interviews are informal and relatively short (up to an hour).

During the first such interview, the family is told that the interviewer (ethnographer) is interested in what it has been like to visit with a professional about something that is happening in their family. "By the way," the interviewer will say, "What do you call it when you go to see Dr. Smith?" "We call it 'going for meetings.' " "Please tell me what it has been like to go for meetings as if I'm someone you know who is interested in doing the same thing. Tell me a story about what your meetings are like." The interview becomes a reflective listening exercise on the part of the ethnographer with the goal of having the family "teach" the interviewer what their experience of therapy has been. The interviewer is careful not to "lead the witness" but rather let the family tell their story as they perceive it. Families typically talk about not knowing what to expect of therapy, parents are relieved to find that the therapist is not judgmental, and the adolescent drug abuser is usually waiting for the "ax to fall" so says nothing or tells the parents and the therapist what "I think they want to hear." An in-depth summary of what emerges during such interviews is available elsewhere (Newfield, Kuehl, Joanning, & Quinn, 1989).

At the end of each ethnographic interview, the family is asked what, if anything, the interviewer may share with the therapist and/or team about what the family has said. Families typically place no restrictions on the interviewer but will occasionally ask that some comment (usually about the therapist) be withheld. It is imperative that the interviewer has a clear agreement with the family about what is going to be shared with the family. This caveat goes beyond confidentiality to include securing the family's trust during subsequent interviews.

Typically a family is interviewed by the ethnographer once or twice during treatment and again after therapy is completed. These later sessions again provide feedback to the team but also allow the interviewer to ask the family to further clarify or confirm "domains of meaning" the ethnographer is constructing to describe the family's experience of treatment. For example, the ethnographer may mention in a follow-up interview, "Earlier you told me that going to meetings is an ordeal, but a necessary evil. Could you clarify what you meant?" or "Other families have told me that although they are very aware of the team at first, they become more comfortable with their unseen presence and generally don't desire to meet them. How does that observation fit with your experience?"

As these examples illustrate, the ethnographic interviews move from reflecting what the family has said in the first interview to constructing a "domain" or meaning system that captures the essence of the family experience of their treatment and compares their personal story with those of other families. Consequently, not only does the treatment team receive immediate feedback about the impact of their work with a particular family but the team and other professionals gain valuable information about the overall experiences of families who seek family therapy. Again, a more complete description of how to conduct ethnographic interviews and distill the resulting "domains of meaning" into a complete ethnography is given elsewhere (Newfield et al., 1989). An ethnography is the final written account of an interviewer's experience of interviewing "informants" (in this case, families) around a cultural theme, in our work, family therapy.

In addition to ethnographic interviews between sessions and following the completion of treatment, we also have the interviewer "gossip" with the family if the team is taking a long break (15 to 30 minutes) to discuss some aspect of the treatment session on a given day. Our experience, and that of others conducting process research on family therapy (Pinsoff, 1987), has indicated that families become apprehensive or bored if left alone for more than a few minutes while the team consults. Consequently, we send an interviewer in to talk with the family about their experience of therapy that day. We call these brief interviews "gossip sessions" because the family is simply asked "How's the session going for you today?" They typically respond in a fashion similar to what a person may tell a friend after just returning from a visit to a physician.

Interestingly, families tend to "lay it on the line" and "tell it like it is" even though they know the team may be listening. It has been fascinating to us to note that the family will spontaneously "fill in" the ethnographer while not telling the therapist their reaction to the session. In fact, our follow-up ethnographic interviews have revealed that if the family does not like the therapist or the team's intervention they may often "act polite" and "say we'll do it" when they have no intention to carry out the suggestion or intervention introduced by the therapist. Consequently, introducing the gossip session during treatment sessions and ethnographic interviews between every three or four sessions has saved us from "spinning our wheels" with families who are not "buying" our interventions but do not tell us they disagree.

Further, we have moved from perceiving some families as "resistant" to viewing lack of movement by the family as indicative of our needing to spend more time exploring the family's view of the problem. In short, we have learned to have great respect for the evolutionary nature of therapy and to increase the number and quality of recursive information feedback cycles between the team and the family.

When we first began to incorporate ethnographic interviews and gossip sessions into our treatment model, we were concerned that too much time would be involved to be practical in a nonresearch setting. Interestingly, the total amount of time we spend with a family, approximately 12 to 15 hours over three to four months, has not increased but the apparent degree of change among family members has. In sum, spending some time interviewing families about their experience of treatment has not lessened the total amount of time spent in treatment sessions but has led to the family being more satisfied with treatment and the adolescent's behavior. We are presently researching whether having the family "feel" better about therapy correlates with decreased drug use among family members. To date, we have noted a decrease in drug use among family members as reported by other family members, an improvement in adolescent school attendance and performance, and a decrease in adolescent legal infractions. We are presently preparing a controlled outcome study that will compare family systems therapy with ethnographic interviews to family systems therapy without interviews. Our goal is to test whether or not the use of ethnographic interviews improves treatment outcome sufficiently to justify their continued use.

The last five years of researching family therapy as a treatment for drug abuse has increased our respect for the context provided by family members and the format of treatment. We have come to realize the importance of being aware of how the family experiences therapy so as to not waste our time by pursuing a treatment strategy that is not connecting with the family's experience of reality. Furthermore, we now believe that adopting a constructivist stance as therapists helps us avoid the presupposition that there is a correct way to do therapy with all families. Rather, we believe that each family has an unique world view or epistemological stance of its own, that our world view must connect with theirs through the therapeutic format employed, and that therapy is a coevolutionary process involving therapist/team and the family.

References

Dell, P. (1982). Beyond homeostasis: Toward a concept of coherence. *Family Process, 21*, 21–41.

Frazier, S. (1982). Structural & strategic therapy: A basis for marriage or grounds for divorce? *Journal of Marital and Family Therapy, 8*, 13–22.

Haley, J. (1976). *Problem-solving therapy.* San Francisco: Jossey-Bass.

Haley, J. (1980). *Leaving home: The therapy of disturbed young people.* New York: McGraw-Hill.

Joanning, H., Gawinski, B., Morris, J., & Quinn, W. H. (1986). Organizing a social ecology to treat adolescent drug abuse. *Journal of Strategic & Systemic Therapy*, *5*, 55–61.

Joanning, H., Newfield, N., & Quinn, W. H. (1988). Drug "use" or "abuse": A systemic perspective. Manuscript submitted for publication.

Joanning, H., Quinn, W. H., Arrendondo, R., & Fischer, J. (1984). *Family therapy versus traditional therapy for drug abusers*. National Institute on Drug Abuse Grant # 501DA03733.

Keeney, B. (1983). *Aesthetics of change*. New York: Guilford Press.

Maturana, H. (1980). Autopoiesis: Reproduction, heredity, and evolution. In M. Zeleny (Ed.), *Autopoiesis, dissipative structures, and spontaneous social orders*. Boulder, CO: Westview Press.

Minuchin, S. (1974). *Families and family therapy*. Cambridge, MA: Harvard University Press.

Minuchin, S., & Fishman, C. (1981). *Family therapy techniques*. Cambridge, MA: Harvard University Press.

Newfield, N., Kuehl, B., Joanning, H., & Quinn, W. H. (1990). A mini-ethnography of the family therapy of adolescent drug abuse: The ambiguous experience. *Alcohol Treatment Quarterly*, *7*(2), 57–79.

Palazzoli, M., Boscolo, L., Cecchin, G., and Prata, G. (1978). *Paradox and counterparadox*. London: Jason Aronson.

Pinsoff, W. (1987, November). *Research for the clinician: Integrating qualitative and quantitative methods*. Annual Conference of the American Association for Marriage and Family Therapy, Chicago.

Stanton, M., & Todd, T. (1982). *The family therapy of drug abuse*. New York: Guilford Press.

CHAPTER NINE

Drug-Abusing Families: Intrafamilial Dynamics and Brief Triphasic Treatment

DENNIS M. REILLY, M.S.W., A.C.S.W.
Southeast Nassau Guidance Counseling Center
Wantagh, New York

Since 1972, the Southeast Nassau Guidance Counseling Center has maintained an ambulatory, drug-free treatment program for youthful drug abusers and their families. This program, a branch of SNG's community mental health center, serves a suburban, largely white, middle-class Long Island population within commuting distance of New York City. The majority of the drug-abusing clients are between the ages of 12 and 25. The most common drugs of abuse are, in descending frequency of use, marijuana and alcohol, barbiturates and minor tranquilizers, amphetamines, cocaine, and hallucinogens. Only about 12 percent of the population abuses heroin, methadone, or other opiates. Most are polydrug abusers.

The findings reported in this chapter are based on our 15 years of experience with this population. We believe that much of what we have noted concerning the functioning and treatment of drug-abusing families can be generalized to other treatment populations. However, this should be done with caution, as our observations rest on a rather restricted sample, one that is geographically limited and racially and economically homogenous.

As a result of our work with youthful drug abusers and their families, we have come to see the family as the interface between the individual and his or her society. The family is the fulcrum, the pivot point, the mediator, and the interpreter between its members and their culture. As such, it is particularly influential in the socialization of its members, whether into "prosocial" or "antisocial" roles. It is a semipermeable membrane that regulates the flow of either prosocial or delinquent influences from the outside world of peers, class and group interests, media, social values, and so on. It is a social lens mechanism that may either selectively magnify and focus socially deviant influences on its individual members, or screen and filter them out. It is the disturbed family system that creates in its individual members—the identified patients or "symptom bearers"—a vulnerability to antisocial or "prodrug" influences of peers, media, or subcultures. It is the disturbed family system's need for a delegated family black sheep, scapegoat, or deviant that makes a young person particularly susceptible to the adoption of delinquent or drug-abusing values and behavior. It is the disturbed family system that "pushes" the black sheep into the arms of a drug-abusing peer group. This helps to explain why one young person may choose to "differentially associate" (Sutherland & Cressey, 1955) with a drug-abusing peer group, while another choose a prosocial one. Finally, it is the disturbed family system that "nominates" the drug abuser and "elects" him or her to the office of scapegoat.

Characteristic Interactions in Drug-Abusing Families

As we have noted previously (Reilly, 1975a, 1975b), our experience makes it possible to construct a tentative profile of a family system that tends to produce drug-abusing behavior in its members. Such a profile must remain, however, something of an "ideal type," as no one family will manifest all of its characteristics in real life. It is a type that must remain "culturebound" to the extent our research sample is unrepresentative of the general population. It is a profile that is relative, a matter of degree. Drug-abusing families carry trends moderately extant in all families to a pathological extreme. With these points in mind, we can move on to an examination of some of the common interactional themes manifested by the drug-abusing families under study.

Negativism

Drug-abusing families often describe family life as dull, deadened, alienated, lifeless, and shallow. They feel isolated from one another, encapsulated, out of touch. Communication occurs in primarily negative ways via criticism, complaints, blaming, nagging, and corrections. In such families, members quickly learn that the only way to introduce a modicum of "life" or excitement into the system is to precipitate a crisis. Children swiftly learn that the only way they can consistently gain attention is to make trouble or create problems—"the squeaky wheel gets the oil." Acceptable behavior is rarely praised or recognized, indeed, it is generally ignored, whereas "bad" behavior is unfailingly reinforced with attention and a surge of heightened excitement and involvement, rare and treasured commodities in such households. By the time the children are old enough to enter the adolescent subculture, they are already primed to discover an enormously convenient and sure-fire means of stimulating family system excitement and provoking negative adult attention: drug abuse.

Parental Inconsistency

Parents in many of these families seem incapable of setting clear and consistent rules or limits to govern their children's behavior. The same unit of behavior that they ignore one moment, they may punish or reward the next. They often disagree as to whether and how to discipline. Children get very confused and ambivalent messages concerning what is right or wrong, acceptable or unacceptable. This situation creates in the children an enormous hunger for clarity and structure, and they tend to engage in behavior designed to provoke either the parents or parental substitutes into taking a definite stand. Drug abuse often serves this function admirably. The young person will, sometimes even half consciously, flaunt his or her drug involvement in a cry for help, attention, and concern. He will leave drugs around the house in places easily accessible to his parents, or she will advertise her drug abuse in front of teachers at school or police on the streets.

Parental Denial

As the young person escalates attempts to "set himself or herself up" and get caught, his or her parents often respond by escalating their denial of what is occurring. They manage not to see the drugs "hidden" in obvious places, not to notice their child's altered behavior. Often this denial persists until outside authorities are forced to intervene. And even then—even at that late date—the parents' response is often, "No, you're mistaken, it can't be *my* child!"

Vicarious Parental Behavior

Often parents have a vested interest in "not seeing," and therefore not stopping, their children's drug abuse. These are parents who, despite conscious disapproval and verbal condemnations, unconsciously envy the hedonistic freedoms they attribute, rightly or wrongly, to today's youth. Though they may not be able to indulge themselves in these "forbidden pleasures," they are able to gain a great deal of secondhand gratification by covertly licensing them in their children. They clearly convey to their children this morbid fascination, whether it relates to drugs, sexuality, violence, or general lifestyle. Finally, their messages concerning drug use are ambivalent in the extreme, usually taking the form, "Don't let me catch you using drugs," with the emphasis on not getting caught or not letting the parents "know" that they are using drugs.

Miscarried Expression of Anger

These families have problems expressing feelings in general, positive as well as negative, with open expressions of anger considered as especially dangerous. Family members already feel deprived of love, affection, and attention, and this state of emotional deprivation creates an enormous sense of rage and frustration. However, this very rage is suppressed and repressed for fear that it will lead to further rejection and loss of love, or to complete loss of control over potentially murderous impulses. Instead of expressing it directly, a youth in such a family comes to discharge anger indirectly. Drug abuse is an excellent vehicle for misdirected rage. It allows one to express it passive-aggressively through spiting one's parents. In such a case the drug abuse (and, more important, getting caught in the drug abuse) is a hostile and rebellious act. For some, the drug abuse is symbolically murderous, a kind of parenticidal gesture. This is illustrated by the number of young people who say, "If my parents knew I used drugs, it would kill them," and who then promptly arrange to get caught using drugs in a manner designed to be as embarrassing as possible to their parents. Drug abuse is also an excellent way to misdirect anger in an intropunitive way, to take it out on oneself. Such an adjustment is quite common among drug abusers and leads to a more or less chronically depressed state, a poor self-image, a self-defeating lifestyle, a tendency to be accident prone, occasional suicidal ideation or attempts, and a number of masked suicides disguised as overdose deaths.

Self-Medication

As has been commonly observed, the youthful drug abuser is usually not the only person in his or her family to ingest mood-altering substances. Often the entire family defends against unpleasant effects and seeks pleasurable sensations and experiences via taking something to relieve anxiety or depression, to bolster self-esteem, or to feel "alive" or "human." Whether this something is a mild tranquilizer prescribed by a doctor, an over-the-counter sedative, alcohol, coffee, cigarettes, or junk food, the message is clear: If life is hard to swallow, then swallow something to make it bearable.

Pathogenic Parental Expectations

Parents in such families often manifest extremely unrealistic expectations of their children. When these are too high, love is made conditional on success, and a young person will often turn to drugs, which serve a double function, for they not only allow one to spitefully revenge oneself upon demanding parents but also provide a tailor-made excuse for every failure — "What can you expect of me? I'm just a junkie (or pothead, or speed-freak)." In other cases parental expectations are unrealistically low: Almost from birth, the parents predict that the youth will fail. They expect the worst, and the child learns to fulfill the self-fulfilling prophecy, to play out his or her negative life-script in an attempt to live down to the parents' expectations — to give them what they want.

Underlying Family Themes

We have described several interactional patterns rather characteristic of drug-abusing families. However, the question remains as to why the families behave in this unfortunate manner. We believe that the answer lies in two related underlying themes usually present in the family system: impaired mourning and homeostatic collusion in the symptomatic behavior.

Impaired Mourning

The families of drug abusers are, in our experience, intensely preoccupied with the issues of attachment and separation, fusion and individuation, dependence and autonomy, loss and restoration, and death and rebirth. The parents of youthful drug abusers have often suffered profound emotional losses within their own families of origin. They have a strong sense of having lost their own parents via death, divorce, rejection, or neglect. The conflicts over this loss have never been worked through; mourning is incomplete and the love/hate ambivalence so characteristic of such relationships is never resolved. The ties to the lost love objects of the family of origin are never given up, and the individual is never able to transfer affections fully to new love objects (such as the spouse and children in the family of procreation).

Traditional psychoanalysis describes how such impaired mourning can lead to melancholia, a condition in which the ego is identified with the lost object; by castigating itself, via intropunitive depressive symptoms, it symbolically punishes the ambivalently loved object by proxy. This simultaneously accomplishes object conservation (keeping the object alive within oneself) and revenge (Freud, 1959).

The parents of drug abusers handle their impaired mourning in a different way (Reilly, 1975a). Often they manage to avoid the painful experience of melancholia or reactive depression, to defend against the pains of loss and abandonment, by projecting their conflicts over loss and separation onto their present-day families. Their unresolved grief survives intact and contaminates their families of procreation. It creates the dull, deadened, negativistic, lifeless, and loveless atmosphere so characteristic of drug-abusing families.

In order to achieve object conservation, in order to guard against loss and the recognition of loss, the parent will reincarnate his or her ambivalently loved and lost object in first one, then the other, of the current family members. He or she will re-create a lost parent or sibling in a spouse or a child. Children who are the object of such "irrational role-assignments" (Framo, 1972) are "parentified"; often their roles are "chosen for them before they are born" (Framo, 1969). They are turned into revenants, ghosts from the past. The hostility originally felt against the abandoning object is then displaced onto the child, who serves as designated proxy (Boszormenyi-Nagy, 1969). In our experience, it is often the drug-abusing child who has been selected to reincarnate or stand in for his or her parents' lost objects. He or she is named after, or seen as taking after, or resembling the lost objects. The family role of the drug-abusing child is to function as the black sheep or scapegoat whose bad behavior both provokes and justifies the parents' ambivalent attachment to him or her and their hostile overinvolvement. Identifications are confused with relationships, ego boundaries are weak, and ego fusion and diffusion are high. And since the parents have never adequately mourned or accepted the loss of their own parents, they are quite unable to tolerate the loss of their children, particularly the child who has been selected as proxy for the lost object. Thus, despite a deceptive facade of encapsulation and noninvolvement, all family members are covertly enmeshed in sticky, ambivalent ties and snared by a high degree of reciprocal separation anxiety. Finally, as Paul (1967) points out, families that have failed to cope with losses suffered early in their life cycles often develop a family style characterized by "a relative paucity of empathy," a "lack of respect for individuality," attempts to "deny the passage of time," and the tendency to unwittingly keep a family member "in an inappropriate dependent position." This is an excellent description of a typical drug-abusing family.

Familial Collusion

Drug-abusing behavior within a family system operates as a homeostatic regulatory device. As we have seen, it serves to rationalize the parents' hostile overinvolvement with the drug abuser, thus maintaining him or her in the ambivalently-regarded revenant role. Consequently it makes possible object conservation, revenge, and the deferment of long overdue mourning. The obstacles posed by the drug abuse, its inertia and its drag, are sufficiently powerful to prevent the youthful drug abuser from achieving the escape velocity necessary for departing from the family's orbit. Achievement of separation and autonomy is forestalled and the parents need not suffer the pains of an empty nest. The drug abuse may serve as a means of saving the marriage, as it conveniently distracts the parents from having to deal with personal or marital problems. Also it serves to precisely equilibrate the emotional distance between the parents. When they drift too far apart and greater closeness is desired, it can unite them in a joint rescue mission to save the drug abuser's soul; when things get too close for comfort and increased distance is sought, the drug abuser can come between them to give them breathing space (Reilly, 1977). Drug abuse also conveniently provides the nondrug-involved siblings with a handy negative role model, allowing them to feel successful against the backdrop of the identified patient's failures. Finally, the drug abuser's symptoms often operate as a cry for help from the entire family; they serve a flagging or signal function, an SOS from the family begging for outside assistance.

Our findings concerning the collusive involvement of the family system in drug abuse are in line with the reports of other researchers in related works. Boszormenyi-Nagy and Spark (1973) see delinquent adolescents as "loyal traitors" fulfilling a negative loyalty commitment to their families. Stierlin (1974) has described troubled youth as "bound delegates" sent out on "delinquent missions" by vicarious parents. Alexander and Dibb (1975, 1977) point out the central role played by dependency/autonomy struggles in drug-abusing families and allude to the failure of the parents to support movement towards adult responsibility on the part of the drug abuser. Harbin and Maziar (1975), in a comprehensive review of literature dealing with the families of drug abusers, note widespread support for the idea of intrafamilial etiology. Noone and Reddig (1976) utilize Jay Haley's (1973) concept of a symptom as a single that a family has become stuck at a crucial point in its lifecycle. They see drug abuse as a sign that the family has failed to cope adequately with the normal adolescent separation crisis and task. For them, drug abuse is a way for the adolescent to remain rebelliously dependent on his or her parents, a way of staying at home without losing face. Cannon's (1976) study of drug-abusing families noted a parental tendency to "infantilize" the drug abuser, to perceive him or her as weak, and to encourage him or her to escape frustrations rather than overcome them. Finally, it is interesting to note that a poll (Gallup, 1977) reports that adolescents throughout the country perceive drug abuse as "the biggest problem facing their generation," with "the inability of parents and children to communicate and 'get along' with each other" a close second.

Treatment

We have found a course of brief, triphasic, and time-limited conjoint family therapy to be most effective with our client population. We try to limit the treatment course to 15 sessions and state this limit clearly at onset of treatment. We find that the time limit is extremely helpful in maintaining focus and motivation, that it aids in specification of goals, and that it makes possible a timely crisis intervention. In addition, the time limit forces the family to confront the issues of separation, loss, and abandonment in vivo as part of the treatment process and in the person of the therapist. The limit provides a timely reassurance to family members who resist initial involvement (this too shall pass) and those who fear that therapy will be interminable. Our strong expression of confidence that meaningful change really can occur in as few as 15 sessions provides a powerful placebo effect, a potent therapeutic use of suggestion, and a strong dose of hope to people who may have seen the situation as hopeless. Finally, it serves as a living challenge to the myth of mutual helplessness that surrounds a long-standing drug-abuse problem.

Early Phase

In the beginning we concentrate on redefining the problem as the family system, rather than as the drug abuse itself. We challenge the myth of the designated patient, the idea that the drug abuser alone is, as Bowen (1969) says, the sick one. We ask all family members both what they like about the family and each other, and what they would like to change. Blaming is discouraged, and negative comments are often relabeled (Haley, 1973) or reframed (Watzlawick, Weakland, & Fisch, 1974) as positive signs of concern or caring. The emphasis is on how the situation can be changed rather than on how things got this way. The therapist teaches and models communication skills, the use of behavioral contracts, mutual exchange contingencies, and reciprocal positive reinforcement. Bargaining and compromise are encouraged. The family is confronted about its tendency to reinforce negative behavior with attention; expressions of affection are encouraged, and the family is helped to praise, attend to, and reward "good" behavior and to withdraw attention from "bad" (Lieberman, 1972).

The family is helped to identify specific everyday family events that serve to cue or reinforce drug-abusing behavior. Once identified, the family is encouraged to stop this offending behavior and find a substitute mode of interaction. Initially anger is handled by helping the family members to express it openly, to render it overt rather than covert. Once they are capable of this, the therapist shifts gears and, in a seemingly paradoxical way, relabels the anger as a positive demonstration of concern and involvement. This is done to defuse the situation and to render it more amenable to compromise and the use of behavioral contracts. During this stage, our focus is overwhelmingly on restructuring the family; on establishing or strengthening generational or subsystem boundaries (Minuchin, 1974); on extricating the children, particularly the drug abuser, from enmeshment in the parents' marital conflicts; and in "remarrying" the parents.

Often this focus on restructuring the family, improving the marriage, emphasizing the positive, and changing the contingencies of social reinforcement for everyday behavior is enough to bring about the desired changes. When a family seems to be responding well to this approach and when, by the fourth session or so, we see a diminution of drug abuse and an increase in positive family interaction, we maintain this strategy for the duration of treatment, with little recourse to alternate techniques. We find that this approach is extremely effective with our working-class, blue-collar, or action-oriented families who often appreciate a present-centered, process-focused, and enactive (Minuchin, 1974) approach.

However, some families seem to bog down in this initial stage, and by the fourth session still show no willingness to relinquish their old negativistic patterns of interaction. When this occurs, we move into a secondary treatment phase in which we concentrate more on the past and its effect on the present. At this point we focus on the issue of impaired mourning. This is often necessary for middle-class families, and especially for excessively intellectual and insight-oriented families who refuse to make any progress until therapy bestows upon them the obligatory eureka, the depth insight into past traumas they have come to expect from treatment.

Secondary Phase

In this phase, we help the family to work through their conflicts concerning impaired mourning, attachment, separation, and loss — conflicts that are at the root of the family's scapegoat system and collusive investment in the pathology. We ask, in effect, "Who are the ghosts haunting this family? Whom do they possess and how can we exorcise them?" We seek to identify the projections, identifications, and displacements contaminating the family. We ask about parental losses and try to determine whether impaired mourning has led to reincarnation of a lost object in a scapegoated spouse or child.

We explore the family naming process, since family names present valuable clues in our attempt to trace family identifications. We ask who the parents and the children are named after. How were the names chosen? By whom? Which names were discarded? What are the family nicknames? Whom do parents and children seem to take after? Of whom do other family members remind them?

The Romans had a proverb, *nomen est omen*. They saw a predictive, prognostic, and prophetic quality in names. They were right. In the unconscious, names are magical and powerful. Naming often confers not only an identity on a child but also an identification.

When a father named Stephen names his son Stephen, Jr., we might suspect that he may have a greater than usual investment in his son functioning as a surrogate, as an extension of himself. We may suspect further complications should he name a daughter Stephanie. Names may also reveal fixed parental expectations, directives, and role allocations, thus functioning as self-fulfilling prophecies. Parents may name a daughter Eve because they need her in the role of temptress or seductress, or they may name her Virginia because they need her to remain virginal. They may name her Dawn because, in shared subconscious fantasy, they see her as a savior who will alleviate a depression and bring hope, light, and a new day to a failing marriage and a bleak life. A weak, emasculated, and ineffective father may name his son Lance or Victor, or another name that has a strong masculine, phallic, or heroic ring. A mother who has recently lost her own father may quickly arrange to have a baby as a replacement, naming it after the deceased in an attempt to effect a reincarnation, a literal renaissance.

Thus, by asking how the parents and children were named and by exploring the implications of that process, we can help the parents to understand better the ways in which they are tragically burdening themselves and their children by confusing identifications with relationships and births with reincarnations.

Throughout this phase the parents are encouraged to discuss their families of origin in detail; they are helped to recognize the ways in which they have been attempting to gain belated mastery over archaic relationship patterns arising in their families of origin within the inappropriate context of their family of procreation.

Haley's (1969, 1973) and Watzlawick, Weakland, and Fisch's (1974) paradoxical techniques of "prescribing the symptom" or encouraging patients to deliberately produce heretofore spontaneous behavior can be adapted for use in this phase. Parents can be directed to keep lists of all the ways in which the identified patient resembles or reminds them of the lost love object. Within the session they are encouraged to engage in roleplaying by relating to the drug abuser as if he or she really were the lost object. Forcing them to do overtly what they have been doing less than consciously all along is frequently far more effective in stopping the inappropriate behavior than is an intellectual interpretation.

As this phase concludes, our goal is to help the parents to finally and belatedly complete their griefwork in relation to their lost love objects. We encourage the emergence of the previously blocked affective constellations—feelings of abandonment, disappointment, anger, and guilt, and later sadness, longing, forgiveness, tenderness, and hope.

Final Stage

Once the parents' regressive attachments to their own lost objects are loosened via mourning, they become better able to let go of their children, to allow them to separate and individuate. Since they no longer require that their children stand in as reincarnations or revenants, since they no longer need them to be possessed by the ghosts of lost objects, they can now afford to be less possessive (1975a). They become better able to treat their children like real people in their own right, and are less likely to cast them in fixed, stereotyped, and ambivalent roles.

In the final sessions, both treatment course and the gains made by the family are reviewed. The therapist helps everyone to work through their feelings concerning termination of treatment and separation from the therapist. Confidence is very strongly expressed in the family's ability to make it on its own, to function independently, to maintain gains, and to resolve future problems without ever necessarily needing further treatment. Should a return to treatment ever be indicated, it is not defined as a failure or a relapse. Rather, it is reframed as a sort of a booster shot, checkup, refresher course, or reinforcement designed to help the family help itself through a difficult period.

Case Illustration

Throughout most of this chapter, we have concentrated on the unmarried drug abuser living at home with his or her parents. However, our technique can be adapted to other situations, including that of a married drug abuser living with a spouse in his or her own household. Discussion of such a case will help to illustrate an array of treatment interventions.

Bill, 21, and his wife Dierdre, 22, had been married for one year. Bill had smoked marijuana and gone out drinking with his friends several times a week since his early teens. Dierdre was aware of this when they married. However, recently Bill had increased his smoking and drinking, and had begun using amphetamines rather heavily as well. Dierdre insisted Bill apply for treatment and both were assigned to conjoint marital therapy.

Bill was the oldest of several siblings. Both his parents were alive, and the father was an alcoholic. The mother was the dominant spouse and, according to Bill, often treated the father like one of the children. She was very strict and controlling with the children. Dierdre was an only child. Her mother had also been the dominant spouse, the father having been "kindly, but weak and sickly all his life."

In the first treatment phase, the therapist redefined the problem as the marital relationship rather than Bill's substance abuse. The therapist had the couple review what they liked about one another, all the good times they had in the past, and the tender and happy moments they still shared. That they had entered counseling, the therapist indicated, was a sign of their mutual concern and proof of their maturity, courage, and foresight.

Dierdre complained about Bill's drug and alcohol abuse. Bill objected that Dierdre was exaggerating and felt that she was being "contaminated" and "recruited" by his own mother, who had gotten her to join his mother's Al-Anon group.

The therapist explored the situations that cued Bill's substance abuse, his binges. Invariably they began rather harmlessly with both Bill and Dierdre have a social drink in a restaurant or smoking a small amount of marijuana at a party. The problem would begin with Dierdre's attempts to control Bill. While they were both in the middle of their first drink, for example, she would start to warn him that he should not get drunk. He would grow resentful and begin to drink just to spite her. She would escalate her warnings and he would escalate his drinking until he could hardly stand.

The couple was helped to see that Dierdre's attempts to control Bill merely provoked the undesired behavior. Dierdre was instructed to ignore Bill's drinking or drug use at the next party they attended; controlling himself would be his responsibility, and if he failed, the unpleasant results would be his problem, not hers. She was successful in doing this, despite Bill's attempts to provoke her into resuming her strict mother role. After a few unpleasant mornings after, Bill spontaneously reduced his drinking and drug use at parties.

The directive to Dierdre not to reinforce Bill's substance abuse with attention resulted in a reduction in his alcohol and marijuana use to sub-culturally normal, social levels within four weeks. He ceased all amphetamine use by the fifth week. In the seventh week, following an argument with Dierdre, he took several uppers in a highly theatrical and ostentatious fashion. He was, he admitted later, "trying to get Dierdre's goat." She remained calm and he abandoned the attempt. Following that incident, there were no recurrences of amphetamine abuse.

However, an interpersonal problem remained. Bill feared Dierdre wanted to trap him with commitments; he saw her as overly demanding, draining, and a crybaby. Dierdre felt he was aloof, insensitive, and uncaring. She wished he would not avoid her as much as he seemed to, that he would spend more time with her. A reciprocally reinforcing behavioral contract (Fischer & Gochros, 1975; Knox, 1971) was set up in which Dierdre would allow Bill a specific amount of time "out with the boys" in exchange for his guaranteeing her a specific amount of conversation and closeness each night.

In the second treatment phase, which was considered necessary because of this couple's difficulties with intimacy, the therapist concentrated on the naming process and on unresolved grief in the spouses concerning events in the families of origin. Dierdre said she has been named after a fictional folkloric character, "Dierdre of the Sorrows" — or at least that was her mother's association with that name. Her middle name, Veronica, was a character in a soap opera her mother used to listen to before her birth; it was also, her mother told her, the name of the grieving woman in the New Testament account of Christ's crucifixion. When Bill heard how Dierdre had been named, he joked, "Boy, that's really you! With names like those, no wonder you're a crybaby! You're a walking soap opera; everything's a tragedy to you." Throughout her life, Dierdre had been a worrier, especially concerning her father's health. He had died two months before the couple entered treatment. It emerged that Dierdre had begun to worry about Bill's health and his alcohol and drug use right after her father's death. It was then that she first began to see Bill as weak, needing her and her help as her father had. By selectively attending to the weak parts of Bill's personality, she unwittingly reinforced them and thus succeeded in reincarnating her father in Bill. Now she would worry about Bill and sacrifice for him as she had for her father.

Bill was a junior, named after his father. From birth, he was seen as the family black sheep, as taking after his father. His mother was especially fearful that he would become an alcoholic like her husband. Consequently she was stricter with him than with the other children, often taking special care to warn him away from the evils of drink. Naturally this approach resulted in precisely the opposite of what she consciously intended. Bill was clearly convinced that he would turn out like his father; however, his response was, "What the hell, I might as well enjoy it since it's inevitable anyway." In his late teens he described himself as a "hell raiser." However, after his marriage, he settled down. When Dierdre's loss of her father precipitated her attempts to rescue and control him, he began to develop an "allergic" reaction to her. She began to remind him more and more of his controlling mother. Part of him enjoyed being mothered again—it gave him an excuse to abdicate responsibility: "It was as if I'd never left home; I didn't have to look out for myself because my mother or Dierdre would do it for me." But another part of him resented the outside control, feeling trapped, annihilated, and swallowed up, this part rebelled. If his mother or Dierdre wanted him to drink less, "by God, I'd drink more." His ambivalent response to Dierdre's attempts at control not only exacerbated his substance-abuse symptoms and his tendency to avoid and distance himself from her, but is also reinforced her own counterproductive attempts to rescue him. Both were caught in a vicious cycle.

The therapist helped Dierdre to become more consciously aware of her lifelong role as sorrower, rescuer, and martyr, and assisted her in belatedly mourning her father. This freed her to see Bill as a real person, distinct from her father; it also permitted her to regard his drug and alcohol use more realistically, as being essentially nonproblematic unless he and she colluded to make it a problem. It also gave her the security to let go of Bill a bit, to allow him the breathing space he seemed to need in the marital relationship if he was not to feel trapped. The therapist helped Bill to confront his lifelong role as a black sheep and a stand-in for his alcoholic father. He came to realize that he need not necessarily follow the script his parents had unwittingly written for him. He was helped to mourn that his mother's love was ambivalent, and to come to terms with it, so that he no longer needed Dierdre to reincarnate his controlling, intrusive mother. This simultaneously freed him to show an increased degree of closeness and tenderness toward Dierdre.

At the conclusion of therapy Bill and Dierdre's relationship was markedly improved, and substance abuse was no longer a problem.

Assessment

We have been very encouraged by the success of this triphasic conjoint family therapy approach. As the family's investment in the drug-abuse symptom falls away, the drug use itself occasionally shows a complete cessation. More often, it decreases in frequency, or a switch from the harder to the softer, less dangerous drugs occurs. Simultaneously there is a notable improvement in family communication and relationship patterns.

Of course the extent to which this technique can be confidently generalized to other socioeconomic or treatment populations is undetermined. However, it does seem potentially adaptable, at least to a variety of youthful populations. One of its virtues, at least in our eyes, is that it is a rather eclectic and flexible method. Depending on the case at hand, one might utilize techniques borrowed from the structural family therapy school or the communications theorists in one phase, and the insights of the object-relations school in another. The freedom to do so is refreshing. Too often internecine rivalry between the varying family therapy schools (Ferber, Mendelsohn, & Napier, 1973; Foley, 1974) blocks the creative synthesis of diverse approaches so necessary if our field is to remain viable and if we are to remain vital and helpful as therapists.

References

Alexander, B. K., & Dibb, G. S., (1975). Opiate addicts and their parents. *Family Success, 14,* 499–514.

Alexander, B. K., & Dibb, G. S., (1977). Interpersonal perception in addict families. *Family Process, 16,* 17–28.

Boszormenyi-Nagy, I., (1969). Intensive family therapy as process. In I. Boszormenyi-Nagy & J. Framo (Eds.), *Intensive family therapy.* New York: Harper & Row.

Boszormenyi-Nagy, I., & Spark, G., (1973). *Invisible loyalties.* New York: Harper & Row.

Bowen, M., (1969). Family psychotherapy with schizophrenia in the hospital and in private practice. In I. Boszormenyi-Nagy & J. Framo (Eds.), *Intensive family therapy*. New York: Harper & Row.

Cannon, S. R., (1976). *Social functioning patterns in families of offspring receiving treatment for drug abuse*. Roslyn Heights, NY: Libra Publications.

Ferber, A., Mendelsohn, M., & Napier, A., (1973). *The book of family therapy*. Boston: Houghton Mifflin.

Fischer, J., & Gochros, H., (1975). *Planned behavior change*. New York: Free Press.

Foley, V., (1974). *An introduction to family therapy*. New York: Grune & Stratton.

Framo, J., (1969). Rationale and techniques of intensive family therapy. In I. Boszormenyi-Nagy & J. Framo (Eds.), *Intensive family therapy*. New York: Harper & Row.

Framo, J., (1972). Symptoms from a family transactional viewpoint. In C. Sager & H. Kaplan (Eds.), *Progress in group and family therapy*. New York: Brunner/ Mazel.

Freud, S., (1959). Mourning and melancholia. In *S. Freud, Collected Papers* (Vol. 4). New York: Basic Books.

Gallup, G., (1977). Drugs, parent relations are top problems. *Newsday*, May 18.

Haley, J., (1969). *The power tactics of Jesus Christ*. New York: Avon.

Haley, J., (1973). *Uncommon therapy*. New York: Ballantine.

Harbin, H., & Maziar, H., (1975). The families of drug abusers: A literature review. *Family Process, 14*, 411–431.

Knox, D., (1971). *Marriage happiness: A behavioral approach to counseling*. Champaign, IL: Research Press.

Liberman, R., (1972). Behavioral approaches to family and couple therapy. In C. Sager & H. Kaplan (Eds.), *Progress in group and family therapy*. New York: Brunner/Mazel.

Minuchin, S., (1974). *Families and family therapy*. Cambridge, MA: Harvard University Press.

Noone, R., & Reddig, R., (1976). Case studies in the family treatment of drug abuse. *Family Process, 15*, 325–332.

Paul, N., (1967). The use of empathy in the resolution of grief. *Perspectives in Biology and Medicine, 2*, 153–169.

Reilly, D., (1975a). Family factors in the etiology and treatment of youthful drug abuse. *Family therapy, 2*, 149–176.

Reilly, D., (1975b). Legislative testimony. In *Anomalies in drug abuse treatment*. State of New York Legislative Document # 11. New York: New York State Legislature.

Reilly, D., (1977, May). *Theory of family therapy*. Panel presentation at National Drug Abuse Conference, San Francisco.

Stierlin, H., (1974). *Separating parents and adolescents*. New York: Quadrangle/ New York Times Book Co.

Sutherland, E., & Cressey, D., (1955). *Principles of criminology* (5th ed.). Philadelphia: Lippincott.

Watzlawick, P., Weakland, J., & Fisch, R., (1974). *Change, principles of problem formation and problem resolution*. New York: Norton.

CHAPTER TEN

Adolescent Substance Abuse: Multidimensional Family Therapy in Action

HOWARD A. LIDDLE, ED.D.   GAYLE A. DAKOF, PH.D.
Temple University   *Temple University*

GUY DIAMOND, M.A.
Philadelphia Child Guidance Center

Drugs are news. In contemporary America, perhaps as never before, a preoccupation about drug use and abuse pervades our culture. This is appropriate since the United States has the highest rate of adolescent drug use among the world's industrialized nations (Falco, 1988). The range and diversity of drug abuse and drug-related problems of adolescents, the number of teenagers in need of treatment or care, and the costs to society are enormous (see Carnegie Council on Adolescent Development, 1989; Dryfoos, 1990; Institute of Medicine Report, 1989). Public opinion polls

Acknowledgments are due to the dozens of staff who worked on the Adolescents and Families Project (AFP) since its inception in 1985. Special recognition is due to Ken Parker, Ph.D., and Raquel Garcia, B.A., and to Kim Barrett, Ed.D., and Geoffrey Shaskin, M.S.W., and to the family therapists on the AFP: Jacqueline Arroyo, Ph.D., Nancy Allsop, M.A., Joyce Burel, M.A., Randy Cheek, M.A., Janece Dagen, M.A., Steve Eckert, M.S.W., Lucia Gattone, M.S.W., M.F.C.C., Paul Guillory, Ph.D., Michelle Holt, M.S.W., Steve Parson, M.A., Kim Sutterfield, Ed.D., Sam Tuttleman, M.S.W., and Michael Watson, M.A. Appreciation is expressed to Jacqueline Arroyo, Guy Diamond, and Michelle Holt, who were the therapists for the cases presented in this chapter and who participated in the transcript production and commentary. This research was supported by a grant from the National Institute on Drug Abuse (1RO1 DA3617) to Howard Liddle in 1985. Finally, we gratefully acknowledge the families who participated in our project. Correspondence concerning this chapter should be addressed to Dr. Howard Liddle, Temple University, Weiss Hall, Philadelphia, PA 19122.

proclaim the drug problem to be our country's greatest social dilemma, and once again our nation's president has declared a "war on drugs." Frequently, this battle is waged primarily in the domain of law enforcement. The drug-related stories that appear on the evening news highlight videotapes authenticating seizures of large illegal drug shipments. Our society still fumbles to formulate effective policies that will address the "national tragedy" (Daruna, 1990) of adolescent drug abuse. We remain in an era that seeks simplistic answers to the etiology (e.g., peer influence) and treatment (e.g., "Just Say No") of complex, multilevel problems. As Nadelman (1989) warns, a narrowly conceived national policy that continues to overemphasize strategies such as curtailing supply and discouraging use by fear-inducing tactics is likely to be counterproductive.

Less visible, sensational, and funded are treatment efforts, especially those targeted at adolescents. Often characterized as "just experimental users," teenagers who abuse drugs and alcohol typically cannot command research and treatment support. Failing to develop and evaluate drug treatment programs for adolescent users yields serious consequences to both the adolescent and society (Coombs, 1988; Dryfoos, 1990). Newcomb and Bentler (1988), for example, have documented the long-term negative consequences of adolescent drug abuse on mental health, social connectedness, dating and marriage patterns, work stability, and educational aspirations.

Systematic studies on adolescent drug-abuse treatment has not only been sorely neglected but those few psychotherapy outcome studies of adolescent problems (Kazdin, Bass, Ayers, & Rodgers, 1990) have yielded distressing conclusions for those who wish to take therapeutic outcome seriously. Meta-analyses reveal that good therapeutic outcome with teenagers is a very difficult proposition (Casey & Berman, 1985; Tramontana, 1980; Weisz, Weiss, Alicke, & Klotz, 1987). Moreover, Weisz and colleagues (1987) found that problems of undercontrol (e.g., aggression, impulsivity) were less successfully treated than problems of overcontrol (e.g., shyness). Given conclusions of this nature, and since drug abuse can best be considered a problem of "undercontrol," it is reasonable to conclude that constructing and testing effective treatment programs for adolescent drug abusers presents a formidable challenge for those who attempt treatment and research in this area.

In the mid-1980s, the National Institute on Drug Abuse (NIDA) launched an initiative to address the possibilities of constructing family therapy models to treat adolescent drug abuse. Since a successful family therapy approach for drug abuse had been empirically established by teams led by clinical researchers such as Stanton (Stanton & Todd, 1982) and Szapocznik (Szapocznik, Kurtines, Santisteban, & Rio, 1990), as well as others (see review by Bry, 1983), NIDA was interested in whether effective family therapy treatment models could be developed with adolescents (*Con-*

gressional Record—Senate, 1990; National Institute on Drug Abuse, 1983).[1]

This chapter presents aspects of a family therapy treatment model developed in a NIDA-funded study—the Adolescents and Families Project.[2] Rather than presenting the entire approach, our aim here is to offer certain key units of the family therapy treatment manual that directed our clinical work.[3]

Multidimensional Family Therapy

Multidimensional family therapy (MDFT) is a multisystemic treatment approach for adolescent substance abuse and its correlated behavior problems (Liddle, 1991a, 1991b). With its roots in the integrative structural-strategic family therapy tradition (Fraser, 1982; Stanton, 1981; Todd, 1986), MDFT incorporates additional notions about the targets, mechanisms, and methods of change. It is a reformulation of the structural-strategic family therapy of Liddle (1984, 1985).[4] The model's refinement was driven by the mandate of our research project: to construct a specialized treatment model for adolescent substance abuse. This activity, the refinement of an existing integrative approach, was influenced by the contemporary general spirit in drug-abuse treatment (Liddle & Schmidt, 1991; National Institute on Drug Abuse, 1991) and psychotherapy (Miller & Prinz, 1991) of *treatment development* (i.e., greater particularization of treatment models, population-specific treatment manuals, theory-specific outcome, therapy process specification) and *model enhancement* (i.e., the reconstruction of treatment packages for specific purposes).

Conceptually, MDFT reflects a trend in the literature to conceive of adolescent problems such as drug use and delinquency as correlated behaviors. Current thinking in this area is captured in Dishion, Reid, and Patterson's (1989) argument for understanding drug abuse and delinquency as "somewhat different aspects of a unified behavioral process" (p. 189). This perspective typifies the current thinking and research in this area. An extensive literature review concluded a strong relationship of adolescent substance abuse to conduct disorder (Bukstein, Brent, & Kaminer, 1989). There is a growing consensus among investigators and clinicians on the importance of understanding adolescent problems in a multivariate, multisystemic, nonreductionistic fashion (Loeber, 1985; Elliot, Huizinga & Ageton, 1985; Fishman, 1986; Henggeler, Rodick, Bourdin, Hanson, Watson, & Urey, 1986; Jessor & Jessor, 1975; Kazdin, 1987; Pandina & Schuele, 1983).

The MDFT approach has several distinguishing characteristics relative to many contemporary family therapy models. First, it is a *research-based approach.* Although there are several well-articulated, empirically based family treatment models for adolescent problems (e.g., Alexander & Parsons, 1973; Alexander, Klein, & Parsons, 1977; Barton, Alexander, Waldron, Turner, & Warburton, 1985; Henggeler et al., 1986; Robin & Foster, 1989; Szapocznik, Perez-Vidal, Brickman, Foote, Santiseban, Hervis, & Kurtines, 1988; Szapocznik, Perez-Vidal, Brickman, et al., 1988), others exist outside of the context of systematic evaluation and research (Fishman, 1988; Jurich, 1990). Family therapy, however, is now in a new era, one that is less tolerant of approaches that lag behind in evaluation, or worse, are less amenable or receptive to research (Erickson, 1988; Liddle, 1991).

Second, MDFT is a *specialized model,* developed in a specific context for particular purposes. It specializes in treating the problem behavior syndrome (Jessor & Jessor, 1977) or the cluster (Kazdin, 1987) of adolescent problems of substance abuse and conduct problems. Philosophically, it is syntonic with those urging greater specialization of therapy model construction (Achenbach, 1986; Goldfried & Wolfe, 1988; Gurman, 1988; Liddle, 1990; Pinsof, 1989).

Third, this approach is appreciative of the problems with and the tendency of some models to endorse family reductionism — the crediting or blaming of health and pathology on the family. Accordingly, MDFT *emphasizes individuals* as systems and subsystems more than many other contemporary family therapy approaches.

Its *multidimensional focus* is a fourth distinguishing feature of this model. For example, integrating assessment dimensions, such as cognitive attributions, affective states, and recollections of the past, with communication and social skills training is not the usual fare for family therapy models. Another aspect of multidimensionality is the importance of extra-familial factors (e.g., educational, juvenile justice systems) in instigating and maintaining adolescent problems. Peer, educational, and juvenile justice systems, for instance, must remain primary areas of assessment and intervention in any multisystemic, multidimensional model.

A fifth factor concerns the *integrative* nature of the model. Although still lagging behind the psychotherapy field, the integrative tradition in family therapy is beginning to take hold (Lebow, 1987). Still, most family therapy integrative models, particularly ones designed for adolescent drug abuse, have relied on models of family therapy for their sources of integration. For instance, approaches for adolescent substance abusers such as those outlined by Ellis (1986), Lewis and associates (1990), and Todd and Selekman (1990b) rely primarily on structural, strategic, brief therapy, behavioral, and systemic schools of family therapy. Existing within a family psychology framework (Kaslow, 1987; Liddle, 1987a, 1987b), the foundation of multidimensional family therapy aims to be more comprehensive than contemporary family therapy models. Many of these approaches, for instance, underutilize basic knowledge of psychological principles and content (Liddle, in press-a).

A sixth distinguishing characteristic of MDFT concerns the *degree of emphasis that it places on the adolescent* in the context of family therapy for adolescent problems. The adolescent is a prominent figure in the successful conduct of this therapy, and treatment is seen as disadvantaged if he or she does not participate fully. Engagement, therefore, is a primary emphasis of the clinician's early work. We help the adolescent feel that therapy can be a context in which his or her individual concerns can be met. This chapter focuses on the crucial engagement phase of treatment.[5]

The seventh distinguishing aspect of MDFT relates to its integrative nature, emphasis on individuals, and extent of focus on the adolescent. Because of its centrality in MDFT and the degree to which other family therapy models make fallacious assumptions about adolescent development (e.g., Pittman, 1987), minimize individual adolescent development issues in the process of emphasizing parental empowerment (Haley, 1980) and correction of "incongruous hierarchies" (Madanes, 1981, 1985), or ignore normative content altogether (Fisch, 1989), we signify the *incorporation of empirical findings of developmental and adolescent psychology into our clinical model* as our final core characteristic. Although some have appreciated the need for this activity in family therapy (e.g., Stratton, 1988), we concur with the conclusions of those who argue that not enough has been done to place clinical interventions within a developmental framework (e.g., Furman, 1980; Kendall, Lerner, & Craighead, 1984; Shirk, 1988).

The MDFT approach, for instance, uses existing knowledge of how families serve as buffering or protective mechanisms to protect against the influence of deviant peer and societal influences (e.g., Burke & Weir, 1978; 1979; Greenberg, Siegel, & Leith, 1983; Larson, 1983; Steinberg & Silverberg, 1986; Wills, 1990), as well as empirical data on how positive family relations in the adolescent years fosters adolescent competence in a variety of ways (e.g., *self-confidence* [Ryan & Lynch, 1989], *self-regulation* and *exploratory behavior* [Hartrup, 1979; Hill & Holmbeck, 1986], *autonomy* [Steinberg, 1990], and *ego development of the teenager* [Hauser & Follansbee, 1984] *and the parent* [Hauser, Borman, Jacobson, Powers, & Noam, 1991]).

We should note that although family therapy certainly has had a broad-level appreciation of the role of family life cycle thinking in clinical practice for some time (Carter & McGoldrick, 1986; Falicov, 1988; Haley, 1973; Liddle, 1983; Solomon, 1973), the emphasis suggested in MDFT differs from a broad-level appreciation of the family life cycle paradigm, for instance. Many family therapists have a general sense of the importance of developmental principles as overarching metaphors in their work (Liddle, 1988a), but, in practice, do not utilize developmental knowledge in any substantive or systematic way. The case vignettes provide some examples of how this developmental content guided our interventions and assessment. Another publication details the fuller implications of the adolescent development literature in the construction of MDFT (Liddle, Schmidt, & Ettinger, in press).

Conceptual Framework of Multidimensional Family Therapy: An Overview

This approach draws from contemporary work emphasizing the continuous interplay and reciprocally determining *relationship between cognition, affect, behavior, and environmental input and feedback* (e.g., Bandura, 1978; Greenberg & Safran, 1984; Mahoney, 1984; Wachtel, 1977).

> *Conceptions of human behavior in terms of unidirectional personal determinism are just as unsatisfying as those espousing unidirectional environmental determinism. . . . Rather, human functioning is explained in terms of a model of triadic reciprocity in which behavior, cognitive and other personal factors, and environmental events all operate as interacting determinants of each other. (pp. 22–23, 18)*

Fundamental to the treatment model as well are the *ecological* (Bronfenbrenner, 1983), *dynamic-interactional* (Lerner, 1978), and *interactional* (Magnusson, 1988) perspectives on human development. This holistic conception of development underscores "the organization and integration of capacities in various developmental domains" (Rieder & Cicchetti, 1990, p. 382). A final area of influence has been the still-emerging domain of *developmental psychopathology* with its basis rooted in a thorough understanding of problems in their developmental context (Achenbach, 1990; Cicchetti, 1984; Kazdin, 1989; Rutter & Sroufe, 1984).

Key assumptions of MDFT, drawn in large part from the theories briefly mentioned above, include the following:

1. People function simultaneously in numerous domains of human existence (e.g., affective, cognitive, behavioral, temporal, moral/ethical, spiritual, interpersonal).[6] This premise is hardly a new revelation. For over 20 years, the social cognition area, for instance, has contributed substantially to our understanding of the links between cognition, emotion, and behavior (Shantz, 1983). This sensibility is clearly present in contemporary mainstream psychotherapy as well (e.g., Greenberg & Safran, 1987).

2. These domains of human existence are interconnected, yet the mechanisms that govern these relationships are not always apparent.

3. In therapy, human problems can be accessed through these related domains of functioning. And, by implication, solutions to these prob-

lems can be generated within any one (or more) of these domains of human functioning.

4. Therapists are handicapped if they conceive of the primacy of one domain over another, or intervene only into one domain. MDFT aims to avoid a univariate focus at assessment and intervention levels.

5. At the level of intervention, in part due to our beliefs about the nature of human problems, a clinician is advantaged by having available multiple targets for change (i.e., human functioning is understood best by a multivariate focus and facilitated by a multimodal[7] therapist stance).

Overall Goals of Treatment

These are derived from the family's presentation of what each member wants from treatment as well as from generic formulations about families with adolescents (i.e., the importance of understanding both parental and adolescent subsystems). We do not see adolescent substance abuse as a manifestation of the "faulty launching" of the adolescent (Reilly, 1975, 1979, 1984), nor as a problem of failed separation (Levine, 1985). Models of this nature have, unfortunately, been developed on the basis of previous clinical work and research on young adult (vs. adolescent) drug abusers (Stanton & Todd, 1982). They are based on anachronistic conceptions of adolescence (e.g., a one-sided accenting of emotional detachment and separation). Models of this type also fail to take into account notions of interdependence (Steinberg, 1990) and autonomy-connectedness (Grotevant & Cooper, 1983).

Blechman (1982) warned the substance abuse field that the conventional wisdom of the times may not always be correct. Following this, for example, the enmeshment of the drug abuser with his or her family, and the inevitability of all adolescent substance abusers coming from dysfunctional families are two pieces of such "conventional wisdom" that have failed to be confirmed in recent research (Friedman, Utada, & Morrissey, 1987; Volk et al., 1990). Preliminary results from the AFP also indicate that our clinical families tended more toward disengagement than enmeshment (Liddle, Dakof, Parker, & Diamond, 1991).

With the developmental literature as a guide, MDFT signifies interdependence (Cooper, Grotevant, & Condon, 1983; Hill, 1980; Steinberg, 1990) in the parent-adolescent relationship as the delicate process we seek to foster. The continuing and redefined *attachment* of parents and teenagers (e.g., Greenberg, Siegel, & Leitch, 1983), tailored to fit the developmental idiosyncrasies of the second decade of life, and not detachment of the adolescent from the parents, orients the goal-setting process. Although we have speculated on the reasons why myths about adolescence endure (Eisner

& Liddle, 1991), considerable agreement exists on the field's movement toward fresh thinking about adolescence. This modern era relies on empirical formulations rather than psychodynamically oriented speculations (Blos, 1979; Erickson, 1968; Freud, 1958; Hall, 1904). It transcends the narrow conception that adolescence is only about emotional separation from one's parents and advances multidimensional and ecologically oriented notions of adolescent psychology (Feldman & Elliott, 1990; Steinberg, 1990).

Multidimensional Assessment and Intervention

The approach assesses and intervenes into:

1. *Multiple Domains in Which People Exist (e.g., cognitive, affective, behavioral, temporal).* Human beings and human problems are complex and multifaceted. Following this appreciation, contemporary psychotherapy challenges us to construct sufficiently complex models of assessment and intervention. Any single approach, particularly one that resides in a singular, "pure" model tradition, may be too limited in scope and not specific enough for particular clinical phenomenon and populations. This position asserts that the *schools of family therapy,* as we have known them in the past at least, have outlived their usefulness (Liddle, 1990).

2. *Multiple Subsystems in Which People Reside (e.g., individual, marital, parental, extrafamilial, peer, sibling).* Modern-day family therapy recognizes the difficulties inherent in family reductionism.[8] Family systems work does not infer that the entire family should be the only unit of focus. In addition to extrafamilial contexts such as the juvenile justice system and the schools, MDFT places primary importance on the therapeutic alliances between therapist and parent(s) and between therapist and teenager.[9] These are distinct relationships with their own course, expectations, and contract for what therapy can and will be. Success with one family member does not in the least guarantee success with the other. In fact, the complex connection between these relationships is revealed when we consider that success in one of these relationships (e.g., the therapist-parent[s] subsystem) may in fact lead to difficulties in the other (e.g., the therapist-teenager relationship).

3. *Multiple Content Realms in Which Personal and Relationship Problems Reside (drug and alcohol abuse, family and individual development, problems as they exist in the present and are remembered from the past).* This area refers to the fact that human problems may be presented in a clinical situation in various forms. We believe that the context of therapy is vitally important — that clinicians make decisions about specific content themes that will be carried forward throughout therapy. These content

themes are varied and can be transformed during the course of treatment. They are related to generic themes of family life, as well as to a family's idiosyncratic "big questions" (Liddle, 1985, 1988). MDFT devises its content themes from the generics of family life, as well as from the particulars of family life with adolescents and the individual and subsystem development of each member. We actively incorporate research findings from the adolescent development literature into our clinical work. For example, findings that indicate how adolescent identity development is fostered through a continued familial interdependence rather than an emotional separation (Grotevant & Cooper, 1983) or the influence of different parenting styles on adolescent personality development (Baumrind, 1991; Steinberg, 1990) become guides to goal setting and intervention.

4. *Multiple Methods and Pathways to Prompt Change.* The approach works for in- and out-of-session change, and assumes change to be multiply determined. Such change, occurring at individual, dyadic, multiperson, or familial levels, can be prompted in myriad ways (e.g., via reformulation of cognitive attributions, practice via behavioral rehearsals, greater acceptance of another through emotional expression and clarification). This change has affective, cognitive, and behavioral components; it is not simply continuous *or* discontinuous in nature, as some would have it (Hoffman, 1981) (both are in operation; see Liddle, 1982). MDFT recommends a flexible, multimodal therapeutic stance and uses several key modules or units of treatment across cases. This chapter deals largely with the adolescent module in MDFT.

Drugs, Etiological Agents, and Problematic Epistemologies

Multidimensional family therapy is a subsystem therapy[10] designed to alleviate the presenting problem of drug abuse. Adolescent drug abuse is defined contextually. It is not seen as a disease of the adolescent, or, necessarily, as an addictive process. Although proponents of the disease model of adolescent substance abuse, or chemical dependency as it is also called, express a righteous certainty in their view, years of careful research do not support these firm assumptions. Despite warnings about the difficulties in identifying and differentiating between antecedents, concomitants, and consequences of adolescent drug abuse (Kandel, Kessler, & Margulies, 1978), reductionistic thinking is in no short supply in the adolescent substance abuse field (Alexander, 1990; Peele, 1986b).

In the MDFT approach, the abuse of drugs is understood in the ecology of the teenager's life, which is frequently manifested by multiple problems, such as poor relationships, cognitive and problem-solving skills, learning and school difficulties, low self-esteem, family stress or dysfunction, and movement onto a trajectory of failure and incompetence. Substance abuse is thus defined as existing in a context of other, interrelated problems, each of which might have to be addressed.

Just as the model is defined multidimensionally, problems are defined multidimensionally — as having several facets that must be assessed and targeted for change. This perspective is drawn from modern-day thinking and research about drug abuse and other behavior problems of adolescents. Several causal factors are related to drug use initiation and maintenance (Newcomb, Maddahian, & Bentler, 1986). For Brook and colleagues, there exists a network of influences on adolescent drug involvement (Brook, Nomura, & Cohen, 1989).

Today, unidimensional theorizing about the etiology and treatment for adolescent drug abuse is a distinct minority position. The cutting edge of thinking and research in this area has moved beyond articulating single variables or domains that influence initiation and maintenance of adolescent drug abuse, to questions about the interconnection and interaction of these individual factors.

> *Drug use among teenagers is one component of an integrated life-style involving attitudes and other behaviors. Thus a strict focus on teenage drug use will be too limited for effective prevention or treatment. At an individual level, the surrounding and correlated aspects of drug use must also be carefully considered and integrated in programs (Newcomb & Bentler, 1988, p. 236)*

Many other contemporary theorists and researchers have called for a similar approach to understanding adolescent drug abuse. Often referred to as a *problem behavior syndrome* view (Jessor & Jessor, 1977), this framework casts the deviant behaviors of adolescents within a network of other correlated behaviors (Loeber, 1985; Elliot, Huizinga, & Ageton, 1985). In a careful meta-analysis of 143 adolescent drug prevention programs, Tobler (1986) concluded that simplistic, information-only approaches to prevention were ineffective. Because drug-abuse problems are complex, Tobler recommends that programs for teenage drug use should be multidimensional and linked with other interventions, such as the teaching of coping skills and the generation of realistic alternatives to drug abuse.

Pandina and Schuele (1983) have also recommended a multivariate approach to adolescent drug abuse. They suggest a multicausal, interactive framework that considers intrapersonal, extrapersonal, and sociocultural levels of analysis, with factors from each level acting simultaneously to influence use behavior.

> *A major implication of this view is that efforts toward prevention and rehabilitation aimed at changing adolescent alcohol and drug use may not be*

maximally effective if they are limited in focus to the use behavior itself or on an isolated domain of the adolescent's life. Instead, interventions should focus simultaneously on multiple domains. (Pandina & Scheule, 1983)

In his work with antisocial child behavior problems, Kazdin's (1982) guidelines for treating the problem behavior syndrome are also applicable to adolescent substance abuse. Kazdin's *cluster theory* formulation includes the idea of "response covariation" (i.e., the interaction of problem behavior with other problem behavior and with other behaviors in general) as a method to conceptualize the nested relationship of problem behaviors to each other.

Research on response covariation has potentially important implications for administering treatment. Changes in problems presented in treatment can be achieved in different ways. The most obvious way is to focus directly on the problem, the usual thrust of treatment, even though the presenting problem is defined quite differently across treatments. Alternatively, a particular problem area may be altered by focusing on a correlated area of performance. At first glance, there may be no obvious value in attempting to treat a problem indirectly by focusing on a correlated response. Yet, for some clinical disorders, the correlated behaviors that may influence the target problem may be more readily accessible or responsive to the intervention. (Kazdin, 1982)

These frameworks would give the term, *substance abuse problem,* a less precious and specialized ring to it than is frequently the case, especially in the chemical dependency community. Thus, we stand with Peele (1986b) in objection to the connotations and consequences of mindlessly adapting models of addiction to adolescents.

The 250 teenagers in the Adolescents and Families Project had significant problems with life, in addition to their problems with the abuse of drugs and alcohol. Adolescent drug abuse creates a developmental lag in teenagers' maturation (Baumrind & Moselle, 1985); as a result, adolescents who abuse drugs often fail to learn necessary life skills, and contribute to the creation of a family context characterized by disorganization, distance, and despair. In light of the considerable evidence on the family's capacity to serve as a buffer against the drug abuse of its youth (Baumrind, 1991; Brook, Brook, Gordon, & Whiteman, 1984; Brook, Brook, Lettieri, & Stimmel, 1985; Brook, Whiteman, Gordon, & Brook, 1985; Burke & Weir, 1978; Glynn, 1984; Gorsuch & Butler, 1977; Greenberg, Siegel, & Leitch, 1983; Larson, 1983; Wills & Vaughn, 1989), the promising effects of family therapy for adolescent substance abuse (see reviews by Davidge & Forman, 1988; Stanton, 1991), and the consensus on the need for multivariate conceptualization of adolescent problem behavior, it clearly seems wise to invest in family systems models of treatment.

Engaging the Adolescent and Setting the Foundation for Therapy

Working with adolescents and their families necessitates serving at least two masters: the parent(s) and the adolescent. Structural and strategic models of family therapy have primarily focused on instituting parental control and authority by establishing the hierarchical organization of the parents vis à vis the teenager (Haley, 1980; Madanes, 1981, 1985; Minuchin, 1974). The goal was to have hierarchical incongruity corrected (i.e., parents in charge of their children). Although we appreciate the importance of parental empowerment in the realm of control, there are additional aspects of parenting adolescents that have been found to be important (Baumrind, 1991; Greenberg, Siegel, & Leitch, 1983; Siegel, 1982) (i.e., empowerment is possible in other realms as well).

Beyond Control: Facilitating Development in Multiple Realms

The MDFT approach urges greater attention to other dimensions in the therapy in addition to parental hierarchy. Although authority and control are important dimensions in therapy with teenagers, they are by no means the only or even the primary variables of our interest or focus. In fact, in therapy with adolescents, *overfocusing* on the reestablishment of parental control is developmentally inappropriate and hence could be counterproductive to the accomplishment of key therapeutic goals. Pragmatically speaking, an overemphasis in this direction can also prevent the therapist from engaging the adolescent effectively in therapy, which will of course deter opportunities to establish an agenda for the teenager. The phrase we used with the adolescents, "There can be something in this for you," literally and metaphorically represents an important aspect of MDFT.

This engagement of the adolescent and the definition of an agenda for him or her in therapy is a primary goal in MDFT. It requires the therapist to work with both parental and adolescent subsystems simultaneously, even though the activities in each may seem contradictory.[11] The therapist can increase the probability of success with the teenager by taking a posture of respect and support for the adolescent's personal experience, both inside and outside his or her family.

This therapeutic posture is not one of "child saving" (i.e., a unidimensional, partial perspective that ignores the realities and experiences of the parent[s]), but rather one of acknowledging that the adolescent has his or her own story to tell. The therapist must honor the therapeutic promise to the teenager that his or her story can be "heard" in this therapy. This is especially important because drug-using teenagers have been found to experience a lack of personal agency or control over their own lives, and relatedly, feel a profound meaninglessness or lack of direction (e.g., Newcomb & Harlow, 1986). MDFT addresses these influential, organizing themes by, among other interventions, working alone with the adolescent for significant periods at all stages of therapy.

In this chapter, by analyzing portions of actual therapy sessions from the AFP, we will illustrate how we work with drug-abusing teenagers and their families.

Case 1: "There Is Something in This for You"

The following case excerpts, which come from the end of session 1 and the beginning of session 2, illustrate how one might develop and work with the *content theme* that we call "There is something in this (therapy) for you." The adolescent, in this case, is a 16-year-old boy, Sam, who is the youngest of four children. At the time he entered therapy, Sam regularly used alcohol and marijuana. He had severe school and behavior problems since the second grade. Sam had difficulty expressing himself verbally, and instead often resorted to violence. This seemed to be his predominant way of dealing with his hurt, anger, and disappointments. By the time Sam came to the Adolescents and Families Project, most everybody else (i.e., schools, other therapists, probation officers, his parents) had given up on him. They had judged Sam to be too out of control, too violent, too incompetent, and too unintelligent to be a good therapy candidate. One goal with Sam was to support his feelings, while at the same time, help him change how he expressed those feelings. We tried to transform his language and behavior in a more civilized and appropriate direction. Although his parents separated a year ago, they both agreed to attend therapy.

The therapist[12] spent most of the initial session talking with the parents about family history and current problems. During this discussion, Sam was somewhat indifferent and periodically belligerent. He was seen alone for the last 10 minutes of the session.

"I Think We Could Do a Lot Here"

Therapist (T): So what do you think of this?

Sam (S): It's cool.

T: You've never been in therapy like this, have you?

S: No, not like this.

T: Do you feel nervous, do you feel . . .

S: No. (matter of factly) It's just another counseling.

T: I don't think it's going to be another counseling. That's not the way I work. I think we could do a lot here. But I guess one thing I want to know is whether you're going to work with me. You know what I mean by that? (Sam nods.)

T: (a few minutes later) You see, I'm really interested in who you are, and I really want to know more about you. I want to know who you are in this family, and who you want to be, as your own person, Sam. But I'm going to need your help. Do you think you can help me with it?

S: I can try.

The therapist begins to set the foundation for engaging the adolescent in therapy. The therapist established his expertise and confidence, tested whether Sam is willing to accept an injection of optimism, and acknowledged that he has a point of view that needs to be expressed. Since the family, schools, police, and juvenile justice systems generally see these adolescents along constricted, pathological lines (antisocial, addicted, disturbed), asking for a teenager's help can create a new relational experience that counters the biased conceptions that the adolescent has about adults in authority. The attributional set of adolescents, parents, extrafamilial sources of influence, *and* the therapist are all equally central to this approach.

"That's Something We Could Do Here"

T: Well, you told me last week that when the big fight happened with your father, you don't like dealing with your anger that way.

S: I don't, man, but that doesn't mean any of you are gonna make me change. . . . Maybe I'm wrong, I'm not saying I'm not.

T: Would you be interested in learning how to deal with things better?

S: (pauses) Yeah. I am.

T: That's something we could do here. (pause) You know, you didn't look so happy when you were hitting your dad. (Sam kicked and hit his father in the family assessment the previous week.) And you told me you hate when you get mad at him. I didn't think you looked too happy. Tonight I felt like there were times when you weren't happy. You didn't like what they were saying, maybe you don't feel like they understood you enough. Maybe you feel like you get in between them. You know, it's a hard situation, your parents being split up. They're still working out their things. It's going to influence you. I know that's rough. So, I want to help you work through some of that in a way that would work out good for you. But I'm gonna need your help.

We look for opportunities to develop positive themes and goals with the adolescent and parents (i.e., behaviors that need to occur more frequently). In addition, the therapist actively searches for and emphasizes the adolescent's thinking and feelings about his or her current circumstances. And, with even the most profoundly abdicating parents, there is often something in what they say that can be embellished and expanded into a theme ("I'm worried about him" or "I wish I could be a better parent"). With the adolescents, in order to help craft themes, we search for some—

even slight — indication that he or she is unhappy and might like something changed. These nuggets of possibility, often obscured in a larger stream of unproductive conclusions, must be recognized, highlighted, and carried forward within sessions and from one interview to the next. In the previous sequence, for instance, the therapist reminds Sam of a previous statement he made about not being happy when he lost his temper with his father. Statements such as these are used as motivation-enhancing reference points throughout treatment.

We utilize the social reality of the adolescent already being "on the record" (i.e., having said that his behavior makes him unhappy or that he is willing to examine or try and change). We *carry forward* these themes, or "partial truths" (Minuchin & Fishman, 1981), and lend them back to the adolescent or parent. It is often most important to remind the client of this sometimes forgotten theme during times of difficulty in treatment, such as when the motivation of the adolescent or parent is flagging. In the case under discussion, by latching on to Sam's previous statement about how he would like to find a better way to handle his anger, the therapist demonstrated to Sam that his words are remembered and taken seriously. This statement on the teenager's part, which sometimes appears as an afterthought or as a minuscule part of a broader message, is used to remotivate the adolescent during difficult times, or, in the early stages of work, to help depict therapy's possibilities.

As we said, Sam was presented to our project as a teenager who was a poor therapy candidate. The area of Sam's feelings was something that most people believed should be avoided. He was typecast as a youngster whose predominant feelings (and those that he was most adept at communicating) were anger. We began our work with Sam with the multidimensional assumption that Sam's affective world was more complex than anger. Although clinicians often avoid an adolescent's emotional world, assuming they are unable to work in this realm, we have a different orientation in this regard. Working the affective realm with adolescents alone early in therapy potentiates access to other areas of functioning (e.g., core cognitions about self and others). Further, it can facilitate engagement and establish an agenda for them in the therapy. Importantly, it distinguishes the therapist as a person who can understand them, confirm their right to have and present their perspective,[13] and as one who, sometimes at least, takes their side.

"Will You Let Me Challenge You?"

T: What does that all sound like? Do you want to give it a try?

S: (indifferently) Yeah.

T: Would you like to see things change?

S: Sure.

T: What kind of things? What would you say?

S: I don't know, just how I get along with everybody.

T: Do you feel like you get along with your mom now?

S: Yeah. Better than I used to.

T: How about your dad?

S: All right.

T: It sounds like he would like to be closer to you. Is that something you share also?

S: I don't know.

T: You don't know? Hum . . . Well (pauses) . . . it's perfect that you say that, because that's exactly the kind of thing I'm gonna ask you *not* to do. I'm going to ask you to struggle with things in here, and say "Yeah, this is what I hate or this isn't what I want." Even when it's difficult. Because I know you've got a voice in there that wants things. But sometimes they're hard to say. You're afraid you're gonna hurt somebody, or get angry at them, or you might not get what you want. But I want to help you to be more straight with them.

Assessment and challenge are two important themes in this sequence. The dialogue served simultaneously as an intervention and assessment. The therapist attempted to obtain answers to the following questions: Is the adolescent willing to respond to the framework that the therapist is offering? Can the teenager identify with these concerns and begin to articulate his own story? What are the adolescent's leanings about the possibility of a therapeutic relationship at this early point?

Whereas some adolescents will quickly respond to the therapist's offer of empathy and understanding, others remain not only distrustful but hostile toward the therapist's attempt to access their emotional life or private thoughts. However, it is important to recognize that the teenagers' suspicions or apparent emotional fragilities are not the only determinants of their degree of disclosure. Intellectual ability and interpersonal skills also affect the adolescent's capacity to have the kind of discussion we seek.

Another theme here concerns the definition of a relationship that will serve as a context to develop new relational and conceptual skills. In essence, the therapist tells the teenager that it is important for him or her to communicate more effectively with the world, and in a sense with himself or herself, about one's reactions and experience.

In the above segment Sam's tentative responses are a cue not to push too much at this point. In establishing alliances and content themes, the therapist continually calibrates the pace of setting the therapeutic agenda according to family members' receptivity. By meeting Sam's pace, but sometimes extending the apparent limits, the therapist and Sam together coestablish a session's pace. During this session the therapist said, "Listen. There is no reason that you should trust me yet. Think over what I have been saying and let's talk about it next week." Here, the therapist intends to reduce the pressure on Sam, show him respect, define what some elements of therapy might be, and help him participate in modulating therapy's process.

"Can You Be Straight with Your Parents?"

Establishing a link to the first interview, the therapist began the second session by meeting with Sam alone. New information, as it emerges, must be factored into therapy.[14] Prior to this session, Sam had received the news that his probation officer wanted to send him to a boys' camp for one year because he hit a teacher at juvenile hall. We used this crisis to heighten the importance of Sam's participation in treatment. The segment begins with Sam explaining that if he is sent to the camp, he will run away.

S: I mean, I don't care about doing time—even if my parents. . .

T: What do you mean, you don't care about doing time?

S: Oh, I care about doing time, but I mean, I'm not . . . I mean it's not . . . it's just that I don't want to be that far away from my parents where I can't . . .

T: Sam! I don't get it. I appreciate that you want to be around them, but how does it happen that you get in such tangles with them?

S: Just when they keep . . . I know it's stupid, but they just start . . . I don't know, man, my dad just starts arguing and I snapped out. I know they're not going to get back together, but it still hurts me when they start arguing, even if it's over pity shit. It was over the food . . . I don't know, man.

T: I want to ask something of you tonight, and it's going to be really hard, because I think you're in a lot of pain in this family, right?

S: Kind of.

T: What?

S: Yeah. Maybe.

T: You admitted it to me the first time we met!

S: I know.

T: Within five minutes. Why don't you like to admit it?

S: I'm just trying to be . . . I don't know, man. (starts to cry) Everything is just messed up.

T: So, you try to be tough so nobody knows you're hurting? Does it feel safer that way, or . . .

S: Yeah, usually then people don't ask me what I'm feeling.

T: People don't ask you questions because they just think you're wild and out of control? (Sam nods) Well, that's what I want to know if you'd be willing to do tonight.

S: Do what?

T: To really talk with your parents about how upset you are. Because I think they would have a whole different take on you if you could be straight with them.

Sam begins an important process. He is starting to share, what we might call, the story of his life. The segment illustrates how the affective realm is used, in part, to engage the adolescent into the therapeutic process of examining one's life and generating alternatives. (Obviously, work in the emotional domain is also done with the parents as well). Again, MDFT targets multiple realms of life for assessment and intervention. The affective realm is but one of several targets of the therapy. Not all teenagers are willing or able to talk about their emotional disappointments, *nor is it necessary for every adolescent to do so.* To clarify: In this approach, catharsis or emotional expression, *per se,* is not a goal of the therapy. However, conversations about one's feelings are one important aspect of multidimensional work. They are a pathway to creating individual change, solidifying engagement, establishing and maintaining alliances, and helping family members establish new and salubrious ways of being with each other.

In this sequence, the therapist facilitated Sam's description by empathically appealing to the affective side of the story. Affective content became a therapeutic foundation with Sam and his family. This addresses the question: "Can I create a setting in which (partly as a result of his interactions with me) Sam can relate to his parents in new ways?"[15] At the outset of such hoped-for transactions, as was the case here, it is sometimes sufficient simply to have adolescents sort out, in conversation with the therapist, their many and frequently overwhelming feelings. Ultimately, however, an important goal with this teenager, and with many others, was the development of a *new language.* This term is a metaphor to describe new ways of adolescents relating their experience to the world. This expanded self replaces the defiant acts and self-administered anesthesia (e.g., alcohol and drugs) with more functional thoughts about self and others, feelings, and behavior.

Subsystem Work: Wholes and Parts   Finally, we understand these conversations as both wholes and parts, in part, thanks to the conceptual work of Koestler (1979, p. 33) and the application of his work in family therapy by Minuchin and Fishman (1981, p. 13). Each conversation between therapist and adolescent (and therapist and parent) has potential value, in and of itself. Contrary to what a radical family therapy philosophy would have us believe, people do not change only in relation to other family members. One aspect of change occurs, as it might be put, at the level of the individual, as a system (and a subsystem in relation to the family and other social systems).

Reductionism at the family level is changing in family therapy (Liddle, 1991a). Thankfully, and as strange as it may sound, there is a renewed sense of the *importance of individuals* in family therapy (Nichols, 1987; Schwartz, 1987, 1988). In individual sessions in MDFT, teenagers can be heard and responded to, sometimes as never before. Family members can be helped to sort out their intensely experienced and tangled feelings and thoughts, and, by using progress in these realms, they become more skillful communicators. The increased competence of the adolescent and the parent creates a new, motivating reality for the other.

This is the "whole" aspect of the clinician-adolescent subsystem therapy. But this subsystem work can also be considered as a "part." Conversations such as the one with Sam illustrated above, which can occur at any stage of therapy, also serve a *preparatory function*. As we have said, for various reasons, the teenager or parent at the outset of therapy may not be able or ready to begin talking with the other. For instance, how does a clinician understand the adolescent's lack of ability? Skill deficits, a lack of readiness, the blocks of emotional history, as well as strong negative attributions may all interfere with effective communication. While the conversation with Sam has potential healing functions with the adolescent as a self, it simultaneously readies Sam for action in relation to his parents.

Case 2: Shifting Domains of Operation in a Session

The next case elaborates the idea of *preparation for enactment*. Now we examine the preparation of both the daughter and the mother, and detail the "thought rules" and techniques of initiating a conversation about a disturbing family theme. In the following segments, we see how a therapist shifts focus when his in-session assessment indicates limited results with a straightforward problem-solving approach. Learning the skills of and developing personal ground rules for *therapist improvisation*—the change of one's intentions in a session—is the heart of clinical technique. Too often our teaching fails to help students acquire an appreciation of how to think through interventions and intervention planning to this level of detail. Consensus on how these instincts can be taught and how evaluation should proceed in this area has not been reached (Avis & Sprenkle, 1990; Liddle, 1991c).

"I Want My Daughter Back"

Jim and Marina, divorced for many years, have two daughters: Sally, age 15, who resides with her mother and stepfather, and Cynthia, age 20, who lives on her own. Marina sought treatment for her younger daughter's drug use (marijuana and alcohol), poor grades, and their progressively distant relationship. Sally's stepfather was decidedly uninvolved in childrearing tasks. Marina was concerned with Sally's drug use as well as with Sally's increasing involvement with her girlfriend's family. Marina believed that her daughter was drifting away from her toward what Sally called her "adopted" family. This environment permitted drinking and other freedoms that ran counter to Marina's values.

Abandonment was a central theme in this case. Themes such as this one exist in and can be accessed through a variety of domains. For instance, in the temporal realm, it is difficult to imagine addressing the topic of emotional or physical abandonment without dealing with issues of the past. Exploring attributions about abandonment makes available the relevant core cognitions (e.g., "Perhaps I am unworthy of love"). Perhaps the most commonly thought of way in which the theme of abandonment is materialized in sessions is through the affective realm. The intense feelings that come with the memories of being abandoned or neglected, as well as those feelings that accompany the parents' experience of their own behavior, are key domains of therapeutic operation.

In this case, the daughter felt abandoned by her mother, who said explicitly that she was choosing to protect her second marriage at the cost of isolating her daughter. Marina, seemingly unaware of the impact of this stance on her daughter, felt abandoned by her daughter as well. Sally's emotional involvement with her new family, although it gave attention and security to Sally, was difficult for Marina to accept. In situations like this one, in which there are powerful affective themes, problem-solving and negotiation strategies can easily fail.

Therapist Improvisation: Shifting Domains of Operation The key principle illustrated in the following sequences is the therapist's shift from a problem-solving to an affective dimension. A multidimensional model allows the clinician maximum flexibility for in-session work. In the present case, at the previous session and the beginning of the current session, Marina expressed extreme pessimism about her daughter. The clinician was aware of mother's pessimism and was looking for productive ways to address and, if possible, counteract it. The therapist decided to challenge mother's pessimism in a straightforward, problem-solving way by trying to work a conversation about mother and daughter having dinner together (a rare occurrence). When the therapist assessed that this approach was not working, she shifted the focus from the problem-solving on this content to the affective dimension. In the first segment, we see a lack of movement in the behavioral and cognitive dimensions.

"Let's Get Something Accomplished"

The therapist is clarifying her rationale for requesting mother and daughter conversations in the session.

T: What's this about? Well, it's about having a relationship with your daughter. It doesn't necessarily mean it has to be as formal as a date.

Mother (M): (interrupts; seems *frustrated*) Well, it does because she doesn't want to have *anything* to do with me. I mean, like if I walk in and talk to her . . .

T: But you can do stuff together. What about dinner, what about doing stuff, you know . . .

M: She won't have dinner with me. She *will not* sit down. She *has not* sat down and had dinner with me for two years.

T: Would you like her to have dinner with the family?

M: Sure, it's normal. Sure.

T: So, what do you have to do? What are the kinds of things that go into this? Let's not assume that that's out the window.

M: It *is* out the window. (discouraged)

T: Mmm.

M: Well, I mean, after two years it is.

T: (sits forward and addresses father) Jim, can you convince this lady that she's got more influence over this kid?

M: (interrupts, sounding a bit insulted) Well, I don't have the energy to go in and scream and yell and pull her out everyday. I mean it's . . . You guys make this sound like it's really easy, and it isn't.

Working to forge an agreement about having family dinner together, the therapist begins to realize that work on this problem is both complex and intertwined with other issues. The intervention targets the cognitive (i.e., the level of meaning of an event in the family) and behavioral realms (i.e., logistics and skills in making the plan happen). As the therapist continues to focus on the possibility of mother and daughter achieving greater contact through the dinner, the mother's pessimism emerges. The father is included as a temporary move on the therapist's part to help change the mother's mind. However, mother felt pushed and unsupported within the context of a relationship with her daughter that itself felt unsupportive. In this situation, the therapist must change her stance immediately or risk mother's disengagement.[16] The therapist makes a dramatic shift.

Intentionally Shifting Focus in a Sequence   The therapist asks Sally to leave the session for a few minutes.

T: (to mom) I wanted Sally to step out because I think you're feeling ganged up on, and that's not what . . .

M: (interrupting) I feel *really* ganged up on. You guys make it sound real easy and it's not. (Mom laughs nervously)

T: That's not what I'm about, okay? That's not what I'm about. I'm here to try to make life easier for you. Do you believe that?

M: Well, maybe. I don't know. (laughs; doesn't sound convinced)

T: No. You don't. Okay.

M: I'm really tired of convincing others . . .

T: If that's where it's at, then that's what we need to be talking about. (pauses) Are you mad at me right now?

M: No. I'm just mad at the whole thing. I'm mad . . . Sally doesn't care about having a relationship with me, and it seems like if I try it's . . . you know, after a while you think, gee, this kid just does not want a mother. Maybe she doesn't want a father. She doesn't care at all. (sounds upset, discouraged, frustrated)

This type of dialogue continued for about 20 minutes. It ends with the following statement from the therapist that reaches Marina.

T: (to mom) So why are you doing this (coming to therapy, trying to reach out to your daughter)? You're doing this because you *love* her and you're *concerned* about her. You've already lost your older daughter to drugs. And you don't want this for Sally. You never wanted this for your older daughter. And it's *painful* and it tears you apart, and *that's* why you're here (in therapy) . . . that's why you want to do this, as *hard* as it's going to be. (pause) And I don't want you to feel like I am ganging up on you, or Jim is ganging up on you. I want to be here for you, Marina. Because I've seen how tough this is. I know it's *tough*. And my heart goes out to you, and I will do everything I can to be supportive of you.

This segment contains several important shifts. First, the therapist shifts the focus of the session from the daughter (e.g., "Are you interested in having more of a relationship with your mother?") to the mother (e.g., "I think you're feeling ganged up on"), and, perhaps more importantly, to the therapeutic alliance between Marina and herself (e.g., "Are you mad at me right now?"). By asking Sally to temporarily leave the session, the therapist sends a signal of respect to the mother (i.e., "I sense your upsetness and I want us to deal with that").

The shift from mother-adolescent problem solving attends to Marina's experience and individual needs of the mother. Another shift occurred in the locus of the therapeutic action. Instead of working either directly or indirectly with the mother-adolescent interaction, the therapist brings herself and the mother into the center of the process. This use of self by the therapist is constituted by a willingness to address her relationship with Marina. These moments illustrate the sincerity and credibility that have been established between therapist and mother. The therapist draws on this capital in times of crisis.

These are difficult moments to manage. Even with a clear session plan, a clinician's failure to read the feedback of the moment, especially in the affective and therapeutic alliance domains, increases the risk of iatrogenic effects. Feedback about a family member's reaction to the session's events (and to the therapist) are a challenge to read and to know how to respond. The ground rules for being attentive to and reading feedback can be made explicit and depend on lucid personal judgment under difficult conditions (Liddle, 1985). In this sequence, although the therapist had a specific agenda for the session, she appropriately adapted her style, content, and focus to accommodate to the feedback from her interventions.

In this segment, Marina and the therapist deal with hopelessness and the difficulty of resuscitating parental commitment. Aspects of this conversation include: (1) confirming the mother's anger ("I think you're feeling ganged up on") and despair ("You are really angry and frustrated"); (2) compassion for the difficulty of her situation ("This is really hard for you"); (3) normalizing the behavior ("Anyone would find this hard"); and (4) offering new explanations ("She is not used to you reaching out to her") and resuscitating commitment ("You love this child"). While recalibrating the session's emotional tone, the conversation also influences, in the moment at least, the mother's attributional set. It redirects her from a set that negatively connotes Sally's feeling state (e.g., "'My daughter doesn't care about having a relationship with me") and lack of motivation for a relationship with her mother (e.g., "This kid just does not want a mother").

Preparing the Daughter   In the previous segment, the therapist asked Sally to leave the room so the parents could be talked with alone. Before she asked Sally back into the session, the therapist met briefly with her alone. She tried to prepare Sally for subsequent work with her mother. Sally was challenged to "rise to the occasion" and take her own desire for independence more seriously.

T: (to Sally alone) Go back in there. Don't be a kid with your mom. Don't protect her. Be straight with her and let's see where it can go. I'll be there to help if you need it. I'll support you in this.

Sally agreed to try and therapist and Sally went back to the session.

In the next segment, the mother's change in affect and intent is clear. The previous therapist-mother interaction helped Marina out of a blamed and blaming posture and placed her in a vulnerable spot vis à vis her daughter. She is now ready to reach out to Sally, perhaps in a way that could move her daughter to complementary behavior. By meeting alone with Sally, the therapist tried to facilitate her accessibility to Marina. As she asks mother and daughter to try again, the therapist must monitor Marina's ability to remain in this emotionally available position. As the conversation unfolds, the therapist tracks Sally's understanding of what her mother is doing and, ideally, helps her to respond in kind. In tandem with this, the therapist tracks Marina's continuing ability to maintain the positive tone she has achieved.

Sally originally sat on a couch with her mother, across from Jim. In order to intensify the mother-child proximity, the therapist moved Sally to the chair across from her mother on the couch.

T: (To Sally) I want you to turn your chair to your mom. Your mom has told me some things just now that I thought were really important. And I want her to have a chance to say these things to you directly, because I was very moved by some of what she said. Okay? (The pace is intentionally deliberate and the tone is serious.)

M: (sadness in mom's voice) Well, first of all, it's very hard for me to talk, because I feel so bad about all this. I feel the loss of a daughter. I *miss* you. There's things that I want to do with you. I want you to be my *daughter.* I mean . . . and you don't want any part of it. That's very hurtful. (pause) I see mothers with their daughters — they enjoy each other's company and I just feel like you want nothing to do with me. (Mom begins to cry) You're home only because you have to be home. We have to make all these rules just so that maybe I can squeeze in some time to be with you. You really don't want any part of that. (the upset emotional tone changes slightly) I came from a family of mothers and daughters. I was close to my grandmother who had daughters. I was close to my mother who had daughters. I was even close to her sister, who also, you know, kind of adopted Auntie and I because we were daughters. That's a very special thing. (becoming upset again) I lost one daughter (a reference to mother's estrangement from her oldest child) and now I'm losing another daughter . . . It's not . . . (stops talking, at momentary loss for words)

T: And you don't want to lose her.

M: No. (emphatically)

T: And you don't want to have to make rules, but you don't know how to connect with Sally, you don't know what to do. (Sally was, up to this point, not responding very much to her mother's efforts. The therapist continues to encourage her.)

T: (in a soft voice to Sally) Your mother is being particularly open right now, Sally. She's not saying this to hurt you, she's saying it because she feels so sad and she loves you so much. Help your mom right now. Help her to know how to have a relationship with you. (pause) I don't believe for a minute that you don't miss it too, Sally.

Sally has her head down and is crying. The therapist hands her a tissue.

T: I think that's why you're crying right now. I don't think you want your mom hurting like that. Why is that? I think it's because you love your mom. Talk to her, Sally. (long pause. The therapist gets up and moves next to Sally. She puts her arm around the girl's shoulder.) She's hurting. Do you want her to hurt like this? I know you don't. Talk to her. She *loves* you. She's frustrated, she's hurt, but she loves you and she wants to talk. (pause) Would you like to try? (pause) Would you like to try? (long pause. Sally continues to cry quietly while her face is buried in her hands behind her hair.) Okay, come with me. (Sally accompanies the therapist out of the session.)

Shifting gears, the therapist now attempts a "hallway intervention." She has attempted to help Sally respond more clearly to her mother, but on this occasion, it is difficult for the daughter to do any more than she has done. The therapist, so as not to unduly disrupt the session and to give this conversation a reasonable chance of achieving even more success, speaks to Sally in the hallway. The intent is to assess quickly Sally's feelings about what is happening, as well as determine her willingness to respond a bit more fully with her mother. They return to the session with the therapist not sure how far Sally is willing to go on this occasion.

T: So, Sally, tell your mom what's going on.

S: I don't know. (sobbing voice)

T: (challenges) What do you think about the things she said? (pause) Sally, why are you crying right now? (Sally's head is bowed and her hands are still covering her face.)

S: (to mom, in a sobbing voice) Because I . . . I don't want you to feel that way.

M: Well, how else can I feel? I mean . . .

T: (strong, challenging) Why don't you want your mom to . . . Why do you care? Why?

S: Because I love her.

T: Then, tell her you love her. Tell her what it means to see her in so much pain. Tell her about that. (pause; voice softens) Your mom needs to know you love her.

S: She knows.

T: No, she doesn't know, Sally.

S: (to mom) You don't know?

M: Well, I think you sort of love me, but I think you sort of love to be away from me. You don't want anything to do with me. Nothing.

T: That makes you feel unloved.

M: Very unloved.

T: That's why I'm saying—I don't think your mom really knows that. Loving someone means, "I want a *relationship* with you. I want a connection with you. I want you to know when I'm scared. I want you to know when I'm happy." (pause) I'm saying you need to let your mom know. If that's how you feel, then you let her know. You love her, then let her know. (Sally still averts eye contact with her head down and her hands and hair covering her face.)

This sequence is facilitated by many key components. The mother's affect/intention remained productive, as did the content. The therapist nurtured this mood and discussion. If Marina were to get off track, the therapist would reenter the conversation and help her return to this effective posture. Family members often need more coaching during these early change attempts.

With Marina doing some excellent work, the therapist turns to Sally.

In a sequence such as this one, therapists are taught to have an active mind and to listen to the conversation in an anticipatory way. On this occasion, several questions might occupy one's thoughts.

What will it take for the daughter to respond at the same level as the mother?

Has enough groundwork been laid with the daughter individually?

Does the daughter believe that her mother really wants to hear what she might have to say?

To what degree should the therapist encourage the daughter to express herself (versus involving the mother in the encouragement)?

What are some reasonable outcomes for this sequence on this occasion? And, is it not possible that asking Sally to respond in this session may be reaching too far at this time?

Questions such as these inform a clinician's judgment on a moment-to-moment basis. How to recalibrate one's interventions in the action of a session is one of the most complex of all therapy skills.

Although Sally had shared in individual sessions ideas about what she wanted in a new relationship with her mother, as well as her feelings of abandonment by her mother, Sally did not discuss these issues with Marina in this interview, despite the therapist's urgings.

Given these circumstances, the therapist concluded that this sequence had progressed as far as it could on this occasion. Here we are careful to check ourselves for what might be called *in-session reductionism*. This is a malady of clinicians, common among structural therapists of bygone eras, which assumes that the only locale of change is within the session.[17] A related form of this disorder is *in-session reductionism — overdramatic type,* which proffers unrealistic expectations for the outcome of any particular sequence one facilitates. The genesis of this disorder is commonly believed to be the beloved, but sometimes dangerous, *edited training videotape.*

We were satisfied with the outcome of this session. The mother's stance toward Sally remained emotionally available and nonblaming. The daughter made it clear that she was touched by the mom's sincere efforts. Said Sally, "I don't want you [mother] to feel that way," in response to mother wondering whether or not her daughter cared about her. And in response to the therapist's question, "Why don't you want her to feel that way?" Sally responded, "Because I love her."

In this final sequence, sensing that there is a long way to go in furthering the kind of process that had occurred in this session, and realizing too that there were still some loose ends about what was discussed, the therapist worked to construct a useful ending to the session.

T: I don't think that we can have a sense of closure tonight on this topic. This is a huge and very important topic, but what I want to know is (to mom), is there anything that you can get . . . that you need from Sally right now, before you leave this room? Because, Marina, I have to say that I was very, very moved, as I think everybody in this room was. I know what you said was very hard, and you said a lot of things, and I was very, very moved. And I think that you certainly deserve some support, and I'm wondering if there's anything that you need from Sally before you leave this room tonight.

M: (pauses, then in a tender voice) I'd kind of like a hug. (then, with more firmness) I want a hug! (Mom and daughter reach out simultaneously and embrace one another—both sobbing. The therapist then ends the session.)

In this session the supervisor and therapist sometimes tried too hard to engineer the Big Bang—the breakthrough event that comes every so often in therapy. Further, we also realized that we had preconceptions about what this process would look like. Such expectations can create problems. On this occasion, these expectations almost helped us not to notice the change that was happening. This sequence reminds us that each participant in the conversation does not participate in the same way or at the same pace, nor is it important for them to do so. In this example, Marina recovered some of her positive motivation after the therapist's attention to her relationship with Marina. Further, Marina extended herself to Sally in an emotionally touching way. On this night, Sally did not respond as some of our other teenagers had. Still, in her own style and to the degree that she was able and willing in this session, Sally did indeed respond to her mother, and Marina recognized and appreciated her degree of response. A sequence of this nature also reminds us of the challenge to implement the multidimensional philosophy. That is, an overemphasis on emotional expression can miss cognitive or behavioral possibilities.

Finally, this sequence presents an opportunity again to remember the focus in this approach on an *incremental* or successive approximations view of change. This is our emphasis despite the fact that change can be defined as having both continuous and discontinuous elements (Liddle, 1982). We focus on working and framing change for family members as a series of small steps. These are defined by Mahrer (1988b) as "good moments" of therapy (i.e., processes that are instrumental to change). As Greenberg and Pinsof (1986) have put it, outcome should be broken down into the small *o*'s (small outcomes) that comprise a ground level view of the therapy process. Fixation on the final product, the Big *O* of a final outcome or a Big Event, can instigate unrealistic expectations and a focus at the wrong level of detail. Attention to these Big *O*'s would be like trying to hit a home run every time up at bat.[18]

Case 3: Apology and Forgiveness as Facilitators of Development

The previous case illustrated a flexible therapeutic stance that constantly assesses progress and shifts to different dimensions of human functioning and intervention as needed. It highlighted how to deal with commonly occurring circumstances that stop progress in the problem-solving realm.

This case explores another dimension of parent-adolescent relationship problems. It concerns the process of retribution, or, as the adolescent would sometimes call it, "payback," to the parent. In a payback scenario, the teenager feels that she or he has gotten a bad deal in the family and wants to repay the parent for her or his misery. As with all themes, this one is shaped both by the therapist and the family. The payback theme is not the only background process that inhibits normal developmental transitions. It is simply one of several potentially useful themes. Nonetheless, because of its affective power, this theme is one that we attended to quite carefully.

Although understandable from the viewpoint of the family's history, the payback process deters the adolescent's and parents' development. It derails the necessary negotiation of the teenager-parent relationship, making it difficult to deal with anything but issues relating to the payback scenario. Challenging the adolescent quite directly on this issue, the therapist might say, "You need to talk to your father and mother in new ways. It should be done in a way in which they can respond. The payback mode only feels good because you feel hurt. You know it won't help in the long run."

Some family therapists, especially those with a strategic orientation (Jurich, 1990) seem unnecessarily reluctant to challenge adolescents this explicitly. Developmentally speaking, we confirm the adolescent's attempts at self-definition, expression, and assertion, yet urge and teach new ways of accomplishing these. As we know, however, although preparation of the teenager is important, and the steps to ready the adolescent for more productive interchanges with his or her parent(s) are capable of specification, the results of clearly articulated plans do not always coincide with therapist intentions.

The following case illustrates successful interchanges between a mother and daughter. Although we have largely discussed the benefits of this kind of healing conversation for the adolescent, these processes can have profound impact on the parents as well. One aspect of this change process involves the rekindling of the parents' commitment to their teenager. More basically, conversations in this realm can help parents realize their *continued* importance in their child's socialization process. Changes made by parents in this regard also give adolescents some needed hope that their parents can indeed change in outlook and behavior.

Roni is a 16-year-old who dropped out of school at age 13. At the start of therapy, she had just ended 10 straight days of "speed bingeing" (amphetamines) and had been staying with her 19-year-old drug-dealer boyfriend. She had recently been hospitalized for her second suicide attempt. Roni lived with her mother, Jan, a recovering alcoholic, for the last six years.

The following segments all come from the third session. Roni wore dark glasses, long black gloves, a black shirt and skirt, and long black leather boots. As this sequence begins, the therapist is presenting an aspect that might be possible in therapy.

"Will You Let Your Mom Know You?"

Therapist: Roni, you said something very important. You said to your mom, "You don't really know who I am so you cannot really say anything about me." And that's part of who you are. You keep yourself very private. But I hear Jan (mom) saying that she would like to know you a little bit more (Roni starts to shake her head, saying "no" with this gesture) — things like what you are thinking and feeling. Could we use some of this time in therapy for letting her get to know *you*, the real *you*?

Roni: Every time — No. I'm so . . . I don't want anybody to know me, because when they know me, they know how to hurt me, and when they know that, they do it and it hurts.

T: And that's happened to you before?

R: Many, many, many times. Countless times. And I've finally gotten to this point that I've been striving for for years, where *nobody* knows me. Nobody can! Nobody can barely even look at me in the eye anymore. I wear my sunglasses constantly because I believe — and I don't know if you guys are gonna think I'm crazy but — I believe the eyes are the doorway to the soul and that when you really look into somebody's eyes dead on without anything in between, there's like a connection. And then you really know somebody. And because of that, I always wear my sunglasses.

T: Are you afraid your mom might hurt you?

R: Uh-huh. She has in the past.

T: She has in the past?

R: Very much so!

The therapist helps Roni to explain her emotional world and her drastic coping strategies. Roni protects herself from further hurt with her sunglasses and long black gloves. Later, Roni explained that her persistent involvement in the drug culture was related to a profound unhappiness with her life. Roni had made two serious suicide attempts. Despite her negating the possibility of trying new ways of involvement with her mother, Roni's openness gave us some hope. In assessing Jan's contribution to the current stalemate, we wondered whether she could respond to the frank discussions that the daughter seemed able to instigate.

Problems in Problem Solving As we have said, part of this model involves straightforward problem solving. Everyday life problems comprise the content of these discussions. Parents are supported to discuss age-appropriate expectations of their adolescent, and teenagers are helped to negotiate with their parents. However, when working with adolescents and parents whose past together has been tumultuous over a period of time (e.g., neglect, abuse, alcoholism and drug abuse of parents or other significant adults), problem-solving or skill-training approaches in the usual sense can have their limitations. That is, although this remains an empirical question, it was our clinical impression that the problem solving could not be about the day-to-day problems but about these fundamental relationship breaks and transgressions, some of which have been active for 10 or 15 years. Thus, the content of the problem solving was critical to its success.

Attention to and work in the parents' and adolescent's affective realm were a matter of course in our work. Although this focus might be seen by some as a return to age-old, hydraulic thinking (i.e., penetration to deeper levels of awareness as key to therapeutic unlocking resistances), work in this realm can motivate and provide an effective *foundation* for problem solving and skill training. Enactment is also conceived as a multistaged procedure. As we have said, the whole-part metaphor helps the therapist to remember that facilitating effective communication and problem solving does not only occur in therapist-guided parent-adolescent enactments.

In the final case, attempts at straightforward problem solving yielded generally limited results. The dilemma was framed: What alternatives exist when one's best efforts at facilitating a problem-solving sequence have met with only limited success? A multidimensional approach suggests a variety of alternatives may produce equally positive results. In the final case, motivational issues were considered primary. The therapeutic problem became how we could materialize the reasons *why* mother and daughter should want to be in a position of negotiation and dialogue with each other. In these situations, MDFT relies on a "first-things-first" philosophy.

At an impasse, the therapist asks, "What might be the *next* thing that has to happen for progress (e.g., a reasonable conversation on realistic content) to be made?" We realize, of course, that there might be many "next" things that need to occur, and hence it would be a problem to search for the one correct key to break a stalemate. Again, change, at least the "change" that therapists can have most immediate access to, is viewed in terms of successive approximations.[19]

With Jan and her daughter, our judgment became: Something else had to happen before mother and daughter could negotiate and problem solve. Our therapists were advised to keep in mind some guiding questions to orient and track their work. A central question in this case (which was also a generic question used with other cases was: *What is the missing event (conversation, statement, condition) or pattern (the interactional dimension of the missing event) that could move this process along?*[20]

In this case, both Jan and Roni had legitimate claims against each other, and neither was able or interested in helping the other solve their shared problems. Indeed, in a typical scenario such as this one, problems are *not* seen as shared (as ours) but as residing within the other (as "your problem"). The transformation of this attribution is a primary task of family therapy, even though it is not frequently cast in this way.[21] With Jan and Roni, themes of rejection and retaliation permeated their interactions. Movement toward reconciliation, as we have said, is not a simple task. Problem-solving attempts often become mired in the adolescent's retribution and in parental resignation.[22]

Given these conditions, family therapists in the Adolescents and Families Project were trained[23] to facilitate in-session shifts as solutions to in-session stuck points. These were shifts of focus, of domain of operation, and of content in a session. We look to different levels of meaning or different domains of communication for a way out. Overriding questions in these circumstances become:

Am I focusing on the useful content?
Is this conversation at an appropriate level of detail?
Is the territory in which this session is now operating on target?

These kinds of questions are asked of oneself during the session. They help develop an intentionality and criterion-driven methodology for moment-to-moment decisions. The following segments exemplify an intentional shift of domain of operation in the session, and were achieved through a process like the one we have just described.

"What's Getting in the Way Here?"

R: (angrily) You think that I'm really irresponsible, and I can't do shit.

Mom: (curtly) That's not true.

R: Yes, it is.

M: No, it's not. (The negative tone continues, and perhaps is escalating.)

T: (leans forward, trying to cut the sequence and get each person's attention) Is that really why you're so mad? Is that really the core of all this? I think you're just talking about the superficial stuff. I don't think that's where it's at. I want to know what makes this so hard. What's getting in the way of you two working out day-to-day problems? Why is there so much anger and resentment?

R: The list could go on and on and on of the things that she's done to me.

T: Think of the worst things.

This meaningful interchange puts the problem-solving quest into a new light. By amplifying the discussion to include the affective realm, which in this situation includes past resentments and hurts, the therapist creates a shift in the interview. The tone changes dramatically as possibilities for discussing core affective themes (e.g., forgiveness) appear. Although no single intervention exists to tap the territory of relational expectations and regrets, focus and persistence are extremely helpful. We ask each family member, repeatedly if necessary: Why is this so hard? What's getting in the way? The goal is to help each family member define for himself or herself, sometimes alone and other times in the presence of others, what each perceives to be the barriers to progress. Leading a family to explore and create a new story about a significant trauma can be risky, difficult, and upsetting for all those in the room, including the therapist. Work in this realm of strong emotion requires a clinician's compassion and commitment to enable each family member to address the fundamental issues. In the acting profession, there is a saying having to do with "getting at the truth" of a scene or character. Effective family therapy with teenagers and their parents gets at the truth or the essence of these tormented relationships — family ties that have been stretched to the breaking point.

In the next segment, the theme of forgiveness has been reintroduced into the discussion. It had been developed previously as a necessary theme and goal.

T: Roni, what's the part that hurts the most? What's the part that you have the most difficulty forgiving her for?

R: Abandoning me. She abandoned me.

T: How did she do it? How did she abandon you?

R: (fidgeting with her hair, continuing to cry) We were a family once a long time ago. We were a family! I had my friends over and I had little birthday parties and slumber parties and . . . (starts to cry).

T: What happened?

R: Mom decided she can't stand our town and wants to move to the big city. As soon as we get here, it's like all of a sudden she wasn't mommy. She moved here all by herself with her two kids on welfare and she just got all these strokes for it. Everybody said, "Oh Jan, oh Jan, honey, honey (mockingly pats mother on the back), I'm so proud of you. I can't believe you did this all by yourself." And she got so caught up in this, it was like I didn't even exist anymore.

T: Say more, Roni.

R: I mean, I would ask, "Can I go out, Mommy?" "Sure, go ahead, have fun." While she's sitting there, with all her friends getting all these strokes.

T: So, she didn't do all that she's trying to do now.

R: She didn't do anything!

T: Is she trying now to be the mother she wasn't for all those years?

R: Maybe. But it's too late now. I don't want it! I won't take it! It's like saying, "Oh, I'm so sorry, honey, I didn't give you a Christmas gift for the past 50 years but that's okay, I'll give you a toy car now to make up for the one I didn't give you when you were six." Well, it doesn't work like that.

T: So you're saying she'll never be able to make up for all the lost time and all that she hasn't given and what she took away.

R: I'm not saying that. I'm saying that she can't start treating me like I'm 12 now just because she didn't treat me like I was 12 then.

This segment reveals principal aspects of the healing conversations we attempt to promote. Important relationship issues have become articulated. Roni's longing for the parenting her mother once provided ("we were a family a long time ago"), her ability to define the problem in her own words ("you were too into your own thing to pay attention to me"), and a beginning specification of the conditions under which change could occur (e.g., there are some ways in which mother cannot make up for the past and an implication that there are some ways in which she can). Revelations are not the goal. Articulation of this content serves to form the arena within which the next conversations will occur. Progress with Roni, however, is half the battle, since it is equally important to develop mother's views on this same topic.

Helping the Adolescent Take Responsibility   Sessions may have extensive discussions of past events. However, getting history on the table of therapy merely begins the necessary therapeutic process. As past events loosen their grip, other themes gain salience. Although the events themselves are in the past, the feelings and thoughts about them often remain as vibrant as ever.

Discussions regarding each person's responsibility for present behaviors and commitments to future actions are also important components of the therapeutic fabric. The segment below shows how the therapist confronted Roni's use of her past hurts for current purposes.

T: Why is coming home on weeknights unreasonable?

R: Because I work on Friday and Saturday day, which means I cannot go out on Friday and Saturday nights or else I'll be too tired to work. I'm off on Tuesdays and Thursdays, which means my nights out should be Mondays and Wednesdays.

T: Are you saying that you're willing to live in the house if your mother is more reasonable?

R: It depends on how reasonable is reasonable.

T: See, Roni, I think you're teasing her. You're being unfair to her in a very basic way. On some occasions, you'll say, "Mom, I'm your daughter and, yeah, we'll dance like it's a mother and daughter thing and we'll talk about negotiation, and about when I come home and when I stay out, and all of that." But there's a certain point in that discussion where you say, "No more," where you say, "No, I've just changed the rules on you. *Now* we are just going to be friends." And that's not a good scene, Roni. That's no good.

R: Well it gets to a certain point where I can't take it any more.

T: I understand that. But I think you have the capacity to deal very directly with your mom about things that are upsetting you. But because you are so smart, you keep changing the rules. In addition to making her squirm and kicking her, it creates constant instability for the two of you. She's your mom for that three minutes and then for the next two, you're just gonna be friends. You say she comes on harsh to you, but you're making her crazy. Anybody would feel crazy.

Here, the therapist introduced a number of themes that will be developed throughout treatment. First, Roni's protective strategies are understood as part of her contribution to the present difficulty. This challenge, and its correlates to be developed later, encourage Roni to seek developmentally appropriate alternatives to her current conflict resolution tactics. Roni is invited to transform her victimized, powerless position and replace it with an increased sense of agency.

The adolescents are challenged, as we put it, for revoking their mother's or father's "parenting license." They are told, as in this sequence, that although their complaints may have some validity and should be responded to by the parent, the manner in which they express their concerns is ineffective. The therapeutic relationship and the context of therapy are offered as forums where they can be assisted in expanding their repertoire of expression and action.

Finally, the challenge in the previous sequence lends some needed support to Jan. If Roni's perspective was to become the sole focus of the treatment, the mother would clearly question the goals of the therapy (indeed, this would be a sure sign of a therapy badly out of balance). Multiple alliances and appropriately complex themes must always be developed in this work.

This support for Jan might be related to how she moves into an emotionally open position with her daughter in the following "confessional" dialogue. Mother is moved by Roni's revelations. It prompts similar behavior from her.

Affirmation Fights Abdication

Roni is looking down with her head in her hands.

M: (to Roni) I'm certainly open for discussions about whatever it is you feel you need to explore. Even if it means in the larger sense of our relationship. Because I think it's more than you staying out on weeknights. I think it's *way* more than that.

This is significant since it implies that mother realizes tne importance of having a conversation at the right level of detail and content.

T: What do you mean? What do you think it is?

M: I think it goes deeper than that.

T: Well, say what you think.

M: I think she's pissed off at my leaving her father and leaving that family unit — the traditional family unit. We were in a middle-class, all-American family situation and I left that, ended up on welfare, you know, and the list goes on and on from that.

T: Right. What else?

Roni continues. Crying, she confronts the mother with the fact that while mom was drunk, the son of mother's best friend sexually abused Roni. Jan admits she was intoxicated at the time but, at the same time, she shows a willingness to discuss this incident with her daughter. The therapist probes to see if there are other issues or events between them that should be explored. Jan replies.

M: Well, there was my drunkenness, my drug use, my open relationship attitude. I think my boundaryless relationships affected a lot of people, including my children, and I think that's *really* done some incredible damage.

Jan gives a powerful acknowledgment of her daughter's reality for the past dozen years. Further, Jan discussed her need to gain more skills ("Yes, maybe I do need more skills, that's why I'm here") and to be more consistent in her parenting. Roni was attentive during her mother's discussion of these important matters. Conversations that acknowledge hurts and involve new, openly-stated levels of responsibility taking promote healing of torn parent-adolescent relationships. Although they are certainly not the only means through which such healing can occur, they are prime examples of the kind of therapeutic events we seek to sponsor.

Setting the Agenda for Future Sessions   Content themes are established and constantly revised and reworked throughout therapy. The following segment shows how closure is brought to the session. The interview's content is identified as central themes for future work. This procedure, importantly, links the therapy over time. In this case, this content became the starting point for the next session. Not uncommonly, these themes attained greater richness and complexity as they were discussed in each following session.

T: So, Roni, is there no forgiveness forthcoming? (pause) Would you be willing, Roni, to talk with us about what forgiveness is — what it means to you?

R: I could try but I don't really even know what forgiveness is, I don't forgive people. I'm there and I love them and I'm loyal to them until they fuck me over, and then after they fuck me over, they don't exist.

T: And that's what we have here. Okay—that's what I mean. So you *do* have a sense of what is in the way here. That is good. I'd like to suggest this. (Hesitating, and momentarily incapacitated by Roni's extreme stance about forgiveness and not exactly sure how to create an opening for future work in this area, the therapist wonders: "Has Roni closed this theme off from work?") (Now talking to both mother and daughter, the therapist decides to let them in on his thinking about how this theme can guide their work together.) In the normal course of events, we would be discussing things like pragmatics and logistics—day-to-day problem-solving things. But, obviously, there's so much stuff that exists between the two of you that these discussions would not be fruitful. What we need before any problem solving gets done is to decide what discussions need to occur between the two of you. What's the stuff that's still in the way of achieving progress on pragmatics, such as decisions about where Roni's going to live, where she's not going to live, and so on? And, I think two of the areas we've got to get to are the two I've mentioned. One is, what will it take for Roni to offer some *forgiveness* to her mom? And the other is, how can Jan begin to prove herself as more *believable* to her daughter? Forgiveness and believability are the two themes.

Roni, like many of the teenagers we have seen, did not believe that life with her family might have some value to her. Over the years, Jan's inconsistent availability and ineffective protection left Roni with, at best, ambivalent feelings toward her mother. We were often reminded of Patterson and colleagues' work on parental monitoring as a critical aspect of a healthy family environment (Dishion, Patterson, & Reid, 1988; Patterson, Dishion & Bank, in press). Roni's search for independence and identity did not evolve from a secure base (Bowlby, 1988). She seemed to be running from the chaos and unpredictability of her youth. The therapist established order to the therapy by naming some benchmarks by which progress could be measured. In this case, Roni was challenged about what we called the "kicking quota" (a retribution system) in which she seemed to operate. We asked her when would she be done "kicking" or paying back her mom? Was there no end to it or could it be altered by building in new ways of relating in the present? As we have said, these behaviors are challenged quite directly. A pragmatically useful and hope-inducing assumption, stated explicitly to the adolescent and parent, is that the adolescent can do better at communicating and negotiating the parent-adolescent transition.

Achieving these transitions (e.g., decreased hierarchy of the parent-adolescent relationship and age-appropriate connectedness) are hindered by many things, including carried-over issues from the family's past together. Mother's responsiveness, which we facilitated and amplified in individual sessions, was certainly vital to our success in this domain. Roni's newfound abilities (e.g., to think complexly about and manage some degree of forgiveness), which were also accessed and accentuated by work with her alone, were equally important to the advancement of a new process between mother and daughter.

Conclusion

Although the family therapy approach, developed in the Adolescents and Families Project, both in name and in practice is multidimensional, this chapter, by design, has focused on a selected number of dimensions (e.g., the adolescent, the affective realm). Nevertheless, we hope that the basic thrust of the multidimensional approach has been visible. Existing in the contemporary movement of integrative therapeutic models that construct comprehensive, specialized treatment manuals for particular problems and populations, Multidimensional Family Therapy (MDFT) operates in several domains simultaneously:

1. MDFT considers *multiple realms of human functioning* and *targets of intervention* (e.g., affective, cognitive, motivational, behavioral).
2. MDFT has *multiple foci of the interventions* (e.g., adolescents, parents, adolescent-parent interaction, whole family, extrafamilial).
3. MDFT has *multiple content themes of therapy* (e.g., substance abuse, past hurts and disappointments, ineffective parenting styles, difficulties in renegotiating parent-adolescent transition, individual skill deficits, as well as those in adolescent-parent communication, abdication of parental responsibility).
4. MDFT uses *multiple types of interventions* (e.g., in-session and out-of-session problem solving, understanding and reworking the past, reformulation of cognitive attributions, facilitation of forgiveness, resuscitation of parental devotion and love).

Although the approach is multidimensional and integrative, it is not an unsystematic potpourri of interventions (quite to the contrary, since it aims to be systematic and specialized). It is systematic in that the model consists of a protocol for working among the multiple dimensions outlined earlier. It is specialized in that this protocol has been developed specifically for substance-abusing and conduct-disorder adolescents and their families and not as a general model of family therapy. The major benefits of such a model are that it is tailored to the particular problems and needs of adolescents and their families, it can be scientifically evaluated, and it can be readily disseminated.

Walking the Tightrope   Can we identify a process that exemplifies the difficult work of family therapy with adolescents and their parents? When working with adolescents and their families, clinicians must learn how to walk the tightrope. They must establish and maintain alliances with both the adolescent and the parents; hence, at one time they must be the voice of the adolescent, at other times they serve the same role with the parent(s). To support and speak for both parents and teenagers while also taking into account extrafamilial systems such as juvenile justice and school is a daunting task. Yet, maintaining multiple alliances is not only possible but essential to successful therapy with drug-abusing adolescents and their families.

Since this chapter focuses primarily on the adolescent side of the equation, we will summarize certain basic principles of working with the adolescent.

Our initial challenge is how to engage adolescents in the therapy. The majority of substance-abusing adolescents will come to therapy only because either their parents or the juvenile justice system has ordered them to do so. Since we have found that active participation by the teenager in the therapeutic process increases chances for success, it is vital to help the adolescent formulate a personal therapeutic agenda. Without this viable agenda, engagement will be compromised.

Establishing the adolescent's agenda is one of the primary and first therapeutic challenges. The adolescent must be convinced that therapy can be worthwhile for him or her personally. To accomplish this goal, the therapist must show the teenager, through both words and actions, that therapy will be more than just helping the parents to be more powerful and controlling. Engagement and alliance-building strategies are continued throughout the therapy. Examples of adolescent engagement and agenda-setting strategies were most clearly seen in the treatment excerpts of Sam and his family.

As mentioned in the introduction, MDFT tries to facilitate both in-session and out-of-session change. Fostering in-session change through enactment, as can be seen in the excerpts, is a core component of this approach. We are very careful to adequately prepare the adolescent, the parent(s), and other family members for these conversations. This step maximizes possibilities for success. Preparation consists of meeting with each family member alone to explore, highlight, question, and acknowledge personal beliefs, attitudes, opinions, and feelings about self, other family members, and the family as a whole. We try to help each family member figure out how he or she feels and what he or she thinks about important content themes that either the therapist or family member has brought to the therapy.

By working individually with each family member before the enactment, the therapist is able to (1) solidify alliances so that the therapist will be free to challenge in the upcoming enactment sequence, (2) help each family member formulate the content and style of what he or she wants to say to other members, and (3) elicit from each member his or her most helpful statements. The definition of *helpful statements,* of course, will vary from family to family, person to person, and issue to issue. An example of a helpful statement would be a parent's stated willingness to listen to his or her adolescent's perspective despite many previous disappointments and hurts. Preparation of this sort was illustrated in segments from the last case of Roni and her mother, Jan.

Many substance-abusing adolescents feel that they have little control of their emotions, thoughts, behaviors, and daily life. Although they may not be able to articulate precisely how they experience the world, many adolescents have an unmistakable sense that something in their life is desperately wrong. Several interventions are used to alter this experience. First, we have high expectations for the adolescent, and we attempt to increase his or her own self-expectations by providing alternatives — holding up certain desirable behaviors and in essence saying, "This is what you can do, this is what you can be, this is how you can get along in the world, and this is how you can interact with your parents." For each family we may use different materials to sketch this portrait of higher expectations (e.g., attributions, emotions, the past, etc.), but the message is always the same: You can do better *and* I'm going to help you do better.

We also present to the adolescents our high expectations of their parents. We tell the teenagers about our goal of helping their parents be better parents — to be more fair, to listen and acknowledge them, and to be more responsive. By talking to the adolescents about their parents' parenting, we counter the teenagers' realization that responsibility for change does not lie solely with them. This serves to counter some of their pessimism as well. It can be a difficult balance to maintain, but we want adolescents to feel *some degree* of responsibility to help alter their parents' behavior, but not too much responsibility. The therapist creates a partnership with the teenager that, among other things, helps deal with parents and about how those parents treat the teenager. Adolescents appreciate having and often need a spokesperson, even one that is not always completely on their side. They are accustomed to a world that does not respect them, expects them to be unreasonable, and, in general, understands adolescence (incorrectly so) as a time of necessary storm and stress (Offer, Ostrov, & Howard, 1981).

In addition to increasing expectations, we help the adolescent, literally and figuratively, find a different language, and thus a different way of being in the world. With our initial case in this chapter, the therapist tried to help Sam communicate his unhappiness and frustration through words rather than through violence and self-destructive actions. With Roni, the therapist helped her talk to her mother about past hurts and betrayals rather than continuing to indirectly punish her mother by severe drug use and suicide attempts. With Sally, the therapist helped her to begin communicating how much she cared for and loved her mother. The language that we aim for is one in which the adolescents can, to the best of their ability, explain their subjective experiences, world views, hopes and dreams, complaints and disappointments. Again, although not discussed in this chapter, it is important to remember that we also work just as intensely with the parents so they will be receptive to their adolescent's new language.

Coda

By virtue of its built-in comprehensiveness, flexibility, and specificity, multidimensional therapy offers therapists and families the necessary tools for repairing family functioning and, as a result, reducing or eliminating the adolescent's self-destructive behaviors such as drug abuse, suicide attempts, school failure, and violence. We aim to mend these relationships by establishing and maintaining strong alliances, by raising expectations for the self and other family members, by preparing family members to have conversations on topics that relate to core family themes, by helping family members to engage in effective in-session and out-of-session problem solving and negotiation, and by assisting them to practice new behaviors and accommodate when necessary to the changes of others. These are the necessary concomitants of change.

In AFP's families, the adolescent-parent(s) relationship is in severe disrepair. These are families full of misunderstandings, hurts, disappointments, hopelessness, and betrayals. Living in a land of extremes of thought and action, these individuals, understandably, come to devalue family relationships. These intense feelings and processes must be dealt with in a forthright manner. Starkly stated, the families seem to experience their lives as their own private hell. It is the therapist's job to venture into this ominous territory with courage, conviction, compassion, and, of course, great skill. The families need and deserve no less.

Endnotes

1. NIH Guide for Grants and Contracts; Volume 12, Number 8, August 19, 1983—National Institute on Drug Abuse Program Announcement titled "Family Therapy and Prevention Research."

2. The Adolescents and Families Project began in 1985 at the University of California, San Francisco, and moved for its final year of operation to Temple University in April of 1990.

3. Although not without its critics (Stanton, 1988), the treatment manual tradition that is currently flourishing in the psychotherapy research world (Lambert & Ogles, 1988) has been a source of inspiration and guidance in the development of multidimensional family therapy (MFT). For instance, Kaufman (1985) has supported the development of treatment manuals that would be accompanied by intensive training and supervision for the family therapy of drug abuse. The family therapists in the Adolescents and Families Project were trained in the MFT ap-

proach prior to seeing cases and were supervised via live supervision throughout the research project.

4. Although Todd (1990) has stated that the MFT model used in the Adolescents and Families Project was based on and was a test of the Stanton and Todd (1982) structural-strategic approach, this is not the case. Liddle's (1984, 1985) initial version of structural-strategic therapy was much more clearly related to the structural-strategic approaches of Stanton (1981) and Todd (1986) than is MDFT. The approach developed for the Adolescents and Families Project, for instance, does not use paradoxical interventions, does not employ a function of the symptom concept, does not primarily draw from other schools of family therapy for its tenets and methods, is not ahistorical in its focus, uses adolescent development research to guide its assessments and interventions, and works with individuals in the course of treatment more than the structural-strategic models. It should be noted, however, that Stanton's own work has evolved and recent publications seem to take remove him from the structural-strategic realm (Stanton, 1984). Todd's (Todd & Selekman, 1990a) more recent work seems to have changed less than Stanton's relative to the original Stanton and Todd (1982) model. Todd integrates aspects of other brief family therapy models (e.g., the DeShazer, White, and Milan systemic model) into the basic structural-strategic (Stanton & Todd, 1982) model.

5. Other components of MDFT include work with other individuals (each parent alone, the teenager's friends), other subsystems (parental and sibling), and extrafamilial systems (school and probation personnel). The skills and special problems associated with these components are the subject of other publications.

6. With this said, we must heed the caution issued by Lazarus, Coyne, and Folkman (1982) on the topic of apparently neat classifications and distinctions between these realms of human existence: "Thoughts, emotions, and motives are inferred from observations of the person . . . how we partition these concepts and punctuate theoretical sequences is often a matter of theoretical and methodological convenience" (p. 232). While realizing the usefulness of separating these domains of existence and experience, Folkman, Schaefer, and Lazarus (1979) have argued for an understanding of the realms and acknowledging their constant interplay.

7. Although this is not a specific reference to the multimodal therapy of Arnold Lazarus, his model should be recognized as one of the best contemporary examples of integrative theorizing and therapy model construction.

8. Family reductionism commits the same conceptual error that family therapy was invoked to alter. Reductionism at the level of the family places the onus for health and pathology at the doorstep of the family, ignoring other relevant systems of influence. Family therapy's rediscovery of the individual is, to adapt a concept from modern-day economic theory, part of a *conceptual "correction."*

9. The concept of the therapeutic alliance in family therapy remains, as yet, underdeveloped. Pinsof and Catherall (1986) provide an example of the kind of work needed in the family systems field that appreciates the tradition, conceptual developments, and research on therapeutic alliance in the individual psychotherapy field, and builds concepts and research methods for use in family therapy.

10. Subsystem therapy is used to portray an approach that does not only work with the entire family unit. Separate sessions with the key subsystems, the adolescent (which sometimes includes siblings and peers) and the parent(s), are fundamental to this model. Although family therapy models moved in a reductionistic direction, some of the field's most prominent approaches (e.g., Bowen, Brief Therapy Model, Milton Erickson) regularly see individuals alone.

11. This chapter emphasizes the skills of doing a multidimensional, multi-systemic therapy through the adolescent subsystem. This is not meant to imply that the skills needed to work for adolescent, parent, and family change through the parental subsystem are somehow less vital. The modules for working such subsystems as the parental and extrafamilial subsystems are developed in other publications. Important themes in the parental subsystem, for example, have included the establishment or rekindling of parental hopes, dreams, and aspirations for their adolescent. This revitalization of a parent's commitment, which could be said to address the so-called parental imperative, can be accomplished through interventions that promote compassion, perspective taking, and a stance of negotiation on the parents' part. As one can see, this genre of intervention can serve as a necessary complement to the control and authority-oriented interventions commonly thought of in work with the parents of teenagers.

12. Howard Liddle was the coordinator of the family therapy condition on the project. He supervised cases using live and videotape methods.

13. *Understand* and *confirm* perhaps do not carry enough of the connotation of how these realities are both understood/confirmed *and* shaped, simultaneously. At this stage of therapy, however, given the developing therapeutic alliance between therapist and teenager, it is probably more accurate to say that we aim for a more "pure" understanding and confirmation of the reality of the adolescent's life as he or she experiences it.

14. One of the most difficult challenges for any therapist concerns how to do therapy with a consistency of themes (which, of course, develop and evolve over the course of therapy), while at the same time maintain the ability to incorporate new content into these themes. This new content often serves as a major factor in the themes' transformation.

15. Although *modeling* certainly is a factor in a change process of this nature, our conception of change centers more on the work that occurs in the therapeutic relationship between therapist and adolescent, and on the changes that are practiced outside of the therapy session, rather than on a modeling theory per se.

16. Just as the concept of the therapeutic alliance is still in formation in family therapy, the notion of splits or ruptures in the therapeutic alliance (Safran et al., 1990) await conceptual and empirical inquiry.

17. A related but converse disorder, of course, is *out-of-session reductionism,* in which it is assumed that change happens outside of sessions, primarily as a result of a therapist's directives.

18. Extending the metaphor, although it is easy to think of affective break-throughs as "home runs," other, less dramatic moments and events in therapy can have more solid, long-lasting consequences. Cognitive understanding, downplayed by such theorists as Haley (1976), can serve as a powerful foundation for, or post hoc organizer of, behavioral change. In general, family therapy has, unfortunately, not appreciated the role of individual differences on these dimensions in the change process.

19. The version of change that is referred to as *discontinuous* (Hoffman's "leap theory" of change) seems, at least according to the way we do therapy, as more out of reach and ephemeral in the clinical realm. It seems to promote a magical thinking rather than a hands-on, "what is the next step in the change process?" attitude on the therapist's part.

20. The language here clearly avoids the connotation of the question: What needs to happen for things *to be solved?* There is rarely such finality and surety in

human interaction and problem solving. The intent is to create a system of expectation with the families that problems are not "cured" by therapy; they may indeed arise again. The difference would be that they have new ways of looking at and skills for solving the life events and problems that will come their way.

21. The cognitive revolution that has swept psychology has been slow, thus far at least, to take hold in family therapy. Its impact in family psychology and marital and family studies, however, has been marked (e.g., Epstein & Baucom, 1988; Finchman & Bradbury, 1988).

22. Taking our cue from the process research literature and its methodology, we have begun to identify the specific markers that evidence poor problem solving in parent-adolescent communication (and hence the need to change focus) (Diamond, 1990).

23. The best representation of the family therapy training philosophy used in AFP can be found in Liddle (1988a, 1988b).

References

Aber, J. L., Allen, J., Carlson, V., & Cicchetti, D. (1989). The effects of maltreatment on development during early childhood: Recent studies and their theoretical, clinical, and policy implications. In D. Cicchetti & V. Carlson (Eds.), *Child maltreatment: Theory and research on the causes and consequences of child abuse and neglect.* New York: Cambridge University Press.

Achenbach, T. M. (1986). Developmental perspectives on psychotherapy and behavior change. In S. L. Garfield & A. E. Bergin (Eds.), *Handbook of psychotherapy and behavior change.* New York: Wiley.

Achenbach, T. M. (1990). What is "developmental" about developmental psychopathology? In J. Rolf, A. S. Masten, D. Cicchetti, K. H. Nuechterlein, & S. Weintraub (Eds), *Risk and protective factors in the development of psychopathology.* New York: Cambridge.

Alexander, B. K. (1990). The empirical and theoretical bases for an adaptive model of addiction. *The Journal of Drug Issues, 23,* 37–65.

Alexander, J. F., Klein, N. C., & Parsons, B. V. (1977). Impact of family systems intervention on recidivism and sibling delinquency: A model of primary prevention and program evaluation. *Journal of Consulting and Clinical Psychology, 45,* 469–474.

Alexander, J. F., Parsons, B. V. (1973). Short-term behavioral intervention with delinquent families: Impact on family process and recidivism. *Journal of Abnormal Psychology, 81,* 219–225.

Avis, J. M., & Sprenkle, D. H. (1990). Outcome research on family therapy training: A substantive and methodological review. *Journal of Marital and Family Therapy, 16,* 241–264.

Bandura, A. (1978). The self system in reciprocal determinism. *American Psychologist, 33,* 334–355.

Bandura, A. (1986). *Social foundations of thought and action: A social cognitive theory.* Englewood Cliffs, NJ: Prentice Hall.

Barton, C., Alexander, J. F., Waldron, H., Turner, C. W., & Warburton, J. (1985). Generalizing treatment effects of functional family therapy: Three replications. *The American Journal of Family Therapy, 13,* 16–26.

Baucom, D. H., Epstein, N., Sayers, S., & Sher, T. G. (1989). The role of cognitions in marital relationships: Definitional, methodological, and conceptual issues. *Journal of Consulting and Clinical Psychology, 57,* 31–38.

Baumrind, D. (1991). The influence of parenting style on adolescent competence and substance abuse. *Journal of Early Adolescence, 11,* 56–95.

Baumrind, D., & Moselle, K. A. (1985). A developmental perspective on adolescent drug abuse. *Advances in Alcohol and Substance Abuse, 4,* 41–67.

Blechman, E. A. (1982). Conventional wisdom about familial contributions to substance abuse. *American Journal of Drug Alcohol Abuse, 9,* 35–53.

Blechman, E. A. (1990). The knowledge base of family therapy. Review of M. McGoldrick & B. Carter (Eds.), *The changing family life cycle: A framework for family therapy. Contemporary Psychology, 35,* 812.

Blos, P. (1979). *The adolescent passage.* New York: International Universities Press.

Bowlby, (1988). *A secure base.* New York: Basic Books.

Bronfenbrenner, U. (1979). *The ecology of human development.* Cambridge, MA: Harvard University Press.

Bronfenbrenner, U. (1983). The context of development and the development of context. In R. M. Lerner (Ed.), *Developmental psychology: Historical and philosophical perspectives* (pp. 147–184). Hillsdale, NJ: Lawrence Erlbaum.

Brook, J. S., Brook, D. W., Gordon, A. S., & Whiteman, M. (1984). Identification with paternal attributes and its relationship to the son's personality and drug use. *Developmental Psychology, 20,* 1111–1119.

Brook, J. S., Brook, D. W., Lettieri, D. J., & Stimmel, B. (1985). Adolescent alcohol and substance use and abuse: A cause of concern or for complacency. *Alcohol and Substance Abuse in Adolescence, 4.*

Brook, J. S., Nomura, C., & Cohen, P. (1989). A network on influences on adolescent drug involvement: Neighborhood, school, peer, and family. *Genetic, Social and General Psychology Monographs, 115,* 123–145.

Brook, J. S., Whiteman, M., Gordon, A. S., & Brook, D. W. (1985). Father's influence on his daughter's marijuana use viewed in a mother and peer context. *Alcohol and Substance Abuse in Adolescence, 4,* 3–4.

Bry, G. H. (1983). Family-based approaches to reducing adolescent substance use: Theories, techniques and findings. NIDA Monograph 47.

Bukstein, O. G., Brent, D. A., & Kaminer, Y. (1989). Comorbidity of substance abuse and other psychiatric disorders among adolescents. *American Journal of Psychiatry, 146,* 1131–1141.

Burke, R. J., & Weir, T. (1978). Benefits to adolescents of informal helping relationships with their parents and peers. *Psychological Reports, 42,* 1175–1184.

Burke, R. J., & Weir, T. (1979). Helping responses of parents and peers and adolescent well being. *Journal of Psychology, 102,* 49–62.

Carnegie Council on Adolescent Development. (1989). *Turning points: Preparing American youth for the 21st century.* The report of the task force on education of young adolescents. New York: Carnegie Corporation.

Carter, B., & McGoldrick, M. (1986). *The changing family life cycle.* Boston: Allyn and Bacon.

Casey, R. J., & Berman, J. S. (1985). The outcome of psychotherapy with children. *Psychological Bulletin, 98,* 388–400.

Cicchetti, D. (1984). The emergence of developmental psychopathology. *Child Development, 55,* 1–7.

Congressional Record—Senate. (1990). Using family therapy to treat adolescent drug abuse (H. Joanning, R. Lewis, & H. Liddle). May 1, 1990, S5506–S5507.

Coombs, R. (1988). *The family context of adolescent drug abuse.* New York: Haworth.

Cooper, C. R., Grotevant, H. D., & Condon, S. M. (1983). Individuality and connectedness in the family as a context for adolescent identity formation and role-taking skill. In H. D. Grotevant & C. R. Cooper (Eds.), *New directions for child development: Adolescent development in the family* (Vol. 22, pp. 43–59). San Francisco: Jossey-Bass.

Coyne, J. C., & Liddle, H. A. (in press). The future of systems therapies. *Psychotherapy.*

Daruna, J. H. (1990). Preventing substance abuse: Directions for action. Review of B. S. Brown & A. R. Mills (Eds.) (1987). *Youth at high risk for substance abuse.* ADAMHA Publication, Rockville, MD.

Davidge, A. M., & Forman, S. G. (1988). Psychological treatment of adolescent substance abusers: A review. *Children and Youth Review, 10,* 43–45.

Diamond, G. S. (1991). *Resolving a parent child conflict: A discovery oriented process study.* Presentation at American Association for Marriage and Family Therapy Annual Conference Research Institute, October 1991, Dallas, Texas.

Dishion, T. J., Loeber, R., Stuthamer-Loeber, M., & Patterson, G. R. (1984). Skill deficits and male adolescent delinquency. *Journal of Abnormal Child Psychology, 12,* 37–54.

Dishion, T. J., Patterson, G. R., & Reid, J. R. (1988). Parent and peer factors associated with drug sampling in early adolescence: Implication for treatment. In E. R. Rahdert & J. Garbowski (Eds.), *Adolescent drug abuse: Analyses of treatment research.* NIDA research monograph 77, 69–93.

Dishion, T. J., Reid, J. B., & Patterson, G. R. (1989). Empirical guidelines for a family intervention for adolescent drug use. In R. H. Coombs (Ed.), *The family context of adolescent drug use.* New York: Haworth.

Dryfoos, J. G. (1990). *Adolescents at risk: Prevalence and prevention.* New York: Oxford University Press.

Eisner, L., & Liddle, H. A. (1991). Myths of adolescence: What clinicians need to know. Submitted for publication.

Elliott, D. S., Huizinga, D., & Ageton, S. S. (1985). *Explaining delinquency and drug use.* Beverly Hills: Sage Publications.

Epstein, N., & Baucom, D. (1988). *Cognitive-behavioral therapy with couples.* New York: Brunner/Mazel.

Erikson, E. H. (1968). *Identity: Youth and crisis.* New York: Norton.

Erickson, G. D. (1988). Against the grain: Decentering family therapy. *Journal of Marital and Family Therapy, 14,* 225–236.

Falco, J. (1988). Preventing abuse of drugs, alcohol, and tobacco by adolescents. Working paper for Carnegie Council on Adolescent Development. Washington, DC.

Falicov, C. (1988). *Family transitions: Continuity and charge over the life cycle.* New York: Guilford.

Feldman, S. S., & Elliot, G. R. (1990). *At the threshold: The developing adolescent* (pp. 388–413). Cambridge, MA: Harvard University Press.

Finchman, F. D., & Bradbury, T. N. (1988). The impact of attributions in marriage: Empirical and conceptual foundations. *British Journal of Clinical Psychology, 27,* 77–90.

Fisch, R. (1989). Training in the brief therapy model. In H. A. Liddle, D. C. Breunlin, & R. C. Schwartz (Eds.), *Handbook of family therapy training and supervision.* New York: Guilford.

Fishman, H. C. (1988). *Treating troubled adolescents: A family therapy approach.* New York: Basic Books.

Folkman, S., Schaefer, C., & Lazarus, R. (1979). Cognitive processes as mediators of stress and coping. In V. Hamilton & D. M. Warburton (Eds.), *Human stress and cognition: An information-processing approach.* London: Wiley.

Fraser, J. S. (1982). Structural and strategic family therapy: A basis for marriage, or grounds for divorce? *Journal of Marital and Family Therapy, 8,* 13–22.

Freud, A. (1958). Adolescence. *Psychoanalytic Study of the Child, 13,* 255–278.

Friedman, A. S., Utada, A., & Morrissey, M. (1987). Families of adolescent drug abusers are "rigid"'" Are these families either "disengaged" or "enmeshed," or both? *Family Process, 26,* 131–148.

Furman, W. (1980). Promoting social development: Developing implications for treatment. In B. Lahey & A. Kazdin (Eds.), *Advances in clinical child psychology* (Vol. 3, pp. 1–40). New York: Plenum.

Glynn, T. J. (1984). Adolescent drug use and the family environment; A review. *Journal of Drug Issues, 2.*

Goldfried, M. R., & Wolfe, B. E. (1988). Research on psychotherapy integration: Recommendations and conclusions from an NIMH workshop. *Journal of Consulting & Clinical Psychology, 56,* 448–451.

Greenberg, L. S., & Pinsof, W. M. (1986). Process research: Current trends and future perspectives. In L. S. Greenberg & W. M. Pinsof (Eds.), *The psychotherapeutic process* (pp. 3–20). New York: Guilford.

Greenberg, L. S., & Safran, J. D. (1984). Integrating affect and cognition: A perspective on the process of therapeutic change. *Cognitive Therapy and Research, 8,* 559–578.

Greenberg, L. S., & Safran, J. D. (1987). *Emotion in psychotherapy: Affect, cognition, and the process of change.* New York: Guilford.

Greenberg, M. T., Siegel, J. M., & Leitch, C. J. (1983). The nature and importance of attachment relationships to parents and peers during adolescence. *Journal of Youth & Adolescence, 12,* 373–386.

Grotevant, H. D., & Cooper, C. R. (Eds.) (1983). *Adolescent development in the family.* San Francisco: Jossey-Bass.

Gurman, A. S. (1988). Issues in the specification of family therapy interventions. In L. C. Wynne (Ed.), *The state of the art in family therapy research: Controversies and recommendations.* New York: Family Process Press.

Haley, J. (1973). *Uncommon therapy.* New York: Norton.

Haley, J. (1976). *Problem solving therapy.* San Francisco: Jossey-Bass.

Haley, J. (1980). *Leaving home.* New York: McGraw-Hill.

Hall, G. S. (1904). *Adolescence: Its psychology and relation to psychology, anthropology, sociology, sex, crime, religion, and education.* Englewood Cliffs, NJ: Prentice-Hall.

Hartrup, W. (1979). Two social worlds of childhood. *American Psychologist, 39,* 955–960.

Hauser, S. T., Borman, E. H., Jacobson, A. M., Powers, S. I., & Noam, G. G. (1991). Understanding family context of adolescent coping: A study of parental ego development and adolescent coping strategies. *Journal of Early Adolescence, 1,* 96–124.

Hauser, S. T., & Follansbee, D. (1984). Developing identity: Ego growth and change during adolescence. In H. Fitzgerald, B. Lester, & M. Yogman (Eds.), *Theory and research in behavioral pediatrics.* New York: Plenum.

Hauser, S. T., Houlihan, J., Powers, S. I., Jacobson, A. M., Noam, G. G., Weiss-Perry, B., Follansbee, D., & Book, B. K. (in press). Adolescent ego development within the family: Family styles and family sequences. *International Journal of Behavioral Development.*

Hauser, S. T., Powers, S. I., Noam, G., & Bowlds, M. K. (1987). Family interiors of adolescent ego development trajectories. *Family Perspective, 21,* 263–282.

Hauser, S. T., Powers, S., Noam, G. G., Jacobson, A. M., Weiss, B., & Follansbee, D. J. (1984). Family context of adolescent ego development. *Child Development, 55,* 195–213.

Henggeler, S. W., Rodick, J. D., Bourduin, C. M., Hanson, C. L., Watson, S. M., & Urey, J. R. (1986). Multisystemic treatment of juvenile offenders: Effects on adolescent behavior and family interaction. *Developmental Psychology, 22,* 132–141.

Hill, J. P. (1980). The family. In M. Johnson & K. J. Rehage (Eds.), *Toward adolescence: The middle school years. Part I.* Chicago: University of Chicago Press.

Hill, J. P., & Holmbeck, G. N. (1986). Attachment and autonomy during adolescence. In G. T. Whitehurst (Ed.), *Annals of child development* (Vol. 3, pp. 145–189). Greenwich, CT: JAI Press.

Hoffman, L. (1981). *Foundations of family therapy.* New York: Basic Books.

Institute of Medicine Report. (1989). *Research on children and adolescents with mental, behavioral & developmental disorders.* U.S. Department of Health and Human Services, Public Health Service, Alcohol, Drug Abuse, and Mental Health Administration.

Jessor, R., & Jessor, S. L. (1977). The social-psychological framework. In R. Jessor & S. L. Jessor (Eds.), *Problem behavior & psychosocial development: A longitudinal study of youth* (pp. 17–42). New York: Academic Press.

Jurich, A. (1990, July/August). The jujitsu approach: Confronting the belligerent adolescent. *Family Therapy Networker, 43–45,* 47, 64.

Kandel, D. B., Kessler, R. C., & Margulies, R. Z. (1978). Antecedents of adolescent initiation into stages of drug use: A developmental analysis. *Journal of Youth and Adolescence, 7*(1).

Kaslow, F. W. (Ed.). *Voices in family psychology, Volumes I and II.* Newbury Park, CA: Sage.

Kaslow, F. W. (1987). Trends in family psychology. *Journal of Family Psychology, 1,* 77–90.

Kaufman, E. (1985). Family systems and family therapy of substance abuse: An overview of two decades of research and clinical experience. *International Journal of the Addictions, 20,* 697–916.

Kazdin, A. E. (1982). Symptom substitution, generalization, and response covariation: Implications for psychotherapy outcome. *Psychological Bulletin, 91,* 349–365.

Kazdin, A. E. (1987). Treatment of antisocial behavior in children: Current status and future directions. *Psychological Bulletin, 102,* 187–203.

Kazdin, A. E. (1989). Developmental psychopathology: Current research, issues and directions. *American Psychologist, 44,* 180–187.

Kazdin, A. E., Bass, D., Ayers, W. A., & Rodgers, A. (1990). Empirical and clinical focus of child and adolescent psychotherapy research. *Journal of Consulting and Clinical Psychology, 58,* 729–740.

Kendall, P. C., Lerner, R. M., & Craighead, W. E. (1984). Human Development and Intervention in Childhood Psychopathology. *Child Development, 55,* 71–82.

Koestler, A. (1979). *Janus.* New York: Basic.

Lambert, M. J., & Ogles, B. M. (1988). Treatment manuals: Problems and promise. *Journal of Integrative and Eclectic Psychotherapy, 7,* 187–204.

Larson, R. W. (1983). Adolescents' daily experiences with family and friends: Contrasting opportunity systems. *Journal of Marriage and the Family, 45,* 739–750.

Lazarus, R., Coyne, J., & Folkman, S. (1982). Cognition, emotion, and motivation: The doctoring of Humpty-Dumpty. In R. W. J. Neufeld (Ed.), *Psychological stress and psychopathology.* New York: McGraw Hill.

Lebow, J. L. (1987). Developing a personal integration in family therapy: Principles for model construction and practice. *Journal of Marital and Family Therapy, 13,* 1–14.

Lerner, R. M. (1978). Nature, nurture and dynamic interactionism. *Human Development, 21,* 1–20.

Levine, B. L. (1985). Adolescent substance abuse: Toward an integration family systems and individual adaptation theories. *American Journal of Family Therapy, 13,* 3–16.

Lewis, R. A., Piercy, F. P., Sprenkle, D. H., & Trepper, T. S. (1990). Family-based interventions for helping drug-abusing adolescents. *Journal of Adolescent Research, 50,* 82–95.

Liddle, H. A. (1982). Review of *Foundations of family therapy: A conceptual for systems change. American Journal of Family Therapy, 10,* 76–83.

Liddle, H. A. (Ed.) (1983). *Clinical implications of the family life cycle.* Rockville, MD: Aspen Publications.

Liddle, H. A. (1984). Toward a dialectical-contextual-coevolutionary translation of structural-strategic family therapy. *Journal of Strategic and Systemic Therapies, 4,* 66–79.

Liddle, H. A. (1985). Five factors of failure in structural-strategic family therapy: A contextual construction: In S. Coleman (Ed.), *Failures in family therapy.* New York: Guilford.

Liddle, H. A. (1987a). Family psychology: The journal, the field. *Journal of Family Psychology, 1,*(1), 5–22.

Liddle, H. A. (1987b). Family psychology: Tasks of an emerging (and emerged) discipline. *Journal of Family Psychology, 1,*(2), 149–167.

Liddle, H. A. (1988a). Developmental thinking and the family life cycle: Implications for training family therapists. In C. Falicov (Ed.), *Family transitions.* New York: Guilford.

Liddle, H. A. (1988b). Systemic supervision: Conceptual and pragmatic guidelines. In H. A. Liddle, D. C. Breunlin, & R. C. Schwartz (Eds.), *Handbook of family therapy training and supervision.* New York: Guilford.

Liddle, H. A. (1990). What's wrong with family therapy? Presentation at symposium "What's wrong with family therapy?" at the 1990 AAMFT meeting, Washington, DC.

Liddle, H. A. (1991a). The adolescents and families project: Multidimensional family therapy in action. In *ADAMHA monograph from the first national conference on the treatment of adolescent drug, alcohol and mental health problems.* Washington, DC: United States Public Health Service, Government Printing Office.

Liddle, H. A. (1991b). Engaging the adolescent in family systems therapy. In T. Nelson (Ed.), *Interventions in family therapy.* New York: Haworth.

Liddle, H. A. (1991c). Family therapy training and supervision: A comprehensive review and critique. In A. Gurman & D. Kniskern (Eds.), *Handbook of family therapy* (2nd ed.). New York: Brunner/Mazel.

Liddle, H. A. (1991d). Empirical values and the culture of family therapy. *Journal of Marital and Family Therapy, 17,* 327–348.

Liddle, H. A., Dakof, G., Parker, K., & Diamond, G. (1991, August). *Anatomy of a clinical research project.* Paper presented at the American Psychological Association Meeting, San Francisco.

Liddle, H. A., & Schmidt, S. (1991). *Family therapy with drug abusing adolescents: The state of the art.* Invited technical report prepared for the NIDA meeting on the five year plan for the Treatment Research Branch, Bethesda, Maryland, February 7–8.

Liddle, H. A., Schmidt, S., & Ettinger, D. (in press). Adolescent development research: Guidelines for clinicians. *Journal of Marital and Family Therapy.*

Loeber, R. (1985). The patterns and development of antisocial child behavior. *Annals of Child Development, 2,* 77–116.

Madanes, C. (1981). *Strategic family therapy.* San Francisco: Jossey-Bass.

Madanes, C. (1985). *Behind the one way mirror.* San Francisco: Jossey-Bass.

Maddahian, E., Newcomb, M. D., & Bentler, P. M. (1986). Adolescents' substance use: Impact of ethnicity, income, and availability. In *Alcohol and substance abuse in women and children.* New York: Haworth Press.

Magnusson, D. (1988). *Individual development from an interactional perspective: A longitudinal study.* Hillsdale, NJ: Lawrence Erlbaum.

Mahoney, M. J. (1984). Integrating cognition, affect, and action: A comment. *Cognitive therapy and research, 8,* 585–589.

Mahrer, A. R. (1988a). Discovery oriented psychotherapy research: Rationale, aims and methods. *American Psychologist, 43,* 694–702.

Mahrer, A. R. (1988b). Research and clinical applications of "good moments" in psychotherapy. *Journal of Integrative Eclectic Psychotherapy, 7,* 81–93.

Miller, G. E., & Prinz, R. J. (1991). Enhancement of social learning family interventions for childhood conduct disorders. *Psychological Bulletin, 108,* 291–307.

Minuchin, S. (1974). *Families and family therapy.* Cambridge, MA: Harvard University Press.

Minuchin, S., & Fishman, H. C. (1981). *Family therapy technique.* Cambridge, MA: Harvard University Press.

Nadelman, E. A. (1989). Drug prohibition in the United States: Costs, consequences, and alternatives. *Science, 245,* 939–947.

National Institute on Drug Abuse (Treatment Research Branch). (1991). Meeting on the five year plan for the Treatment Research Branch of NIDA, Bethesda, Maryland, February 7–8.

Newcomb, M. D., & Bentler, P. M. (1988). Impact of adolescent drug use and social support on problems of young adults: A longitudinal study. *Journal of Abnormal Psychology, 97,* 64–75.

Newcomb, M. D., & Harlow, L. L. (1986). Life events and substance use among adolescents: Mediating effects of perceived loss of control and meaninglessness in life. *Journal of Personality & Social Psychology, 51,* 564–577.

Newcomb, M. D., Maddahian, E., & Bentler, P. M. (1986). Risk factors for drug use among adolescents: Concurrent & Longitudinal analysis. *American Journal of Public Health, 76,* 525-531.

Nichols, M. (1987). *The self in the system.* New York: Brunner/Mazel.

Offer, D., Ostrov, E., & Howard, K. I. (1981). The mental health professional's concept of the normal adolescent. *Archives of General Psychiatry, 38,* 149-152.

Pandina, R. J., & Schuele, J. A. (1983). Psychosocial correlates of alcohol and drug use of adolescent students and adolescents in treatment. *Journal of Studies on Alcohol, 44,* 950-973.

Patterson, G. R., Dishion, T. J., & Bank, L. (in press). Family interaction: A process model of deviancy training. In L. Eron (Ed.), special edition of *Aggressive Behavior,* in press.

Peele, S. (1986a). The "cure' for adolescent drug abuse: Worse than the problem. *Journal of Counseling and Development, 65,* 23-24.

Peele, S. (1986b). The dominance of the disease theory in American ideas about and treatment of alcoholism. *American Psychology, 323.*

Peele, S. (1986c). The implications and limitations of genetic models of alcoholism and other addictions. *Journal of Studies on Alcohol, 76,* 63-73.

Pinsof, W. M. (1988). A conceptual framework and methodological criteria for family therapy research. *Journal of Consulting and Clinical Psychology, 57,* 1-7.

Pinsof, W. M., & Catherall, D. R. (1986). The integrative psychotherapy alliance; Family, couple and individual therapy scales. *Journal of Marital and Family Therapy, 12,* 137-151.

Pittman, F. S. (1987). *Turning points.* New York: Norton.

Reilly, D. M. (1975). Family factors in the etiology and treatment of youthful drug abuse. *Family Therapy, 2,* 149-171.

Reilly, D. M. (1979). Drug-abusing families: Intrafamilial dynamics and brief triphasic treatment. In E. Kaufman & P. N. Kaufmann (Eds.), *Family therapy of drug and alcohol abuse.* New York: Gardner Press.

Reilly, D. M. (1984). Family therapy with adolescent drug abusers and their families: Defying gravity and achieving escape velocity. *Journal of Drug Issues, 14,* 381-390.

Rieder, C., & Cicchetti, D. (1990). Organizational perspective on cognitive control functioning and cognitive-affective balance in maltreated children. *Developmental Psychology, 25,* 382-393.

Robin, A. L., & Foster, S. L. (1989). *Negotiating parent adolescent conflict: A behavioral-family systems approach.* New York: Guilford.

Rutter, M., & Sroufe, L. A. (1984). The domain of developmental psychopathology. *Child Development, 55,* 17-29.

Ryan, R. M., & Lynch, J. H. (1989). Emotional autonomy versus detachment: Revising the vicissitudes of adolescence and young adulthood. *Child Development, 60,* 340-356.

Safran, J. D. (1990a). Towards a refinement of cognitive therapy in light of interpersonal theory: I. Theory. *Clinical Psychology Review, 10,* 87-105.

Safran, J. D. (1990b). Towards a refinement of cognitive therapy in light of interpersonal theory: II. Practice. *Clinical Psychology Review, 10,* 107-121.

Safran, J. D., Crocker, P., McMain, S., & Murray, P. (1990). Therapeutic alliance rupture as a therapy event for empirical investigation. *Psychotherapy, 27,* 154-165.

Schwartz, R. C. (1987). Our multiple selves. *The Family Therapy Networker, 11,* 25–31, 80–83.

Schwartz, R. C. (1988). Know thy selves. *The Family Therapy Networker, 12,* 21–29.

Shantz, C. V. (1983). Social cognition. In J. H. Flavell & E. M. Markman (Eds.), *Handbook of child psychology, Vol. 3: Cognitive development* (pp. 495–555). New York: Wiley.

Shirk, S. R. (Ed.) (1988). *Cognitive development and child psychotherapy.* New York: Plenum.

Siegel, I. (1982). *Parental belief systems.* Hillsdale, NJ: Lawrence Erlbaum.

Solomon, M. (1973). A developmental conceptual premise for family therapy. *Family Process, 12,* 179–188.

Stanton, M. D. (1981). An integrated structural/strategic approach to family therapy. *Journal of Marital and Family Therapy, 7,* 427–439.

Stanton, M. D. (1984). Fusion, compression, diversion, and the workings of paradox: A theory of therapeutic/systemic change. *Family Process, 23,* 135–168.

Stanton, M. D. (1988). The lobster quadrille: Issues and dilemmas for family therapy research. In L. C. Wynne (Ed.), *The state of the art in family therapy research: controversies and recommendations* (pp. 7–31). New York: Family Process Press.

Stanton, M. D. (1991). *Outcome research on family treatment for drug abuse: Implications for practitioners.* Presentation at the NIDA Conference on Drug Abuse Research and Practice. Washington, DC, January 12–15.

Stanton, M. D., Todd, T. C., and associates. (1982). *The family therapy of drug abuse and addiction.* New York: Guilford.

Steinberg, L. (1990). Autonomy, conflict, and harmony in the family relationship. In S. S. Feldman & G. R. Elliott (Eds.), *At the threshold: The developing adolescent* (pp. 255–276). Cambridge, MA: Harvard University Press.

Steinberg, L., & Silverberg, S. (1986). The vicissitudes of autonomy in early adolescence. *Child Development, 57,* 841–851.

Stratton, P. (1988). Spirals & circles: Potential contributions of developmental psychology to family therapy. *Journal of family therapy, 10,* 207–231.

Szapocznik, J., Kurtines, W., Santisteban, D. A., & Rio, A. T. (1990). Interplay of advances between theory, research, and applications in treatment interventions aimed at behavior problem children and adolescents. *Journal of Consulting and Clinical Psychology, 58,* 696–703.

Szapocznik, J., Perez-Vidal, A., Brickman, A. L., et al. (1988). Engaging adolescent drug abusers and their families in treatment a strategic structural systems approach. *Journal of Consulting and Clinical Psychology, 56,* 552–557.

Szapocznik, J., Perez-Vidal, A., Brickman, A. L., Foote, F. H., Santiseban, D., Hervis, O., & Kurtines, W. M. (1988). Engaging adolescent drug abusers and their families in treatment: A strategic structural systems approach. *Journal of Consulting and Clinical Psychology, 56,* 552–557.

Tobler, N. (1986). Meta-analysis of 143 adolescent drug prevention programs. *Journal of Drug Issues, 16,* 537–567.

Todd, T. C. (1986). Structural-strategic marital therapy. In N. S. Jacobson & A. S. Gurman (Eds.), *Clinical handbook of marital therapy* (pp. 71–105). New York: Guilford Press.

Todd, T. C. (1990, November). Presentation at ADAMHA Conference on Mental Health and Drug Abuse Problems of Adolescents. Washington, DC.

Todd, T. C., & Selekman, M. D. (1990a). Beyond structural-strategic family therapy. In T. Todd & M. Selekman (Eds.), *Family therapy with adolescent substance abusers*. Boston: Allyn and Bacon.

Todd, T. C., & Selekman, M. (1990b). Principles of family therapy for adolescent substance abuse. In P. H. Tolan (Ed.), *Multisystemic structural-strategic interventions for child and adolescent behavior problems* (pp. 49–70. New York: Haworth.

Tolan, P. H. (1990). Introduction: Treating behavioral problems from a multi-level structural-strategic approach. *Journal of Psychotherapy and the Family, 6,* 1–8.

Tramontana, M. G. (1980). Critical review of research on psychotherapy outcome with adolescents: 1967–1987. *Psychological Bulletin, 88,* 429–450.

Volk, R. J., Edwards, D. W., Lewis, R. A., & Sprenkle, D. H. (1989). Family systems of adolescent substance abusers. *Family Relations, 38,* 266–272.

Wachtel, P. L. (1977). *Psychoanalysis and behavior therapy: Toward an integration*. New York: Basic Books.

Weisz, J. R., Weiss, B., Alicke, M. D., & Klotz, M. L. (1987). Effectiveness of psychotherapy with children and adolescents: A meta-analysis for clinicians. *Journal of Consulting and Clinical Psychology, 55,* 542–549.

Wills, T. A. (1990). Social support and the family. In E. A. Blechman (Ed.), *Emotions and the family: For better or worse*. Hillsdale, NJ: Erlbaum.

Wills, T. A., & Vaughn, R. (1989). Social support and smoking in early adolescence. *Journal of Behavioral Medicine, 12,* 321–339.

CHAPTER ELEVEN

Stepfamilies and Substance Abuse: Unique Treatment Considerations

JUDITH ZUCKER ANDERSON, PH.D.
University of California, Irvine

Stepfamilies may prove to be the traditional American family of the next century. The rising divorce rate and high incidence of remarriage have resulted in the stepfamily becoming an increasingly common phenomenon. It has been estimated that over 35 million adults are stepparents and that one in every five children is a stepchild. Demographers anticipate that 45 percent of American children born in the 1980s will experience a parental divorce and 35 percent will live with a stepparent before their eighteenth birthday (Glick, 1984).

In our experience, we would predict these numbers to be even greater in families where at least one parent is a substance abuser. Substance abusers frequently come from as well as create stepfamilies. The substance abuser often has a history of marital instability and difficulty sustaining intimate attachments, yet, with strong dependency needs, he or she is likely to remarry and often create a series of blended families as marriages fall apart and children are left behind. It is also common for the substance abuser to have had a family of origin experience of parental strife, divorce, and several remarriages (as is true in many dysfunctional families) (Kaufman & Kaufmann, 1979).

Despite the tremendous growth of stepfamilies in the general population, there has been a dearth, until recently, of empirical investigation into the nature of interaction among stepfamily members, the stages through which stepfamilies go in order to form a family unit, and how they are similar to or different from intact families. Indeed, most of the early literature on stepfamilies consists of case studies and anecdotal reports focusing primarily on clinical, dysfunctional samples of such families. This has led to a rather gloomy portrait of stepfamily life and supports folktales and myths about "evil stepmothers" and the fear of being "treated like a stepchild." In American culture, the primary model for normal family life has long been the nuclear family unit of two parents and their offspring. Although this image of the family is no longer normal in the statistical sense, it is still held as an ideal in terms of its cultural, social, and psychological desirability. Stepfamilies and therapists alike have a tendency to evaluate the stepfamily by using the nuclear family as the ideal.

This creates a deficit model that is both inaccurate and damaging for stepfamilies. Stepfamilies need to be evaluated by use of their own norms. It is crucial for family therapists to expand the traditional concept of normal family processes to include what a well-functioning stepfamily looks like and to know the typical patterns of dysfunction. In the past decade, much more empirical and clinical information has become available to comprehensively delineate stepfamily processes and to develop stepfamily norms that refute many old stereotypes while still emphasizing the complexity and formidable nature of blending families.

The relevance of an identified patient's symptoms to unresolved issues related to stepfamily formation are often not even considered in treatment planning. Or, other times, armed with only a nuclear model of family functioning, the therapist may examine stepfamily issues, but may select inappropriate or even destructive goals for the treatment of step-relationships. Of course, stepfamilies may end up feeling like a failure because they cannot re-create a nuclear family structure and feel like they should. The therapist should not reinforce such maladaptive ideas.

It seems obvious to state the necessity for clinicians working with substance abuse families to be well versed in the field of chemical dependency. Yet, since such a large percentage of these substance-abusing families will also be stepfamilies, so too is it necessary to understand the unique and inherent clinical issues involved in stepfamily systems.

An extensive literature search in 1989 showed only two articles that even remotely discussed any issues of stepfamilies and substance abuse (Blechman, Berberian, & Thompson, 1977; DeBlois, 1983). This chapter will address the important issues involved in treating stepfamilies and highlight the particular aspects of substance-abusing stepfamilies. It should be emphasized that adding substance abuse as an extra factor to the process of stepfamily integration can intensify and complicate matters exponentially. The focus of this chapter will include (1) key inherent differences between stepfamilies and nuclear families, (2) major developmental tasks of stepfamily formation, (3) assessment of stepfamily functioning, and (4) effective intervention techniques for dealing with stepfamily issues.

Key Inherent Differences between Stepfamilies and Nuclear Families

Many problems in stepfamilies are found in all family relationships yet are often exaggerated due to the complexity of the stepfamily structure. There are many unique characteristics that inherently create obstacles in the process of stepfamily formation that are simply "givens" in providing members of a nuclear family with a sense of identity and belonging.

The psychic and physical boundaries that provide structure and comfort in the nuclear family are much more permeable in a stepfamily. The most basic physical boundary of the family home needs to be expanded to include other households so that stepfamily members can maintain access to their biological parents or children living elsewhere. The physical boundaries of home get blurred as children continually leave and return from their visits. Affectional bonds and loyalties cross boundaries to the noncustodial parent. Parental authority is often shared by an ex-spouse residing in another household.

Decision making regarding children can become quite complex when effective coparenting involves not only the two parents in the family working together but requires the negotiation of a cooperative relationship with the noncustodial parent. Cooperation between households is also necessary to reduce many of the loyalty conflicts that arise for children when their parents are divorced and a new adult has entered their lives as an additional parenting figure. Such conflicts are simply not issues in nuclear families.

Unlike "given" relationships in the nuclear family, roles and relationships are ambiguous and lack clear cultural guidelines. Children growing up have not played house practicing how to be a stepparent. Finally, the stepfamily lacks a history of shared experiences and rituals that aid a family in building relationships and maintaining its own unique identity. Many stepfamily members often speak of "culture shock"—an acute feeling of an unfamiliar, sometimes alien, environment that is very disorienting to their basic sense of what "my family" is.

For nuclear families, the usual ups and downs of daily living have an underpinning of a largely unconscious foundation of thousands of moments of shared experience and caring. This missing foundation in the stepfamily necessitates that its primary task be the integration of separate individuals from different family cultures into a new workable family structure.

Major Stepfamily Developmental Tasks

A new stepfamily's main goal is to create a new family culture and to develop a positive identity as a viable family unit. "The primary source of problems in remarriage involves the children from the first marriage and their resistance to accepting the remarriage family" (Kaufman & Kaufmann, 1979, p. 430). Approximately 40 percent of remarriages end within five years, with the presence of children from a previous marriage cited as the key factor in the divorce (Glick & Sungshin, 1986; Visher & Visher, 1988).

Many of the problems that paralyze remarried families are created by their intense struggle to feel like a "real" family. As Visher and Visher state, "Adults and children in stepfamilies come together suddenly with little connectedness or trust. As they work to gain their equilibrium, it is not that the homeostasis of the family has broken down; rather, new stepfamily groups have never had stability. Achieving this basic stability is their task" (Sager, Brown, Crohn & Walker, 1983, p. 22).

There are many ways therapists can help stepfamilies negotiate this complicated journey. First, the therapist should view the stepfamily as working through a series of developmental stages that are unique to step-families. The following are the stages a stepfamily must resolve in order to achieve the basic task of stepfamily integration before they can begin dealing with the issues that take place in all types of families. These stages are discussed at length elsewhere (Minuchin & Fishman, 1981; Visher & Visher, 1979, 1988). It is generally agreed that it takes from 1½ to 2 years for most stepfamilies to reach this basic level of integration. (Hetherington, Cos & Cox, 1985; Visher & Visher, 1988). These stages are:

1. Mourning the losses
2. Establishing a strong couple bond
3. Structuring of family rules and roles
4. Creating a parenting coalition
5. Accepting of stepparent by stepchild and vice versa

Mourning the Losses

Stepfamilies are born of previous losses through divorce or death. The need to resolve earlier losses before being ready to form new attachments is the first developmental task in all stepfamilies. Children and adults in stepfamilies often have different timetables for resolving their mourning processes because the impact of the losses varies. The more typical losses for children are having to let go of the fantasy that the biological parents will reunite and fearing the loss of contact with the noncustodial parent. In divorce or death, remarriage often underscores the idealized image of the absent parent and triggers conflict about having to replace him or her with a stranger.

Sometimes children have reasonably resolved mourning the death or divorce experience if many years have passed. Great turmoil can be experienced instead in the loss of their special role and the intense closeness to their parent that evolves in a long-term single-parent family. Giving up the privileged position of being mom's little man of the house or dad's special girl can be very difficult. The losses can be more intense when the noncustodial parent in the original family has been a substance abuser. In that case, it is likely that the custodial parent and opposite sex child have been enmeshed and the child has been elevated to a quasi-spousal position, not just since the divorce, but for years.

The adults in stepfamilies may have to mourn the failure of a previously shattered marriage or the pain of an unexpected death before they can fully invest in their new marriage. A stepparent who has never married before may have to grieve the loss of his or her fantasy of "perfect marriage dreams," which usually do not include someone else's children.

Dealing with such painful and messy emotions can seem contradictory to the joy of a new marriage. Many adults, caught up in the glow of new love and the hope of new-found happiness, will deny their own darker feelings and exert covert pressure to move on from the past quickly and get involved in the new family. Yet empathy and respect for each family member's differential readiness to complete any unfinished mourning and overt permission to have those feelings is exactly what is needed.

Since a hallmark of substance abuse is denial and self-medication to avoid emotional pain, one can easily see how a substance-abusing parent or stepparent can pose a major obstacle to the resolution of this task for the entire family. In a similar vein, a substance-abusing adolescent, who denies his or her internal reality, is likely to stay stuck in this stage and be unable to develop new attachments in the stepfamily. It is important to emphasize that once the substance abuser is abstinent and in treatment, and the veil of denial is lifted, the intensity of these unexpressed losses may come flooding out in full force. The family's denial lifts only if they have lived with the substance abuser long enough to develop denial patterns.

Establishing a Strong Couple Bond

A key developmental task in a stepfamily is the establishment of a strong couple bond to provide the basic glue necessary for holding the family together. A primary difficulty in nurturing coupleness in a remarriage, of course, is the immediate presence of children. The luxury of a "honeymoon phase" with lots of private time, taken for granted in first marriages, is simply nonexistent. The remarried couple may enjoy occasional privacy when their children are away visiting the noncustodial parent or when the stepparent's children are not visiting them. These special times should be nurtured and guilt about enjoying them relieved.

To nurture a couple's bond effectively requires that the adults actively give their relationship a high priority and be able to set clear boundaries for privacy despite the children being around. One couple, for example, put a sign on their bedroom door occasionally that reads "Please don't knock unless you are bleeding or the house is burning down!" The children learned in a playful yet serious way that the adults' time alone was to be respected.

It is also necessary to respond flexibly to the children's needs versus the couple's needs in any given situation and to be willing to sacrifice one's own immediate wishes at times. This is, or course, much harder to do as a stepparent when he or she may not have an inherent investment or be attuned to the children's needs.

When the stepparent is also a substance abuser, it is likely that he or she will be more self-focused and lack the flexibility to be sensitive to the subtle needs of others. It is also likely that both the substance abuser and the codependent partner have had problems in being intimate in relationships in their past. Such a deficit in knowing how to connect intimately to another person will certainly increase their ambivalence in making their coupleness a priority.

Structuring of Family Rules and Roles

Stepfamilies are instantly expected to function as a family unit with no guiding foundation, unlike first-marriage families, where the rules and roles governing family behavior gradually evolve over many years. Thus, an important task in creating a basic level of family organization is to make explicit how basic operations of daily living may be different now that the families have merged.

It is important to acknowledge feelings of "culture shock" that are expectable reactions to different ways of living. A seemingly minor shift like changing the usual family dinnertime from 5:30 to 7:00 P.M. because stepfather works later can trigger intense reactions.

Rules about discipline and decision making must be clarified, particularly to outline clearly what role the stepparent will take. This requires that the adults, first, be frank and direct with each other about their wishes and expectations. Then, depending on the ages of the children, more or less input regarding their preferences can be elicited.

There is a wide range of what is viable in terms of a stepparent role— adult friend, supporter, or monitor of the biological parent's discipline; an additional parent figure; or a true substitute parent when the noncustodial parent is dead or absent. It is easiest for a stepparent to take a more active parenting role when children are young, and usually extremely difficult to parent adolescents directly as a new stepparent.

Another important issue that must be addressed in this stage is the preservation of the specialness of the biological relationships in the stepfamily that predate the new marriage. As noted earlier, many children suffer an extreme sense of loss in the connection they had enjoyed with their biological parent prior to the remarriage. They need to be reassured, both in words and actions, that their special bond is still there. In the interests of creating a new family and being fair to everyone, the reality of stronger alliances existing between biological relationships over step-relationships is often denied or seen as something bad. Children need some time alone with their biological parent. (Just as couples need to nurture their new bond, children need the reassurance that their old bond continues.)

When one of the adults is a substance abuser, there is likely to be difficulty in problem solving in a straightforward style. Substance abusers are not accustomed to tackling problems head-on and dealing with touchy issues directly. When one or more of the children is a substance abuser, there may be so many immediate acting-out crises to respond to that push the parents toward a tendency to overcontrol and to be less receptive to creating a more negotiable structure that chaos may result. The stepparent may get fed up quickly and want to give up parenting or the marriage.

Creating a Parenting Coalition

Once bonding between the new couple has taken place and suitable stepparenting roles have been established, the next task is to figure out a cooperative system of sharing childrearing responsibilities with the children's other household. This concept of a "parenting coalition" includes all the primary caretaking adults in both households after one or both spouses have remarried (Sager, Brown, Crohn, & Walker, 1983). It is an expanded definition of the recognized ideal of "coparenting" as a key factor in children's adjustment after divorce. That is, research and clinical observation strongly indicate that maintaining parent-child contact with both parents is most advantageous for children, although it may pose great difficulties for the adults involved (Hetherington, Cos & Cox, 1985; Wald, 1981).

Children function better and are happier when their parents and stepparents have civil and cooperative relationships. Many of the loyalty conflict that arise after remarriage can be alleviated when children are kept out of the middle of adult struggles. Also, if a child's fear of losing contact with his or her noncustodial parent is ameliorated, the child is more likely to form a better relationship with a new stepparent (Hetherington, Cos, & Cox, 1985; Sager et al., 1983). In addition, when children can visit comfortfortably between two households, the remarried couple can occasionally have some "time alone" to nurture their own relationship.

Of course, developing such clear and cooperative relationships between custodial parents, noncustodial parents, and their new spouses and ex-spouses can be a formidable task. It requires a level of maturity that encourages the primary focus to stay consistently on the best interests of the child, despite unavoidable emotional sidetracks triggered by old marital conflicts or new competitive jealousies. Coparenting agreements that may have been workable prior to one spouse's remarriage usually need to be renegotiated once a stepparent becomes involved in childrearing responsibilities. The crucial task is for the adults to set up a structure of nurturance and discipline that defines for the children clear yet permeable boundaries between the households. Children can adjust to different standards and rules in each household as long as the adults stay clear and consistent. When biological or stepparents are unclear or inconsistent about their roles, children are very likely to use the ambiguity to manipulate.

Before encouraging the formation of a parenting coalition, however, it must first be clear that there are no factors that make such an arrangement unadvisable. When the noncustodial parent is a substance abuser, the child may be at physical or emotional risk if allowed to have regular, prolonged visits. Any indications of parental nonresponsibility or potential dangers must be carefully assessed along with the extent of the substance abuse.

If a serious problem is validated, then monitored visitation may be necessary. For instance, the child may maintain contact by having brief visits with another responsible adult present or perhaps in the grandparents' home. It should be emphasized that maintaining minimal contact with the dysfunctional parent can be crucial for children, except in truly dangerous situations. It is crucial because an absence of contact can seriously lower a child's self-esteem as the parental withdrawal is often personalized. That is, the child feels that he or she must have done something terribly wrong that caused the parent to disappear from his or her life. Or, if the child understands that the parent has a drinking or drug problem that prevents contact, he or she may think, "If daddy really loved me, he would stop drinking so he could see me" or "If I only knew what to say or do, I could stop it." And when it does not happen, the conclusion of not being loved is devastating.

Accepting of Stepparent by Stepchild and Vice Versa

It is generally agreed that a major developmental task of stepfamily integration involves resolution of the dilemma of inclusion versus exclusion of step-related persons into the family unit (Sager et al., 1983; Visher & Visher, 1979). That is, in order for successful stepfamily integration to occur, the child must reach a level of acceptance of the stepparent as a permanent part of his or her new definition of family. Similarly, the stepparent must come to terms with the reality that his or her spouse's child is part of the package in this new marriage. The stepparent must then develop some way of including the child in his or her concept of the new family unit.

Acceptance is the key attitude. This does not mean loving each other. Expectations to love instantly often make it impossible to just accept each other's presence. Yet, until basic acceptance occurs, step-related persons cannot really begin to consider investing an attachment in this new person. Other factors that pose obstacles to acceptance are loyalty conflicts on both sides; that is, the stepchild's fear of attaching to a stepparent as a sign of disloyalty to the noncustodial parent, or the stepparent's guilt at building a relationship with the stepchild and not giving to his or her own biological children living elsewhere or even in the home.

When the stepchild is a substance abuser, the stepparent is often frustrated and angry at having to deal with all the crises and the amount of attention required by the biological parent to handle the acting-out. The stepparent will then resist accepting the stepchild as part of his or her life with the understandable attitude of "I did not bargain for all this trouble and high drama."

When the stepparent is a substance abuser, the stepchild may experience the stepparent's often unpredictable behavior as a basis to mistrust or disrespect him or her. If the child's natural father was also a substance abuser, and mother has remarried another substance abuser, as is often the case, the child may shut down all possibility of connecting to the stepparent. The child's internal belief that it is not safe to count on a father in any consistent way will be confirmed and he or she will often take the position that "this guy does not belong in my family and I wish he would go away and leave us alone." The oldest child may also exhibit extreme protectiveness toward his mother, seeing it as his job to protect her and the family from further trauma.

Assessment of Stepfamily Functioning

With such a developmental perspective as outlined above, the therapist is in a position to assess at which stage the stepfamily seems stuck. If all stepfamilies go through these stages, it is important to know what factors are involved in those who make the transition successfully and those who get stuck. Following are assessment guidelines for therapists based on the most current clinical and research information. Particular emphasis is placed on how stepfamily functioning is different from what may be expected from traditional intact family norms (based on family systems theory).

Marital Subsystem

A basic family systems theory axiom is that where there is a symptomatic child, a distressed marriage is generally likely. Current research suggests that many stepfamilies may have very good marital relationships and still develop family dysfunction. To put it another way, stepfamily dysfunction does not necessarily signify a poor couple relationship (Anderson & White, 1986; Crosbie-Burnett, 1984; Sager et al., 1983). In fact, when compared to dysfunctional nuclear families, dysfunctional stepfamilies have significantly better marital adjustment (Anderson & White, 1986). The clinical implication is that the therapist should not assume marital difficulty when a stepfamily presents itself for treatment.

How can it be explained that dysfunctional stepfamilies do not fit the expected family system hypothesis? It may be that family dysfunction in nuclear families is due to marital conflict that spills over into the general family functioning. This is supported by marital research indicating that many unhappy first-marriage couples stay together for the sake of the children, or at least delay divorce until the children are grown (Glenn & Weaver, 1978; Kanoy & Miller, 1980). Thus, children are the glue holding the unhappy marriage together, which creates a fertile ground for family dysfunction. On the other hand, in a remarried family, the husband and wife have already been through a divorce and have chosen to marry each other in spite of the possible unhappiness of either partner's children. The glue in this case is the marital bond rather then the couple's mutual concern for the children.

In sum, a couple bond provides the necessary glue to hold the family unit together, but is not sufficient to ensure that a positive step-relationship will develop. And, it is critical that a somewhat positive step-relationship ultimately develop. Many stepfamilies are splitting up, despite marital satisfaction, when step-relationships remain extremely distant or conflictual. This is dynamically a very different phenomenon than in first marriages.

Stepparent-Stepchild Subsystem

Reciprocally positive parent-child bonds are a hallmark of a functional family. Research consistently confirms that the parent-child relationships in nuclear families are stronger and more positive than the stepparent-stepchild bonds in stepfamilies.

The many cultural, legal, biological, and psychological factors discussed elsewhere (Visher & Visher, 1979, 1988) that pose inherent obstacles in stepfamilies to the typical parent-child bonding process suggest that it may be unreasonable to expect the same quality and degree of involvement as in nuclear families. An important issue is to what extent stepparent and stepchildren can form positive and reciprocal relationships. One must understand the qualitative differences between well-functioning and dysfunctional stepfamilies to use a more appropriate yardstick rather than measuring against intact family norms.

In well-functioning stepfamilies, the stepparent-stepchild relationship is characterized by a mutually positive but not very intense involvement. Both stepparent and stepchild are willing to invest in each other as a source of emotional gratification to a moderate degree. And both seem to accept each other as part of their new definition of family (Anderson & White, 1986).

This contrasts sharply with the extremely distant and/or rejecting stepparent-stepchild relationships found in dysfunctional stepfamilies (Anderson & White, 1986). Clinical impressions indicate that pressure for premature cohesion often results in just the opposite. Anecdotal data from stepchildren in treatment suggest how pushing for closeness backfires: "I wish they didn't make me call him 'dad'—he's not my dad—they can't make me love him, too!" or "My mom says I should be close to him, but I really miss my dad and don't want anything to do with him."

Not only is a lack of connection in step-relationships found in dysfunctional stepfamilies but often there is an active desire to exclude the other person from the family entirely. Research supports the clinical speculation that unresolved feelings of exclusion between stepparent and stepchild may impede stepfamily integration and relate to family dysfunction. The data specifically showed that in dysfunctional stepfamilies, 57 percent of the children assigned strong exclusion statements to their stepfathers and 44 percent of the stepfathers expressed a strong desire to exclude their stepchild from the family, Yet, in functional stepfamilies, only 12.5 percent of stepchildren and 6.3 percent of the stepfathers wished to exclude each other from the family. None of the children in either group assigned exclusion statements to their biological parent (Anderson & White, 1986). These results suggest that the functional stepfamilies have more successfully resolved the task of inclusion versus exclusion and are perhaps more able to proceed with establishing step-relationships. The issue of exclusion seems to rest mainly in the stepparent-stepchild relationship in dysfunctional stepfamilies. This need to exclude is even stronger when the stepparent or stepchild is a substance abuser.

Parent-Child Coalitions

Family theorists maintain that dysfunctional families are characterized by parent-child coalitions that disrupt effective family functioning. Inherent in the stepfamily is an imbalance in the structural arrangement of the biological, legal, and developmental ties husband and wife share toward the children they parent. The given asymmetrical position of the parent from the beginning creates a fertile ground for the development of natural parent-child coalitions. It is simply impossible for the stepparent to compensate for the lacking biological bond and powerful ties created over years of shared history. That is, the strength of the biological parent-child bonds creates a preference for biological over step-relationships even in a well-functioning stepfamily.

Functional stepfamilies exhibit a tendency for having natural parent-child coalitions. Dysfunctional stepfamilies demonstrate a significantly different, more extreme pattern of strong biological parent-child coalitions accompanied by a nonreciprocal or negative relationship with the stepparent-stepchild (Anderson & White, 1986). This suggests that when stepfamilies are compared with each other, rather than against nuclear family norms, a stepfamily can have moderate levels of parent-child coalitions and still function effectively as a family unit. But such a preference for biological relationships that may be workable in functional stepfamilies seems to be exaggerated and represents a more problematic pattern in dysfunctional stepfamilies.

Let us look at a typical stepfamily interaction described by a number of families in treatment that illustrates how parent-child coalitions can lead to family dysfunction. The child misbehaves and the stepparent attempts to discipline the child. The child resents the stepparent's attempt at authority and complains to her parent. The parent sides with the child without consulting the stepparent. The stepparent feels his actions have been undermined and, feeling tentative about his parental rights, he angrily withdraws. The child experiences the stepparent's withdrawal as rejection and further justifies his lack of involvement with this unavailable person.

Unintentionally or not, the parent has created a triangle that reinforces the parent-child coalition and that blocks interaction between stepparent and child. The ironic aspect is that even though the natural parent has largely contributed to this process, he or she may become unhappy with the stepparent's lack of involvement with the child and blame him or her for withdrawing, or blame the child for being so difficult.

The therapist must understand that such patterns develop not necessarily because there is a poor marital relationship but because the couple has not developed a clear parental subsystem that clearly defines and supports the stepparent's role and promotes direct contact between stepparent and stepchild. The active substance abuser's stepparent role will be even more undermined by each episode of intoxication or substance-abuse maladaptive behavior.

Adolescents in Stepfamilies

The developmental needs of an adolescent to separate and individuate are often in direct conflict with the stepfamily's need to build a cohesive family unit. Adolescents are more able to make conscious decisions than younger children about their desires to be an insider or outsider in the stepfamily. Their more sophisticated understanding of the complexities of family relationships can enable them to give valuable input to the family's formation as well as to know exactly how to be divisive.

Adolescence is often a time of changing long-standing custody arrangements. This can represent a child's positive developmental need to have increased contact and more identification with the noncustodial parent (usually the father) or it can be a potentially negative solution to the unresolved difficulties of stepfamily formation, especially between the stepparent and the adolescent.

The combination of stepparent-adolescent relationships is likely to create a lot of stress. Loyalty conflicts and difficulty with discipline from the stepparent are the major issues. Whiteside (1989) emphasizes, "In this combination of age and family stage, there should be no expectation that the stepparent will be able to assume an effective authoritative position directly in relation to the child" (p. 153). A useful parenting strategy for the stepparent of an adolescent is to support the parent in childrearing and discipline and to take a secondary parenting role, rather than attempting to move in and "shape up the kids."

All therapists working with stepfamilies hear the war stories of the many backfired attempts of stepparents jumping in with a heavy hand to put an unruly adolescent in line. Although the intervention may be based on the good intention of rescuing an overwhelmed partner who has never been able to control his or her teenager, the stepparent inevitably fails and the family remains fragmented.

When the adolescent is a substance abuser, a destructive discipline pattern is even more likely to evolve. That is, the teenager is more likely to act out and misbehave and the stepparent is drawn into disciplining him or her with more authoritative methods, especially if the parent has been ineffective. The parent may be protective of the child and disagree with the harshness of the stepparent, further reinforcing an intense parent-child coalition.

If this pattern escalates without interruption, a typical dysfunctional solution is what Sager and colleagues (1983) call the "adolescent extrusion syndrome" in the stepfamily. This syndrome is a systematic problem where "a reciprocating negative interaction between youth and adults builds up to an ultimate crescendo that eventuates a self-imposed or commanded banishment" (p. 259).

In extrusion there is the fantasy that if the adolescent physically leaves, the problems of the family will vanish. A common scenario is the teenager comes home in the middle of the night obviously loaded for the nth time. An argument ensues that culminates in threats such as, "Look what you are doing to our family" or "We cannot handle this anymore—you better go live with your father."

The threats of extrusion are more likely to be carried out when the stepfamily's consolidation is tenuous. The couple may have developed limited skills in resolving conflicts without rigid rule setting, and when the rules fail to control behavior, the fear of another marital/family failure becomes overwhelming. Unfortunately, in situations of severe substance abuse, neither biological parent's household really welcomes the adolescent and a shuttling back and forth occurs with each crisis.

Intervention Techniques with Stepfamilies

The following list emphasizes key interventions that are useful in facilitating the process of stepfamily integration. Although some of these are techniques common to family therapy in general, their purpose and implementation is somewhat different when working with stepfamilies.

1. *Use of Genograms.* Although genograms are a useful tool with all families, they are a critical component of stepfamily treatment. They provide crucial information for the therapist in clarifying the often confusing array of family members—which children belong to whom; who lives where, when, and for how long; when marriages and divorces occurred; and the composition of the various households and how they may fluctuate according to changing custody arrangements. Sometimes the task itself of sitting down together and outlining all the players and the timing of key events in the family drama can be enormously reassuring as the stepfamily can concretely see the overwhelming complexity of their situation in a more organized fashion.

When substance abuse is a factor, the genogram provides a matter-of-fact way to make explicit the patterns of substance abuse in the current family, both prior families, as well as the families of origin. For example, if mother has remarried another alcoholic and both adults came from alcoholic families of origin, predictable issues impacting their formation as a stepfamily can easily be identified. That is, the family can look at the repetition of substance abuse and the particular patterns of loss and disruption that permeate their family histories and may create special sensitivities that intensify their current reactions to the inherent conflicts of stepfamily formation.

2. *Sharing Past History.* Extensive historical work is often not necessary with other families, yet is a crucial aspect of stepfamily therapy. The impact of helping stepfamily members exchange past memories and important life events, a seemingly mild intervention, is often unexpectedly powerful in stepfamilies. Since stepfamilies have no shared history, their lack of a sense of belonging is a painful deficit. Stepfamilies often report feeling "like a stranger in a strange land." Like any strangers, the sharing of past personal histories, joys, and struggles underlines humanness and helps create a context for their current family unit.

In the revelations of past family and marriage experiences, the meaning of those losses and their influence on current unspoken expectations can be clarified. The building of empathy for each family member's different timetable in mourning those losses can also occur.

When substance abuse is involved, it is likely that much of the stepfamily interaction is limited to discipline, polite conversation, or tense conflict. For example, if stepchildren can hear a newly recovering stepparent share his loss of everything in his prior family, the personal devastation of the substance abuse and his struggles to maintain sobriety, they can see him in a broader, more human way, which is helpful for positive bonding. Similarly, when a stepparent can hear from her stepchildren the pain they experienced in growing up in an alcoholic family, she is more likely to be able to not personalize their rejecting behavior and understand their difficulties in forming new attachments.

3. *Use of Educational Interventions.* A greater amount of direct educational work is involved in treating dysfunctional stepfamilies. This is often uncomfortable for therapists who are mainly trained in a nuclear family model that often devalues the use of direct education as being therapeutic. However, there are a number of therapeutic benefits that come from direct education of stepfamilies about typical stepfamily processes.

Stepfamilies make the same mistakes about themselves as do inexperienced stepfamily therapists. They hold unrealistic goals, they expect to be able to love each other instantly, they feel disappointed in not being able to re-create an intact family feeling, and so on. The therapist can help alter the family's cognitive model of what a stepfamily realistically can be like. This can effectively reduce anxiety and guilt about failing to achieve the intimacy level of a well-functioning intact family.

For example, the therapist can help educate stepfamilies that, even in well-functioning stepfamilies, less intense interpersonal involvements between stepparent and stepchild are expected to develop than is usual in biological parent-child relationships. The therapist can normalize the tendency for the natural parent and child to feel closer and be more involved with each other than the stepparent and stepchild, while simultaneously intervening to diminish excessively intense biological parent-child coalitions. The therapist can reframe the step-relationship from one that is a poor substitute for a biological parent to one that is a unique relationship in its own right. The stepfamily can be taught that a gradual evolution of closeness seems to work best and how to learn ways of establishing their own levels of closeness and distance.

When substance abuse is also a factor, stepfamilies will need to be educated in how issues related to substance abuse create special sensitivities in various areas that will likely intensify, perhaps exponentially, an already stressful process.

4. *Structuring and Reducing Intensity.* When working with step-families, it is helpful to think of the therapeutic task as being "structuring" rather than the typical "restructuring." That is, since they lack a basic structure to begin with, a main goal of stepfamily therapy is to intervene actively in the formation of a viable family system. Many family therapy techniques are intended to create intensity and induce a crisis in order to interrupt chronic, repetitive family patterns that are immune to gentler strategies. These kinds of restructuring techniques are useful and quite effective in nuclear families. The deep family loyalty and longstanding ties in nuclear families allows them to tolerate the chaos and upset of such unbalancing techniques (Messinger & Walac, 1981). Stepfamily structure, however, is much more fragile and undeveloped. There is little family loyalty or "we-ness" until basic integration has occurred. Thus, such intense restructuring techniques may be intolerable and cause fragmentation. The techniques used should be oriented to reducing tension and helplessness and to increasing mastery and control. For example, when to see the whole family together is a more difficult decision with stepfamilies than in traditional family therapy. If the bonding between the couple does not seem strong enough to allow the adults to work together and to tolerate the potential onslaught of resistance from the children, it is better to work with the couple alone first after an initial family evaluation. As Visher and Visher (1988) state, "In our experience, seeing the entire household unit too early can cause stepfamily disintegration rather than having an integrative effect because of the strong emotional pulls that exist along biological lines" (p. 66).

5. *Using Correct Relationship Language.* One of the most frequent mistakes made by therapists working with stepfamilies is to use inaccurate language when referring to step-relationships. That is, the therapist will simply address the adults as "mom and dad" or refer to a child as "your new son" and ask him to talk to "your new dad" about an issue. This can instantly call into question the therapist's credibility in understanding the complexity and confusion that underlies the formation of attachments in a stepfamily.

The therapist must help each stepfamily find labels that feel most congruent with their particular situation. It is crucial to elicit the internal meanings attached to various words in order to understand fully the importance or discomfort in using certain labels. For example, one girl, who was actually quite fond of her stepfather, said, "I feel close to him, but I'm not ready to call him 'dad.' Maybe someday I could call him 'pops' or 'poppa,' but not 'dad.' I only want one dad." On the other hand, another child said, "I feel good about calling my stepdad 'dad' when we are together as a family and calling my real dad 'dad' when I'm with him – but if we are all together, like at a school play and I have to introduce my family to others, then I call him my stepdad because I think it might hurt my dad's feelings to say anything else."

The therapist must help the family respect each other's feelings about being pressured to use titles that signify a deep bond before one actually exists. Stepfamilies often mistakenly think that "if we act like a happy family and call each other by family names, we will start feeling like a family." As mentioned earlier, this pressure for premature cohesion usually backfires.

Overall, the primary clinical implication of this chapter is that the clinician must approach a dysfunctional stepfamily differently from a dysfunctional nuclear family in various ways discussed above. Also, the therapist needs to expand the traditional concept of "normal family processes" when working with stepfamilies so as to include what could be considered to be functional for well-functioning stepfamilies. That is, one should avoid trying to fit a stepfamily into a nuclear family mold. Rather, knowledge of typical patterns found in functional stepfamilies is a more effective basis from which to evaluate and treat stepfamily dysfunction.

This chapter emphasized that adding substance abuse as an extra factor to the process of stepfamily formation can intensify and complicate matters exponentially. Examples are given throughout to highlight aspects of substance-abusing stepfamilies. Substance abuse creates such additional turmoil, in large part, because the characteristics required for successful stepfamily integration are often the very qualities that are likely to be deficits for the substance abuser. This underscores the importance of a committed recovery process as a crucial antecedent to the establishment of effective stepfamily relationships.

References

Anderson, J. A., & White, G. (1986). An empirical investigation of interaction and relationship patterns in functional and dysfunctional nucleus families and stepfamilies. *Family Process, 25,* 407–422.

Blechman, E., Berberian, R., & Thompson, W. (1977, December). How well does number of parents explain unique variance in self-reported drug use? *Journal of Consulting and Clinical Psychology, 45*(6), 1182–1183.

Crosbie-Burnett, M. (1984). The centrality of the steprelationship: A challenge to family theory and practice. *Family Relations, 33,* 459–463.

DeBlois, S. (1983, June). Marital histories of women whose first husbands were alcoholics. *British Journal of Addiction, 78*(2), 205–213.

Glenn, N. D. & Weaver, C. N. (1978). A multivariate, multisurvey study of marital happiness. *Journal of Marriage and the Family, 40,* 269–282.

Glick, P. C. (1984). Marriage, divorce and living arrangements: Prospective changes. *Journal of Family Issues, 5,* 7–26.

Glick, P. C., & Sungshin, L. (1986). Recent changes in divorce and remarriage. *Journal of Marriage and the Family, 48,* 737–747.

Hetherington, E. M. (1987). Family relations six years after divorce. In K. Pasley & M. Ihinger-Tallman (Eds.), *Remarriage and stepparenting: Current research and theory.* New York: Guilford Press.

Hetherington, E. M., Cos, M., & Cox, R. (1985). Long term effects of divorce and remarriage on the adjustment of children. *Journal of the American Academy of Child Psychiatry, 24,* 518–530.

Kanoy, K., & Miller, B. C. (1980). Children's impact on the parental decision to divorce. *Family Relations, 29,* 309–315.

Kaufman, E., & Kaufmann, P. (1979). *Family therapy of drug and alcohol abuse.* New York: Gardner Press.

Messinger, L., & Walac, K. (1981). From marriage breakdown to remarriage: Parental tasks and therapeutic guidelines. *American Journal of Orthpsychiatry, 51,* 429–438.

Minuchin, S., & Fishman, C. (1981). *Family therapy techniques.* Cambridge, MA: Harvard University Press.

Papermon, P. (1984). The stepfamily cycle: An experiential model of stepfamily development. *Family Relations, 33,* 355–363.

Sager, C., Brown, H., Crohn, H., & Walker, L. (1983). *Treating the remarried family.* New York: Brunner-Mazel.

Visher E., & Visher, J. (1979). *Stepfamilies: A guide to working with stepparents and stepchildren.* New York: Brunner-Mazel.

Visher, E., & Visher, J. (1988). *Old loyalties, new ties, therapeutic strategies with stepfamilies.* New York: Brunner-Mazel.

Wald, E. (1981). *The remarried family: Challenge and promise.* New York: Family Service Association.

Wallerstein, J. S., & Kelley, J. B. (1990). *Surviving the break up: How children and parents cope with divorce.* New York: Basic Books.

Whiteside, M. (1989). Remarried systems. In L. Combinck-Graham (Ed.,), *Children in family contexts.* New York: Guilford Press.

CHAPTER TWELVE

Behavioral Treatment of the Alcoholic Marriage

BARBARA S. MCCRADY, PH.D.
Center for Alcohol Studies
Piscataway, New Jersey

Alcoholism treatment approaches have derived from a variety of theoretical models, including psychodynamic, disease, and learning models. Since the 1940s, behavior therapists have developed models for conceptualizing and treating alcoholism and alcohol-related problems. Early behavioral models drew heavily on the concepts of operant and respondent conditioning, whereas newer behavioral approaches have incorporated advances in social learning theory. General behavioral principles, such as conditioning, reinforcement, expectancies, and modeling, have been applied to the understanding of the relationships between alcoholics and their spouses, with research focusing both on understanding the interactions in alcoholic relationships and on developing treatment models. In addition to the development of theoretical models, all behavioral approaches stress the importance of empirical tests of the efficacy of treatment approaches, and behavioral marital approaches with alcoholics have been no exception. This chapter will outline some of the major assumptions of behavioral approaches to treating alcoholic marriages, and then describe a model for assessment and treatment of these couples.

Assumptions of the Behavioral Model

Four major assumptions underlie our approach. First, we assume that there are identifiable *events* in the environment that are associated with an increased probability of drinking. In behavioral terms, these are called *cues* or *antecedent stimuli,* but with clients, we use the term *triggers.* These events do not *cause* an alcoholic to drink, but increase the probability of drinking because drinking has been reinforced in these situations in the past. These antecedents may relate primarily to individual, intrapersonal issues of the client; they may relate to the client's relationship with his or her family; or they may relate to other interpersonal relationships.

A second major assumption of behavioral approaches is that there are internal, *organismic* events that occur in response to triggers, and that these internal responses form the basis for the client's decision to drink. These internal events are of three types: physiological responses, cognitive responses, and affective responses. For example, if a client is physically dependent on alcohol, then the passage of time (the trigger) will lead to withdrawal symptoms (the organismic response). The onset of these symptoms will also result in certain cognitive reactions, such as thinking "I need a drink to calm down." Other antecedents will also result in cognitive and affective responses. A family argument might lead to feelings of anxiety or anger in the alcoholic, and might also lead to thoughts such as "I'll show him that he can't push me around" or "I really need a drink now to get control of myself."

A third assumption of behavioral approaches is that there are identifiable *consequences* of drinking, and that some of these consequences reinforce or maintain the drinking. These consequences may be individual, such as the alleviation of withdrawal symptoms; they may relate to the family, such as a spouse providing increased attention to the alcoholic when drinking; or they may relate to other interpersonal relationships, such as feeling more comfortable at a party when drinking than when sober. In addition to the positive consequences of drinking, behavioral approaches assume that there are delayed, negative consequences of drinking. Unfortunately, these negative consequences usually occur well after the positive consequences, so they do little to deter the alcoholic from further drinking.

The fourth assumption of behavioral approaches is that there is a *circular relationship* among antecedents, drinking, and consequences. Thus, a couple might have an argument, the alcoholic might drink in response to that argument and then feel bold enough to "tell off" his wife (a positive consequence of drinking, from his perspective), setting the stage for another argument (a delayed negative consequence), which then serves as a cue for further drinking.

Thus, in behavioral approaches, we attempt to identify antecedents (triggers) for drinking in three different realms—those that relate to the alcoholic, those that relate to the family, and those that relate to other interpersonal relationships. We then attempt to identify the thoughts and feelings that the alcoholic has in response to these situations. Finally, we attempt to identify consequences of drinking in these situations. We also assume that some antecedents, cognitions, and affects are directly related to drinking, whereas others represent broader areas of dysfunction, which

TABLE 12–1 • *Sample Elements in a Functional Analysis of Drinking*

Individual	Family	Other Interpersonal
Antecedents		
Time of day	Family drinking	Work-related drinking
Drinking environment	Family celebration	Drinking buddies
Failure experience	Spouse nagging	Offers of alcohol
	Spouse-control behaviors	Social situations with alcohol
	Marital problems	Conflict with coworker or boss
	Child problems	
	Conflict with parents	
Thoughts		
Positive expectancies about alcohol use	Retaliatory thoughts	Belief in increased social acceptance if drinking
Negative self-statements	Negative thoughts about family control behaviors	Belief in increased social competence if drinking
	Thinking of alcohol as way to escape	Concerns about others' negative evaluations if don't drink
	Self-blame for family or child problems	Belief that client is inferior to other people
		Belief that should always please others
Feelings		
Inadequacy	Inadequacy	Inadequacy
Anxiety	Anxiety	Anxiety
Depression	Depression	Depression
Anger	Anger	Anger
Guilt	Guilt	Guilt
Physiological		
Withdrawal symptoms	Anger-related arousal	Anger-related arousal
Headaches	Anxiety-related arousal	Anxiety-related arousal
Premenstrual syndrome	Sexual arousal	Sexual arousal

TABLE 12–1 • *Continued*

Individual	*Family*	*Other Interpersonal*
Positive Consequences		
Decreased withdrawal symptoms	Increased assertiveness with family	Feeling socially accepted
Forgetting failure	Positive attention from family	Decreased social anxiety
Anxiety reduction	Avoidance of responsibilities	Feeling more socially adept
Enjoyment of taste	Retaliation toward family	
Relaxation	Protection from negative consequences of drinking	
Negative Consequences		
Physical problems	Marital conflict	Conflict with friends
Legal problems	Communication problems	Loss of friends
Emotional problems	Child behavior problems	Work problems
Financial problems	Conflict with parents or in-laws	Conflicts with co-workers or supervisors
Job loss	Physical or sexual abuse	Embarrassing behavior in social situations

may set the stage for drinking or make continued recovery difficult. Table 12-1 provides examples of a variety of antecedents, cognitions, affects, and consequences that may be associated with drinking.

Overview of Behavioral Approach

Therapeutic Stance

When approaching a couple from a behavioral perspective, the therapist takes a particular stance with them. The therapist's role is that of an expert consultant who can provide information and tools to the couple. The therapist generally provides a clear rationale for therapeutic interventions, and takes on the role of teacher. The therapist works with the couple to articulate goals for the therapy, and helps the couple develop the skills that they need to achieve these goals. The therapist will demonstrate or describe new skills, and help the couple practice these skills through rehearsal and feedback in the therapy session, and homework assignments to facilitate the couple's learning.

Assessment and Treatment Overview

Treatment is divided into several steps. First, the therapist assesses the couple for any emergency situations. These may include the need for supervised detoxification, the need for immediate medical or psychiatric care, or the need to protect a family member from physical or sexual abuse. The therapist cannot proceed with any other parts of assessment or treatment without determining the need for immediate care.

The second step is to conduct a comprehensive assessment of the couple. In the approach described in this chapter, almost all assessment and treatment is conducted with both the client and spouse present. Conjoint assessment and treatment is seen as the *treatment of choice*. By being involved from the beginning of the treatment, the spouse can learn about alcoholism and the process of change, can learn ways to cope both with drinking and sobriety, and the couple can learn how to solve their problems together. This approach is different than traditional, disease-model approaches, which state that couples should not be seen conjointly until well into separate recovery programs through Alcoholics Anonymous and Al-Anon.

Assessment of the couple falls into three domains—evaluation of the drinking problem, evaluation of the individual needs of the client and partner, and evaluation of the marital relationship. Assessment includes the use of interviewing, standardized paper and pencil tests, use of self-recording procedures, structured observations of the couple, and use of physiological measures. Each of these approaches will be described in detail in the next section.

Treatment also covers three basic domains—helping the client develop skills to attain and maintain abstinence from alcohol; helping the spouse learn skills to support abstinence and to respond more productively to drinking situations; and helping the couple to improve their marital relationship. Techniques for each of these domains will be discussed below.

Behavioral Assessment

The Interview

In the initial interviews with a couple, the therapist wants to establish rapport with the couple and instill a sense of hope, provide the couple with information and a model for understanding their problems, engage both partners in the treatment, and gather concrete information. As with all therapies, the therapist's characteristics and behavior are important. The behavior therapist uses reflective listening, open-ended questions, empathy, and warmth as basic therapeutic tools. The therapist also uses standard couples interviewing techniques, such as directing questions openly to the couple to see who responds and eliciting responses from the quiet partner.

Certain content areas are covered in the initial interviews. The therapist assesses the couple's presenting problems and reasons for seeking treatment, as well as which partner initiated treatment. Current and past alcohol and drug use are assessed, and the need for detoxification is evaluated. The spouse is actively involved in providing information, because clients may forget information, minimize the severity of problems, or, under some circumstances, lie about their actions. In addition, the therapist inquires about ways that the drinking has impacted on the family and how the family has attempted to cope with this problem. Usually, taking such a history with both present results in each partner hearing new information. The therapist frames the experience of learning new information as an example of ways in which the couple's communication has broken down, encouraging them to view learning new information about each other as the first step in the change process.

In addition to assessing drinking and drug use and its impact on the family, the therapist also assesses other areas of life functioning. These include: (1) occupational and financial status and concerns; (2) issues related to the children (if present), including the current functioning of the children and how discipline and time with the children are managed: (3) legal status and problems; (4) residential circumstances and problems; (5) affectionate and sexual relationship and problems; (6) distribution of role responsibilities (e.g., housework, cooking) and problems; (7) leisure and recreational activities; (8) families of origin and problems associated with them; (9) religious orientation; (10) physical health and medical problems; (11) emotional health and problems; and (12) general views of the marital relationship, including its strengths and weaknesses. Making at least brief inquiry into each of these areas allows the therapist to have a fuller picture of the couple's functioning.

Questionnaires

A variety of self-report questionnaires have been developed to assess alcohol and drug use, the consequences of use, and patterns associated with use. In our work, we use the Alcohol Use Inventory (Horn, Wanberg, & Foster, 1977) or the Alcohol Dependence Scale (Skinner & Horn, 1984) to obtain a picture of the extent and severity of the client's drinking-related problems. To assess triggers, thoughts, and feelings associated with alcohol use, two scales are particularly helpful. The Drinking Patterns Question-naire (Zitter & McCrady, 1979) lists 260 situations that clients have reported as antecedents to drinking. These are divided into 10 face-valid scales (e.g., Environment, Emotions, Parents). Clients check off all situations that they perceive as antecedents to their drinking, then rank order the scales in importance to their drinking. An alternative scale, the Inventory of Drink-ing Situations (Annis, 1982), provides a profile of situations in which the client drank heavily over the past year. Either of these scales is useful in more accurately pinpointing antecedents to drinking.

In our work, we ask both partners to complete one of these question-naires, to obtain both of their perspectives on the client's drinking cues. Agreement between partners is usually high (McCrady & Zitter, 1983), but each partner usually has some unique perspective to contribute.

Questionnaires can also be used to assist the therapist in identifying spouse patterns for coping with the partner's drinking. We have modified the Spouse Behavior Questionnaire (James & Goldman, 1971) so that it yields four types of information: spouse behaviors that appear to cue drinking, spouse behaviors that may reinforce drinking, spouse behaviors that protect the client from the aversive consequences of drinking, and spouse behaviors that may reinforce abstinence. Review of responses to this questionnaire can help the therapist and the couple identify spouse behav-iors that cue or reinforce drinking, as well as identify deficits in positive, supportive behaviors associated with abstinence. Having both the spouse and the client complete this questionnaire provides two perspectives on the spouse's behavior. In addition, it forces the drinker to begin to think seriously about ways that his or her drinking has affected the partner.

A third domain that can be measured with questionnaires is the current marital relationship. A variety of marital satisfaction questionnaires are available, including the Marital Adjustment Test (MAT) (Locke & Wallace, 1959), the Dyadic Adjustment Scale (DAS) (Spanier, 1976), and the Areas of Change Questionnaire (ACQ) (Margolin, Talovic, & Wein-stein, 1983). The MAT and the DAS are general measures of marital satisfaction that are widely used. Both are brief and easy to complete, and yield a single score that provides information about each partner's marital happiness, in comparison to a normal control group. The DAS includes a brief subscale measuring closeness to divorce, which often provides the therapist with his or her first information about the potential stability of the relationship.

The ACQ uses a rather different format, in which each marital partner is asked to rate how much change is desired from the partner in each of 34 areas of relationship functioning (e.g., doing housework, getting together with friends, having interesting conversations). After rating the 34 requests for partner change, the person completing the questionnaire then has to identify how much change he or she thinks the partner wants in the same 34 areas. This questionnaire then forces both partners to think not only about their own complaints but also those of their partner. Thus, the questionnaire itself pushes the couple to think empathically about the other's wishes. Sample items from each of these questionnaires are included in Table 12-2.

Self-Recording

A third assessment tool is that of self-recording. Clients are given small index cards and are instructed to complete these cards daily. Each day, they are to record any alcoholic drinks they consumed, the number and intensity of urges to drink that they experienced, and a daily marital satisfaction rating. On the back of the card, they are instructed to record the situation associated with drinking or drinking urges. Clients are instructed to carry a card at all times and are urged to be honest in their responses. The therapist emphasizes that being honest is the only way that treatment can be successful. As the client records drinks and drinking urges, the couple and the therapist can obtain more information about cues for drinking, as well as deficits in the client's skills to deal with those situations without drinking.

A comparable self-recording card is provided for the partner. Once a day, the partner is instructed to estimate the amount of drinking (if any) by the alcoholic partner, and also estimate the degree to which he or she thinks the alcoholic spouse experienced urges to drink. The spouse also makes a daily rating of marital satisfaction. We provide spouses with these self-recording cards because we believe that spouses are already observing and estimating their partners' drinking, and that making the observing overt removes some of the controlling aspects from the behavior. It also provides the therapist with a second source of information about the client's success or problems with abstinence. Sample self-recording cards for clients and spouses are reproduced in Figures 12-1 and 12-2.

Structured Observations

To conduct effective couples therapy, the therapist benefits from having a specific and detailed picture of the way that the couple communicates and tries to handle their problems. Obtaining information about the couple's communication patterns early in treatment enables the therapist to focus on these communication deficits whenever they arise. There are two approaches to assessing communication. The first is to merely observe the couple's behavior during the therapy session. The therapist can observe interruptions, who talks the most, the degree to which each partner listens to and understands the other, and the affective tone of the communication. A more formal supplement to informal observations in the session is to ask the couple to discuss a problem of concern to them and to observe their

TABLE 12-2 • *Sample Items from Self-Report Questionnaires*

Questionnaire	Sample Items	Scale
Drinking Severity		
Alcohol Use Inventory (Horn, Wanberg, & Foster, 1977)	"Does your social life require you to drink?"	Yes/No
	"Do you sometimes neglect your work because of drinking?"	No/Somewhat/ To a great extent
Alcohol Dependence Scale (Skinner & Horn, 1984)	"Do you often have hangovers on Sunday or Monday mornings?"	No/Yes
	"Do you panic because you fear you may not have a drink when you need it?"	No/Yes
Drinking Pattern		
Drinking Patterns Questionnaire (Zitter & McCrady, 1979)	"I sometimes drink or get an urge to drink when passing a particular bar or restaurant."	Yes/No
	"I sometimes drink to be part of the group."	Yes/No
Inventory of Drinking Situations (Annis, 1982)	"I drank heavily when I had an argument with a friend."	Never to Almost Always
	"I drank heavily when I would have trouble sleeping."	Never to Almost Always
Spouse Behavior		
Spouse Behavior Questionnaire (James & Goldman, 1971)	"When he gets drunk, do you keep out of his way?"	1x/week or more to Never
	"Have you complimented him on his actions when he has been sober?"	1x/week or more to Never
Marital Relationship		
Marital Adjustment Test (Locke & Wallace, 1959)	"State the extent of agreement or disagreement between you and your mate on the following items: Handling family finances Demonstrations of affection"	Always Agree to Always Disagree

TABLE 12–2 • *Continued*

Questionnaire	Sample Items	Scale
Dyadic Adjustment Scale (Spanier, 1976)	"Indicate the extent of agreement or disagreement between you and your partner for . . . sex relations."	Always Agree to Always Disagree
	"How often do you discuss or have you considered divorce, separation, or terminating your relationship?"	All the time to Never
Areas of Change Questionnaire (Margolin, Talovic, & Weinstein, 1983)	"I want my partner to participate in decisions about spending money."	Much less (−3) to Much More (+3)
	"It would please my partner if I had sexual relations with him/her."	Much less (−3) to Much More (+3)

interactions. Their interaction can be observed from behind a one-way mirror or can be videotaped or audiotaped. The couple is usually instructed to discuss the problem for about 10 minutes and to attempt to solve the problem during those 10 minutes. The therapist can then observe positive and negative verbal and nonverbal behaviors, problem-solving behaviors, interruptions, and so on.

In research-based treatments, the videotaped segment can then be coded, using a structured coding system such as the Marital Interaction Coding System (MICS) (Hops, Wills, Patterson, & Weiss, 1971), or the Communication Skills Test (CST) (Floyd & Markman, 1984). Even if no formal coding is done, however, observing the couple's interactions can provide the therapist a much fuller picture of the couple's communication skills and deficits.

Physiological Measurements

Two major types of physiological measures are used in behavioral alcoholism treatment. A simple breath analyzer may be used at the beginning of each treatment session. If the breathalyzer reading indicates that the client is intoxicated, the therapy session is rescheduled. Clients are informed of this plan at the beginning of treatment and are told that therapy cannot be productive if the client is high. The breathalyzer communicates to the couple that the therapist is serious about treatment and about abstinence, and prevents the therapist from getting into the position of trying to "guess" whether or not the client had been drinking.

FIGURE 12–1 • *Sample Client Self-Recording Card*

Name_____

Date_____

Urges to Drink		Drinks			
Time	How Strong (1–7)	Time	Type		How Much

Marital Satisfaction (1–7):

Comments:

A second physiological measure used with some clients is monitoring a liver enzyme, the GGTP (gamma-glutamyl transpeptidase). GGTP is sensitive to recent heavy drinking and, therefore, if monitored periodically, can provide the couple and the therapist with objective feedback about the course of treatment.

Putting Together the Assessment Information

At the completion of the assessment, the therapist usually sits down with the couple to provide feedback about the assessment, and to come to agreed-upon goals for the treatment. In this feedback session, the therapist identifies major triggers for drinking, major positive consequences that the client appears to be obtaining from drinking, major spouse behaviors that trigger or reinforce drinking, and a view of the major strengths and weaknesses in the couple's relationship. The therapist helps the couple see the

FIGURE 12–2 • *Sample Spouse Self-Recording Card*

Rating Scale: 1 2 3 4 5 6 7

			very low								greatest ever

Spouse Monitoring

Day	Date	Drinking	Urge Intensity	Marriage Satisfaction
		NO L M H	0 1 2 3 4 5 6 7	1 2 3 4 5 6 7
		NO L M H	0 1 2 3 4 5 6 7	1 2 3 4 5 6 7
		NO L M H	0 1 2 3 4 5 6 7	1 2 3 4 5 6 7
		NO L M H	0 1 2 3 4 5 6 7	1 2 3 4 5 6 7
		NO L M H	0 1 2 3 4 5 6 7	1 2 3 4 5 6 7
		NO L M H	0 1 2 3 4 5 6 7	1 2 3 4 5 6 7
		NO L M H	0 1 2 3 4 5 6 7	1 2 3 4 5 6 7

NO = no drinking
L   = light drinking
M = moderate drinking
H = heavy drinking

relationships between their behaviors, drinking, and consequences, by using "trigger sheets" that demonstrate graphically the connections described. Figure 12–3 provides sample trigger sheets for a couple previously described by the author (McCrady, 1982).

The therapist actively involves the couple in the feedback process by asking their reactions to the therapist's formulation. The therapist then goes on to outline the plan for therapy, including the level of care and frequency of visits (if outpatient), the goals for the therapy, and the responsibilities of the couple and the therapist in the treatment. If the couple agrees with the formulation and treatment plan, then treatment can proceed.

Behavioral Treatment

Treatment Overview

There are four major components of the treatment: (1) helping the drinking partner to stop drinking and to develop skills both to maintain abstinence and to deal effectively with other life problems, (2) helping the spouse learn skills to respond more effectively to drinking and to absti-

FIGURE 12–3 • *Analyzing Drinking: "Gerry"*

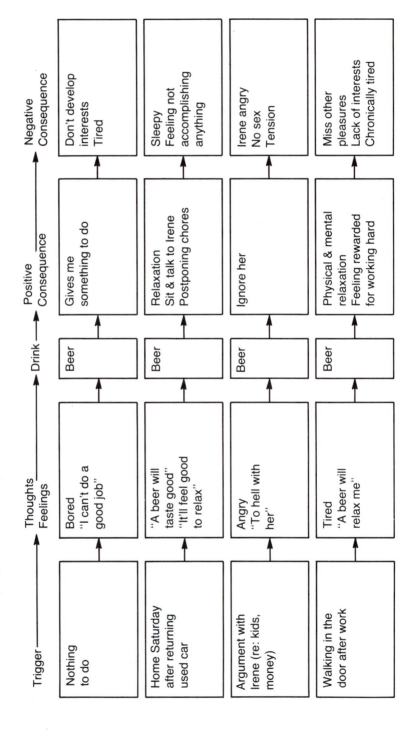

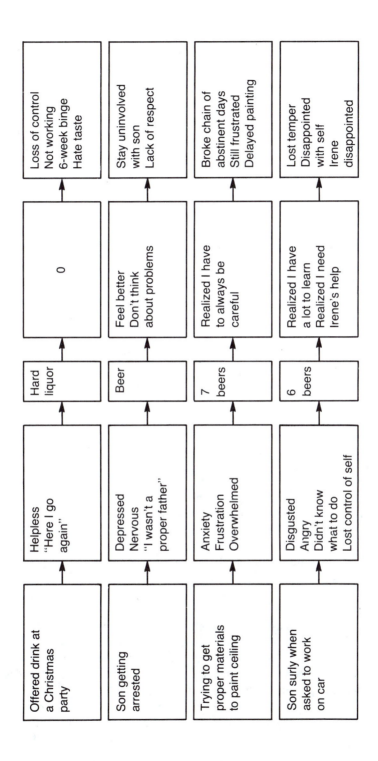

203

nence, (3) helping the couple learn how to cope with alcohol and alcohol-related situations differently, and (4) helping the couple change their relationship to make it more positive and satisfying to them. In our approach to treatment, we work with the identified client and spouse *conjointly* from the beginning of treatment, providing separate treatment sessions only under special circumstances, such as marital violence or significant individual psychopathology of one spouse.

Treatment is not strictly sequenced, but the early sessions are usually devoted almost exclusively to issues related to the client's drinking, with minimal efforts directed toward helping the spouse change, and minimal focus on the relationship per se. Any treatment focus on the spouse's behavior is directed at helping him or her learn skills to support changes in the partner's drinking, and to be prepared to deal with relapses. By treating the couple conjointly during these early sessions, however, the therapist is able to use the sessions as a vehicle to help both the client and spouse understand more about the phenomenology of alcoholism, and to help the spouse learn that may behaviors attributed to the alcoholic's "personality" might actually be attributable to the drinking problem. For example, a husband who views his wife as forgetful might learn that she was experiencing blackouts. Or a wife that viewed her husband as irritable and nervous might learn that he was showing signs of alcohol dependence and withdrawal.

The alcohol-focused content of the early part of treatment can also be used as an initial vehicle to help each member of the couple develop more understanding and empathy about the partner's experience of the drinking problem and change during treatment, and can also be used to help the couple begin to develop skills to discuss and solve problems.

The focus of treatment gradually shifts from alcohol-focused material to more general issues for the couple. As treatment progresses, more session time is devoted to treatment interventions designed to increase the positive, reinforcing value of the relationship, and then to treatment interventions that teach communication and problem-solving skills.

Abstinence Skills

The early sessions of treatment focus primarily on skills to help the alcoholic stop drinking and maintain abstinence from alcohol. There are a number of excellent books that describe individually oriented behavioral approaches to alcoholism treatment, and the reader is referred to these for more detail (e.g., Hay & Nathan, 1982; Marlatt & Gordon, 1985; Miller & Munoz, 1982). Clients are taught to keep track of drinking and urges to drink, using the self-recording cards described earlier in the chapter. From these cards, and from the use of structured questionnaires, the client, spouse, and therapist identify a variety of high-risk situations associated with drinking.

After identifying high-risk situations, the client develops a variety of plans for ways to deal with these situations. These plans might include avoidance of certain triggers (such as heavy drinking friends), rearranging triggers (such as socializing with heavy-drinking friends only through non-drinking activities, such as going to a movie and out for ice cream), or learning how to respond differently to triggers (such as learning effective ways to refuse drinks offered by heavy-drinking friends).

A second important component of the individually focused treatment is the use of a variety of techniques to enhance the client's motivation or desire to stay abstinent. Techniques might include having a client create a list of positive consequences associated with abstinence and negative consequences associated with drinking, or writing an autobiography about his or her drinking history (Marlatt & Gordon, 1985). The client would be taught ways to keep memories of the seriousness of the drinking clearly in mind, and would be taught how to review these consequences when feeling tempted to drink. The client also might be taught self-reinforcement techniques (such as rewarding himself for successes with abstinence, or mentally giving herself a "pat on the back" for coping with a difficult situation).

A third aspect of abstinence-related skills involves teaching the client skills to cope with life problems that might set the stage for a relapse. The client might be assisted in learning different ways to cope with interpersonal discomfort, anxiety, or self-defeating or irrational thinking. A variety of behavior therapy techniques can be used, such as assertiveness training, relaxation training, or cognitive restructuring.

Any aspects of therapy that focus primarily on teaching the client skills for attaining and maintaining abstinence are provided with the spouse present. Our approach assumes that it is essential that the spouse understand both the difficulties that the alcoholic experiences in not drinking, as well as understanding the steps that the alcoholic is taking to change. Often, the spouse may unwittingly sabotage treatment through lack of comprehension of the process of change, rather than through any psychological desire to see the alcoholic continue to drink.

Spouse Skills

At the same time that the alcoholic is learning skills to change the drinking, the spouse also needs to learn new ways to respond to drinking, threats of drinking, his or her own feelings about the drinking, *and* abstinence. From the beginning of treatment, we attempt to help the spouse discuss ways that he or she has tried to cope with the drinking in the past, and to discuss feelings about the drinking. We emphasize that most spouses try their best to cope with the drinking, and empathize with the helplessness and frustration that the partner has experienced. The therapist uses questionnaires and interviewing to identify specific dysfunctional ways that he or she has responded to drinking in the past.

Some of these behaviors we define as "triggers" for the client's drinking—actions on the part of the spouse that *increase the probability* that the client will drink. This is a subtle concept to convey to the spouse—the therapist is not trying to define the spouse as *causing* the drinking problem, but rather is trying to help the spouse realize how ineffective and counterproductive some of these actions might have been. For example, one spouse we treated would call her husband late in the afternoon and ask him when he'd be home, hoping that the call would encourage him to come right home. She and her husband were asked whether or not the call had the desired effect. Her husband gave her feedback about the impact the phone call on him, telling her that he knew she was trying to get him to come home and not drink, and that he resented the call and felt like drinking when she called. Such feedback helps the spouse sort out the difference between effective and ineffective ways of coping with the drinking.

Once the spouse identifies some of his or her ineffective coping approaches, the therapist helps the spouse learn some alternative approaches. Conceptually, we are teaching spouses to decrease spouse cues for drinking, and teaching them to allow aversive consequences of drinking to occur naturally, so that continued drinking has more negative consequences associated with it. For example, the therapist might use assertiveness training approaches to help the spouse learn how to express drinking-related feelings more directly. As a result, the spouse in the above example might, when anxious about whether or not her husband was going to drink, learn to express this anxiety directly, in terms of her own feelings, rather than converting her anxiety into an attempt to control his behavior.

Roleplaying is used to help the spouse practice these new skills and to help the client learn how to respond to the changed behavior of his or her partner. Spouses are also taught to decrease attention to drinking, to stop protecting the client from naturally occurring negative consequences of drinking. In addition to roleplaying, spouses may use "covert rehearsal," in which they visualize different coping responses, to help them learn new behaviors.

In addition to learning how to cope differently with drinking and drinking-related situations, we believe that it is important for spouses to learn ways to interact *positively* when the client is not drinking. Conceptually, we are attempting to teach spouses to provide positive reinforcement for a desired behavior (abstinence). However, most couples find the notion of reinforcing each other rather repugnant, so we frame reinforcement as feedback, sharing, or support. We encourage spouses to identify things they could say that would indicate positive feelings about the drinker's changes. We have had spouses say everything from, "It's great that you're not drinking," to "I love having my husband back," to "You're doing well." Couples vary greatly in the ways that they are comfortable sharing positive feelings, and the therapist must be careful to help the couple practice interactions that will be reinforcing for them. In addition to helping spouses tell their mates positive things, some spouses also may do positive things. In fact, for some couples, concrete forms of positive feedback are more comfortable than verbal interactions. So, one wife might make sundaes for her husband each evening, while another husband might give his wife a backrub.

Alcohol-Focused Couples Interventions

A third major focus of treatment is the use of drinking interactions as a vehicle to begin to change the couple's interactions in general. Most couples enter treatment expecting to discuss drinking, and many are reluctant to focus on topics that appear to be unrelated to drinking, such as their own relationship. However, couples have to cope with a variety of problems when the alcoholic first decides to change, and we use these problems as a way to begin to affect the couple's interactions in a more general way.

A variety of alcohol-related topics confront any couple for whom drinking is a problem. Will alcohol be kept in the house? Will they attend social functions where alcohol is served? What will be said to family members? What will be said to friends? How will the couple handle situations where the alcoholic is offered alcohol? Are there ways that the partner can respond that would be helpful when the alcoholic is experiencing urges to drink? How will the couple handle relapses if they occur?

Each of these questions may be answered unilaterally by either or both partners. Unfortunately, if the couple handles such issues separately, the probability of conflict and ineffective coping is high. For example, an alcoholic wife might decide to confide in her closest friends about her drinking problem and decision to stop. Her husband might want to cover up the drinking, feeling that his wife's drinking would be viewed as an indication of his failure as a husband. Thus, while he was inventing stories to cover for his wife, she might be being honest and frank. Such a conflict of approaches would be sure to generate embarrassment and conflict between them.

As an alternative, if the couple does not raise questions such as the above, the therapist explicitly asks the couple if they have considered these questions and how they have begun to handle them. Usually, the couple has difficulty discussing these topics because of deficits in communication and problem-solving skills. The therapist uses these discussions to begin to help the couple learn to identify and explain their own feelings about situations, listen to and understand the other's feelings, offer solutions, compromise, and try out solutions that the couple has agreed on. Through the process of discussing alcohol, which is a "safe" topic for the couple, a variety of relationship issues emerge, making easier the therapist's gradual shift to focus on these broader relationship issues.

Relationship Change

The fourth major component of our behavioral approach to couples alcoholism treatment is a direct focus on the couple's relationship. We do not initiate direct attention to these issues until the alcoholic has stopped drinking and has had some weeks of fairly continuous abstinence. As noted above, relationship issues are first introduced in the context of discussions of how to handle alcohol-related situations. However, the therapist gradually introduces other relationship issues into the therapy, if the couple does not raise these issues themselves.

Behavioral marital therapy (e.g., Jacobson & Margolin, 1979; Stuart, 1980) for any type of relationship distress has two major foci: increasing the reinforcing value of the relationship, and improving communication and problem-solving skills. Behavioral marital therapy assumes that distressed couples have an excess of negative interactions, and that they have learned to control each other's behavior through negative or coercive exchanges. The first goal in treatment is to attempt to increase positive exchanges, setting the change for the couple to be more amenable to the hard work involved in learning new communication skills.

In working with alcoholic couples, the therapist may use a variety of techniques to increase positive exchanges. (The reader is referred to Jacobson & Margolin [1979] or Stuart [1980] for more complete information on these techniques.) The couple may be assigned the task of finding an activity that they could share and enjoy once during the week. These activities may be as simple as going out for pancakes or going to a flea market, or as elaborate as dinner and theater. The therapist emphasizes that the couple has not had many opportunities to really enjoy time together because of the drinking, and that they should find ways to treat themselves for the hard work that they have been doing related to the drinking.

A second set of techniques for increasing positive exchanges focuses more directly on interactions between the partners. Stuart (1980) uses a technique called "Caring Days" in which each spouse selects a day to do as many small, positive things as he or she can think of to make his or her partner happy. Another technique, called "Catch your spouse doing something nice" (Stuart, 1980), asks each spouse to write down at least one action of the partner that they liked each day, and then to tell him or her about it.

Such a technique encourages spouses to focus on positive behaviors, rather than focus only on negative partner behaviors.

Communication and problem-solving skills are varied. The therapist needs to assess carefully each couple's communications skills and deficits before intervening. Couples often need to learn how to listen accurately, how to understand the other's position even if they do not agree, how to express their own feelings rather than attacking the partner, how to identify problems in terms that facilitate problem solving, how to make specific requests for change, how to brainstorm solutions, and how to select and carry out solutions.

The behavior therapist working with an alcoholic couple uses a range of behavioral marital therapy techniques to accomplish these goals. Couples may be taught communication skills in a structured manner, practicing each skill individually, through roleplaying in the treatment session and at home. Couples also are given feedback about specific communication skills as they discuss a problem, and are helped to try different communication skills as the interact in the session. (The reader is referred to Gottman, Notarius, Gonso, & Markman [1976] for a clear, readable book about communication training for couples.)

This chapter has presented an approach to couples alcoholism treatment that is based in behavioral theory and techniques. A number of controlled research studies have evaluated the effectiveness of this approach to treatment (see McCrady [1989] for a review). Behavioral approaches have consistently been found to have equivalent or better treatment outcomes than alternative couples approaches, and consistently better outcomes than other approaches that do not fully involve the couple in the treatment.

Behavioral approaches clearly are not as popular as family systems and family disease model approaches to alcoholism treatment. However, until other approaches to treating alcoholic couples and families have similar research studies to support their effectiveness, we challenge the clinician to justify the use of unproven approaches, or to develop the kinds of research studies that will provide information about the effectiveness of alternative approaches to family-based treatment.

References

Annis, H. M. (1982). *Inventory of drinking situations (IDS*-100). Toronto, Canada: Addiction Research Foundation of Ontario.

Floyd, F., & Markman, H. (1984). An economical observation measure of couples' communication skill. *Journal of Consulting and Clinical Psychology, 52,* 97–103.

Gottman, J., Notarius, C., Gonso, J., & Markman, H. (1976). *A couple's guide to communication.* Champaign, IL: Research Press.

Hay W., & Nathan, P. E. (1982). *Clinical case studies in the behavioral treatment of alcoholism.* New York: Plenum Press.

Hops, H., Wills, T. A., Patterson, G. R., & Weiss, R. L. (1971). *Marital interaction coding system, Technical report No. 8.* Portland: University of Oregon, Department of Psychology.

Horn, J., Wanberg, K., & Foster, M. F. (1977). A differential assessment model for alcoholism: the scales of the Alcohol Use Inventory. *Journal of Studies on Alcohol, 38,* 512–543.

Jacobson, N., & Margolin, G. (1979). *Marital therapy.* New York: Brunner/Mazel.

James, J. E., & Goldman, M. (1971). Behavior trends of wives of alcoholics. *Quarterly Journal of Studies on Alcohol, 32,* 373–381.

Locke, H. J., & Wallace, K. M. (1959). Short marital-adjustment and prediction tests: Their reliability and validity. *Marriage and Family Living, 21,* 251–255.

Margolin, J., Talovic, S., & Weinstein, C. D. (1983). Areas of change questionnaire: A practical approach to marital assessment. *Journal of Consulting & Clinical Psychology, 51,* 920–931.

Marlatt, G. A., & Gordon, J. (1985). *Relapse prevention. Maintenance strategies in the treatment of addictive behaviors.* New York: Guilford Press.

McCrady, B. S. (1982). Conjoint behavioral treatment of an alcoholic and his spouse. In W. M. Hay & P. E. Nathan (Eds.), *Clinical case studies in the behavioral treatment of alcoholism.* New York: Plenum Press.

McCrady, B. S. (1989). Outcomes of family-involved alcoholism treatment. In M. Galanter (Ed.), *Recent developments in alcoholism, Volume VII: Treatment Issues* (pp. 165–182). New York: Plenum Press.

McCrady, B. S., & Zitter, R. (1983). The Drinking Patterns Questionnaire: An approach to identifying drinking situations. Unpublished manuscript.

Miller, W., & Munoz, R. (1982). *How to control your drinking.* Englewood Cliffs, NJ: Prentice-Hall.

Skinner, H. A., & Horn, J. L. (1984). *Alcohol Dependence Scale (ADS) users guide.* Toronto, Ontario: Addiction Research Foundation.

Spanier, G. (1976). Measuring dyadic adjustment: New scales for assessing the quality of marriage and similar dyads. *Journal of Marriage and Family, 38,* 15–28.

Stuart, R. (1980). *Helping couples change: A social learning approach to marital therapy.* New York: Guilford Press.

Zitter, R., & McCrady, B. S. (1979). The Drinking Patterns Questionnaire. Unpublished questionnaire.

CHAPTER THIRTEEN

Willpower: A Major Issue in the Psychotherapy of Adult Children of Alcoholics

TIMMEN L. CERMAK, M.D.
Clinical Director
Genesis Psychotherapy Center

ALVIN A. ROSENFELD, M.D.
Director of Psychiatric Services
Jewish Child Care Association

Twenty-eight million Americans have at least one alcoholic parent (Hindman, 1975–76). Most of the early research on this population focused primarily on the deleterious effects during childhood of living in an alcoholic family (El-Guebaly & Offord, 1977; Whitfield, 1980). The literature identifies problems such as fetal alcohol syndrome, child abuse, attention deficit disorders, eating disorders, stress-related medical disorders, and conduct disorders such as school problems, truancy, runaways, and delinquency. Studies have also described "invulnerable" children who do exceptionally well despite their early experiences in alcoholic families (Keane, 1983).

Current work now demonstrates that children of alcoholics (COAs) remain at risk for maladaptive behavior later in life. For example, COAs are at high risk for developing alcoholism themselves or marrying someone who becomes an alcoholic (Miller, 1977). Adult children of alcoholics (ACAs) are prone to suffer from low self-esteem and compulsive achieving, to attempt or commit suicide, and to experience serious difficulty maintaining satisfying intimate relationships (Wegscheider, 1981). Recent studies of employee assistance programs demonstrate a disproportionately high percentage of ACAs among referrals (Lavino, 1982). ACAs in group therapy demonstrate restricted emotional spontaneity, denial of personal needs, unclear bound-

This chapter originally appeared in *Advances in Alcohol and Substance Abuse, 6* (4), copyrighted by Haworth Press.

aries of interpersonal responsibility, difficulty trusting, and pervasive fears of abandonment (Cermak & Brown, 1982).

The number of ACAs that suffer from some or many of the above symptoms and problems is, to date, unknown. But in those ACAs who have been carefully observed, one general, strikingly persistent dynamic has been noted — conflicts around a number of *control* issues (Cermak & Brown, 1982). ACAs commonly react to the interpersonal and intrapsychic complications of life by increasing their efforts to control both internal and external events. Whether the mechanism for maintaining control is mastery, manipulation, denial, or obsession, the maintenance of control is unquestioned as a universal ideal; and the loss of control precipitates significant existential fears and self-deprecation. When circumstances are threatening, ACAs characteristically defend themselves psychologically by sheer force of will power. The striking intensity of this show of will represents an important legacy from the experience of growing up in an alcoholic family.

We do not wish to imply that the dynamics found in adult children of alcoholics are unique to this population. Parallels exist in other populations that were under chronic stress during childhood, especially the stress of being physically or severely emotionally abused.

Alcoholism and Control

Some therapists unfamiliar with alcoholic families may find the emphasis on control by the offspring to be in stark contrast to the alcoholic parents. Closer investigation reveals that the attitudes and beliefs of these children are an acceptance rather than a rejection of their family's value system.

Alcoholic parents frequently praise their children for achieving high, even precocious levels of mastery and self-control. One motivating factor is their unrealistic devotion to will power, which nearly always lies at the core of an alcoholic's world view (Bateson, 1971). It might seem paradoxical that anyone committed to such a struggle for control should be so prone to relapses. This is best explained by the fact that alcoholics are actually using control in the service of denial; will power cannot achieve an alteration of the reality that they have the disease of alcoholism. Alcoholics often devote enormous attention to the issue of control. The intensity with which they struggle to master (i.e., deny) their disease becomes a primary source of pride and self-worth. The tragic struggle, rather than the resolution of the struggle, equals virtue. The extent to which the alcoholic can mount an epic struggle in the face of certain defeat becomes enobling. To challenge the demons in the bottle face-to-face epitomizes the struggle of human frailty against the forces of darkness. Except for hubris, the battle might be won. Instead, it inevitably descends into pure bathos.

To the nonrecovering alcoholic, self-mastery is a more important goal than sobriety itself. The individual believes that only by proving he or she is "strong" enough to drink normally can he or she reclaim self-respect. All too frequently, spouses and friends share in this belief system and base their own self-esteem, and their evaluation of others, on the ability to control their world. Too often this includes a belief in the ability to control the alcoholic's addictive behavior. Whether or not this degree of control is ever achieved, or even achievable, children naturally incorporate their parents' attitudes, beliefs, and value systems, and thus learn to value themselves more highly the more capable they become of managing their lives through will power and denial of human frailties. In overvaluing the pseudomaturity and precocity of COAs, we may be focusing too much on the behavior and too little on the underlying attitudes and motivations (Rosenfeld, Wenegrat, et al., 1982). To be more succinct, ACAs have a legacy from their families of origin of unrealistically assessing the limits and glorifying the pathway of self-control.

Rather than rejecting their parents' distorted attitudes, ACAs often believe that their parents failed because they were not sufficiently powerful. Had they been stronger, they would have overpowered their addictions. Although there is a seductive quality to such a moralistic viewpoint, most alcoholics do not seem to have the inner resources to recover on their own, despite prodigious efforts. Recovering alcoholics typically discover that it was their persistent belief that they should be able to overpower their illness that kept them drinking and prevented them from getting realistic help. Although ACAs may not drink problematically, many do retain this belief in controlling what is beyond their limits to control. As a result, they replay the dynamics of their parents' addiction in other circumstances, with similar reproach for their apparent inadequacies.

Much more documentation is needed before concluding that the characteristics described above are more common among alcoholics and their families than among other dysfunctional families. On the other hand, since accepting a revised view of self-control and the proper role of will power in one's life is generally believed to play an integral role in the treatment of alcoholism, it is justified to assume that these same factors will also play some role in treating the family members.

Codependency

It is important to acknowledge that the nonalcoholic parent very frequently becomes an active participant in building the edifice that protects the alcoholism from being seen realistically. The bricks of this edifice are all the lies, half-truths, and ignored perceptions that we call denial; and the mortar is will power. This tendency to enter into the alcoholic's distorted perspectives is labeled *codependency,* and is a concept with proven therapeutic value in the chemical dependency treatment field.

Human beings who spend an extended period of time in a committed relationship with an alcoholic frequently develop codependent personality traits that take on a life of their own, and may require intensive therapy to recover. Codependents invest their self-esteem in the ability to influence/control feelings and behavior, both in themselves and in others. They experience anxiety and boundary distortions around intimacy and separation, often confusing intimacy with fusion (i.e., poor ego boundaries) Cermak, 1985). They end up living a life that is characterized by denial, compulsions, constricted feelings, low self-esteem, and stress-related medical complications (Wegscheider-Cruse, 1985).

The characteristics of codependents place them in perfect complementary relationships with active alcoholics. Any blame that the alcoholic projects, the codependent accepts. Whenever the alcoholic relapses, the codependent feels personally inadequate. Proof of the codependent's own adequacy becomes based on his or her ability to keep the alcoholic sober. In other words, alcoholic and codependent world views are absolutely consistent. Alcoholics think other people make them drink, and codependents think they should be able to make the alcoholic not drink. The same unrealistic efforts to gain self-esteem by controlling the uncontrollable is often modeled by both parents in an alcoholic family.

Post-Traumatic Stress Disorder and ACAs

Persistent personality traits are generally overdetermined. Such is the case with control issues found in ACAs. In addition to initiating the alcoholic's and the codependent's overemphasis on control, a second genetic dynamic lies in the degree of stress experienced by a child trapped within an alcoholic family.

Within the framework of DSM-III, Axis IV provides guidelines for assessing an individual's level of stress. Listed under family factors for children and adolescents are the following: (1) cold, distant, or hostile relationships with or between parents; (2) physical or mental disturbance in family members; (3) parental intrusiveness and inconsistency; (4) insufficient parental control; and (5) loss of parents. Although alcoholism is not mentioned directly, the entire list serves as a description of dynamics in an alcoholic family. For some COAs the stress is overt, such as abuse, neglect, and a chaotic living situation. For others the stress is less obvious, such as having one's perceptions invalidated or interacting with a parent who is incapable of focusing attention and whose emotional responsiveness is chronically drug affected. This chapter is guided by the hypothesis that the degree of stress experienced by children of alcoholics is far greater than generally believed.

One argument in favor of this hypothesis is that Post-Traumatic Stress Disorder (PTSD) serves as a useful model for understanding most of the characteristics found in ACAs (Cermak, 1984, 1985). In its charter statement, the National Association for Children of Alcoholics coined the term *Adjustment Reaction to Familial Alcoholism*. As defined by DSM-III, adjustment reactions represent maladaptive behavior "in *excess* (author's italics) of the normal and expectable reaction to the stressor." Furthermore, adjustment reactions are expected to remit once the stressor ceases. The implications are that the source of difficulties during adult life experienced by COAs lies within themselves. Such a view is at significant variance with the implications of PTSD, which succinctly describes the characteristics of ACAs and implies etiologic factors that pertain in alcoholic families.

First, the symptoms of PTSD are consequences to be expected in most individuals subjected to sufficient stress. These symptoms involve both an intrusive ailment and the byproducts of excessive denial. The intrusive features, by which the trauma is reexperienced, include (1) obsessive thoughts, images, and feelings; (2) recurrent dreams; and (3) the sudden recrudescence of behavior and feelings associated with the trauma in the fact of its symbolic equivalent. The effects of excessive reliance on the mechanism of denial leads to psychic numbing, characterized by (1) a sense of estrangement and detachment and (2) a constriction of emotions, especially in situations demanding intimacy, tenderness, and sexuality. Additional symptoms of PTSD include hyperalertness (leading to startle responses, excessive autonomic arousal, and chronic anxiety) and survivor guilt (often manifested as chronic depression).

Adult children of alcoholics frequently complain of difficulties that resemble the symptoms of PTSD outlined above. They complain of not being able to stop thinking of their family and not being able to separate emotionally even with 3,000 miles between them. Whenever they sense rejection, there is the sudden reemergence of grief, fear, and inadequacy, leaving them feeling suddenly very unadult. At other times, particularly when called on to be present in a relationship and honest about their needs, ACAs complain of going blank, feeling numb and unaware of their emotions. They constantly expect catastrophe, especially after anything good has happened. And they sense a sourceless guilt, as though they are responsible for everyone else's pain. They lose themselves in their efforts to gain safety by pleasing other people. In other words, their own codependent traits emerge whole cloth in the face of stresses that resemble alcoholic family dynamics (inconsistency, arbitrariness, denial, secrets, intrusion).

Second, the symptoms of PTSD are more likely to occur if the precipitating stress is a prolonged series of traumatic events, if the trauma is perceived to be of human origin, and if the social system surrounding the individual is closed to new information or alternate perspectives. All of the above etiologic factors are descriptive of the experience for many children of alcoholics.

Third, the diagnosis of PTSD can be made if, and only if, the psychologically traumatic events are considered of sufficient severity as to lie *outside the range of human experience usually considered to be normal,* and therefore expected to evoke significant symptoms of distress in almost all individuals. The implications of PTSD point in a direction opposite to that of adjustment reaction. The source of difficulties for ACAs is now posited in the intensity of the stress experienced during childhood, rather than in the ACAs distorted reactions to that stress. Such a view validates the degree of stress, without dismissing the ACAs responsibility for acting in the present to recover from the posttraumatic effects.

The diagnosis of PTSD was initially applied to Vietnam veterans and was essentially an update of the concepts of shell shock (World War I) and war neurosis (World War II). Its applicability to children and adolescents in nonmilitary situations is demonstrated by Terr's (1983) study of the Chowchilla school bus kidnapping. After only 27 hours of utter vulnerability and terror, 100 percent of the children developed posttraumatic symptoms. Most intriguing among those symptoms, from the standpoint of understanding similar effects on children stressed by living in alcoholic families, are what Terr described as mortification (extreme shame for permitting oneself to be so powerless) and a belief in omens (retroactive distortions of memory, presumably motivated on an unconscious level to deny that one was as powerless as one in fact was).

In the final analysis, whether the trauma is overt or covert, children of alcoholics frequently develop a self-protective stance that object relations theory has described as characteristic in physically abused children. The chilling words of Vaillant (1983) help summarize why such a self-protective stance might be necessary: "Outside of residence in a concentration camp, there are very few sustained human experiences that make one the recipient of as much sadism (read "stress") as does being a close family member of an alcoholic."

Parallels to Physical Abuse

The model of physically abusive families developed by Wasserman and Rosenfeld (in press) appears relevant to an understanding of ACAs. They begin with the well-known premise that a parent-child bond is the first stage in forming relationships. The social relatedness initiated by such bonding is one hallmark of our biological heritage as primates.

All mammalian children require adequate parental nurturance, care, and protection to survive. Since human offspring require an extraordinary degree and duration of such nurturance, a repertoire of biological and psychological mechanisms has evolved that enables infants to elicit parental bonding behavior and to maintain relatively constant interpersonal contact.

When an infant's efforts to bond are undertaken in a chaotic family and only inconsistently responded to by parents, anxiety becomes potentially overwhelming. Many children build rational explanations for irrational events to defend against this anxiety. Wasserman and Rosenfeld (in press) point out that such a defense arises because young children (especially in the early school years) cognitively believe that all events are causally linked. Perhaps more importantly, these children need the illusion of constancy and benevolence in their relationships with people they cannot conceive of living without—their parents. Children in arbitrary and chaotic families are constantly uncertain about who takes ultimate responsibility for the family's and for their own safety. To prevent this chronic stress from becoming intolerable and their own personalities from fragmenting, some children need to find a reason for their suffering. They often do so by interpreting the cause of their intermittent abandonment to be their own "badness." This conclusion, although erroneous to an outside observer, serves an important defensive function for the child. Because it creates the illusion of internal control of one's fate, the child maintains a basis for hope. To paraphrase Fairburn, it is better to live as a sinner in a world ruled by God than as a saint in a world ruled by Satan. Hope stems from the belief that once the child learns how not to be "bad," the world will be as Eden again.

To a young child, home is the universe; parents are giants and gods. But for the children of alcoholics, the universe of interpersonal interactions is deeply chaotic. Each god has many faces, depending on his or her state of sobriety. The gods are capricious (e.g., seductive or angry without discernible reason). At times one or both of the parental gods is physically present but emotionally absent—stuporous in body or dead in spirit. Home is a profoundly insecure place, whether or not actual physical abuse occurs or is even threatened. The parent who is a playful pleasure at noon may become an abusive, assaultive monster by mid-afternoon. Rules and punishments announced to the child while the parent is intoxicated are treated as nonexistent the next morning. (One patient recalled being mocked by his father for not leaving the house after dinner for a week. This man had been afraid to point out that it was the father who had grounded him. Only after learning about alcohol-induced amnesic episodes did this patient begin to make sense of his earlier experience.)

Why do children of alcoholics and children who are physically abused feel relieved, more secure, and hopeful after concluding that they are the cause of their parents' inconsistent and often frankly incompetent parenting? Because by assuming responsibility, a child also concludes that destiny is under his or her control. "If what is happening to me is all my fault, then all I have to do to live in a good world is to change myself." When the child's attempts fail to alter the parents' behavior, those who retain hope try harder, redoubling their efforts and setting standards of perfection which, if attained, will lead to their having "good" parents and a happy family.

One ACA patient told of beating herself* for failing to put napkins on the table after fully preparing the meal by herself. She imagined that, had she done so, she might have prevented a particularly ugly family argument that broke out that evening. Omnipotent fantasies become exaggerated to the point that the child believes if only she chooses her actions carefully enough, she can control her parents' behavior. While this appears to an outsider as highly irrational, from the child's standpoint it makes psychological sense. If the child of an alcoholic accepts the reality that her parents' drinking is outside her control, she is left with no leverage for improving her circumstances. This leads to feeling more intensely insecure and often hopeless. Children of alcoholics who react in this "realistic" way may actually experience more profound disruptions in their development, leading to antisocial behavior, behavior disorders, and inadequate coping skills.

The dynamics outlined above hold equally for many children from physically abusive, grossly neglectful, and alcoholic families. The common factor is that to psychologically survive circumstances many of us imagine would be intolerable, the child develops coping mechanisms that are based on interpersonal boundaries distorted to include important aspects of the environment, such as parental behavior, as well as developing an omnipotent sense of what the child ought to be able to control. This is all for the purpose of enhancing the child's sense of security and hope. Without such defenses, the eventual level of social adjustment during adulthood can be severely compromised. However, because of the defenses "successful copers" develop during childhood, they often continue to have a poor internal adjustment. As adults, their personalities are characterized by a distorted belief in their own omnipotence and a tendency for depression when the expectable disappointments of life puncture this "megalomania."

Psychotherapeutic Implications

Several implications for psychotherapy with adult children of alcoholics stem from the critical role that control issues play in their sense of self-esteem, from the existence of PTSD symptoms and from their codependent tendency to equate intimacy with loss of ego boundaries. Therapists who evaluate ACAs with these implications in mind can often enhance the effectiveness of their work.

To begin with, it is useful to assess the degree of PTSD present, and especially to ascertain whether a preponderance of intrusive symptoms (i.e.,

---

*The pronouns *she* and *her* are used to refer to children of alcoholics in order to reflect the tendency for a higher percentage of ACAs seeking treatment to be female.

reexperiencing the trauma) or denial symptoms (psychic numbing) exist. Lessons from the treatment of Vietnam veterans (Schwartz, 1984) and theoretical considerations regarding distortions in the normal stress response, provide important guidelines for responding to each of these PTSD phenomena. Horowitz (1976) has shown that "stress response syndromes" such as PTSD, represent a failure of the normal modulation between denial and intrusion needed to break a stressful event down into resolvable portions. While the urge to facilitate catharsis in patients with psychic numbing is understandable, too rapid or intense release of affect may overwhelm the patient. What is required is a measured catharsis that validates the need to pull back from emotional overload and helps the patients to manage their anxiety more effectively. The proper therapeutic response to most PTSD symptoms is to concentrate on freeing the pendulum that must swing back and forth between denial and intrusion. By helping patients experience a successful modulation between these two normal responses to stress, therapists can usher ACAs into a more confident willingness to begin acknowledging feelings at the moment they are happening.

Second, it is important to assess how actively codependent ACAs are. The more deeply they invest their sense of self-esteem in others and the more completely they confuse intimacy and enmeshment, the more likely they are to suffer from severe psychopathology. Early deprivation can clearly lead to primary borderline personality disorders in children of alcoholics. On the other hand, secondary borderline behaviors appear as a result of intense codependency. ACAs who are *capable* of maintaining intact ego boundaries can often latch onto therapists in a very borderline manner in the assumption that intimacy is achieved by relinquishing boundaries. The "learned boundary deficits" can lead therapists to set treatment goals appropriate for active borderlines, but inappropriately limited for codependent ACAs. The more actively codependent an ACA is, the more valuable a referral to Twelve Step programs with a focus on ACAs can be. Healthy Al-Anon and ACA meetings can provide the validation of peers and a structured program for helping members learn detachment (i.e., appropriate interpersonal boundaries). Therapists with a working knowledge of the Al-Anon program rarely experience conflicts between these self-help groups and their own therapeutic goals. Quite the opposite, therapy in conjunction with Al-Anon can often be more effective than either one alone.

Third, the core issue of basing self-esteem on the ability to control life represents a fundamental barrier to successful therapy. In the chemical dependency field, it is generally assumed that alcoholics only begin their recovery in a meaningful way when they become willing to call into question their relationship to willpower. Up until that point, most therapeutic efforts are directed toward helping them explore in detail how they attempt to control the world, why it does not work, and what price is being paid for their devotion to unworkable solutions. Nor surprisingly, ACAs must also confront their control issues directly if they ever hope to receive substantial benefit from therapy.

It is useful to the therapist to understand the probable resistances ACAs will have to relinquishing their devotion to willpower. Not only is the unrealistic belief in self-control used by the ACA as the foundation for security and hope, not only is self-control a defense against feelings of isolation, abandonment, and loss, but it is also an identification with the beliefs of parental figures and thereby serves as a source of connectedness with the past. As such, it is both an identification with the aggressor and a genuine wish to retain respect for what was cherished by one's parents. Furthermore, control often represents a reenactment of a real experience in the child's past, since the child probably played some role in holding the parent or family together. Successfully functioning in such a role may have provided an understandable basis for the child's sense of pride. If self-discipline can be made to control their world during adulthood, ACAs can become living proof that their parents' approach to live was valuable and correct. Whether the parents could live up to their own standards is irrelevant to the illusion that one has received the gift of high standards from them.

Adult children of alcoholics will tend to resist any perceived attack on their strategy of managing life by force of will. As the therapist begins to question the effectiveness of self-control, he or she will be ignored, misunderstood, or resented. The ACA will frequently react by redoubling efforts to maintain control. After all, ACAs have direct personal evidence from the past that supports the importance of this strategy as a survival mechanism. Pressure applied by an inexperienced therapist to abandon control measures often reinforces the perceived need of the ACA client to maintain the defensive armor. In effect, a self-validating fallacy exists: If life can be happy only if one controls one's life and the lives of others, then any sign of *un*happiness is naturally seen as inadequacy on one's part, and evidence that increased vigilance and effort is required to regain control.

Even as therapy progresses and the therapist becomes more of an ally, every time ACAs reassess the realistic limits of control, they suffer anxiety and pain. This examination calls into question cherished illusions that have guided and sustained life, and maintained ties to the childhood gods—the parents. These illusions are integral to the ACAs psychic defense structure. Relinquishing them quickly would set the ACA adrift in uncharted waters (an extremely "out-of-control" feeling). Even examining this defense is painful because it automatically involves a more realistic assessment of past family circumstances, which were painstakingly distorted and guarded against to preserve self-esteem and hope. Once ACAs become more realistic about how limited their powers were in childhood, the image they created of their "good" parent is deeply challenged. They become anxious because history must be revised and brought into greater alignment with reality. The alternative is to pay the price of continued denial and distortion. Facing reality collapses the illusion of a benevolent universe, created at such personal effort and expense during childhood. At this point in psychotherapy, the ACA may still not perceive that the world offers much to replace this forsaken illusion. During these first departures from a codependent world view, the therapist can become very important as a mooring in present reality.

For all these overlapping reasons, ACAs almost invariably pass through a grief reaction with each step they make toward greater maturation and acceptance of their past. It is important for therapists to anticipate that the loss of illusion may be as significant as the loss of a body part. In general, ACAs will only consider relinquishing their devotion to control after a supportive, trusting therapeutic setting has permitted acknowledgment of the overwhelming evidence that their strategy has been the cause of great personal suffering, and that the risk of letting go of the strategy is worth taking. However, the therapist who recognizes the purposes these defenses have served realizes that undoing them is risky in psychologically fragile patients. Even in relatively well put together patients, relinquishing belief in omnipotent control will precipitate a grief reaction, since they will then have to face the depression they have been avoiding since childhood. The therapist who is alert to this dynamic is better able to help ACAs make sense of their therapeutic experience and to use the opportunity to do the grief work needed to build a more realistic and satisfying world view. This work is heightened during the important event of termination, with all of its sense of loss and abandonment.

While grief reactions by ACAs often lead to the possibility of more mature individuation, two factors present obstacles to the therapeutic process: First, each loss during therapy can be expected to resonate with a host of unresolved past losses. Alcoholic families tend not to tolerate genuine feelings of loss and sadness. Therefore, ACAs will often have a backlog of feelings around abandonment and loss that are activated as the belief in superhuman control is relinquished. Second, the arousal of grief will be sensed by many ACAs as further and potentially overwhelming loss of control. The fear is often that sadness will become unending, or that destructive, uncontrollable rage will result. Therefore, grief reactions are frequently disguised, turned inward, and manifested as frank depression. Intensification of self-recrimination is frequently an effort to reestablish the degree of control and to ward off grief.

As ACAs recover, they often benefit from a consistent therapeutic relationship during the period of relinquishing their illusions. The therapist with a working knowledge of alcoholic/codependent belief systems will better understand these moments when transference is likely to be most intense with ACAs, and will be sensitive to when and why nonjudgmental support is most effective. Such a relationship permits the corrective experience of decreasing isolation and increasing trust as the illusion of control is traded for living in a less controllable, yet more nourishing, rich, and delightfully unpredictable world.

It is particularly poignant and powerful for therapists to display an understanding of one of the ACAs core dilemmas—while their experience tells them that the locus of control in their lives is often *external,* their values tell them that self-esteem depends upon an *internal* locus. A sound psychotherapeutic relationship can provide the arena for challenging the alcoholic family belief system that perpetuates this dilemma. In its place, a new belief system can be built—one that is based on a more realistic assessment of the role of will power in our psychic lives and that legitimizes self-acceptance.

References

Bateson, G. (1971). The cybernetics of "self": A theory of alcoholism. *Psychiatry, 34,* 1–18.

Cermak, T. (1984, Summer). Children of alcoholics and the case for a new diagnostic category of co-dependency. *Alcohol Health and Research World, 8*(4), 38–42.

Cermak, T. (1985). *The adult children of alcoholics as chemical dependency therapists.* Presented at NCA Forum, Washington, DC, April 21.

Cermak, T., & Brown, S. (1982, July). Interactional group therapy with the adult children of alcoholics. *International Journal of Group Psychotherapy, 32*(3), 375–389.

El-Guebaly, N., Offord, D. (1977, April). The offspring of alcoholics: A critical review. *American Journal of Psychiatry, 134,* 86–91.

Hindman, M. (1975–76, Winter). Children of alcoholic parents. *Alcohol, Health and Research World NIAAA,* 2–6.

Horowitz, M. (1976). *Stress response syndromes.* New York: Jason Aronson.

Keane, J. (1983, April). *Factors in the healthy adjustment of CoA's.* Presented at the NCA Forum, Houston.

Lavino, J. (1982). *CoA's in the workplace.* Presented at the Governor's Conference on Children of Alcoholics, New York.

Miller, D. (1977). *Children of alcoholics: A twenty-year longitudinal study.* San Francisco: Institute for Scientific Analysis.

Rosenfeld, A., Wenegrat, A., et al. (1982). Sleeping patterns in upper middle-class families when the child awakens ill or frightened. *Archives of General Psychiatry, 39,* 943–947.

Schwartz, H. (1984). *Psychotherapy of the combat veteran.* Jamaica, NY: Spectrum Publications.

Terr, L. (1983, December). Chowchilla revisited: The effects of psychic trauma four years after a school-bus kidnapping. *American Journal of Psychiatry, 140,* (12) 1543–1550.

Vaillant, G. (1983). *The natural history of alcoholism* (p. 20). Washington, DC: Howard University Press.

Wasserman, S., & Rosenfeld, A. (in press). The dynamics of child abuse. *Bulletin of the Academy of Psychiatry and the Law.*

Wegsdcheider, A. (1981). *Another chance.* Palo Alto, CA: Science and Behavior Books.

Wegscheider-Cruse, S. (1985). *Choicemaking.* Health Communications, Inc.

Whitfield, C. (1980, June). Children of alcoholics: Treatment issues. *Maryland State Medical Journal,* 86–91.

CHAPTER FOURTEEN

The Therapist's Relationship with Couples with an Alcoholic Member

DAVID BERENSON, M.D.

Alcoholics and their families are notoriously frustrating for therapists of all theoretical persuasions. As family therapy of alcoholism evolves, it focuses increasingly on changing relationships within the family rather than on interpreting the client-therapist relationship. This chapter presents a way of understanding and utilizing isomorphic therapeutic relationships to achieve practical clinical results. Its focus will be on enabling the therapist to take a clear, nonreactive stance as a means to potentiate wider changes in the family system. The changes are directed through conjoint family sessions or by coaching an individual on altering relationships within his or her family of origin. I prefer this approach to other forms of therapy that concentrate on interpreting transference or directly altering family structure or communication patterns.

Previously I presented an overview of an approach to alcohol problems that integrates Bowen's Family Systems Theory with Alcoholics Anonymous and Al-Anon (Berenson, 1976), an approach that subsequently has been further developed by Bepko and Krestan (1985). This chapter will address specific issues that arise in the course of the therapist's relationship with couples in the "wet" phase of alcoholism, and this therapeutic approach will be placed in the wider context of general systems theory.

In general systems theory, the term *isomorphism* means having the same form. Here, it refers to the tendency within systems for patterns to replicate themselves. A similar process may occur at all levels within a given system, with variations in surface manifestation. Isomorphism also carries a holistic connotation. An obvious example of isomorphism in therapeutic relationships is the transference process, wherein the client replicates previous relationship patterns in his or her relationship with the therapist. The interaction and resolution of transference is the foundation on which psychoanalysis is based.

The relationship between therapist and families with alcohol problems frequently mirrors events within those families. For example, the wife of an alcoholic may veer between rescuing and persecuting her husband. Some therapists follow a similar pattern with alcoholic patients. At first they may allow the alcoholic to do anything, even come to sessions drunk, then shift to a punitive stance and terminate therapy angrily or demand that the alcoholic sober up before they will treat him. In both situations, spouse and therapist are caught up in a system of automatic emotional reactions to the alcoholic. Neither has a clear view of how the system operates and neither is self-determined in his or her own behavior.

Historically, therapists have had difficulty treating alcoholism because of a traditional reliance on words or content. We are taught to point out, interpret, and clarify problems verbally. This method of working again parallels patterns within the alcoholic family. An alcoholic's wife may point out for years the destructive effect of her husband's drinking behavior. The alcoholic becomes extremely adept at agreeing with her verbally while dramatizing his disagreement through his actions. When a therapist's work with an alcoholic is primarily verbal, it only perpetuates existing patterns. To treat alcoholism effectively, the therapist must take into account the total pattern that exists within both family and treatment situations, striking a balance between overinvolvement and detachment, which enables the therapist to modify the family system. This continuum of involvement is what Minuchin calls "joining" or "restructuring."

Just as a surgeon maintains a clean operating field, a therapist working with alcohols must establish and maintain a position that affords a clear view of patterns within the family. The goal is to structure treatment to achieve maximum leverage with minimum chaos. A therapist must forgo the initial impulse to focus on changing the most obviously dysfunctional member of the family: the alcoholic. This direct approach only replicates the pattern in which the wife becomes, in Fogarty's (1976) terms, a pursuer and the alcoholic a distancer. No matter how skillful the therapist, any content or process interpretations he or she uses will be rendered ineffective since this approach parallels the wife's pursuit. And the alcoholic has long since perfected the ability to evade and frustrate the spouse's and therapist's efforts to change him, while continuing to drink. As a therapist working to restructure an alcoholic family, my first move is always *not* to pursue the alcoholic.

This does not mean I refuse to talk to alcoholics, but I define my initial responsibility to them as medical and educational, rather than psychotherapeutic. I may diagnose a drinking problem, discuss the disease model of alcoholism, explain the stages of denial, and suggest attending Alcoholics Anonymous or a residential treatment program, all within a single session. I do not expect the drinker to welcome my diagnosis or agree with my recommendations. In fact, I tell the alcoholic explicitly I do *not* expect him or her to be able to follow my suggestions at first, because of the presence of denial. But I also let the individual know that eventually he or she will have to do so if he or she wants to resolve personal and relationship problems. By taking a hard line, I immediately establish a position very different from that of the stereotypical "shrink," who gets lumped by the drinker into the same ineffectual category as the spouse.

If a therapist does not pursue the alcoholic, two options remain: to work with the couple or with the spouse alone. In either case, the focus is on keeping the problem *within* the couple. The therapist must make it clear that he or she is not attached to any particular outcome, but is acting as consultant to the family. In treating alcohol-related problems, either in conjoint sessions or with the spouse alone, the therapist points out transactional patterns and presents behavioral alternatives without getting very involved in interpreting content or trying to impose a change of behavior. The goal is to cool down the entangled emotional system to allow the spouse and alcoholic to gain perspective on their automatic behavior patterns.

By seeing couples, the therapist is immediately protected from the problem of what to do if the alcoholic comes to a session drunk. At the outset of the session, the therapist clearly defines the problem as the *spouse's* rather than the alcoholic's. The therapist discusses with the spouse what options he or she has to respond to the alcoholic's behavior and points out during the session or through viewing a videotape of the session later how drinking affects the couple's interaction. A therapist always has the right to end a session if an alcoholic becomes too disruptive. As therapists, we are responsible for the structure of the therapy, not for what happens within the couple.

Often the alcoholic will try to sabotage therapy by refusing to come to conjoint sessions. The resigned spouse may then shrug his or her shoulders and say, "If he (she) doesn't come, what can I do?," thus effectively passing responsibility to the therapist, just as the alcoholic passes responsibility to his or her spouse. The structure of therapy again replicates the relation between alcoholic and spouse. By clarifying the situation and taking an "I" position with the spouse, the therapist models behavior that the wife or husband can then adapt for use in dealing with the alcoholic. As defined by Bowen (1976a), an "I" position means being self-determined rather than reacting automatically to forces within a system. It means accepting responsibility for one's behavior rather than blaming someone or something else.

There are a few specific steps the therapist must take at the start of therapy. First, he or she must calm the emotional intensity within the sessions and within the family. In the midst of extreme chaos or conflict, few families can stabilize sufficiently to move to another level. Seeing one member of the family may be a first step toward quieting down the system and getting some clarity. The next priority is to create a support system for family members that will help them make needed changes and allow the therapist to function as consultant outside the family system. If a family has social problems related to jobs or housing, or if there is active physical abuse, the therapist will need to mobilize support through the natural system of extended family and friends or draw upon aid from social agencies, vocational training, and protective services. When abuse is more emotional than physical, a referral to Al-Anon or Codependents Anonymous (CODA) can provide a social and emotional support system for the codependent spouse.

I have found Al-Anon to be especially effective in reinforcing my instructions to the client. Following a policy of nonreactive behavior may seem simple and reasonable in the therapist's office, but at home in the midst of chaos, good intentions break down and many people have trouble remembering and acting on therapeutic suggestions. An Al-Anon sponsor, only a phone call away, can provide the emotional support needed to calm a volatile situation. I will usually refuse to take phone calls from clients between sessions if they call during a crisis and have refused to attend Al-Anon meetings. If they are attending meetings and have a problem their sponsor can't handle, then of course I will take their call. But the implied message behind my policy is that therapy is an opportunity for people to look at themselves and take responsibility for their lives, not a place to get sympathy.

A high percentage of spouses will accept referrals to Al-Anon and drinkers to AA if the therapist focuses on two issues: matching the client's background to a specific Twelve Step meeting and directly addressing the issue of shame. I caution my clients that they may feel uncomfortable in AA or Al-Anon for two reasons: because the other people in the group are not enough like them or because they are overwhelmed by the shame associated with addiction.

The first problem can be overcome by referring clients to specific meetings where they are likely to fit in. I tell them to try a number of meetings until they find one where they feel comfortable. The second problem can be eased by educating clients about the shame-driven aspect of the addictive cycle in which they are caught, stressing the fact that AA and Al-Anon are uniquely treatments for shame. If they feel shame, humiliation, and embarrassment at the prospect of attending AA or Al-Anon, I reassure them that they will probably experience considerable relief by the end of the first meeting—a relief that will permeate more and more of their lives if they continue to attend Twelve Step groups.

It is essential that therapists who themselves are working with alcohol-related problems have an emotional support system. The alcoholic frequently transfers his or her anxiety to the spouse, who in turn passes it on to the therapist. The therapist must avoid letting this anxiety touch off a personal reaction that amplifies total anxiety within the therapy and adds it to the family. He or she must be careful to keep responsibility within the family to allow them to deal with the problem. Consultation or supervision on an as-needed basis helps the therapist to maintain clarity. Audio- or videotaping sessions for later review is a good means of reinforcing objectivity, as is discussing with the consultant the emotional reactions triggered in the therapist from dealing with an alcoholic family system. The two most common reactions a therapist will have are overinvolvement, which comes from getting sucked into the system, or a tendency to withdraw or reject the client as a means of self-protection. The purpose of outside consultation or supervision is to maintain perspective on the structure or pattern of the therapy as a whole in order to avoid getting bogged down in its content or "facts."

The therapist *always* has the option to discontinue seeing an individual or family in therapy. In the mental health field, we often make it our duty to see whoever walks into the office on a weekly basis for an indefinite period of time. When a therapist gets sufficiently frustrated at a client's lack of progress, the client may be discharged with what I call a "farewell curse," telling the client he or she is unmotivated or borderline or narcissistic. It is essential that the therapist maintain the option of not treating clients in two situations. The first arises when the therapist realistically recognizes he or she is incapable of handling a particular problem. This usually occurs when the therapist is either inexperienced in working with alcohol problems, or when he or she has unresolved emotional patterns in his or her own family that parallel those of the client. The therapist may then refer the client to Al-Anon or AA, or to another therapist, but must make sure the client realizes the referral is being made because the therapist lacks the necessary skills, not because the client is untreatable.

The second situation arises when, in a therapist's accurate professional assessment, therapy would not help to resolve a client's problems at a particular time. For example, if the client is referred to Al-Anon, refuses to go, and continues in therapy with no improvement, the therapist can point out that unless the client is willing to take this additional step, he or she will probably not get better. The situation is analogous to an internist prescribing penicillin for a patient with pneumonia who refuses to take the medicine and then comes back repeatedly to ask the doctor to treat him or her for pneumonia. A therapist has the right to suspend therapy until the client is willing to follow suggestions or to suggest a viable alternative.

Many clients in therapy have no real intention of changing, but are only looking for support and justification to continue self-destructive patterns. The therapist has a responsibility to disillusion a client who thinks he or she is solving problems when in reality the client is only reinforcing or perpetuating them. This happens in therapy, as it does in marriages, when the alcoholic and therapist or spouse are forever debating the nature of the problem, coming up with new solutions and never quite making any progress. The therapist who concentrates on interpreting content, hoping this will cause the client to change, is stuck in the same futile pattern as the spouse who keeps hoping that he or she can say or do the right thing in the right way at the right time and thereby change the alcoholic. Taking a clear, strong, nonreactive position will have more of an impact on resolving alcohol problems than any amount of brilliant words, interpretations, or tasks.

Once I have the spouse in therapy with a clear contract to work on changing his or her role in the process that maintains alcoholism, I find it useful to present the spouse with three options to resolve the drinking problem:

1. Keep doing exactly what you are doing.
2. Detach or emotionally distance yourself by:
   a. accepting the situation and choosing to live with it, or
   b. doing a family intervention.
3. Separate or physically distance yourself by
   a. leaving, or
   b. having the alcoholic leave.

The first option doesn't look like it would do much to resolve a drinking problem, but if in fact a spouse would consciously *choose* to behave exactly as he or she is doing, rather than blaming others or resisting the pattern, the problem would usually resolve itself. In my experience, however, very few people have been able to use this way to resolve an intense alcohol problem. The main advantage of this option is that one can immediately get down to work in therapy. Given the choice between changing and not changing, most clients will choose not to change, but in a covert way. By suggesting that client continue doing exactly as he or she has been doing, a therapist can undercut this whole pattern. I might tell a client, "You've put up with this for 10 years. I don't see why it can't go on for another 10." This kind of statement places responsibility squarely within the family, not with the therapist. When clients consistently avoid choosing options 2 and 3, the therapist can then point out that they are choosing option 1 by default.

Clients are usually quick to say that keeping the situation as it is would be intolerable, and that they want to move on to the next option — emotional detachment or distance. This option requires the spouse to stop criticizing or denying the alcoholic's drinking. For example, she is asked just to accept his drinking behavior as she continues to live with him, and to accept responsibility for her own feelings and reactions. This is a difficult goal, and in drinking systems with a high degree of emotional intensity, almost impossible. It also presents another isomorphic trap of which therapists and Al-Anon sponsors must beware. The first step in AA is for the alcoholic to acknowledge his or her powerlessness over alcohol. In Al-Anon, the spouse's first step is to acknowledge his or her powerlessness over the alcoholic. Many therapists and Al-Anon members may misinterpret this step to mean the spouse should detach from the alcoholic by *controlling his or her own emotions*. But it is no more possible for the spouse to do that than it is for the alcoholic to control his or her drinking. So option number 2, emotionally detaching from the alcoholic, may also be an "impossible" choice for most spouses.

If the spouse of an alcoholic and other family members have already achieved some detachment, the therapist may choose to set up an intervention. As developed by Johnson (1986), an intervention is a mobilization of the entire social system surrounding the alcoholic, including nuclear and extended family, employer and/or coworkers, friends, and neighbors. The intervention team forms. The members make lists of specific drinking incidents, conduct a rehearsal on their own or under professional guidance, and then stage a surprise confrontation with the problem drinker. They read their lists of incidents to make the alcoholic aware of his or her behavior and of its effect on them. The team has also previously arranged an opening for residential treatment — the goal being to get the drinker into the facility, preferably that same day.

When interventions work, there will be a dramatic improvement. When they don't, a sense of betrayal and bitterness may linger. Problems arise, particularly when the spouse or other family members are not detached but see the intervention and subsequent treatment of the alcoholic as a magical means of change that absolves them of responsibility for their part in the process. Other family members or friends who are actively enabling the alcoholic's drinking may sabotage the intervention, reinforcing the atmosphere of defeat within the family. Because of these risks, I prefer to postpone interventions until family members have begun to shift their reactivity. My adaptation of the intervention technique is similar to that developed by Treadway (1989). I am also likely to invite the drinker to participate in the process rather than springing it on him or her as a surprise.

Option 3 requires a physical separation. If a wife chooses this option, her first thought is usually to get the alcoholic to leave, with the rationale, "I don't want to leave him with all the things I've worked so hard for all these years." Unfortunately, as a general rule in resolving alcohol problems, if a spouse is not prepared to go every step of the way, he or she will suffer repeated defeats. The alcoholic has lots of ways to frustrate the attempts to get him or her out of the house. First, the drinker can simply refuse to leave, or pay lip service to obeying orders of protection and then return unexpectedly. The therapist must allow the spouse to consider the option of the alcoholic leaving, realizing that if that proves impossible, he or she is left with only one option—the spouse must be the one to go. In most cases, a wife will flatly refuse to even consider leaving, since this means facing issues of dependency as well as formidable logistical difficulties.

In effect, the therapist has presented the spouse with three impossible options. The spouse can deal with the alcoholic by adopting one of the three available courses of action and consistently following through, or may despair as he or she exhausts the possibilities of change, realizes his or her powerlessness over emotional reactions to the alcoholic, and admits his or her life has become unmanageable. This is a crucial point in therapy. The therapist must repeatedly clarify that these are the only options available, without expecting the spouse will be able to adopt any one of them right away.

The next phase of therapy allows the client to share feelings of emptiness, despair, failure, and shame at the impossibility of achieving any of these solutions. The goal at this point is for the spouse to "hit bottom" and consequently begin to focus on taking personal responsibility rather than on trying to change the alcoholic. Many people will panic at this prospect and seek to run away from it. At this point I have found it useful to tell the client, "I understand how scary this is. If you can find any other way to resolve the situation, I encourage you to do so. But in my experience there is no other way out, and eventually you will have to choose one of the options we have outlined. To get through this, you may have to experience quite a lot of emptiness, powerlessness, and despair."

The isomorphic trap is that the therapist must beware that he or she is asking the spouse to change, as the spouse has been asking the alcoholic to change. Once the therapist has defined the available options, the spouse must be given time and space to choose one of the alternatives. The fundamental principle both therapist and spouse must remember is that one can never change anyone else; one can only create a context in which another person is allowed the possibility of changing.

If the therapy reaches an impasse, the therapist is faced with the same three options as the spouse. Many fall covertly into option 1, and continue to do whatever has been making the therapeutic situation unworkable. If the therapist chooses the second option, he or she will continue to work with the spouse on issues other than the spouses reactivity to the drinking behavior, but the therapist must make it clear that he or she has no illusions that this sort of work will do anything to resolve the drinking. This is isomorphic, with the spouse continuing to live with the alcoholic while detaching from the alcoholic's drinking. The third option is to interrupt the therapy, giving the client the opportunity to return when he or she is ready to work in therapy. This parallels the choice in which the spouse physically separates from the alcoholic without making any decision about divorce.

The therapist can use systems concepts, such as pursuer/distancer and triangles, as a means to provide perspective for the therapist and the client. By viewing the process connected with drinking as one that oscillates over time and occurs within a wider family context that may span generations, the client can begin to get outside his or her own immediate situation. When a clearer perspective on the family system is seen, the spouse can begin to assume responsibility for her or his own functioning within it.

In seeing a spouse individually, the therapist must beware of becoming personally involved in a triangle with the alcoholic and spouse, which leaves the alcoholic out in the cold. A *triangle* is defined as an automatic emotional system operating with three people (Bowen, 1976a, 1976b; Fogarty, 1976). (It is important to realize that in a chapter of this nature, *triangulation* can only be presented conceptually. Clinical and personal experience are necessary to fully understand this system.) One way to visualize triangulation is to imagine a string connecting you with two other people, or connecting you, another person, and a thing. Every time someone moves, the string maintains the same amount of total distance. For example, in a triangulated family situation, if you move closer to your father, you will mover further away from your mother. In a "threesome," as opposed to a triangle, each member has flexibility to move freely with the other two. In a threesome, you can move closer to your father without distancing yourself from your mother, or feel close to both at the same time, or simultaneously distant from both.

If the therapist is not triangulated into the system, he or she can see the spouse for individual therapy without putting the alcoholic in a distant position where the alcoholic feels persecuted and left out, as though spouse and therapist were conspiring against him or her. Even if therapy sessions are held without the alcoholic, if the alcoholic has a sense of support, he or she may not do much to undermine the situation if he or she feels part of a threesome rather than a triangle. There is no specific form that distinguishes a triangle from a threesome; rather, it is the context or way in which one handles a situation that is relevant. Specific techniques to avoid triangulation include inviting the alcoholic to sessions, letting the alcoholic know he or she is free to choose whether to come or not, or informing the alcoholic of what is happening by telephone.

A crucial phase in therapy is reached when the spouse begins to focus on self, to observe her or his functioning within the system, to accept responsibility for his or her own contributions, and to start focusing on modifying his or her behavior. It is essential for the therapist to point out at this juncture that the alcoholic may get worse. In attempting to avoid the desperation of hitting bottom, the alcoholic may do anything to lure a spouse who is beginning to detach back into entanglement. The drinker may go so far as to get hospitalized, threaten suicide, or increase drunken driving. The alcoholic's anxiety is transmitted to the spouse, who in turn passes it on to the therapist. The therapist must then avoid the isomorphic trap of taking responsibility for the spouse as the spouse has taken responsibility for the alcoholic. If the therapist has predicted to the spouse that the situation is likely to worsen, both will be able to maintain perspective and avoid precipitating a crisis before the spouse is ready to handle it.

It is less likely that the alcoholic will actually damage self or someone else if the spouse is able to detach enough to say, "I don't want you to kill yourself, but I can't stop you." Similarly, if the therapist is detached enough to say to the spouse, "It's okay with me if you want to live with this drinking problem in your marriage for the rest of your life," it is far less likely that the spouse will continue to do so. The trap to avoid here is using the words as manipulation or gimmick rather than creating a context in which it is genuinely acceptable for the therapy either to succeed or to fail. If the spouse or therapist make the above comments sarcastically, or as a way to cover up true feelings, a disaster may result.

Once the spouse has hit bottom and taken responsibility for self, the alcoholic will become more accessible as he or she continues his or her own process of hitting bottom. At this point the drinker may be willing to get sober, usually through participating in Alcoholics Anonymous. It is critical that here, on the verge of success, the therapist, spouse, family members, and friends not rush in with misguided encouragement to "help" the alcoholic to stop drinking. This can wipe out all the progress that has been made. In order for the alcoholic to stop drinking, it is often necessary for him or her to experience emptiness and powerlessness. This may touch off emotional resonances in those close to the alcoholic, which impel the others to offer hope to the alcoholic, which will keep the drinker from hitting bottom.

If one has become a therapist as a way to control unresolved problems of one's own, it will be impossible to treat people at this phase, since what is required here is acceptance and surrender, not control and manipulation.

One becomes empowered only by accepting powerlessness. If the therapist has not personally experienced emptiness and powerlessness as liberating, he or she must be on guard against an isomorphic tendency to impede the system from hitting bottom with "helpful" suggestions, just as spouse, family, and friends keep the alcoholic from hitting bottom with well-intentioned concerns.

In dealing with issues of acceptance, surrender, and recovery, it is useful to extend the isomorphic therapeutic relationship to the ultimate level—to what Alcoholic Anonymous calls a "Higher Power," or God as we understand God. The clinical approach I have developed rests on the confidence that there is indeed a loving, divine presence that is always available to the alcoholic, spouse, and therapist and that can dramatically heal emotional and relationship problems. It is crucial for therapists who seek to treat addictive problems to discover for themselves whether this is truth or merely wishful thinking.

In previous publications, I have sought to address the "allergy" many therapists have to the "God stuff" (Berenson, 1985, in press). Many of us are comfortable with the notion that we are basically biochemical, psychological, or cybernetic mechanisms, or, conversely, that we are "masters of our fate." But we may be profoundly disquieted by the possibility that there may, in truth, be a loving and powerful presence pervading our inner and outer world that transcends our comprehension. The resistance many therapists have to the spiritual message of Alcoholics Anonymous may be isomorphic, with the "drunk pride" many alcoholics exhibit on hearing the same message.

The next decade will likely see an even greater increase in publications, self-help groups, and workshops that directly address issues of spirituality and personal relationship with divinity. Resources that exist for a therapist to get in touch with his or her own powerlessness and Higher Power include specific meetings for therapists within Al-Anon and Codependents Anonymous and workshops on transcendence by this author and others.

When the alcoholic has truly hit bottom, the family system will then move into the "dry" phase, or, in rare instances, directly into sobriety with an integration and transcendence of both "wet" and "dry" feelings and behaviors. At this point, there are new issues to which the therapist must respond, but the principles of creating and sustaining a therapeutic relationship or context remain the same.

References

Bepko, C., & Krestan, H. (1985). *The responsibility trap: A blueprint for treating the alcoholic family.* New York: The Free Press.

Berenson, D. (1976). Alcohol and the family system. In P. Guerin (Ed.), *Family therapy: Theory and practice.* New York: Gardner Press.

Berenson, D. (1985). Foreword to Bepko, B., & Krestan, J. *The responsibility trap: A blueprint for treating the alcoholic family.* New York. The Free Press.

Berenson, D. (in press). A systemic view of spirituality: God and twelve step programs as resources in family therapy. *Journal for Strategic and Systemic Therapies.*

Bowen, M. (1976a). Principles and techniques of multiple family therapy. In P. Guerin, (Ed.), *Family therapy: Theory and practice.* New York: Gardner Press.

Bowen, M. (1976b). Theory in the practice of psychotherapy. In P. Guerin (Ed.), *Family therapy: Theory and practice.* New York: Gardner Press.

Fogarty, T. (1976). Marital crisis. In P. Guerin (Ed.), *Family therapy: Theory and practice.* New York: Gardner Press.

Fossum, M., & Mason, M. (1986). *Facing shame: Families in recovery.* New York: Norton.

Johnson, V. (1986). *Intervention.* Minneapolis: Johnson Institute Press.

Kurtz, E. (1982). Why AA works: The intellectual significance of Alcoholics Anonymous. *Journal of Studies on Alcohol, 41,* 38–40.

Minuchin, S. (1974). *Families and family therapy.* Cambridge, MA: Harvard University Press.

Treadway, D. (1989). *Before it's too late: Working with substance abuse in the family.* New York: Norton.

CHAPTER FIFTEEN

An Abstinence Model of Family Therapy

MARION L. USHER, M.S.S.W.
George Washington University School of Medicine

The initial focus of this treatment model is to engage the family in an ongoing therapeutic process and bring the family into a pattern of abstinence as quickly as possible. Abstinence is a central issue of the treatment contract and represents an important part of the outcome. Several factors enter into the decision to build a treatment model on an abstinence foundation. The insistence on abstinence confronts the problem directly and intrudes on the family's denial patterns. The therapist then can observe how the family tries to organize its behavior into familiar patterns used in the past. The therapist requires abstinence as a parameter of therapy and this parameter has the effect of disrupting the system. This disruption creates a crisis, thereby providing the seeds for family change (Rapaport, 1965).

When the abstinence is not negotiable, the family's task is to discover the best way to achieve sobriety, rather than decide whether alcohol is a problem. The therapist begins to orchestrate the family's interactional patterns by contracting with the individual members to perform specific behaviors. Thus, the therapist establishes an atmosphere in which adaptive familial transactions can take place.

The abstinence model permits the therapist to see how the family functions without alcohol. Since alcohol has been an incorporated part of their daily life, the question is how the family will shape its life without alcohol (Steinglass, 1976). The removal of alcohol from the family system reveals an underlying emotional impoverishment, including feelings of alienation, loneliness, and emptiness that may be experienced by family members (Usher, Jay, & Glass, 1979).

Finally, abstinence is indicated because there may be some genetic involvement. Sufficient evidence now suggests that alcoholism is a familial illness, indicating that returning to drinking is not a viable option (Barnard, 1981, p. 130) (Johnson, 1981–1982).

Abstinence, AA self-help groups, and family therapy comprise the parameters of this model of therapy (see Figure 15–1). These parameters are introduced at the initiation of therapy and are dealt with through-out the course of therapy until they are fulfilled. This process can take from a few weeks to many months or even several years. Even though an alcoholic is abstinent for two years, if the spouse has not attended Al-Anon, the conditions of therapy have not been met. The behavior is seen as noncompliant with the conditions of therapy and, as such, the reasons are explored in therapy.

In this treatment model for working with alcohol-complicated families, there are three phases of therapy. The first phase involves the processes of assessing the family and dealing with the alcohol. The therapist develops a picture of how the family fine-tunes by examining the family's ability to solve problems and by looking at other dimensions of family life, such as communication patterns, roles, the affective involvement of the family members with each other, and the behavioral controls used by the family. The technique of building a genogram and taking an alcohol history results in identifying and labeling the alcohol as a problem for the individual and the family. The family makes a commitment to abstinence through the contracting process. The contract itself calls for the alcoholic to stop drinking and go to AA. The spouse and children are required to go to Al-Anon and Alateen.

The therapeutic task of the second phase of therapy is the reorganization of the family without alcohol. In this phase, the family appears vulnerable and ill-equipped to meet its needs. The feelings of despair and emptiness that arise are labeled by the therapist as the emotional desert. Emphasis is placed on learning skills that will allow the family members to function more effectively as individuals and as a family. The technique of skill building is used to deal with the emotional desert.

The healing of wounded relationships and the ownership of past irresponsible behavior represent the challenge of the third phase of therapy. The therapist encourages the family to enter into this repairing process by using techniques such as identifying old hurts and structuring interactions in the session that will promote adult-to-adult or parent-to-child dialogue. The repairing process should be completed by the family prior to their termination from therapy. The therapist once again evaluates the family at the termination phase of therapy. Criteria considered at this time include length of abstinence, and the instrumental, affective, and structural changes made by the family.

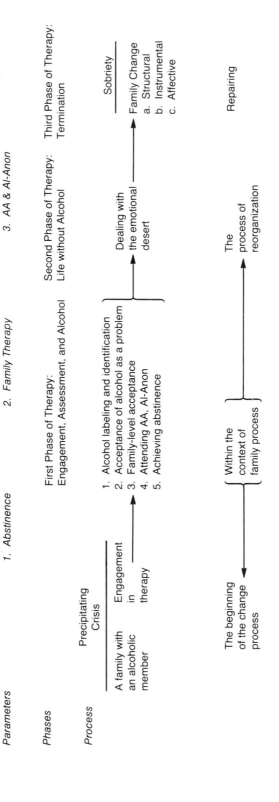

FIGURE 15–1 • A Family Treatment Model for Alcoholic Families

Parameters	1. Abstinence	2. Family Therapy	3. AA & Al-Anon

Phases

First Phase of Therapy:
Engagement, Assessment, and Alcohol

Second Phase of Therapy:
Life without Alcohol

Third Phase of Therapy:
Termination

Sobriety

Family Change
a. Structural
b. Instrumental
c. Affective

Process

Precipitating
Crisis

A family with   Engagement
an alcoholic   in
member   therapy

1. Alcohol labeling and identification
2. Acceptance of alcohol as a problem
3. Family-level acceptance
4. Attending AA, Al-Anon
5. Achieving abstinence

Dealing with
the emotional
desert

The beginning
of the change
process

Within the
context of
family process

The
process of
reorganization

Repairing

The First Phase of Therapy: Assessing the Family and Confronting the Alcoholism

The therapist begins to make clinical judgments when the first contact is made. Requesting the whole family to come to the office tells the contact person that the therapist sees the problem as one with significant implications for the whole family.

Once the family enters therapy, the therapist begins to work with the family to understand the transactional patterns that shape the family members' behavior (Epstein & Bishop, 1981, p. 447). At the end of the assessment phase, the clinician should know what and where the problems are, understand how the family operates, and have an outline of the treatment plan.

This approach to families complicated by alcohol is built on the following assumptions:

1. The presence of alcoholism in the family is an incorporated part of that family's life.
2. Alcohol becomes labeled as a problem when an individual or a group of individuals in the family experiences a disruption in the environment or within themselves.
3. Sobriety achieved through AA and Al-Anon solely does not address the emotional injuries within the family.
4. Families are always in a process of change. At the same time that families are changing, they have a propensity to reestablish familiar patterns of interacting.
5. All the members of a family have a relationship with one another.
6. The family as a system has boundaries and an organizational structure.

This family model has a structural and problem-solving orientation. It focuses on the person in his or her social context (Minuchin, 1974). As the family becomes more effective in solving the problems it faces, the patterns of interaction between the members also change. Satisfying individuals' interpersonal needs becomes possible for the family. One treatment goal is to facilitate this process.

Dimensions of a Family Assessment

The family can be assessed along the following dimensions of family functioning: problem solving, communication patterns, role-affective responsiveness, affective involvement, and behavioral controls the family uses (Epstein, Bishop, & Levin, 1978). The process begins by examining the family's ability to solve its problems. The therapist looks at how the family identifies, grapples with, and resolves its problems. The components of the problem-solving process include identifying the problem, planning a course of action, carrying out the plan, and assessing the effectiveness of the action the family took to correct the problem. For example, in the repeating pattern of a spouse nagging the alcoholic partner to stop drinking, the hoped for solution is that the alcoholic partner would agree to stop drinking. Instead of quitting, the alcoholic responds by picking fights with the spouse. In examining this process, only the spouse identified the problem. They, as a couple, do not agree about the alcoholism — nor do they choose a more effective solution than fighting, such as going to AA and Al-Anon. The clinician observes and assesses inadequate problem-solving processes operating in the family.

Communication patterns involve the exchange of information within the family as well as between the family and its environment. These patterns are analyzed in terms of content and direction. The clarity of any given message moves along the continuum from clear to masked and the direction of any given statement travels from direct to indirect. Verbal communication can be transmitted in any one of the four possible combinations: clear and direct, clear and indirect, masked and direct, and masked and indirect. For example, "All alcoholics are irresponsible" is a communication that is clear in content but is intended to be indirect because it is not person specific.

As the family structure grows and develops, roles are ascribed to and taken by family members. Performance of specific normative roles, such as mother doing the mothering and father doing the fathering, are necessary to sustain the family. Family functioning can be further divided into instrumental and affective areas. The former consists of meeting the provision of daily human needs and the latter is concerned with nurturance and emotional support.

Although some roles can be adaptive, others are not. For example, a scapegoated child used by parents to avoid facing their marital problems is a maladaptive role that the family assigned to the child and a role that the child accepted. Families with an alcoholic member can develop specific roles to continue functioning as they are and to avoid change.

Wegsheider (1981) describes various roles played out in alcoholic families: the enabler, the hero, the scapegoat, the lost child, and the mascot. The *enabler* is the person who protects the alcoholic from experiencing the consequences of his or her behavior. The *hero* (or *heroine*) brings joy to the family. His or her successes are given a disproportionate amount of attention but his or her feelings of loneliness are never addressed. The *scapegoat,* generally the second child, withdraws from the family and relies on friends to meet his or her needs. Often, the acting-out behavior of the scapegoated child brings the family into treatment. The *lost child* often is a loner, who tries to stay out of everyone's way and not cause trouble. The *mascot,* a role generally assumed by the youngest child, is protected by older siblings. The mascot quickly learns to get parental attention by acting precociously. A repertoire of behaviors solidify the role and hinder the individual from developing more constructive behaviors. Each person in the family participates in the masquerade and contributes to the perpetuation of these dysfunctional roles. These roles are dysfunctional since they do not allow the person to have a full range of feelings and behaviors.

By understanding the roles enacted by each person, the therapist can begin to decipher the rules by which the family operates and some of the myths that they hold sacred. For example, a family with an alcoholic member may believe the following myth: They deny that alcohol is a problem for them by stating that the alcoholic works full-time and has done so for many years and, therefore, is not an alcoholic. The myth operating here is that only skid row bums are alcoholics, not working people who live in families.

When a husband wakes up with a hangover too severe to permit him to go to work and his wife calls his boss saying he has the flu, they are acting on their mutual agreement that the wife, as the enabler, should always cover for the husband when he abuses alcohol.

Affective responsiveness refers to the family's ability to respond with emotional appropriateness to a range of stimuli. Feelings range from emotions such as warmth and tenderness to fear, anger, and sadness. In assessing the family's ability to respond, the therapist needs to observe how the family members express their feelings. For example, is the therapist seeing a family that can only express their angry feelings or is this a family that suppresses all emotions and hides them from themselves and outsiders? These observations will reveal a sense of the family's capacity for appropriate affective responsiveness as well as the level of intensity of the responses.

Assessing affective involvement establishes the degree to which family members demonstrate an interest in each other—in each other's values, interests, and lives. The affective dimension ranges from lack of involvement—cold and distant—to symbiotic, or overly defendant, and fusion. At the midpoint on the continuum, the individuals in the family have the capacity to show their concern for each other and to respond to each other with empathy.

The final dimension of this assessment format is an understanding of how the family controls its members. Different behavior may be required for certain situations, for example, little children at the seashore in contrast to the same children at dinner. However, the therapist must evaluate the techniques the family uses to keep members in line. The family style may be rigid, flexible laissez-faire, or chaotic patterns of behavioral control. A rigid control pattern makes no allowance for the differences between individuals or in the context of the behavior. A family that governs its members flexibly is one that is responsive to the circumstances. Decisions are made by evaluating the factors involved in the situation. A laissez-faire style permits the individuals to make their own decisions with little interference from others. Last, a chaotic pattern implies random or no control with no consistency.

Identifying Alcohol Abuse in the Family

A thorough substance-abuse history is part of every family assessment. The identification of alcohol as a problem area for the family is critical to the treatment plan. By discussing possible abuse markers with the family, the therapist will be able to understand the use of alcohol within the family. *Abuse markers* are behavioral indicators of the presence of alcohol abuse. Areas to be explored in this process include the amount of alcohol consumed by each person; when and where it is consumed; the style and pattern of drinking behavior; whether alcohol use affects work, interpersonal, marital, or family relationships; the presence of alcohol-related physical ailments; hospitalizations; the existence of physical side effects of alcohol such as blackouts and hangovers; incidents of physical violence; and the presence of alcoholism in the family history.

Abuse markers can be identified in those behaviors that interfere with role performance at work and in the home. During the assessment, the therapist, in developing a picture of the marital relationship and each spouse's role, finds out about each partner's drinking habits. The clinician will need to understand how alcohol fits into the marital relationship.

The following vignette reveals how an examination into the role performance of the marital partners established that an alcohol problem exists in the family.

> Mr. & Mrs. R came to therapy for marital problems involving communication difficulties and excessive fighting. Alcohol abuse was not mentioned by either individual. During the course of the evaluation, a thorough alcohol history was taken. Their responses to the drinking-related questions differed. She tried to label his alcoholism; he flatly denied it. An opportunity to reveal his denial occurred while discussing what they did in the evening. The fact emerged that they do nothing at night, because he always falls asleep at 8 P.M. from excessive alcohol consumption. Upon further questioning, it became clear that alcohol had also intruded into the emotional and sexual aspects of their lives since they only had sex when he was drunk—something she said she detested. Sexual frequency was also an issue. Most evenings she went to bed alone, leaving him asleep on the sofa in the living room.

This sample illustrates how investigating the marital relationship can also identify alcoholism as a problem.

In taking a history, the way information is revealed and reported are dynamic processes. Are the parents, for example, verbally minimizing the alcohol-related incidents and subsequent fighting, while the children begin to squirm in their seats? Is the teenager the one who "spills the beans" that mother drinks too much and has ceased to perform her functions? Does the family accept the information that is emerging, or have the family members tried to squelch the reporter by denying the facts or negating their validity?

Creating a genogram with the family members is part of taking an alcohol history. The genogram is a structured way to gather critical information—the road map of the family's relationship system (Guerin & Pendergast, 1976). Statistical information on marriages, divorces, remarriages, births, and deaths form the background grid of the genogram. Symbols are used to delineate the information. A picture emerges, showing the structural components of the family. Events such as psychiatric illnesses and hospitalizations are added to the map. As the therapist is coding the information, he or she also should find out how the family responded to these events and how the event affected their lives.

Alcohol information is placed on the genogram by circling the alcoholic person with a double line. Each of the adults is asked to review the people in his or her family of origin. Those who were alcoholic are identified accordingly. In those families where the alcoholism was not seen as a problem initially, the pictorial description helps deal with their denial. The numerous markings stand out and make a statement that increases the family's growing recognition of the role alcohol has been playing in their family. The genogram also serves to underscore the fact that alcoholism has been a family problem through the generations.

Although the genogram is primarily used during the assessment to establish the presence of alcoholism in the family, it can also be used at other times during the treatment process for education and prevention purposes. Children of alcoholic parents have a higher risk of becoming alcoholics themselves or of marrying an alcoholic. One study indicated that 60 percent of nonalcoholic wives married to alcoholic husbands had alcoholic fathers (Wolin, Bennet, Noonan, & Teitelbaum, 1980). Another study reported that 52 percent of the alcoholics in the samples were themselves children of alcoholics (Wegscheider, 1981). In the course of family therapy, these important facts can be given to the children. For example, in those families where the young adult children live out of town, special sessions to include the entire family can be arranged so that the children will understand their vulnerability to alcoholism.

Contracting for the Removal of Alcohol from the Family System

Without alcohol, the family patterns change and the fit between each of the members of the family is altered. Removing the alcohol dissolves the glue that holds the alcoholic family together. As the family moves from living with alcohol to living without alcohol, the balance changes and the system is propelled into another state of flux. The first shift occurs when the family or an individual in the family responds to a precipitating crisis by asking for help. The alcoholism becomes the task to be addressed in therapy after it has been identified and labeled as a family-level issue. The clinician proceeds to contract with the family to remove the alcohol. In introducing the contract and the abstinence, the therapist is capitalizing on the process of change that the family has already started.

Contracting is the way that the therapist enters the family's interactional life. As developing the genogram with the family reframes the problem from an individual one to a matter including the entire family, organizing the contract has the same effect. The therapist enters into an agreement with the family about how abstinence will take place.

The contract consists of a commitment from the alcoholic to stop drinking and to attend AA meetings, for the spouse to attend Al-Anon, the adolescent children to attend Alateen, and to initiate a process of "gift-giving" involving all the family members. The tasks are decided on through several sessions and develop from the content of the sessions. The details of where and when each person will attend their assigned AA and Al-Anon meetings is worked out in the session. Going to AA, Al-Anon, and Alateen is doing something for oneself. Gift-giving involves doing something for another individual in the family. This process offers the family members an opportunity to experience a different interactional pattern. The therapist facilitates the gift-giving process, but the family orchestrates it. In some families, an individual can offer to remove all the alcohol in the house as their part in the gift-giving process. In others, it can be that the whole group plans a family outing together. A spouse may offer to prepare a special dinner. In one family with an alcoholic adolescent, his gift to his parents was to begin to repay a large financial debt he owed them. Some families emphasize creating an elaborate event for their gift-giving, whereas others simply decide to spend time together at home. The process of gift-giving creates the opportunity for each individual to become involved with the other family members in a different way.

The contracting process allows the therapist to see if the family will comply with his or her demands, if they will fulfill the contract, to discover how the family carries out the tasks, and how they respond if the contract has not been completed. The length of time a family takes to fulfill the contract varies. In the following example, one family's experience with the contracting process is described.

> The A family came to therapy because their youngest daughter had received a
> failing report card and was acting sullen. Before this, the family viewed her as
> a very good student with a happy disposition. In the initial interview, both

Mr. and Mrs. A and their two daughters, aged 12 and 10, all complained about the same issues—poor communication and too many fights. The parents felt the children did not do their share in maintaining the house. The daughters grumbled that the parents expected too much from them. As the problems were identified by the family members, Mr. A muttered under his breath, "My wife drinks too much. . . ."

The therapist then addressed the issue of the mother's drinking. Her alcohol intake had indeed been steadily increasing to the point where she was no longer functioning well as a wife and a mother. Increasingly, she was isolated from the life of the family. She was drinking daily, starting earlier in the day and drinking throughout the evening. She had been wrestling with the problem for quite some time but didn't know where or to whom she would turn for help. Further investigation into the alcoholism revealed that Mrs. A's family tree was filled with alcohol problems. All her siblings as well as her father and her grandparents had a history of alcohol abuse. Some were still drinking, others were not. Alcoholics Anonymous had been helpful for some, but not for others. Mrs. A had never been to AA. However, she had an ongoing commitment to Overeaters Anonymous for weight control and found that very helpful. The therapist saw this as Mrs. A's first masked attempt at dealing with her alcoholism since the philosophy, structure, and goals of both self-help groups are similar.

In the first session, a contract was developed with the family. Mrs. A was willing to stop drinking for the next week and made a commitment to do so. Mr. A. was asked what he would like to do to participate in the gift-giving part of the contract. He offered to remove all the alcohol from the house, lock it in the trunk of his car, and take it to the office. The eldest daughter wanted to walk the dog each night and the youngest daughter offered to set the table before dinner. The family actively participated in designing the contract and felt pleased about the work they had done.

At the next meeting, the therapist opened the session by inquiring if the family fulfilled the terms of the contract as it had been designed. The girls both carried out their assignments, recounting anecdotes associated with the tasks that revealed their renewed contact with their mother. Mrs. A did not drink during the entire week and shared with the family what that meant to her and how she had managed to get through the strains and stresses of the week. Mr. A. stripped the house of all the alcohol and put it in the trunk of his car where it remained. He never took the carton of alcohol to his office.

He tried to sabotage ongoing change from occurring. In addition, his behavior might indicate rebellion against the therapist who took his muttering seriously and initiated the contract or perhaps it expressed his lack of total acceptance of his wife's alcoholism.

Mrs. A. was able to address her angry feelings toward her husband; he viewed himself as the innocent victim of her hostility. This interaction was dealt with in the session. The contract was further developed to have Mr. A go to Al-Anon, the daughters to Alateen, and Mrs. A to switch from Overeaters Anonymous to AA. The contract was completed by the family within two months from the start of the therapy.

Outpatient Family Therapy, Inpatient Detoxification, and Residential Alcoholism Rehabilitation Programs

The appropriate treatment to achieve abstinence is selected by evaluating the strengths and the resources of the family by assessing the individual's state of alcoholism and by considering all treatment facilities available in a given community. The treatment is also selected by considering the consequences usually associated with the individual's drinking pattern and the person's ability to achieve specific treatment goals (Pattison, 1979). Treatment selection is a complicated process that involves many factors, and the therapist's recommendation must be accepted by the individual and the family.

The three major options for obtaining initial sobriety are: (1) outpatient therapy for the whole family, (2) inpatient detoxification, and (3) a residential alcoholism-rehabilitation program. The last two options focus primarily on the individual. The family is often included in the process, but is not considered the central focus of treatment. Working with the family is seen as ancillary to the individual's rehabilitation program.

Most families can be helped in outpatient family therapy "to confront the alcoholism, and with the insistence of family members and the therapist, the alcoholic can be convinced within a few sessions to stop drinking and experience initial sobriety" (Usher, Jay, & Glass, 1982, p. 930). Inpatient services are generally not necessary when the family is willing to become involved in ongoing treatment and the family is there to give the necessary support for the alcoholic to achieve abstinence. Since abstinence is the first step in dealing with life problems, carrying out this process in the context of the family and the ongoing daily routine allows the family to reap the benefits of their labors. Removing the alcoholic from the family system produces a break in the family's continuity.

Certain situations, however, clearly indicate a need for hospitalization, even when the family is involved from the beginning of therapy. The presence of psychotic behavior, acts of violence, and medical conditions such as malnutrition, delirium tremens, and convulsions are indications that hospitalization should be provided. Inpatient detoxification is used for acute medical illnesses and emergencies related to alcoholism. The stay in the hospital is brief and after two or three days, the alcoholic returns home. In the past, hospital detoxification was used as a precaution in the withdrawal phase. Few alcoholics, however, are at risk medically during withdrawal (Pattison, 1979, p. 186).

Most residential rehabilitation programs in their present forms are generally a 28-day regime organized around the Alcoholics Anonymous philosophy. Examining the alcoholic's behavior and the consequences flow-ing from that behavior is a priority of the treatment. Educational groups and group therapy are the methods most frequently used. This type of treatment plan, with its emphasis on peer interaction, is designed to break the alcoholic's denial system.

When the alcoholic states he or she cannot stop drinking after several structured outpatient attempts, a course of treatment in a rehabilitation program is appropriate. It stops the cycle of drinking. In the residential program, the alcoholic can reflect on his or her life situation from a distance. The family should be encouraged to participate, when possible, in the program and to continue outpatient family therapy while the alcoholic is in the rehabilitation program. After completing the program, the alcoholic is expected to join the family therapy sessions.

Alcoholics Anonymous, Al-Anon, and Alateen Self-Help Groups

In this treatment model, the AA, Al-Anon, and Alateen self-help groups are used in conjunction with family therapy to assist the family in obtaining and maintaining sobriety. These fellowship groups offer support and friendship, two vital aspects of life that alcoholic families have cut out of their lives. As the alcohol becomes an integral part of the life of the family, links to the outside are dropped and the family becomes isolated from its environment. Forming attachments in self-help groups can be the family's first attempt to reestablish relationships in the environment. AA and Al-Anon are informal groups, with a membership that shares a common problem and accepts those who join their ranks.

The way that change occurs is different in each method. In the self-help groups, the group is the primary medium for change (Davis, 1980). The groups focus on the individual and his or her own issues, not on the individual and his or her relationships as they affect the group. In AA, interaction is discouraged between group members.

In family therapy, change is produced by the family itself. Change emerges from within the family's structure and interactions.

Family therapy and AA self-help groups are similar in that both offer a new, safe environment — a place where emotions can be examined and cooled down. Removing alcohol from the family can create a crisis and stir emotions. Therapy and AA both advocate reducing emotional intensity. Detachment is underscored in Al-Anon as a process for the spouse to examine his or her own behavior, rather than manipulate others in the family system. This represents a first step for the family therapist, who then examines the interaction between the couple and sorts out what each spouse projects onto the other.

Both AA and family therapy encourage identifying feeling and expressing emotions appropriately. Honest communication is a tenet of both methods. Paralleling this, both attempt to reestablish self-esteem in the individual family members (Ablon, 1977).

Both approaches recognize the necessity of involving family members to facilitate change in the alcoholic's drinking behavior. At the same time, both assume that family members can undermine the process of sobriety and can resist change (Davis, 1980, p. 69).

Clinically, a difference exists in the families that resist participating in AA and Al-Anon. First, the resistance can indicate a lack of commitment to the recovery process; it can mean resistance to the entire treatment process. Second, the refusal to go to AA and Al-Anon can be seen as a rigid attachment to the enmeshed position. Some family members are reluctant to change their behavior; they are unwilling to take a risk or take responsibility for their behavior. For spouses to examine their marriage when the alcoholic is sober is threatening. Third, going to AA and Al-Anon not only does something for oneself but also helps one's spouse. Angry feelings that have accumulated through the years can contribute to the resistance and discourage the family member. When one member of the family attends AA or Al-Anon and the other members refuse to go, the reasons for the resistance become an issue in therapy.

AA and Al-Anon are always included in this family therapy model in the initial phases of treatment. These groups help the alcoholic maintain his or her sobriety and support family members to take charge of their lives. AA and Al-Anon is introduced during the contracting phase and is labeled a family activity. Every detail, including the date, time, and place of the meetings, is reviewed with the family until agreement exists about which meetings will be attended in the week. In the next family therapy session, the family's attendance at AA self-help groups is discussed. Resistances are worked with during the session. In the stages of recovery, the central issue related to AA is the actual attendance at the meetings. How the individual feels about attending is secondary to the process. The number of meetings varies with each family. Deciding about the specific number is part of the therapeutic process and is to be negotiated between the therapist and each individual. In some families, once or twice a week is sufficient to maintain sobriety. In others, five meetings a week or even daily attendance may be indicated.

In this model of family therapist and alcoholism, the alcoholism is addressed from the beginning. The AA self-help groups are compatible with this treatment method and are seen as a critical part of the family therapy. The family's attendance at these meetings indicates their commitment to moving to a way of life without alcohol.

The Second Phase of Therapy: The Process of Reorganization

The Emotional Desert

When the alcoholic is removed from the family system, the therapist can determine how the family structures itself and how it operates in its environment. Since alcohol is an incorporated part of the family's life, its removal is seen as a loss. What usually remains after the alcohol is removed is a group of people who lack skills in developing meaningful relationships, have poor communication patterns, and have difficulty constructing appropriate solutions to their problems. The family members appear alienated from one another, are unable to approach each other, and demonstrate little capacity to relate. This family state of isolation is called the *emotional desert* (Usher, Jay, & Glass, 1982).

Formerly, alcohol was a significant part of the family's life. Although the conflicts around the drinking may not have resulted in constructive solutions, these conflicts provided a focus for family interaction. The absence of alcohol thrusts the family into a state of disequilibrium. The arguing and nagging has temporarily stopped. A reshuffling process takes place to reorder the fit between the individual members. The family system becomes reorganized to fill the gap previously filled by the alcoholism. Family members appear as emotionally laden individuals who have no channels for the appropriate expression of their feelings. They do not seem to be autonomous individuals who function in their own right and who relate to and share with other family members.

To address the family's emotional state, the therapist elicits their feelings of despair and emptiness. As these emotions are identified and labeled, the family begins to recognize them. The therapist, together with the family, builds pathways for the appropriate expression of these feelings.

Removing the alcohol from the family not only reveals the emotional impoverishment the family experiences but also crystallizes other significant difficulties previously kept in the background because of the prominence given the alcoholism problem. The following vignette describes the H family after Mr. H had been discharged from a hospital-based alcoholism program. This family is a group of persons who live together but who communicate little interest in the activities and values of the individual members. Since Mr. H stopped drinking, several other family issues were labeled as problems.

Mr. and Mrs. H and their sons—ages 18, 16, and 11—came to therapy on the recommendation of the hospital social worker. During the hospitalization,

Mr. H complied with the rehabilitation program, although he argued against the diagnosis of alcoholism.

From the beginning it was obvious that Mrs. H was the one in the family who was most interested in having the family seen as a whole group. When the sessions were about to start, she was the one who went outside to get the two older boys to come inside the building. The youngest boy would sit in the waiting room chair and would move only after his mother called him a second time. The children all sat around the mother, while the father sat alone separated from the others by the youngest boy. The family stated that they were confused about why they had come for therapy. When this was further explored, they all agreed that Mr. H's drinking was a problem. Mrs. H said that she was worried about her husband and felt the family "didn't act like a real family."

The assessment of the H family revealed they had established a living pattern that allowed for the least possible interaction between Mr. H and the other family members. No one felt good about how the family behaved and everyone felt helpless about things changing.

Mr. and Mrs. H married 12 years ago. She brought her two sons with her to this marriage and had always felt that Mr. H had not performed as the father she hoped he would have been for her boys. Mr. H felt closer to the youngest boy, their biological son. All three boys constantly made requests to spend more time with him. They suggested athletic games and outings. The boys openly approached their father, wanting more contact with him, but he backed off. Throughout the session the eldest boys looked to their mother for assurance, approval, and affirmation. The communication between the father and the boys was limited and only in one direction from son to father.

In the area of problem-solving, Mr. and Mrs. H found a way to provide their children with the basic necessities of life but they never were able to find a solution to Mr. H's evening work schedule. Everyone found Mr. H's work schedule disruptive—he had worked the four-to-midnight shift for 15 years. The family showed no evidence of adapting. Mr. H did not want to change his job, nor did he feel competent to negotiate a different work schedule. He drank nightly with his coworkers and "slept it off" until he went to work again. On weekends he slept late since he often had to work the weekend evening shift. His daily routine, which was entirely different from the other family members, reinforced the disconnected feeling they experienced.

As husband and wife, Mr. and Mrs. H had little contact with each other. They had no couple friends and rarely went out together. They only socialized with Mrs. H's family. Mrs. H complained about their sex life, pointing to the decline in frequency and satisfaction. Mr. H always initiated sexual contact and only when he was drunk. Mr. H complained that he had little sexual interest when he was sober.

Mrs. H had performed very well at work. She had kept the same government job for many years, with regular promotions; Mr. H also reported a good work record.

In the initial phase of sobriety, the family members were alienated from each other and were overwhelmed by their feelings of loneliness. Using the assessment framework previously presented, problems other than Mr. H's alcoholism moved into focus. The spouses, with their different work schedules, spent little time together and seemed to be roommates, rather than husband and wife. Mr. H was alienated from his children; his ability to nurture them and his wife was limited. The emotional life of this family was a desert. When Mr. H was abusing alcohol, the family made few demands of him; they wanted more from him after the alcohol was removed. The family had few skills to deal with their emotional barrenness.

A family's response in the initial phase of sobriety is one of disappointment. The honeymoon is brief and the problems have to be addressed. Contrary to the old myth that life would be wonderful if the alcoholic stopped drinking, the family usually experiences many difficulties. The family is frustrated and surprised that their interpersonal relationships have not automatically improved. Without the alcohol, the family members appear vulnerable and are unsure how to meet each others' needs.

This transition can also be a turning point in the therapy. Moving from a "wet" state to a "dry" state throws the family into flux and an additional crisis is created. The sobriety is fragile and tenuous. Previously hidden emotions are now being addressed. The family must meet the demands of the crisis that sobriety has caused within the family. Family members fear what the future will bring. They doubt their ability to go forward as a family without alcohol and their ability to continue making changes. How they address these fears structures their response to the challenges of living as a family without alcohol.

The family responds to the crisis of sobriety in one of the following ways (Usher, Jay, & Glass, 1982). First, the family may choose to resolve this crisis by reintroducing alcohol into the system, returning to familiar old patterns. The reappearance of the symptom may not only be conveying the family's discomfort in the new balance but also may be a test for the therapist, questioning his or her power and tenacity. The true test for the therapist is whether he or she can help the family understand the return to drinking as a "slip." Viewing this event as a "slip" allows the therapist to follow the family's momentum in the change process that they were in at the outset of therapy. A return to drinking can also represent the family's way of showing the therapist that everyone in the family is not yet in total agreement with the goal of abstinence, which was established at the initiation of therapy. The family is dramatically demonstrating their ambivalence about changing.

The second response to the crisis of sobriety is to maintain the sobriety but to split up the family. After an initial period of abstinence is established, one of the spouses initiates a plan that results in a separation. The emotional barrenness cannot be tolerated and the energy needed to continue the change process is channeled into working out the separation arrangements. Even though abstinence is maintained, this particular solution is neither seen as viable or helpful since the pain and anger each spouse projects onto the other is never dealt with explicitly or clearly understood. These families usually terminate therapy.

In the third response, the family begins the struggle to survive and develop new patterns of interaction to sustain itself without alcohol. To move from a dry alcoholic family to a dry nonalcoholic family is a long and difficult therapeutic process (Steinglass, 1980). In a dry alcoholic family, the central focus is on alcohol and not using it. A family that has grown and developed so that the members carry out their lives without a preoccupation with alcohol is a dry nonalcoholic family.

The dry alcoholic family is still organized around alcohol. Typically, one or more members has directed much energy to obtaining support outside the family. An increased commitment to work, resulting in long hours away from the family, can be supportive to the alcoholic in the early stages of sobriety, but it does little to help the family adjust. Family members have just as little opportunity to interact with the alcoholic as a parent or a spouse as when that person was drinking.

Similarly, an overuse of the AA self-help groups can be used as an excuse to avoid addressing the problems facing the family. In this third response, the chemical addiction is removed, yet no changes have occurred in the family's structure, interactional patterns, or ways of meeting each other's emotional needs. This type of family is considered dry but not sober.

The fourth response places the family in the heart of the struggle to find new paths toward family connectedness. The family makes a commitment to sobriety and to family therapy, through which they can pursue their struggle, reveal their pain, and work toward discovering effective solutions. Ultimately, individual members are able to take responsibility for themselves and can achieve meaningful interaction with each other. Family members experience feelings of closeness and they have developed new skills that will enhance their lives. The alcohol no longer dictates the life of the family; the family moves through life stable and sober.

Predicting the "Slip"

Predicting a relapse or "slip" is used as a therapeutic technique to establish leverage for the therapist. Since the relapse rate for alcoholics is discouragingly high, the therapist is merely stating what can be expected.

With respect to the treatment, this statement can have a significant impact on the therapy. Predicting the slip is a paradoxical message to the family. The therapist has been designing maneuvers to work with the family toward abstinence. By bringing up the slip, the therapist is sending the family a message not to change. The therapist wants the members to resist the message so that they will change (Haley, 1976). Alcoholic families are structurally stabilized to incorporate the drinking members. When the therapy is oriented toward dealing with that problem, the system becomes unstabilized. The family, unsure of its ability to deal with this new situation of abstinence, may return to familiar behavior patterns. Issuing a paradoxical statement speaks to this possibility.

If there are no slips, clearly everyone wins. The family has joined together to prove the therapist wrong. The alcohol remains out of the family system, and the family's process of binding together against the therapist has resulted in a change in the family structure. Specifically, the family has devised a new pattern to deal with the alcohol problem, something that they were unable to do in the past. Not only is the abstinence maintained but the family's ability to solve their problems also has increased. The alcoholic member gains a sense of mastery and experiences some good feelings about himself or herself — two developments necessary for continued success.

If a slip does occur, it can be used as "vehicle of therapy" (Bailey & Leach, 1965). A close examination of the behavior surrounding the drinking episode can yield valuable understanding about each person's role and his or her contribution toward the reappearance of alcohol, as seen in this example.

> After six months of abstinence, Mr. M went out drinking one night. In the next therapy session, both spouses denied that anything significant had occurred in the home or at work. The ongoing issue being explored at that time in therapy was the couple's lack of intimate relationships. This was a painful and difficult area for them to explore. The therapist reminded them of the work they were doing in therapy and suggested perhaps there was a relationship between their feelings about their lack of sexual relations and Mr. M's drinking episode.
>
> Mr. M agreed immediately and proceeded to reveal how he felt when he tried, the night before, to caress his wife, who did not reciprocate the affection. He had made some erroneous assumptions about her response. He did not share his feelings with her nor did he demand a verbal response. He returned to his familiar mode of dealing with his frustration — drinking. In this instance, exploring the alcohol slip in therapy permitted the couple to hear each other's hidden fears about renewing their sexual relations. During the session, the couple explored a more constructive and direct way to communicate with each other.

Skill-Building

The process of skill-building allows the family to learn to negotiate acts and decisions in order to live with each other and in the world as responsible individuals who take charge of their lives. The therapist provides a structure and a safe environment for the family in which they can, as individual members, begin the struggle to find more effective ways of interacting with each other and rewarding ways of meeting their own needs. Reframing the alcohol problem into an issue for the whole family initiates this process.

Carrying out the contract requires the family to organize itself to change the drinking cycle. All the family members have to participate in finding the solution. A breakdown in the family's ability to fulfill the contract gives the therapist the opportunity to help the family acquire the necessary skills to complete the contract. For example, when a family says they do not know where the AA and Al-Anon meeting are in their neighborhood, this problem should be directly addressed in the session. The family decides who will call the AA number, and the telephone contact with AA must be completed in that family therapy session. By executing the contract, the family gains another perspective of itself and its capacity to solve the problems confronting them.

With the contract fulfilled and the alcohol out of the way, the family is free to explore other family issues, label the salient factors in these issues, decide what needs to be changed, devise a course of action, and execute the plan. This process reinforces the learning of problem-solving skills for the family. To carry out the requirements of daily life, families need specific skills. Old patterns of problem solving proved to be ineffective, and resulted in a stagnant and destructive position for the family. New and effective methods of problem solving must be acquired.

To facilitate the skill-building process in the course of therapy, the therapist labels the problems to be solved and works with the family to help them create solutions. In the following example the therapist encourages the parents to address a problem they were having with their son. In the past, they had been unsuccessful in resolving this issue. When the alcohol was eliminated from the F family, several issues surfaced.

> Mr. and Mrs. F were concerned about how their son, Richard, handled money and about his inability to manage his own life. Although the parents agreed these were problems, they differed on the solution.
>
> The F family consisted of Mr. and Mrs. F and their four sons. The two oldest sons were married and living away from home. The youngest son was leaving shortly for the military. Launching the children from the family was not easy for these parents. Before their separation was complete, each of the older boys returned home after the initial exit. Even though Richard went to

school and earned $10,000 a year at his job, his parents thought he was not ready to leave since he could not handle his finances. He also owed them $1,800 and had never successfully dealt with this debt. The parents' lack of problem solving in this area suited Richard jut fine. The more inept they were in disentangling this issue, the less he had to prepare himself to leave home.

The success the family felt in establishing Richard's abstinence allowed them to pursue the next problem of separation, which was pegged to the money issue. The first step in skill-building with the family was to make explicit all of the dimensions of the problem, including where Richard banked, the amounts in his bank accounts, a list of expenses and financial commitments, the exact sum of debts owed, and the amount of income.

Each family member stated how the money should be managed. It became obvious that the parents were far too intrusive in this aspect of their son's life and at the same time were ineffective in enforcing payments from him. Richard chose to convey his attitude to his parents by keeping his finances in a disorderly state. This behavior was translated to the family and Richard was encouraged to organize his money without his parents' help. The therapist asked the parents to negotiate a sum that Richard would pay them every two weeks when he received his paycheck. At first, Mrs. F was to keep the ledger. She did not stick to the rules, however, and kept lending him money on demand. Further discussion resulted in a new plan whereby Mr. F was to keep the books. The system worked well for a few weeks and then Mr. F slipped. He loaned Richard his credit card for gas.

Exploring how each parent participated in this infantilizing process allowed them to discuss how they could support one another, rather than to continue this undercutting process. The therapist regularly inquired about the debt reduction. Within six months, the debt had been reduced to half the amount. This experience provided the F family with some new and effective problem-solving skills. The parents made their expectations clear and designed a plan to achieve this. Since Mr. F took charge of the ledger, he became more involved with his son, which improved the father-son relationship. Mrs. F aligned herself with her husband and some much needed distance was created in the mother-son relationship.

Dealing with Communication Patterns

To mark the boundaries around subsystems and individuals, the therapist frames the interaction in the session to establish (1) that individuals do not speak for others, (2) that communication should be made directly to the person it is intended for, and (3) that the message should be listened to by that person. These requirements produce a communication pattern that consists of clear and direct statements. The family begins to relate to each other differently as they acquire effective communication skills. Inappropriate interruptions are stopped and reviewed by the therapist. The parental subsystem is protected when the therapist stops the children from intruding in their conversation. The opposite is also true. In the same way, the therapist helps the siblings in the family develop a boundary around their subsystem. Delineating boundaries organizes communication between the parents and communication between and among the children separately. Separating the generations helps to clarify the role expectations for each of the individuals in the family.

Restructuring family's patterns of interaction can create different emotional experiences in the session and provide family members with new skills they can use to relate with each other. The therapist addresses the family's disappointment that problems still exist in the sober state. Feelings of hostility, anger, and frustration are labeled.

The therapist guides the direction of the interaction and clarifies the transaction for the individuals involved. The desired result is clear communication with messages sent directly to the person who is able to hear the message and respond appropriately. At the same time, the therapist reaches for, elicits, and emphasizes the nurturing aspects of the family relations. "The focus is on how much and in what way family members can show an interest and invest themselves in each other" (Epstein, Bishop, & Levin, 1978).

The following vignette illustrates the struggle the D family experienced as they were learning new ways to relate to each other. A secret became exposed, confused feelings were unraveled, and together the therapist and family created a resolution. The expression of affect began to fill in the family's emotional desert.

> When Philip, the 21-year-old son, tried to reach out to his father, he had no experience to draw on. Neither of them could remember when he had done so before. At this time in the therapy, Philip had been sober for three months; his father had several years of sobriety. Philip opened a therapy session by saying to his father, "I want to say something to you." He then stopped. He could not continue and felt hopeless about continuing the transaction. Mr. D was asked to change his seat so that he would be sitting closer to his son. Mother started to cry hysterically and began to leave the room. The therapist turned to the mother and asked her to say what was going on for her at that moment. Mother sat down and was able to talk about her pain and her wishes that all this had never happened. She also realized that the scene she was creating distracted Philip and his father from the business at hand. This was a role she often took. Mr. D leaned over to his son and asked him if he could now tell him what was on his mind. The therapist labeled this expression of nurturing, thus reinforcing the father to experience what he had done.
>
> Philip responded to his father with, "You're still an alcoholic." This statement proved to be a very complicated one. Fifteen years ago, Mr. D had given up drinking spontaneously. Philip very much wanted his father to go to AA meetings with him but was afraid to ask. Instead, he blurted out this indirect distancing message. In exploring this communication further, Philip was able to identify his desire to be close to his father but this terrified him.

Philip's body language paralleled his desire to get close to his father. He was reaching over toward his father and was as close as possible without touching him. His body made the statement that he wanted to be held. The therapist pointed out the body language, and then Mr. D reached over and hugged his son. For the D family, the process of eliciting, identifying, experiencing, and sharing their feelings provided them with a different emotional experience — one that helped them feel positively connected to each other. They had created a new bond together.

The technique of siding with the hierarchy of the family (that is, the parents) is used by the therapist to encourage them to take charge of the family. In a family with an unlaunched young adult still living at home and acting irresponsibly, the young adult runs the family. The process of how the parents and the young adult participate in this transaction demands attention. The parents' task is to prepare their child for his or her departure from home and the young adult has the task of leaving. The therapist's role is to help the parents and the child learn the skills required to pursue this separating process. The therapist supports the parents to make their expectations for the young adult's behavior explicit. As his behavior changes and becomes more responsible, the therapist structures the interaction so that the parents praise the child. The parents are encouraged to continue what they are doing. When the expectations are clarified and then responded to, both the parents and the child add to their repertoire of skills and increase their feelings of competence.

These new skills, role behaviors, and communication transactions can also be reinforced by assigning specific tasks for the family to accomplish during the week. The contract establishing abstinence in the family is the first task that the family must complete. Subsequent family homework emerges out of the content of the session. Planning a family outing or a vacation are assignments that can extend the work accomplished in the office.

The Third Phase of Therapy: Sobriety and Termination

The termination process begins when the treatment goals have been accomplished. The family has a sense of itself as a unit, open to its environment and capable of protecting itself when necessary. The individual members of the family exhibit self-reliance and autonomous behavior. The basic foundation is in place for continued growth and development. The alcohol has been removed and the family is equipped to address its problems with its new emotional and interactional life. Several elements must be considered during the termination phase, including abstinence, symptom removal, instrumental and affective change, structural change, and repairing.

Abstinence

The first criteria to be considered at termination is whether or not the alcoholic family member is drinking. Abstinence, as an integral part of this treatment model, must be achieved and sustained before a decision can be made to terminate treatment. The next question to be addressed is what constitutes an appropriate length of abstinence. The reported relapse rate is extremely high, and relapse often occurs within two months after the alcoholic stops drinking (Chalmers & Wallace, 1978). Thus, anything less than six months of sobriety would be considered a short-term recovery, if a recovery at all (Polich, Armor, & Braiker, 1980). In working with families, a year of sobriety is the average length of time in which the necessary work of rebuilding the family structure and its emotional life can be accomplished. This time frame in family therapy creates the opportunity for the family to organize itself into a sober, stable, nonalcoholic family.

Symptom Removal

In the first stage of family therapy, the alcohol is removed. The family members are relieved and exhilarated with the brief honeymoon phase created by the removal of the alcohol. The family may decide to leave treatment at this juncture and choose to ignore other problems revealed to them in the dry state. Change has taken place; abstinence has been introduced. Although this is an admirable achievement in the short run, the chances for this course to be a viable option in the long run are slim.

Another way of conceptualizing symptom removal alone without further therapy is to think of external, as opposed to internal, sobriety. External sobriety can be equated with the beginning abstinence phase. Superficial compliance often is the underlying mechanism motivating its occurrence. The initial sober state generally has little to do with a commitment to oneself and has much to do with quitting alcohol for the spouse, the children, or the employer. Internal sobriety is tantamount to a resolution of a different life experience. The sobriety is internalized and involves a personal commitment to be abstinent and to foster beliefs and values that support this resolution (Chalmers & Wallace, 1978). Openness and a sense of positive self-esteem replace denial and projection as a way of dealing with oneself and the outside world.

Can the alcoholic family move past the initial phase of sobriety and make changes required for their continued growth? At termination, the therapist needs to evaluate how the family operates without alcohol as part of their system. Family therapy with alcoholic families is not short term; the therapist must be prepared to work with the family for an extended period of time.

Instrumental and Affective Change

In the termination phase, the therapist, in coordination with the family, needs to reexamine the degree to which changes have taken place in the instrumental and affective life of the family. Has the pattern of day-to-day life been altered to meet the needs of the family better? If finances were an issue, is more money being generated by the family members?

In one family with a 24-year-old alcoholic son, as the son's drinking problem came under control, the mother's career blossomed. She changed jobs and within three months of taking the new position, she was promoted to director of her department. She requested and received a twenty percent salary increase. The family desired a greater income and obtained what they wanted.

Money is only one way a family takes care of its needs. Role performance is another aspect to be considered. Does the family demonstrate flexibility so that tasks are carried out, as needed, by the various members of the family? Has the family developed the competence required to create the roles that were missing or alter those that were inappropriate? Specifically, has the scapegoated member become an accepted person within the family? Is the alcoholic assuming his or her appropriate responsibilities in the family? Each family member should feel a sense of competence and comfort in the role, such as that of the father or mother, he or she is expected to carry out.

Members of a family begin to feel good about themselves, each other, and the family as a whole when they are able to nurture one another. Smothering and distancing are replaced with nurturing. To grow closer to one another, each person must be able to receive as well as to give nurturing. Compliments are given. An arm affectionately placed around a child's waist or a smile between the spouses are nonverbal examples of nurturing. Alcoholic families come to therapy deficient in this area. At termination, the therapist should observe the family's ability to nurture one another. This is a vital aspect of their lives, which sustains them as individuals and helps to join them as a family.

Anger, the hallmark emotion best describing an alcoholic family, has to be specifically evaluated. Ideally, one would hope the family arguments could be resolved. More realistically, the therapist should assess the family's capacity to resolve arguments without excessive use of blaming or exiting.

To enjoy a full range of affective expression, each person in the family has to feel free to voice both positive and negative emotions. If a child refuses to accept appropriate affection given by one of the parents, why this interaction is unacceptable to the child must be determined. Similarly, if the father relates predominantly to other family members through angry outbursts, the therapist must understand the absence of any other responses. In the termination phase, a full range of affective interaction should exist for the family.

Structural Change

To look at family structure is to look at how a family organizes itself and how the members interact. The family encompasses various subsystems. Boundaries separate subsystems from each other, and the family as a whole from its environment. At termination, the boundary surrounding the family should be permeable and open to stimuli from the outside environment.

For a family to be functional, the parent must be in charge. Parental leadership or lack of it decides the family's ability to manage its problems. At termination, the recovered alcoholic parent should be acting as a responsible adult and parent. The therapist observes and evaluates the parent's progress in assuming responsibility when the family comes to therapy. How the family identifies a dilemma they are struggling with and how they proceed to solve their problems yields the data by which the therapist assesses how and by whom this family is run. Witnessing how the parents orchestrate the problem-solving process allows the therapist to evaluate the changes in roles and structure that have occurred and to assess the impact on the family. At the conclusion of therapy, the rules, leadership patterns, and roles should be altered so that they enhance the emotional life of the family and meet the needs of the individual members. Within this new structure, mutual support and caring can take place.

A family with an alcoholic young adult child still living at home is often developmentally arrested at the "launching" phase. When the young adult should be making an exit from the family, he or she is relying instead on the family to take care of him or her. This phase of delayed launching includes crisis after crisis and can last for many years. The alcoholic child remains dependent on the parents and the parents avoid experiencing the strains and stresses of the "empty-nest syndrome." The parents fear the isolation and emptiness of being alone with each other, and the child is panicked about surviving in the outside world.

At termination, the major structural change in such a family must be that both of the parents have stopped playing the rescue role and have freed the child to lead an independent life outside of the home. The child is allowed to experience the consequences of his or her alcoholic behavior without having a parent place a pillow beneath him or her to soften the fall.

> During the course of treatment of one family, James, the son, was at an out-of-town rehabilitation program, which prevented him from attending the

family therapy sessions for six weeks. The therapy focused on the parents' relationship and the developmental stage they were now approaching. At first they only wanted to talk about James and his problems. Gradually, they brought up their own retirement and the myriad plans they were designing for these years that were soon approaching. They feared that finances might be a problem, especially if they continued to bail James out. They also spoke about their deteriorated intimate life. Mr. E was a recovered alcoholic and felt the area of intimacy and sex had especially suffered since the days of his own drinking. The problem of James's chronic alcoholism served to camouflage the isolation and emptiness existing between the parents. As the parents focused on the deadness of their marriage, James became free to move out of the triangle, maintain his sobriety, sustain regular employment, and live separately. To date, James has been sober for more than a year — a new and different experience for him and the family.

Repairing

Repairing is a process by which the family restores its internal pathways that have become blocked and inaccessible. To complete the repairing is to make amends, to reach out, and to receive acceptance. Repairing contributes to the establishment of intrafamilial connectedness. The intimacy between family members has been destroyed. Repairing the damage helps to heal the old, deep wounds and opens up new emotional options for the family. Without completing the repairing stage, the family remains steadfastly isolated from each other and from others in their network of relationships. The repairing process changes the emotional life of the family.

Repairing takes place when the family can tolerate hearing a young adult say to his father, "I need to tell you how furious I still am for all the times you weren't there for me when I was growing up and you were drunk." The family needs to hear this, but also they need to experience the healing taking place between a parent and a child. To complete the repairing process, the recovered alcoholic has to own his or her irresponsible behavior. He or she has to make amends for the pain inflicted on the members of the family. Taking possession of all of the behavior while he or she was abusing alcohol represents an acknowledgment of his or her part in the interaction as well as owning all of the acts as part of oneself.

The therapist facilitates this process by supporting individual family members to address their unhealed wounds. In a safe environment, each person is encouraged to clear those blocked pathways that exist amongst themselves. This process helps develop a new level of emotional intimacy between the family members. To have permission to be rageful, to be wrong, to be heard, to be accepted, and to be responsible is to repair.

Issues in the Therapeutic Process

Denial

Therapists involved in alcohol treatment agree that the alcoholic's denial of their problem is the greatest obstacle to recovery (Bailey & Leach, 1965). On the other hand, a change in the denial system can be one of the more powerful indicators that treatment will be successful (Williams, Letemendia, & Anoyave, 1973).

Denial is the cement holding together the alcoholic's already shattered self-esteem. Rationalization, projection, and denial are typical of the alcoholic's defense structure.

> *Rationalization is a self-adjusting mechanism by which we first act in response to unrecognized motives, and after the action we offer various supposed "reasons" for our conduct. . . . Projection is directed outward and attributes to others one's disclaimed and objectionable character traits, attributes, motives, and desires. . . . Denial is an intrapsychic defense mechanism by means of which consciously intolerable thought, wishes, facts, and deeds are disowned by an unconscious denial of their existence. (Noyes & Kolb, 1963)*

By insisting that the alcoholic admit his or her alcoholism and stop blaming others, the therapist attempts to intrude upon the denial system. For example, to quote a popular saying in AA, "Take the cotton out of your ears and put it into your mouth."

A typical pattern used by families with an alcoholic member is to deny that alcohol is the problem. For example, if the husband has a drinking problem, the wife may fight about finances rather than address his drinking problem. She denies both his drinking problem and her enabling. Job dissatisfaction, a misbehaving child, a sexual problem, fatigue, and stress are other secondary problems families use to maintain their denial patterns. When the alcoholic denies the impact of his or her drinking on his or her personal, family and work behavior, he or she is denying the impact of the alcohol abuse on the presenting problems identified by the family. Here, denial keeps the family focused on a tangential problem other than the alcoholism. The alcoholism is denied and the culture of the family remains intact.

Alcoholism is not the only problem the family denies. Some families also deny the "emotional desert" encountered in early sobriety and attempt to convince themselves and the therapist that they are functioning well. Family members do not see a need to continue in therapy after the alcohol has been removed. They are extremely reluctant to examine their emotional relationships, which foster distance, deadness, and boredom.

The therapist can also become trapped by denial. The therapist's failure to take a comprehensive alcohol history during the family assessment is an example of the therapist's denial at work. Another denial pattern occurs when the therapist takes an alcohol history but chooses not to notice certain kinds of events or categories of experiences. He or she denies that alcoholism is a serious issue that needs attention or chooses not to recognize the severity of the drinking. The failure of the therapist to take an alcohol history or to recognize important alcohol abuse markers can be due to a lack of knowledge, a discomfort with the problem, an alcohol problem of his or her own that is being denied, an undue pessimism about the prognosis, or a belief emanating from a moralistic value system.

The health care system has a wealth of psychotherapeutic and medical interventions that avoid facing the problem of alcoholism. The stereotypical example is that of the wealthy, successful businessman who is admitted to the hospital for bleeding ulcers—not his alcoholism. The woman whose alcoholism is often bypassed is an upper-class, married professional who is overworked and is experiencing headaches. She is admitted to the hospital for a medical work-up. In the mental health field, a thorough alcohol history is still not a routine part of the initial assessment of all individuals and families. When the clinician continually avoids the alcohol issue, his or her ability to identify it as a problem is weakened. The patient and the clinician dance together to the song called denial. When the alcohol is eventually addressed, the alcoholic rebels and retreats to his or her previous nonalcoholic diagnosis, such as ulcers or depression. This direct family treatment model confronts the alcoholic's games from the beginning and opens up the possibility of change for the family.

The therapist's countertransference feelings toward the family can contribute to his or her collusion with the family's denial pattern. These countertransference feelings can emanate from untreated alcoholism in the therapist's family, reluctance to examine his or her drinking behavior, or negative views about the possibility of successfully treating alcoholism. The therapist does not see the extent of the alcohol abuse present in the family. The therapist's feelings of omnipotence may hinder him or her from labeling the alcoholism and assessing its impact on the family.

Another path that leads to collusion with the family's denial occurs when the therapist becomes overwhelmed by the power of the family and their desire to defeat the therapeutic effort. As a result of this scenario, the therapist begins to act as if he or she needs to "save" a particular person in the family, such as the scapegoated child or the alcoholic. He or she becomes the rescuer (Steiner, 1971). In this role, the therapist is not able to perform as the therapist for the whole family. The therapist no longer is the agent of change; he or she has become an enmeshed member of the family and ineffective in dealing with the family's denial.

Resistance

Resistance is a part of the therapeutic process. It can appear in any phase of therapy and can emanate either from the family or from the therapist. In this broad perspective, resistance is defined as "any phenomenon that arises to thwart or hinder the change process" (Luther & Loev, 1981).

The Therapist's Resistance   One of the first resistances a therapist can experience is the family's reluctance to attend the session. If the clinician has made the decision to include the entire family after the initial telephone contact, he or she is responsible for arranging the event.

Several fears could plague the therapist in handling the arrangement of the first session. Some therapists fear being overwhelmed by the family and being unable to manage the session. Others have stereotyped ideas about the poor treatment outcomes with alcoholic families and don't reach out to establish a working rapport with the family. Beginning clinicians may have concerns about overidentifying with the abusing young adult or not having credibility with an abusing parent, given age and inexperience. Therapists may not have yet adequately resolved their own family struggles (Barnard, 1981). Finally, the therapist may not have the specific skills to recruit and engage the family in therapy. Either alone or in combination these issues can be overtly or covertly transmitted to the family so that they stay away. In some cases, the therapist's inability to engage the family is then projected onto the family and they are labeled "resistant."

The process of recruitment and the family's entrance into therapy is an active one (Stanton & Todd, 1982). The therapist decides who should attend and should personally contact each family member individually. The person who initiated the therapy is not responsible for recruiting his or her family. Timing is important; the sooner the family is contacted and seen, the higher the success rate (Davis, 1977–78). Families also tend to drop out if they have to negotiate the system through a succession of helpers, including intake workers and evaluators (Van Deusen & Stanton, 1980).

The practical aspects of recruitment and the family's cooperation cannot be overlooked. Flexible hours for working families are a must. Home visits are extremely useful to bridge the gap between home and office. The observation of the family in the home environment yields valuable information for the therapist about the family's culture, as well as how they organize their daily life and their interactional patterns in their natural setting (Steinglass, 1981). If the therapy is being carried out in an agency or an institution, administrative support for a family treatment approach must be made clear so that the therapist's efforts are not sabotaged by rigid rules and mixed messages from the administration.

The Family's Resistance   The therapist's resistance is only part of the story; families also resist. During the course of therapy, resistance expressed by the family represents their opposition to change and fear of disruption. Families can have a fatalistic approach toward change (Luther & Loev, 1981). This is particularly true of families that come for help after several failed treatment attempts. They are pessimistic about therapy and are expert at constructing roadblocks for the therapist. Resistance can come from one family member or it can be used collusively by any group within the family. It can also be a response to an inappropriate therapeutic intervention. How the family behaves is a statement about the way the family exists (Dell, 1982). The therapist needs to listen to the family and design specific interventions based on who they are and not who the therapist wants them to be. For example, abstinence is always a requirement of the therapy, but the means of getting it changes with each family.

The following are some resistance maneuvers alcoholic families use. Blaming the alcoholic allows other family members to resist owning their participation in the situation. The enabler does not examine his or her part in the transaction. The cover-up continues undisclosed. In another pattern, family members avoid facing their own alcohol abuse by focusing on the already identified alcoholic. Some nonalcoholic spouses ally themselves with the therapist and try to assume the role of cotherapist. Here, the spouse is attempting to ward off the therapist's efforts to work with them as a couple. The nonalcoholic spouse is trying to maintain the marital imbalance. This stance is partly used to avoid looking at the couple's history of mutual recrimination.

Focusing only on the alcoholism allows the family to avoid dealing with other marital and family problems. During early sobriety, the existence of the "emotional desert" is denied. This denial leads directly into another pattern of resistance—that of terminating therapy after the alcohol has been removed. The family is comfortable with their progress and chooses not to work on any family issues other than the alcohol. Family members address instrumental problems only and refuse to reveal their feelings. Individuals fear their feelings would be unacceptable to and rejected by the others. As in all resistance patterns, this is a way that the family protects itself.

The resistance needs to be recognized, understood, and overcome so that therapy can move forward toward a successful conclusion. Resistance patterns can reflect the politics of the family members' relationship. Deciphering the pattern of the relationships will lead to the understanding of the resistance (Weiss, 1981). This sets up some specific therapeutic approaches to overcoming resistance.

The therapist's first approach is a direct one—joining with the resistance by identifying the individual's fears and worries (Liberman, 1981). An empathic response can convert resistance into compliance and avoid a power struggle between the family and the therapist.

When a direct approach fails, the next effort involves a carefully thought out strategic intervention. Reframing a problem is one example of such a therapeutic tactic. The process of reframing a problem changes the conceptual and emotional viewpoint about the situation, placing the problem in a different context. Family members understand the problem better when it is placed in a new light (Watzlawick, Weakland, & Fisch, 1974), as shown here.

> Mrs. J, a chronic alcoholic, was constantly being "monitored" by her husband. He had specific "tests" by which he evaluated her daily sobriety. Mrs. J was furious at his behavior, which she announced that she hated. Two other problems were being explored during the therapy. Mrs. J had requested Mr. J to take care of her in ways other than being her watchdog. Also, Mr. and Mrs. J worried that their baby would be born with fetal alcohol syndrome, which deforms and debilitates infants born to alcoholic mothers. The therapist's efforts to explore the marital issue of caring and dependence and their concern about the health of the unborn baby were totally unsuccessful. The therapist's attachment to the unborn child and the desire to have Mrs. J stop drinking resulted in the therapist taking Mr. J's side. This was an error. The covert alignment between the therapist and Mr. J led the therapy nowhere.

Perhaps this couple's resistance to focusing on the nurturing aspects of their marriage could have been addressed by reframing the problem as follows: Keeping in mind Mr. J's talents as a "monitor" and Mrs. J's request to being taken care of, Mr. J could have been told to make a list of institutions that would be appropriate for the baby if it were born with the severe effects of fetal alcohol syndrome. He would have been required to develop five questions he would need answered to make a decision about placement. Next, he would have had to rank the institutions, take Mrs. J to visit the first three, and decide with her which one they liked best. The reframing would have taken Mr. J's "monitoring" out of the symptom realm, placing it in another context.

Another strategy to overcome resistance is to establish the current treatment as distinct and special from those that have failed in the past. By taking the role of expert, the therapist gains the leverage needed to make a positive connection with the family. This "take charge" stance helps to create a trusting relationship between the family and the therapist — a relationship in which the family can surrender and begin working.

The therapist adopting a disbelieving stance is another technique that can be effective with families with a history of treatment failures. The therapeutic absurdity serves as a red flag for the couple to attempt to prove the therapist wrong; the couple band together to carry out this task.

In treating Mr. and Mrs. G, the therapist adopted a disbelieving stance from the outset, since Mr. G immediately listed the six treatment places he had attended when he called for an appointment. The first session led to a homework assignment that included AA, Al-Anon, removal of alcohol from the home, and no drinking. Although all the tasks were accomplished, the therapist held on tightly to this doubting attitude, saying, "I can't believe you did all the homework." The next session's assignment included the same agenda plus going out to dinner together, which had been planned during the session. Again, the homework was completed and the therapist remained a "doubting Thomas." After a few weeks, with successful results, Mr. G said to the therapist, "In all my treatment experiences, I never met such a skeptic as you!" He said that this was the longest time he had ever been dry.

Finally, predicting the resistance before it occurs puts the therapist in charge of the therapy. With alcoholic families the therapist predicts the slip, a temporary return to drinking.

These and other strategic interventions are employed to deal with the family's opposition to change. The clinician's judgment designs the strategy and creates the intervention.

Compliance

This model of therapy uses a direct approach regarding alcohol abuse. The therapist expects the family to comply with the direct interventions. The therapist labors with the family to alter the family structure, disrupt the denial patterns, confront the resistance, and initiate change. Direct interventions include advice, commands, explanations, suggestions, interpretations, and tasks that are meant to be taken literally and followed precisely (Papp, 1980). Interventions are used in therapy to change family rules and roles. They also promote sequences that help the family acquire skills with which they can solve their problems. Direct interventions are aimed at promoting open communication, expressing appropriate affect, and interpreting family interaction.

According to Beels and Ferber (1972), family therapists are divided into two categories: conductors and reactors. *Conductors* have a clear sense of their own values and the goals for the therapy. They direct what happens in the session and retain control of the process of therapy. The emphasis is on altering patterns of interaction in order to elicit feelings. The conductor-therapist wants to create a new corrective emotional experience for the family; the session is orchestrated to arrive at this goal. *Reactors* respond to what the family presents in the session. Although they have goals and values relating to the therapy, these remain a secret agenda in the therapy. The reactor-therapist is interested in working through the parental transferences and will join in as a member of the family to sort out the confusion. The conductor remains on the side of the parents, the reactor may align with a child to bring about a change in the network of rules that shape and constrain the family system.

In this direct structural model of working with alcoholic families, the therapist, as a conductor, is in charge of imposing and initiating abstinence. He or she plans how the alcohol will be removed with the family. The therapist expects that the family will comply.

Although the therapist's style may be a central factor in getting the family to comply with the treatment plan, other variables can affect the decision. These variables include the nature of the family's odyssey for help and the precipitating crisis that led the family to seek help.

In the life history of the alcoholic family, many attempts are made to get help from a variety of resources. With each attempt, hope is mobilized. If treatment requires hospitalization, the main focus is on the alcoholic and the family remains on the periphery. A treatment plan that includes the entire family from the beginning capitalizes on the momentum the family initiated in their response to a precipitating crisis. When the family contacts the therapist, they are already in a process of change. The family's involvement during the entire course of therapy shores up the compliance possibility from the beginning.

Who, what, where, and how are important questions around the search for help. Who was the initiator for help in this crisis? Did the alcoholic go to an AA meeting, or did the spouse call the family doctor? Did the nonalcoholic spouse call the local mental health program that had advertised help for alcoholic families? Was this help sought out as a result of the court's initiative? The latter, of course, yields a compliant group for therapy since the court is in a position of imposing severe consequences. Compliance under these circumstances, however, is complicated since "good behavior" is what is called for in this situation for the alcoholic to disengage himself or herself from the legal system. The question of whether the sobriety can be maintained without the external threat of the law can be answered through careful follow-up of these court adjudicated cases.

When a family member voluntarily initiates the contact for help, that act is indicative of a family in an evolutionary state. The contact for help may be a response to a crisis occurring in the family.

The last factor to examine for its contribution to the family's compliance in therapy is the precipitating crisis. Does this crisis have a qualitative difference from the other crises that could bring about compliance? For example, in the past the crises may have centered around the alcoholic's job loss and the family's economic survival. Is the present crisis the result of violence? Families treat crises differently. Some crises are ignored; others create such a disruption in the family system that the members respond to by seeking help.

A precipitating crisis can be seen as a fluctuation in the life course the family is following. "There is always the possibility that one small fluctuation will lead to a larger amplification which will set off a leap to a new place" (Hoffman, 1981). The initiation of therapy and the family's compliance with the treatment demands can be linked in the following way. The initiation of therapy is part of the evolutionary change process experienced by the family and compliance is seen as part of their changing. This direct problem-solving family therapy approach to treatment rides the crest of the already-started change process.

References

Ablon, J. (1977). Family structure and behavior in alcoholism: A review of the literature. In B. Kissen & H. Bigleiter (Eds.), *The biology of alcoholism* (Vol. IV) (pp. 205-242). New York: Plenum.

Bailey, M. B. (1968). *Alcoholism and family casework.* New York: Community Council of Greater New York.

Bailey, M. B., & Leach, B. (1965). Alcoholics Anonymous: Pathways to recovery, a study of 1058 members of the A.A. fellowship in New York City. New York: National Council on Alcohol.

Barnard, C. P. (1981). *Families, alcoholism and therapy.* Springfield, IL: Charles C. Thomas.

Beels, C., & Ferber, A. (1972). What family therapists do. In A. Ferber, M. Mendelson, & A. Napier (Eds.), *The book of family therapy* (pp. 168-232). Boston: Houghton Mifflin.

Chalmers, D.K., & Wallace, J. (1978). Evaluation of patient progress. In S. Zimberg, J. Wallace, & S. B. Blume (Eds.), *Practical approaches to alcoholism psychotherapy* (pp. 255-277). New York: Plenum Press.

Davis, D. I. (1977-78). Forum: Family therapy for the drug user: Conceptual & practical considerations. *Drug Forum, 6,* 197-199.

Davis, D. I. (1980, January). Alcoholics Anonymous and family therapy. *Journal of Marital and Family Therapy, 6,* 65-73.

Dell, P. F. (1982, March). Beyond homeostasis: Toward a concept of coherence. *Family Process, 21*(1), 21-47.

Epstein, N. B., & Bishop, D. S. (1981). Problem-centered systems therapy of the family. In A. S. Gurman & D. R. Kinakern (Eds.), *Handbook of family therapy* (pp. 444-490). New York: Brunner/Mazel.

Epstein, N.B., Bishop, D. S., & Levin, S. (1978, October). The McMaster model of family functioning. *Journal of Marriage and Family Counseling, 4,* 19-31.

Guerin, P. J., & Pendergast, E. G. (1976). Evaluation of family system & genogram. In P. J. Guerin (Ed.), *Family therapy.* New York: Gardner Press.

Haley, J. (1976). *Problem-solving therapy.* San Francisco: Jossey-Bass.

Hoffman, L. (1981). *Foundations of family therapy* (p. 203). New York: Basic Books.

Johnson, N. (1981-82). Effects of family history of alcoholism. *Alcohol Health and Research World, 6*(2), 39-40.

Liberman, R. P. (1981). Managing resistance to behavioral family therapy. In A. S. Gurman (Ed.), *Questions & answers in the practice of family therapy.* New York: Brunner/Mazel.

Luther, G., & Loev, L. (1981, October). Resistance in marital therapy. *Journal of Marital & Family Therapy, 7*(4), 475–480.

Minuchin, S. (1974). *Families and family therapy.* Cambridge, MA: Harvard University Press.

Noyes & Kolb. (1963). *Modern clinical psychiatry.* Philadelphia: W. B. Saunders.

Papp, P. (1980, March). The Greek chorus and other techniques of family therapy. *Family Process, 19*(1), 45–57.

Pattison, E. M. (1979). The selection of treatment modalities for the alcoholic patient. In J. H. Mendelson & N. K. Mello (Eds.), *The diagnosis and treatment of alcoholism.* New York: McGraw-Hill.

Polich, M. J., Armor, D. J., & Braiker, H. B. (1980). *The course of alcoholism: Four years after treatment.* Santa Monica, CA: The Rand Corporation.

Rapaport, R. (1965). Normal crisis, family structure and mental health. In H. J. Parad (Ed.), *Crisis intervention.* New York: Family Service Association of America.

Stanton, M. D., & Todd, T. C. (1982). *The family therapy of drug abuse & addiction.* New York: Guilford Press.

Steiner, C. (1971). *Games alcoholics play.* New York: Ballantine Books.

Steinglass, P. (1976, March). Experimenting with family treatment approaches to alcoholism, 1950–1975: A review. *Family Process, 15*(1), 97–123.

Steinglass, P. (1980). A life history model of the alcoholic family. *Family Process, 19,* 211–226.

Steinglass, P. (1981). The alcoholic family at home: Patterns of interaction in dry, wet & transitional stages of alcoholism. *Archives of General Psychiatric, 38,* 578–584.

Usher, M. L., Jay, J., & Glass, D. (1979). A family therapy approach to restricted emotional interaction following initial sobriety. Paper presented at the Tenth Annual Medical-Scientific Conference at the National Council on Alcoholism, Washington, DC.

Usher, M. L., Jay, J., & Glass, D. (1982, September). Family therapy as a treatment modality for alcoholism. *Journal of Studies on Alcohol, 43*(9), 927–938.

Van Deusen, J. M., Stanton, M. D., et al. (1980). Engaging resistant families in treatment, getting the drug addict to recruit his family members. *International Journal of Addictions, 15,* 1069–1089.

Watzlawick, P., Weakland, J., & Fisch, R. (1974). *Change, principles of problem formation and problem resolution.* New York: Norton.

Wegsheider, S. (1981). *Another chance.* Palo Alto, CA: Science & Behavior Books.

Weiss, R. L. (1981). Resistance in behavioral marriage therapy. In A. S. Gurman (Ed.), *Questions & answers in the practice of family therapy.* New York: Brunner/Mazel.

Williams, P. J. A., Letemendia, E. J. J., & Anoyave, B. (1973, February). A two-year follow-up study comparing short with long stay inpatient treatment of alcoholics. *British Journal of Psychiatry, 122,* 637–648.

Wolin, S. J., Bennett, L. A., Noonan, D. L., & Teitelbaum, M. A. (1980). Disruptive family rituals: A factor in the intergenerational transmission of alcoholism. *Journal of Studies on Alcohol, 41,* 199–214.

CHAPTER SIXTEEN

Integrative, Individual, and Family Therapy, as Told by Debby G.

DEBBY G.

Me: Look, I'm really pissed off at you and I don't feel like I have any control.

Mom: Don't use that kind of language with me.

Me: (at the top of my voice) I'll talk any fucking way I want to. Can't you hear what I'm saying? I'm pissed off and I feel violent. So I'm warning you . . . don't piss me off.

I stomp out of the room.

Later, in my parent's study, my father reminds me that I promised to get into therapy after I got out of the hospital. It has been one year since I went through the drug and alcohol program at Capistrano By the Sea Hospital; when do I plan to start therapy? My stomach hurts as I retort, "Fine. If you pay for it, I'll go," "Fine," he calmly replies, obviously having won the battle.

So, entering therapy was not the calmest decision I ever made in my life, nor did I do it with anything close to complete willingness to get better. Rather, I felt bottled-up and ready to explode most of the time; and it was this incredible anger in sobriety—or more exactly, my inability to express anger in sobriety—that got me into therapy. During the next three years, I would learn that anger was only one small issue I had to deal with. If I had known all the issues I would have to confront, I doubt I would have started therapy at all.

I came to see Ed for the first time at the University of California, Irvine Medical Center. The center is a maze of 1950s buildings of boring shapes and ugly sizes. After hiking from the parking lot through the labyrinth of these buildings, I was nervous and sweaty. That's all—that's all I can remember of my first visit: feeling uncomfortable, nervous, and hot.

We began with private sessions every week and family sessions (my parents and me) once every few weeks. I didn't emote very much in the private sessions, but I would leave feeling a little better than when I came in. In the family sessions, though, I would begin to cry within the first few minutes. I was filled with a pain I had never felt before—not the empty pain I felt while bottoming out on drugs; no, this pain was full and round and grew inside of me. I felt worthless; I thought they felt I was worthless. Worthlessness and feeling judged led to anger, but I didn't know how to express anger, particularly with my parents, and so I turned it back on myself. I would judge myself and believe everything they said; I left these sessions feeling terrible, as if my self-esteem had been smashed. I felt lonely, worthless, afraid, hurt.

I would go to the recovery home I had lived in when I first got sober and talk to the administrator of the house. We had gotten sober and gone through that house program together. He had seen my achievements in sobriety, could love me without judging or criticizing, and helped me rebuild my self-esteem after these family sessions.

The process took about an hour in the beginning, but gradually the time needed to rebuild grew. When it became obvious to me that a two-hour "empowering" session was not healthy after only an hour of so-called "family therapy," I decided I could not participate in family therapy any more. I went to my private session that week and told Ed I couldn't handle another session with my parents; it was undermining my sobriety.

Ed's reply stands out in my mind today as the single most important event in my first year of therapy. He told me I had the mistaken idea that family therapy was a tool only to bring families together. He said in my case he was trying to show me that my family was dysfunctional and that I needed to break away from them. I was amazed and relieved. I knew intellectually that my parents had problems relating to me, but in my heart I thought the problem was me. If only I could change, the problem would be solved; yet, every time I tried to do what they wanted, I invariably felt hurt or angry.

When Ed planted the "breaking away" message, I knew he wasn't lying. He validated my feelings and, because of that validation, I not only felt better but I also drew closer to him. I trusted him a little bit more than I had before.

His validation gave me a new freedom: I could allow myself to feel real anger toward my parents. I was angry at the way my parents had raised me, and I was furious I had the disease of alcoholism. I blamed them for "giving" me the disease. I realized whatever I had done while drinking and using was my fault, but I was *not* a faulty person. My parents did the best they could, but that wasn't good enough; I wasn't ready to forgive them.

The rest of the first year I stayed angry with my parents. I took baby steps in not seeking their approval, support, and love, and I started to accept that they were going to continue to hurt me every so often. This education took the form of not calling them all the time. They live 50 miles away, but I would turn to them for what I thought was approval or love. Every week Ed would ask if I had called them and I would invariably answer, "Yes," then he would ask me to recount these conversations. After some time, I realized that my parents always hurt my feelings in these discussions. I finally acknowledged that I really called them, or at least my mother, to be abused. I was used to it; I thrived on it. I then worked at putting an end to it. (Today, I can almost always judge my self-esteem by looking at my phone bill and counting the number of calls to my parents' number).

I slowly began to separate from my parents, most importantly financially. I learned how to turn down what looked like free gifts but were really attempts to control me. I could say, "No, I won't take whatever you have to offer because I think you mean something else by it." In this manner, I communicated openly with them for the first time. My family used hidden agendas; each of us would say whatever we thought would get us something or somewhere. When I used open communication, not only would the conversation come to an abrupt halt but there was also no way we could take advantage of each other.

Another major breakthrough of this first year was learning how to say, "You hurt my feelings," or "I am angry with you because. . . ." These two phrases were essential keys to recovery; they were the open and honest forms of communication I had never before practiced. As a feeling stuffer, when I felt angry, hurt, or afraid, instead of expressing my feeling during the moment, I reacted later. With my parents, I usually reacted by being angry with my father. When I started to communicate openly how I felt, all the wind was taken out of everyone's sails, including my own. My parents didn't know how to communicate openly or what to do when they heard something that sounded like a plain expression of emotion instead of the highly charged attacks on each other my mother and I were prone to. For me, communicating openly not only helped me to relieve whatever feeling I was experiencing at the time but it also forced me to be myself. I stopped acting out my mother's form of expression of feelings, namely anger at my father, and began to learn what was appropriate for me.

The last lesson involves issues I learned about in family therapy. I call these the present issue, the expectation issue, and the showing love issue. The first, the present issue, is my personal favorite. This one depicts my sick family at its best. My mother believes that she and my father must be completely fair about presents. My parents ,travel quite a bit and they always buy gifts for my sister and me; they almost always buy the same gift — to be fair. They have never (and I say *they* because they say these gifts are from both of them) looked at the fact that my sister and I are two different people, that our tastes and interests differ. As an adult, almost all the gifts I have received from my parents have been cultured pearls, even though I *hate* cultured pearls. In fact, I told them this in family therapy.

However, three years after family therapy, my parents returned from a trip to Thailand and Singapore. Thailand is the ruby capital of the world. Before they left for this trip, I said often, "A ruby ring or little bracelet would really be nice, hint, hint. After all, you'll be back just in time for my birthday." Well, my parents came back from Thailand and Singapore and what did they get me? A cultured pearl pendant!

Overall, there has been improvement. Once, in a family therapy session, my parents announced they were going to France. Because they would miss my birthday, my mother said she had a birthday gift for me — a set of make-up brushes and a photocopied book on how to do one's face. From there we moved to the subject of gifts and gift giving. Ed pointed out that he didn't think make-up brushes were something my father would have thought to give me. My father replied that my mother almost always took care of the present department. Ed asked my father if he liked to pick out presents. He replied that he did, and Ed said that it would be my father's responsibility to pick out a present for me in France. My father got me a bottle of Opium perfume that I love. That one act made a big difference in the relationship between my father and me. I think my father felt good about his choice and I felt a new warmth toward him.

Although this experience was positive, it is not representative of what happened afterward. A year ago, my father and I drove down from northern California to southern California together after visiting my sister, brother-in-law, and newborn niece. During the 10-hour trip, we discussed presents. My father said he had bought an amethyst bracelet for me in Mexico more than 10 years ago, but that my mother would not let him give it to me. He also purchased a piece of scrimshaw in Alaska for my sister 9 years ago that my mother would not let him give to her. I told him my problems with presents and explained that I usually felt hurt and betrayed at the gift-giving ceremonies. He said he understood but didn't know why my mother was the way she was.

It didn't occur to me at the time, but he completely dumped the present issue on her! If he felt so strongly about it, why didn't he just give my sister and me the presents? Throughout the ensuing year, I would occasionally recall our conversation, but we never discussed it openly again. Not until recently, anyway. The morning after my parents gave me the pearl pendant (from Thailand) and I had obviously been disappointed (the pearls were my father's idea), my father said not to worry, there was something else I would get for my birthday. This implied the bracelet from Mexico we had discussed. Then he said my mother mentioned that the bracelet would not fit because my wrist was smaller than hers. I said I would make it fit. My birthday came and my parents took my date and me to a great dinner. They did not give me the bracelet. I felt led on, hurt, and confused. I called my father a few days later and told him how I felt and that I didn't believe the sickness was on my side of the street. He said that he understood and he was trying to resolve the situation.

This time I realized not only was he just as responsible for letting me down as my mother usually was but, in this instance, he was even more at fault. My mother, who did not intend to give the bracelet to me, never mentioned it. My father not only led me to believe I would get the bracelet but turned around and pinned the blame on my mother when "they" chose not to give it to me. Again, if he *really* wanted to give the bracelet to me, he could have done so. After all, he supposedly picked it out and paid for it. I also observed that my expectations were out of line. I expected that because my father and I had talked about this issue, it would be resolved. In my family, that expectation is a false one and I should know better.

Commonly, people in AA refer to insanity as doing the same thing over and over and expecting a result different from what has always happened before. In my situation, I expect certain actions and reactions by my parents over and over, and the results are always different than my expectations. I first learned about false expectations in the family therapy sessions. I learned that sometimes my expectations of my parents are unrealistic and vice versa, but I have had to work diligently at keeping that knowledge alive. Often I have seen myself fall into the expectation trap not only with my parents but also with men in relationships, girlfriends, bosses, and all sorts of people with whom I come in contact. My expectations of people can become either unrealistically high or unrealistically low because, I believe, I learned this behavior from my parents. Their expectations of me are either too high or too low.

My parents expected me to get straight As all through school and couldn't accept that possibly I was a B student in math. I can remember being tutored by my algebra teacher every day at lunch in the eight grade because I had a B in his class. If I didn't improve my grade, I couldn't take a dance class I wanted desperately to take. All through high school and college, grades were almost more important to me than the classes. Driven by my parents to excel, I went to one of the finest universities in the country. Even though I was a practicing drug addict there, I still achieved over a B average. My grades were as good as, and in some instances better than, my classmates, most of whom went on to earn master's degrees or Ph.D.s. Yet when I seriously considered going to law school and we had a special family therapy session toward the end of the first year of therapy to discuss it, my father blatantly said he didn't think I could pass the California bar exam. Where before an unrealistic expectation had been placed on me in my intellectual ability to achieve good grades, in sobriety an unrealistic expectation of failure was attributed to me.

The last item, the expression of love issue, was the easiest problem to resolve. Basically, my father had a great deal of trouble showing love or affection. Ed brought this out openly in family therapy, and I simply asked for more attention. My father immediately took to expressing love and now hugs and kisses me when he sees me; occasionally, he will even hold my hand if we are walking together. This has helped our relationship immensely and he has, to some extent, helped me to express my feelings.

I believe that I too had trouble expressing love, particularly to my female friends. I was not conscious of it before, but I think my father's attempts at correcting something he felt uncomfortable about helped me to do the same. I can now say, "I love you," to my friends on the phone, something I always shuddered at before.

On a deeper level, I think my going through therapy has enabled my father to express his feelings more openly in a number of ways. During my first and second years of therapy, I was asked to speak at several different types of AA and CA meetings and panels. On one of these occasions, I thought it would be nice to invite my parents, Ed, and my sponsor and her husband to hear me speak. I consider it an honor to be asked to tell my story, and I wanted to share this occasion with some of the people I felt close to. I had no idea the experience would be so enlightening.

On the day I was supposed to speak, my mother got sick with a cold, and my father drove from Los Angeles to Orange County (50 miles in rush-hour traffic) without her. At the meeting my father sat near Ed and my sponsor and her husband.

I omitted almost my entire "drugalogue" and focused my sharing on my feelings as a child and an adult, the numbing chill I felt as a practicing addict, and my feelings, experiences, and hopes in sobriety. During my talk I also mentioned that my father was sitting in the room. When I finished speaking, as many people came up to my father as they did to me. So many recovering addicts wanted to tell him how great they thought it was that he came to hear his daughter.

When I was done speaking to those who had questions about the program, I walked over to my father. He was standing with a true rock and roll dude in his mid-twenties, dressed in black leather and chains, who wore his bleached blond hair in a scraggly shoulder-length style. While vigorously shaking my father's hand, the rocker asked my father how he felt about hearing my story. My father answered that he was surprised to hear how differently from his were his daughter's memories of her childhood. When we walked outside my father made some comment about what an inspiration I must be to "those" people. Inside I laughed as I said, "They keep me sober, dad." He was a little taken aback.

Weeks later, though, it was my sister who relayed to me that dad had told the cousins in Canada how proud he was of me. I was amazed: I never thought my parents were proud of me for anything. I instantly felt closer to my father and happy that I could make him feel proud. I also knew that even though he couldn't share his feelings with me, he was beginning to share his feelings.

The speaking engagement had other repercussions for my family, though. I did not doubt that my mother was psychosomatically ill, but I didn't want to accept that fact. However, when she called me to tell me how proud she was of herself because she had been sick and had stayed home, I wanted to scream at her over the phone. When I went to see Ed, he began the session by reinforcing my good feelings about speaking. He told me I was great. Then he asked what my parents had said. I told him I thought my father was proud of me and I told him what my mother had said. He commented that it sounded right to him and I asked him why. That was the day I remember learning exactly what a dysfunctional family is all about.

My mother vies with my sister and me for my father's attention. She cannot handle his giving us more attention than her, so she got sick in order to turn the family attention back to herself. That day I not only learned that my father was capable of feeling pride for his children but that for some reason, either while growing up or throughout my parents' marriage, my mother felt so ignored that she needed to have the family's attention on her constantly.

I don't remember much else about this first year of therapy, except for Ed trying to bring up my relationship with Bob, my boyfriend (whom I had been seeing for 2½ years), which I would always try to dismiss. For some reason, as comfortable as I am discussing sex with just about anyone, I was completely uncomfortable talking about it with Ed. I am not sure if he represented a new form of parent or if it was just a trust issue that made this subject taboo, but since my relationship with Bob was primarily sexual, there was no way I was going to talk about it with Ed. The only other logical reason I can attribute to my guarded avoidance of this topic may have been Ed's role as a reflection of myself. As that reflection, he was forcing to the surface an issue I did not want to, or was not ready to, look at.

Finally, when I was forced to look at my relationship with Bob, I found it more painful than I could have thought in my wildest dreams. Bob and I had a history together — a mentally abusive history for me. Like my mother, Bob criticized me constantly, and I interpreted criticism as love. Although I had stopped calling my mother for criticism, I had not stopped calling Bob. In addition, Bob had seen me through the worst of my drug abuse and now saw the changes occurring in me because of AA and therapy. As I became more whole, the less we got along. He started to lose control over me, both emotionally and sexually. When I was using drugs we had done many unusual sexual acts that I didn't want to do sober. Some of them Bob wanted to repeat, others he wanted to do all the time. The longer we stayed together the more we disagreed and the dirtier I felt after we had sex, but I wasn't strong enough to end the relationship.

As I mentioned, I thought about going to law school, so I decided to take the Law School Admissions Test (LSAT). I didn't have enough money to take a class, so I studied on my on, which required a lot of time and commitment. Before studying for the exam, I went to an AA weekend in Palm Springs. On the way back I stopped in Los Angeles to take Bob to dinner. I didn't call first (the fatal mistake); when I arrived at his house, he wasn't home, so I waited for him to arrive. He did, along with two 17-year-old girls. Without knowing what was happening and feeling as though I was living in a dream, I said I was sorry and left. I drove back down to Orange County in an emotional blackout. I have no idea how I got home, but when I got there I was really afraid I was going to drink. Once again, I turned to the Recovery Home for support. I went over to the house and talked to some people I had gone through the house with until I was calm enough to go home.

In the month that followed, Bob and I continued to see each other, but for me the relationship was over. He wanted desperately to make everything the same again, but we were incapable of communicating about the incident and our feelings. Bob tried to buy my forgiveness and, although I never said anything to him about it, that was his fatal mistake. Being bought made me angry. Also, I knew that any woman to whom I told this story would tell me to dump him, so I didn't talk about it with anyone. Then I began studying for the LSAT. Bob wanted me to come up to LA but I told him I couldn't because I had to study. I began to see him as someone who didn't want me to succeed, someone who was trying to "guilt" me into getting me to do what he wanted. Then I met Doug. He was the sexiest guy I had ever seen at AA, and all I wanted to do was sleep with him. I had no idea he would be the knight on the white horse that would get me out of my relationship with Bob. After seeing Doug for about two weeks, I broke up with Bob. Three months later, of course, Doug and I realized we had only been infatuated with each other and we stopped seeing one another.

For the first time in a long time I was alone—completely alone. There was no one to fall back on, no one to call for abusive criticism, no readily available warmth or sex. I became depressed. I slept a lot and I cried. I had nothing positive to say in AA meetings. I would just go and dump my feelings and leave. I hated work, but at least it was a brief respite every day from my own head. I even cried in Ed's office, which was rare for me in private sessions. I was so out of it I had to ask him what was wrong. He was the one who told me I was depressed. It was this depression, though, that really brought about some major changes for me.

First, Ed was the only person I felt I could turn to who wouldn't tell me to work the AA steps. I was working the steps, but I was still depressed. He seemed to understand that. I placed full trust in him. I confided all about the relationship with Bob to him and he guided me through. I told him how badly I felt about myself, how worthless I felt, how low my self-esteem was.

During that period, I slept around quite a bit, as men had always been a "quick fix" for me. But I did learn to build my self-esteem in other ways. I became friendly with a woman in CA. With her, I began to learn what intimacy was with other women. We helped each other out, and I felt better about myself. I also started to work out at the gym. This really improved my self-esteem and I began to get the glimmer that maybe I was attractive. I also felt good about doing some athletic activity well; I had never felt that I was good at any athletics. I began to read again and although I didn't write, I read over things I had written. That too made me feel good. One of the major challenges I embarked upon was to develop some interests outside of AA because my entire social life had centered on the Program. I began going to Jewish single events and to my university's alumni functions. I even went to a cocktail party for professional singles. Eventually I made a decision not to date men in the Program, which helped my "quick fix" sex problem tremendously.

However, the major obstacle to truly feeling good about myself was my job situation. I had worked before sobriety and for most of my sobriety as a secreatry—not a position I could feel good about. When I went to the winter holiday party for alumni of my university, I felt like an idiot saying that I was a secretary. I had a great boss and had taken on a lot of responsibility in my job, but I didn't see any way out. Ed kept pushing me to look at this area and my AA sponsor suggested that I look through the classifieds just to see what I would be interested in doing. I kept thinking about it and I took my sponsor's advice. All my interests seemed to lean toward editing, publishing, and communications. During this time, our firm merged with a larger consulting firm that had an entire communications division. I was thrilled. I put together a letter with some examples of different writing I had done and went up to the Los Angeles office to speak with the director of the LA communications practice.

He told me that I was completely unqualified for a position in his division, but that I might be interested in a position he was sure would be open soon in the Orange County office. I soon found myself interviewing for an editing position in the Orange County office. As rusty as my skills were, I was hired and have been working as an editorial assistant since.

I recognize now that Ed gave me the encouragement I needed. I was very insecure about interviewing for an editing position, and my parents were anything but supportive. Ed gave me the extra ounce of confidence I needed. He was positive and kind. When I got the job, he congratulated me, implying "You did it!" My mother commented on how nice it was for my old boss to get me the job. The difference two years of therapy made was incredible. I didn't respond when she said it; I just smiled to myself and knew that she would always see it in the negative way she chose to see it.

I visualize the second year of therapy as the emergence of my new self, though I am not sure exactly how this happened. When I asked Ed, all he said was that he reparented me without criticism. He let me be myself. That is not to say I didn't do any work. I believe I did a lot of work, mostly conscious thought and action. I looked at my motives, actions, and reactions, and I consciously changed my behavior patterns. In therapy, I pointed out my behavior patterns to myself and in a safe place learned how to, and made a continuous effort to change them.

The last year of therapy was a blossoming for me. After clearing away the most glaring destructive patterns, working through a depression, and building a little self-esteem, I forged ahead to work on the more subtle problems.

I quit smoking and gained 10 pounds that I needed to gain. I had to become a nonsmoker in order to see what a destructive habit smoking was. During my second year of therapy, smoking was somewhere toward the bottom of my list of issues, but as I started to take better care of myself emotionally, I found a bigger need to take care of myself physically as well. Quitting cigarettes turned out to be a major boost to my self-esteem. For the first time ever, I felt healthy and beautiful.

I developed intimate and rewarding relationships with some very special female friends. Six of these women I got sober with in AA and CA. We formed a group and meet once a month for dinner and a meeting. I now love these women as sisters. I learned through them how to communicate joy and sorrow to a friend and how to say, "You hurt my feelings" and move on. I feel committed to my relationships with them and so I am willing to change my behavior in order to help our friendships. These are new feelings for me. I was never accustomed to risking or being vulnerable with anyone, least of all another woman. Today I have trust and faith. I know if there are confrontations, they will not end the friendship.

Even more significant, though, I developed some special relationships with women outside of AA and CA. Development of friendships with these women has opened many doors of insight, including new perceptions into my behavior at the office and with men.

When I began my job, I felt uncomfortable. At first I thought I felt inadequate because I had done so poorly on the aptitude tests for my position. Then I thought that life at the parent company to which I had transferred was just "different"—harder. Every day I dreaded going to work a little more. Every day I did something else wrong; it never seemed I could do anything right. In addition to feeling inadequate and confused, I was in the difficult transition stage of moving from the position of secretary to professional.

Ed and I discussed the situation, and I looked for new clues and insights each week. Instead of feeling better, I only felt worse as the months dragged on. During this time, I began to make friends with a woman at work. It was through her that I first got an inkling that the problem wasn't me. We opened up and began to talk of our frustrations and she made some observations about my boss that validated my feelings.

Slowly, I began to see that my supervisor did not like me and wanted to hinder me rather than help me. I felt stuck and I couldn't think of any solutions. Finally, toward the end of my last year of therapy many break-throughs occurred at once. I made other friends in my office, both professionals and clerical staff, who all seemed to have the same opinions on my supervisor and manager as I did. I also went to another, much larger office to receive training from three women who had worked for the parent company longer than I had. These women prodded me to talk about how I felt and gave me excellent advice on my choices. They let me know I was not alone and that other people in the firm felt the same way as I did. They understood my predicament perfectly and pointed out that I was completely losing my self-esteem. I realized for the first time that I did have choices and, like all other situations in life, I was not trapped.

I have stuck with my job and forged ahead when I really felt like running. But I also know that I would never have lasted with my self-esteem intact if it were not for these women and the fact that I finally opened up enough to trust them and talk to them. I have stayed in touch with all three of these women and seek their advice and counsel often.

My friendship with the woman in my office with whom I first spoke has grown and deepened over time. She has not only helped me cope from day to day on the job but has also helped me with men and relationships. She has been supportive, understanding, and, when necessary, constructively critical. However, before I could talk to her I had to learn a few lessons on my own. In the last year of therapy I learned where I leave off and others begin and when I am responsible and when the problem is someone else's. I no longer take responsibility for problems that don't belong to me.

Although I do not believe the person with whom I got involved during my last year of therapy is completely emotionally well, he was better than any of the men who went before him. The lesson, though, was in the fact that throughout the relationship I neither felt responsible for his problems nor took his problems on as my own. As the relationship ended, I did not feel like a bad or worthless person. I was angry with him, I was sad, and I missed him. I cried and called girlfriends, but I didn't feel the overwhelming depression I felt after my breakup with Bob; being alone was okay. I could go out and date without jumping into bed.

Afterward, when I found this man to be abusive and manipulative even as a friend, I got angry and stood firm. I chose not to be his friend because he was unable to respect my feelings.

I the last year of therapy I came to accept myself — my good traits and my bad traits. I no longer feel at odds with myself because at times I can be very aggressive, loud, and self-obsessed. I know that I am a good person with a lot to give but, like anyone, sometimes my less attractive traits get in the way of that. Today, I am comfortable with who I am.

When Ed announced my therapy would end soon, I was both excited and fearful. I asked him if people got depressed when their therapy ended and he replied they did. What he didn't tell me was that I would revert to whatever old negative behavior patterns would marginally work and that I might even acquire some new ones!

We had a trial two-month period of no sessions. In that time, I began to go on shopping binges, and I took a man home from a bar — not just any man, but the sickest one I could find: a practicing alcoholic. The next day I was afraid and disgusted with myself. I called Ed, not for support but out of a need to confess. He explained to me that people exhibited all kinds of behaviors and experienced many different feelings when therapy ended; I didn't have to practice this pattern now that I had recognized it. I felt better immediately.

However, my fear returned when Ed told me he wanted me to write about what happened to me in therapy. Although I wrote a great deal throughout my school years and my drug addiction, I had not been able to write creatively in sobriety. Even though this assignment was not "creative," I feared having to write at all. I believe, though, that it has been good for me, not only as a way of seeing my accomplishments but also as a way of resuming my writing.

As therapy ended and the time between sessions increased, Ed said I needed to write about how I felt. I wanted to skip over the end, avoid writing, and pretend it wasn't happening. For several weeks I felt nothing, which I had always found to be the softer, easier way. I asked, "What am I supposed to feel?" He answered with the usual — feelings of loss, grief, sadness, and so on. After talking to Ed, I thought about feeling, but I still didn't really feel anything.

Then things started to pile up at the office — work issues and personality issues. Problems with men followed, and I began searching for someone to talk to. No one quite fit the bill. I began to realize that I missed seeing Ed once a week. He made it possible for me to communicate with myself. Without our sessions it was hard for me to figure out where I stood, let alone listen to myself and make "wise" decisions. Lacking control over the situation at the office, I felt worse and worse; the pressure on me increased until I felt like I would explode. I drove home from work one day crying. I thought I was crying about work, but now I see I was beginning to grieve.

I was not completely depressed throughout those weeks, but I felt shaky, unstable, not well put together, and edgy. I had bad headaches, burning sensations, and severe stomachaches. I often felt like a victim again and I was sad. I seemed unable to focus my feelings directly on therapy and to say that was what I was sad about, but I know it was. Even on vacation I had physical aching symptoms, and the old pattern of getting sick after vacation came back.

At first I worked out at the gym a lot, thinking that would make it better. Then, on vacation in New York, I stopped working out and started eating. I spent my vacation with my parents and fell back into almost every destructive pattern I had ever established with my family. I accepted the free hotel room and meals and had to pay the price of doing exactly what they wanted to do when they wanted to do it. I listened to a constant drone of "I'm right" and "I told you so," the fights about money, and the complaints about everything. These patterns, though, did not change my feelings or help me to escape the sense of pain and loss. After vacation, when I had to fly back to New York for a seminar, I continued to eat and to go on shopping binges.

Often, I felt bewildered and lost, as if I were slipping backward. I felt as though I had all sorts of decisions to make about work and my dating relationships, but I was also afraid of change. I was confused about what I wanted. I felt as though I needed someone to bounce my "stuff" off of, but no one was there for me.

Even on the last day of therapy Ed wanted to talk about my feelings on ending therapy, but I could not get the words out in his office. Just the words, "I'll miss you," were difficult to say. Of course, the minute I got into my car and began to drive out the parking lot, I started to cry.

Later, at a party of a close friend, one of the women from my women's group asked how I was; again my eyes welled up when I answered that therapy had ended that afternoon. She smiled and said, "Hard, huh?" I nodded and walked away until I could calm down. When I left the party and drove home, I allowed myself to really sob. Ed was right: I do find it difficult to express my emotions in the moment. I seem to be most comfortable expressing feelings after the fact.

Since it ended, my feelings about therapy are mixed. Honestly, most of the time I don't even think about it — unless, of course, I happen to remember the deadline on this "chapter" hanging over my head like an ominous cloud. Other times, I miss therapy terribly. I do not always feel "well," and sometimes I can't really recall what I have learned, particularly about men and relationships. I know that my choices in men are vastly better than they were even a year ago, and I know that my behaviors and attitudes are improved, but I still don't feel completely put together in this area. Before therapy ended, Ed mentioned that I may need to come back for counseling when I get into a relationship. Now I see that he may be right.

Other than missing therapy occasionally, I feel good about having finished it. There are few activities in my life that I consider accomplishments, things that I actually saw through to completion; therapy is definitely one of them. I feel that I swallowed some big truths about myself and changed many of my negatives into positives. I feel proud.

It didn't happen in one room, for one hour of the week. It was a process of living life as a trial ground for a new person. It was really a process for which AA has coined the perfect phrase: uncover, discover, and discard. In therapy I did one more thing: build. Not only did I rid myself of the unnecessary baggage I was carrying around but I added a wealth of knowledge and happiness to my life.

Addendum

I have been separated from this chapter for a long time—almost a year. I must apologize to Ed and his editors because I have taken so long to finish this last little section. What is it that went wrong with this piece for so many months? I am not sure. It all seems to stem from some superstitious belief on my part—something about becoming totally well; not being able to return to therapy; truly becoming ready for a healthy and loving relationship. If I finish this piece, I may discover that all of these things are true— even though I know I can go back to Ed whenever I wish. I do have another fear—that I have not gotten any better! One day Ed said in a half joke that if I wasn't in a healthy relationship in two years, I should come back to see him. Well, while I have learned how to get rid of the sick ones almost before any relationship starts, I am not in a healthy relationship. And, while I usually believe that I will end up quite happy and with someone wonderful, I occasionally get down and think I failed in therapy because otherwise I would be in this relationship already.

Anyway, putting all my fears and superstitions aside, I really have gotten significantly better in the last two years. Almost a year ago, I told my parents that I could no longer participate in their dysfunction. I told them this in the most loving way I could, but I was also firm with them. I explained the various roles we played on our family stage and tried to let them know that my part was over.

At that time I also told them I could not look for a partner whom they would necessarily like or who would be Jewish. I quietly made the point that while a Jewish man would make fitting into the family a smoother process, I needed someone who would take my alcoholism very seriously. I explained to them that many of the Jewish men I had dated thus far did not really view me as someone with a problem or as someone who needed to stay involved at some level with AA and CA. They listened attentively to this and did not argue.

A few months later I had to make two decisions: the first was to let my parents know I would no longer accept any kind of money from them, the second was not to sleep in their house. After the trip to New York with my parents, I had decided not to accept any more money from them, which they give in the form of paying for air fare or hotel bills at family weddings. However, I had never actually told them I would no longer accept their money. I let them know this before our trip to Chicago for a cousin's wedding. I don't think I ever enjoyed myself more at a family function than at that wedding, and I am sure it was because I felt no guilt and no pressure about money or doing what everyone else wanted me to do because "they" were paying the bill.

The second decision—not to sleep at my parents house—has been difficult. It is inconvenient to travel to Los Angeles now and ask my cousin or one of my friends if I can stay with them. But the decision has also proven successful. Each time I visit my parents' home, I can see even more clearly the sickness thriving there. The house is crumbling around them; rooms are brimming with junk. My old room is filled so full of stuff and clutter, if you could walk across the floor to the bed, you still wouldn't be able to clear it off enough to sleep in it. What's in that room? Things Miss Havisham wouldn't have kept! The bouquets from my sister's wedding in 1985, huge pots from China, piles of assorted papers, an old coffee table. The closets in that room are filled with hangers. The wallpaper throughout the house is yellowed. The outside needs a paint job so badly, you can see the paint peeling off in large pieces. My parents' house has turned into the ugliest house on their street—a shame because it could be beautiful.

But this is not the important reason why I cannot stay in their home. Really, it's them. They are very critical and negative, and they know no boundaries. In addition, my mother constantly picks on my father. He shuts off his feelings and it all slides off his back. Frustrated, my mother starts to pick on me. Because I experience my feelings today, I become irritated. A friend of mine who came over for dinner one night said afterward that I had learned to build a strong ego because my mother was always attacking me. What he didn't know was how very weak my ego really is.

Probably the best reward from removing myself from my parents' home is that it has opened up my sister's eyes immeasurably. With no support in that house, she too is on the brink of not staying with my parents when she visits, and she is also questioning whether she wants her two small children around them.

I never thought that my actions or my getting well would affect the other members of my family, but in a small way they have. As shown in my discussion with them, my parents have begun to listen to me, and my sister is changing her role of peacemaker ever so slightly. While I do not envision great strides on the horizon, I do see things improving for me and possibly my family. I certainly feel a strong, loving, and supportive bond with my sister and sometimes I feel I am growing closer to my father. I can only hope that my mother is not threatened by these developing relationships, but I am certain she will be.

Well, that is my conclusion to therapy—basically that the growth continues and that the change in one family member definitely affects the rest.

I also want to thank Ed for all the time he spent with me and for gently opening my eyes to both the pain and joy in my life.

CHAPTER SEVENTEEN

The Application of the Basic Principles of Family Therapy to the Treatment of Drug and Alcohol Abusers

EDWARD KAUFMAN, M.D.
University of California, Irvine

The chapters in this book have focused on the multitude of therapeutic approaches that can be helpful in working with the families of substance abusers. The various contributors have emphasized their utilization of a synthesis of many approaches. We would also like to stress that each therapist should choose those systems of family therapy that best suit his or her personality, making use of those techniques that can be grafted onto one's own individual style and family background. The better we, as therapists, understand ourselves and our own families, the better we are able to choose and utilize appropriate therapeutic techniques. It is of interest that the integrative approach that we originally presented has become the primary mode of family therapy as we begin the 1990s.

This final chapter presents a review of the major approaches to family therapy and applies them to the treatment of substance abusers. The five basic approaches have been described by Anderson (1977) as psychodynamic, structural, communications, experiential, and behavioral. Although these five approaches have borrowed greatly from one another to a point where there is substantial integration, there are nevertheless discrete differences which, at times, have led to conflict between them.

Regardless of the approach to family therapy, if the substance abuser is habituated to drugs or is unable to attend sessions without being under the influence of a chemical, the first step is to get him or her off the substance, at least temporarily. Most therapeutic changes in dysfunctional families cannot be initiated until the regular use of chemicals is interrupted. Thus the first goal is to persuade the family to pull together to initiate detoxification. Generally this must be done in a hospital. In some cases it can be done on an ambulatory basis, such as outpatient detoxification from narcotics with methadone. If, after detoxification, the chemical-free state is not maintained, then a drug-aided measure to keep the client from abusing chemicals can be initiated. Antabuse, narcotic antagonists, or short-term, low-dose methadone maintenance can be used in this way. Some individuals will require longer hospitalization, twelve step groups such as AA, CA or NA, a day program, or a residential therapeutic community to ensure sufficient abstinence from chemicals to enable family therapy to occur. Therefore, the second step is to help the family to initiate and support these modalities. In Chapter 14, Berenson has described a system for working with the drinking alcoholic, but that emphasizes the importance of sobriety.

Psychodynamic Treatment

This approach is taken by many different theorists, among whom there have been considerable differences. These include Ackerman (1958), Bowen (1971), Nagy (1973), Zuk (1967), and Paul (1975). Since this author (Kaufman) is psychoanalytically trained, his own ideas about the contribution of this discipline will also be included. This approach has rarely been applied to substance abusers because they usually require a more active, limit-setting emphasis on the here and now than is usually associated with psychodynamic techniques.

Psychodynamic family therapy has come a long way from Ackerman's (1958) initial constructs, which urged the therapist to strip away the defense mechanisms of each family member so that the underlying conflicts become clear. Nevertheless, Ackerman was probably the first to state that family treatment focused on the behavior disorders of a system of interacting personalities — the family group.

The basic principles of the psychodynamic approach are, first, using history to uncover past actions that are inappropriately applied to the present (including the transference), and, second, creating change through insight. This insight is achieved through cognitive or affective reencounter with the past. In Bowen's systems approach the cognitive is emphasized, and every attempt is made to eliminate the use of affect (Bowen, 1971).

Systems theory examines triangulation and uses of the genogram and family chronology. Triangulation implies that whenever there is emotional distance or conflict between two individuals, these tensions will be displaced onto a third party, issue, and/or substance (e.g., alcohol, drugs).

The genogram has become a basic tool in many family therapy approaches. A genogram is a pictorial chart of the people involved in a three-generational relationship system that marks marriages, divorces, births, geographical location, deaths, and illnesses (Guerin, 1976). All significant physical, social, and psychological dysfunctions may be added to it. It is used to examine relationships in the extended family complex. The genogram is the first step for the therapist to take in understanding his or her own family as well as families in treatment. The genogram uses the symbols shown in Figure 17-1 (Guerin, 1976) to illustrate these relationships.

There are two cornerstones for the implementation of psychodynamic techniques: the therapist's self-knowledge and a detailed family history. Every family member will internalize a therapist's good qualities, such as warmth, trust, trustworthiness, assertion, empathy, and understanding. Likewise, they may incorporate less desirable qualities such as anger, despair, and emotional distancing. It is essential that a therapist thoroughly understand his or her own emotional reactions as well as their relationship to the therapist's family of origin (Bowen, 1971) and nuclear family. This self-knowledge can be obtained by some combination of intensive individual therapy, family therapy, and family of origin work. The lack of such knowledge will repeatedly interfere with the therapist's work with families. Some of these problems can be corrected by their being pointed out repeatedly, particularly in live supervision, but others cannot be shifted without psychotherapy or family of origin work. (Live supervision means that a therapist's work is viewed through a one-way mirror and instructions called in during the session or given during a break.)

The more a therapist understands about a family's history and prior patterns, the better he or she will be able to help that family not to repeat dysfunctional transactions or personalized transference reactions. When a couple is stuck, I will frequently use individual sessions for both partners

FIGURE 17-1

☐ = Male (placed to the left)

○ = Female (placed to the right)

△ = Child in utero

△Ab = Abortion

── = Marriage

D╱ = Divorce

| = Offspring (with oldest to the left)

X = Death

that focus on their own family of origin in an attempt to understand and shift patterns that are being repeatedly unchanged over several generations.

The psychodynamic concepts discussed will be countertransference, interpretation, resistance, and working through (Kaufman, 1985).

The Use of Countertransference

Many therapists are unable to utilize supervisory suggestions, even during live supervision. A major reason for this is countertransference. The therapist's uncontrolled emotional reactions may be to either the content or the accompanying affect of an issue being discussed. The therapist may have a countertransference problem toward the entire family or any individual member of the family and may get into power struggles. These are, of course, always to be avoided, and they can be if therapists understand their countertransference.

There are specific types of emotional reactions to substance abusers and their families. The identified patient's (IP) dependency, relationship suction and repulsion, manipulativeness, denial, impulsivity, and role abandonment may provoke countertransference reactions in the therapist. The therapist must be particularly sensitive about becoming a codependent, who tries to protect or is provoked to reject the substance abuser. The relationship between the therapist and the family replicates what happens within the family at home. One example of this is the therapist who alternates between saving and persecution, first allowing the substance abuser to do almost anything, even coming drunk to sessions, and then switching to a punitive position, and, for instance, terminating therapy for a brief slip. Therapists can learn a great deal about a family from tuning into the family's countertransference.

Judicious expression of these feelings may at times be helpful in breaking fixed family patterns. For example, sharing anger at a controlling parent may give the family enough support to express their anger despite their fears.

The Role of Interpretation

Interpretations can be extremely helpful if they are made in a complimentary way, without blaming, guilt induction, or dwelling on the hopelessness of long-standing, fixed patterns. Repetitive patterns and their maladaptive aspects to each family member can be pointed out, and tasks can be given to help them change these patterns. Some families need interpretations before they can fulfill tasks. An emphasis on mutual responsibility when making any interpretation is an example of the helpful fusion of structural and psychodynamic therapy.

Overcoming Resistance

Resistance is defined as behaviors, feelings, patterns, or styles that prevent involvement in therapy or that delay or prevent change (Anderson, 1983). In substance-abusing families, key resistance behaviors that must be dealt with involve the failure to perform functions that enable the abuser to stay "clean." It is important to understand resistances and have methods to overcome them. The greater the resistance by the family, the greater the demand on the therapist's energy and creativity. Resistance may be conscious or unconscious, purposeful or accidental, emanate from one family member or from the entire system (Anderson, 1983).

Some resistances, such as denial, rationalization, somatization, intellectualization, displacement, and acting out, occur in all types of therapy. Other resistances—collusions, myths, family secrets, scapegoat maintenance, pseudomutuality, and pseudohostility—are specific to family therapy (Anderson, & Stewart, 1983).

Every family has characteristic patterns of resistant behavior in addition to isolated resistances. This family "style" may contribute significantly to resistance; some families may need to deny all conflict and emotion and not tolerate any displays of anger or sadness, whereas others may overreact to the slightest disagreement. It is important to recognize, emphasize, and interpret the circumstances that arouse resistance patterns (Anderson & Stewart, 1983). However, the therapist must avoid labeling the behavior as "resistant" or directly confronting it, as this increases hostility and further enhances resistance. Rather, the reciprocal family interactions that lead to resistant behaviors should be pointed out. Anderson and Stewart's excellent book, *Mastering Resistance* (1983), contains many effective methods for dealing with specific resistances. Three general techniques that are widely applicable are (1) asking the family to "try it for just one week," (2) using the extended family and social network, and (3) "shaking things up" or making any change that will challenge the status quo.

Resistance can be focused on in the treatment contract—each family member agrees to cooperate in overcoming resistance. If a family is willing to perform its assigned tasks, then most resistances are irrelevant and/or can be overcome. Resistances such as blaming, dwelling on past injustices, and scapegoating can be directly forbidden by the therapist. The therapist may overcome resistance by joining techniques, including minimizing demands on the family to change so that the family moves more slowly but in the desired direction.

In psychodynamic psychotherapy, the concept of resistance is directly related to change; that is, analysis of resistance is integral and essential to the overall change process. In family therapy, resistance is more often viewed as an obstacle to be overcome. Nevertheless, overcoming family resistance in and of itself may lead to a great deal of positive family change.

Working Through

This important concept, derived from psychoanalysis, is quite similar to the structural concept of isomorphic transactions. It underscores the need to focus for an extended time on many different overt issues, all of which stem from the same dysfunctional core. Thus, in order to have real change, a family must deal with many aspects of a problem over and over until it has been worked through. In analysis, this is termed "the transition from intellectual to genuine or emotional insight." This process is much quicker in family than individual therapy because when an appropriate intervention is made, the entire family system may reinforce the consequent positive change. If the system later pulls the family's behavior back to the old maladaptive ways, then it becomes necessary to work the conflicts through in many different transactions until more stable change takes place.

One critical type of working through that is often neglected in family therapy is termination. Each individual member should be encouraged to share feelings of loss and, after long-term therapy, grief about giving up therapy and the therapist. No matter how skillfully the therapist attributes the family's gains to the family, they will experience loss. Some families will show their readiness to part by referring another family for treatment; on the other hand, some families reject the therapist's value system as a way of expressing their need to terminate (Whitaker, 1976). Sometimes it is very helpful for the therapist to share his or her own grief as a way of tapping these feelings in the family.

Once the names, ages, and dates of the above crucial events are filled in, other relevant facts can be added, including the family's geographical location of each member, frequency and type of contact, emotional and physical cutoffs, toxic issues, and critical historical events (Guerin, 1976).

I was requested to conduct a case conference at an alcoholism treatment program. I had asked to see a family that was receiving treatment at the clinic. Although the therapists there saw many couples, they had only one "family" in therapy, which they presented in absentia. One of the counselors asked the question, "Why should we do family therapy?" and then proceeded to give the family history, which is depicted in Figure 17–2 in genogram format. The identified alcoholic patient was Jim, a 46-year-old former marine. He married June, age 48, in 1975. It was the second marriage for both, and we learned that June's first husband, Joe, had also been alcoholic, and that they had been divorced in 1973. Jim had been married to Betty in 1946, and divorced in 1973. One son from each marriage was involved in treatment, and June's eight-year-old daughter also lived in the family. However, one therapist reported that Jim had two other children from his first marriage. June's therapist stated that June's father was an alcoholic, but no information was known about any of the other parents. (see Figures 17-3 and 17-4).

This points to another function of the genogram — uncovering gaps in information. The genogram also focused on a very crucial, but as yet unemphasized, aspect of this family — that both of June's husbands were alcoholic, as was her father — a critical issue in the treatment of June as well as the rest of this family. We also learned that Steve, a brother whose relevance had been minimized, had frequently drunk with his father and had been brutalized by him.

One session involving the reconstituted family of Jim, Tod, Phil, and Sara had been held. The family scapegoated Jim and ganged up on him about his drinking and brutality. He accepted this passively in the session, but retaliated against everyone as soon as they arrived home. June was held responsible for giving Jim his daily Antabuse, which he stopped taking after a few weeks. The family refused further joint sessions, but June, Tod, and

FIGURE 17-2   FIGURE 17-3

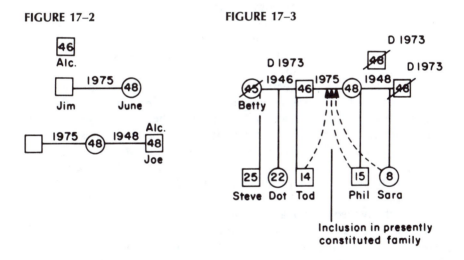

Inclusion in presently
constituted family

FIGURE 17-4

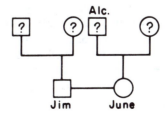

Phil continued to be seen individually. Jim, who was described as racist and sexist, had been assigned a black female therapist, which helped account for his reluctance to continue therapy. June should have been helped to become disinvolved from Jim's alcoholism, and assigning her the responsibility for the Antabuse was antithetical to this. I suggested that she be referred to a group at the clinic for the "significant others" of alcoholics. Tod had already begun to abuse drugs and alcohol, but avoided any discipline or punishment by pretending to behave responsibly and setting Phil up as the guilty culprit whenever his father appeared. Thus Phil would be inappropriately punished, a situation to which he reacted by becoming truant and engaging in an enmeshed, protective relationship with his mother.

Each son was thereby participating in a triangle with the parents, which separated the parental bond. It was suggested that a white male recovering alcoholic be assigned as Jim's individual therapist, with the hope that after Jim had received a few supportive sessions, the staff could utilize the knowledge gained from examining the genogram such that the family could resume conjoint sessions.

Another helpful diagnostic tool that has been developed by systems theorists is the family chronology, which is a time map of the major family events and stresses. The chronology enables the family and therapist to understand the evolution of family patterns over time (Guerin, 1976). The chronology, together with the genogram, "elicits the facts about the structural characteristics, membership, nodal events and toxic events in a family." One of the major benefits of this approach is that many important conflicts and stresses are learned about in the first session or two that otherwise might not come out until much later. The genogram and chronology emphasize another aspect of the systems approach, which is to deemotionalize and objectify data. This is not to deny that strong affect will be released in the early phases of this type of therapy. However, further attempts to achieve insight should be suspended until the initial affect is resolved.

Systems theory emphasizes that family therapy can be done even if only one individual is personally available. This is done in five phases: engagement, planning, reentry work, the work, and follow-through (Carter, 1976). This approach is also helpful in training family therapists to understand that individuation achieved by physical distancing is often only temporary and requires further insight.

My personal experience in the use of past history is that it is extremely helpful if it can be utilized without blaming, guilt induction, and dwelling on the hopelessness of long-standing, fixed patterns. A family chronology of each individual in family treatment is thus extremely helpful in providing information that can be used to enhance change. A psychoanalytic interpretation can be used directly to accomplish immediate shifts in the family system. An example of this technique was used with a family I saw in consultation. The 17-year-old son had lost his driver's license as a result of being in an accident while intoxicated. Immediately after disciplining the son for driving in a car where beer was consumed, the mother embraced and kissed him. When she was given him the task of disciplining him without embracing him, she was asked to remember that discipline did not necessarily mean being held by her feet and dipped head first into a bucket of water, which she had been subjected to as a child. Another mother, who could not ask for support from her husband, was reminded that she was not an army officer as her father, with whom she had identified, had been.

Structural Family Therapy

Although I have used a variety of family therapy techniques for many years, it is only since I have incorporated structural treatment into my methods that I have felt the family treatment of substance abusers has fallen into place. There are two articles on structural family therapy (SFT) in this book, one is by Minuchin, the founder of this system; the other is by Stanton and Todd. Stanton is a former associate of Minuchin who has focused on heroin addicts. Many basic principles of the theory and practice of SFT have not been developed in these chapters, nor applied to substance abusers. The following material on SFT is provided so that the reader may better utilize this relevant therapeutic system with substance abusers.

Family structure refers to the invisible set of functional demands that organizes the ways in which family members interact. The goal of SFT is a more adequate family organization achieved through manipulation and rearrangement of present patterns of interaction (sets) (Minuchin, 1974). Once the genogram has been developed and understood, a family can be examined by mapping boundaries and subsystems. Boundaries are the rules defining who participates in a family and how. These may be represented as (Minuchin, 1974a):

clear, ———— ———— ———— ———— ————

diffuse, or •

rigid. ————————————————————

Subsystems may be formed by generation, sex, interest, or function. The two most common subsystems are executive (parental) and sibling (Minuchin, 1974a).

The relationships between family may be designated as

affiliation or ═══════

overinvolvement. ═══════

Conflict is designated as disruption ──/─── . A coalition is depicted as } . Conflict frequently results in detouring to a third party, hence "detouring." ⊲⊢⊳

The "ideal family" could be mapped as: (M = mother, F = father, C = child)

There are clear boundaries between all individuals, affiliation between parents, and separation of the executive and sibling subsystems. The family therapist functions as a boundary maker who clarifies diffuse boundaries, opens rigid ones, and helps establish generational lines, particularly separating the spouse subsystem from the demands and needs of their own parents as well as those of their children. Probes, which are described later, are frequently used to help delineate these boundaries and their resilience.

The spouse subsystem must have sufficient complementarity and mutual accommodation to implement tasks. If it is dysfunctional, the therapist challenges the process without challenging motivation, and with a complementarity that focuses on the contribution of both parties (i.e., if a husband is controlling, the therapist might focus on the wife for letting herself be controlled). Depending on the family structure, the therapist might ask the husband to make all the decisions and the wife not to undermine them, or the wife to make all the decisions and the husband to support them. The child should have access to both parents but be excluded from spouse function. Parents cannot protect and guide without controlling and restricting. Children cannot grow and become individuated without rejecting and attacking (Minuchin, 1974a).

Therapeutic Tactics

The starting point is always the diagnostic family map, as described earlier, which helps to organize material and set goals. Therapeutic tactics are generally divided into two major categories: joining, which consists of those tactics which are used to enhance the therapist's leverage within the family, and change production, which is composed of strategies designed to change dysfunctional sets (Minuchin, 1974a).

In joining with the family, the therapist alternates between existential engagement and disengaged expert. The therapist must be capable of joining each subsystem, including the siblings. He or she must enable each family member to feel the therapist's respect for each one of them as an individual as well as his or her firm commitment to healing. The therapist must make contact with each family member so that each person is following the therapist, even when the family senses he or she is unfair.

There are three types of joining techniques: maintenance, tracking, and mimesis. *Maintenance* requires supporting the family structures and behaving according to the family's rules. The therapist may initially speak to the family through the family spokesperson or "switchboard." When a family is being pushed beyond its ability to tolerate stress, maintenance techniques can be used to lower stress. Other maintenance operations include supporting areas of family strength, rewarding, affiliating with a family member, supporting a threatened member, and explaining a problem (Minuchin, 1974a).

Tracking involves adopting the content of family communications and using the family's own special language to offer the therapist's ideas. As in hypnosis, if the patient refuses the therapist's suggestions, the refusal is manipulated into a form of obeying the command (Haley, 1977). The therapist enters the family as a supporter of family rules but makes the rules work in the direction of his goals for the family.

Mimesis involves the therapist's adopting the family's style and affect as reflected by the members' actions and needs. If a family uses humor, so should the therapist, but without double binds. If a family communicates through touching, then the therapist should also touch. The therapist might join an isolated father by sharing pipe utensils or by removing his tie or jacket at the same time as the father. Mimesis is frequently done unconsciously and is readily used here in contrast to individual psychoanalytic psychotherapy where it is generally contraindicated, as are most joining techniques. Sharing food in multiple-family therapy (MFT) encourages a joining of all the families present as well as uniting the therapist with each family.

Ultimately, the most significant joining occurs when the therapist communicates to the family that he or she understands them and is working with and for them. Thus, paradoxically, the most profound joining comes when the therapist challenges the family's dysfunctional maneuvers, which gives them hope that the therapist can make them better.

Joining with all family members may be too difficult for one therapist, particularly in families with an adolescent IP. I have often found it necessary to utilize a cotherapist who also treats the adolescent individually and can assume an advocate position in the family sessions. This enables me to better join with parents and facilitate their limit setting. In other cases, the adolescent is begging for limits underneath his or her bravado and a single therapist can easily join with the adolescent as well as the parental system.

Joining Classified by Proximity

In joining families from a close proximity, the therapist must push himself or herself to find positive aspects in all family members, particularly ones who are disliked (Minuchin, 1981). A therapist who finds something positive in someone unlikable will find that he or she then begins to like the individual. Another technique is for the therapist to look into his or her own personality and find similar (but hopefully less exaggerated) characteristics. By confirming these positives, the therapist will enhance the individual's self-esteem and help make the therapist like the person more. In general, pointing out several individual's complementary responsibility for negative behaviors will help the therapist to join with the entire system. In joining from a middle position, the therapist gathers important information by observing his or her own ways of interacting with the family without being incorporated into the family system. Here, it is often important to shift emphasis by tracking from content to process. In joining from a disengaged position, the therapist may have the role of an expert or director. Families who come to a therapist or institution that has an outstanding reputation will readily comply with tasks and other directives. Perhaps even more than most techniques, joining becomes much more spontaneous and less deliberate as therapy progresses.

Change Production or Restructuring   Unlike joining, change production involves a challenge to the family's homeostasis and takes place through restructuring the family sets. In restructuring, the therapist uses expertise in social manipulation, with the word *manipulation* being used in a positive rather than a pejorative sense. Techniques used for change production include the contract, probing, actualization, marking boundaries, assigning tasks, utilizing symptoms, manipulating, mood and support, education, and guidance (Minuchin, 1974a). Frequently a single therapeutic intervention will utilize many of these techniques. Families are motivated to change in three ways: (1) they are challenged in their perception of reality, (2) they are given alternatives that make sense, and (3) alternative transactions provide new types of relationships that are self-reinforcing. The reader is reminded that joining is necessary as a prerequisite and facilitator for change production, and that the therapist may alternate between joining and restructuring as needed.

The Therapeutic Contract   A prerequisite for change is the therapeutic contract (Minuchin, 1974a). This is a decision to concentrate on mutually agreed-upon, workable issues. The contract should always promise help with the problem that brought the family in before it is expanded to other issues. Goals should be mutual. If there is disagreement about them, then work on resolving disagreements should be made a part of the contract.

If family members are seen individually, a contract that everything will be shared with the entire family is preferable but not essential. Some information that is helpful to the therapist should only be revealed if there is specific permission to do so. The length of time that treatment will require should be included in the contract but can be extended at a later date.

Probing   The therapist affiliates with the family system and feels its pressures. Thus the therapist's spontaneous responses will probably be syntonic with the family system. If not syntonic, the therapist's responses will challenge the system and thus be valuable as therapeutic probes (Minuchin, 1974a). All therapeutic maneuvers are probes in that they test the family's resilience and ability to change. Probes may be repelled or may elicit three types of positive responses:

1. Assimilation without difficulty, leading to learning, but not necessarily to growth.

An example of this is a family in which the alcoholic father was deceased and three of the four siblings, who were all drug abusers, were still living with their mother. The fourth was in residential treatment, and the family was in MFT. Two of the drug abusers came to MFT but did not participate because they arrived intoxicated. The oldest daughter did attend MFT and described how she had extricated herself from extreme parental-child responsibilities by disengagement. As a probe, it was pointed out to her that with her pulling out, the drug-abusing siblings had all moved in, and were being taken care of by their mother in a way that was perpetuating their drug abuse and causing the mother to disorganize.

When she next returned to the group, the daughter related that her drug-abusing siblings would have to function on their own, as she was taking her mother to her house and putting her furniture in storage. The sister had reassumed her parental-child role in order to extricate her mother from a bad situation and force her siblings to sink or swim. Although she stated that this would only be until her mother could reestablish herself, she had assimilated the probe and made changes without any personal growth. However, her shift could eventually lead to growth for the family.

2. An accommodation that expands transactional patterns and activates alternative patterns.

This is seen when, without causing stress, probes lead to a decrease of infantilized enmeshed cross-generational ties and begin to build ties between distantiated parties. An example of this is when mothers are readily pulled away from their addict sons and given tasks that build the relationship with the husband or unaddicted children (e.g., buying a wedding dress with a daughter, taking a vacation with a husband).

3. An increase in stress, which, only after it unbalances homeostasis, leads to transformation.

This is a basic principle of all reconstructive therapies. In order to accomplish this, the therapist must have the respect of every family member and may have to unbalance the system in a way which may seem unfair. A common example of this is disengaging a severely enmeshed mother. This may seriously stress and unbalance a family. In some cases, the family may have to weather the storm of the mother's psychosis, depression, or psychosomatic illness. Excluding members from directly attending sessions or having them sit outside the family circle or behind a one-way mirror is a powerful tool that generally is a stressful probe. This kind of family crisis may occur when the addict stops using drugs while living within the family. If the crisis is not anticipated, the family may leave treatment. If it is resolved, the prognosis is quite good.

Alcoholic families frequently gravitate to a rehash of past fights, hoping to entrap the therapist into deciding who started the fight, who is wrong and right, and what the proper decision is. It is critical not to be triangulated into such a position but rather to have the family choose an as yet unresolved conflict and actualize their problem-solving methods or lack of them in the session. The first time a family arrives with an intoxicated member, they should not be dismissed but their actions observed, as this will demonstrate how they interact during a good proportion of their time together. Videotaping the session may provide them with this feedback. Of course, if intoxication is a repeated problem, then the family must develop a system to end the substance abuse.

Most families will enter therapy trying to look as good as possible. Actualizations unleash sequences that are beyond their control and permit the therapist to see the family as it really is. Three progressively elaborated types of actualization are utilized (Minuchin & Fishman, 1981). The first involves sequences that evolve spontaneously as families are permitted to be themselves in sessions. Next, the therapist plans scenarios that permit further natural interactions. These may utilize latent issues that are close to the surface and are beginning to evolve in session. In the most change-oriented types of actualization, the therapist has the family reenact in the session a pattern that is outside of their repetitive, maladaptive system and demonstrates new ways of problem solving.

Actualizing Family Transactional Patterns (Enactment)   Patients frequently direct their communications to the therapist; instead, they should be required to talk to each other. They should be asked to enact and relive transactional patterns rather than describe them (Minuchin, 1974b). They should show how they deal with substance abuse and other family problems rather than talk about them. It is our experience that roleplaying facilitates actualization of patterns (as well as changes them). Manipulating space is a powerful tool for generating actualization. Seating arrangements reveal much about alliances, coalitions, centrality, and boundaries. Asking two members who have been chronically disengaged and/or communicating through a third party to sit next to each other (removing their "switchboard" or "blockade") can actualize strong conflicts and emotions. Enactment minimizes intellectualization and changes boring family sessions into exciting, dynamic ones. It is only when directly observing family patterns in vivo that the therapist can accurately map the family, begin to restructure it, and ultimately evaluate the effects of interventions.

Marking Boundaries   This is achieved by delineating individual and subsystem boundaries (Minuchin, 1974a). Individuals should not answer for others, should be talked to and not about, and should listen to and acknowledge the communications of others. Family members should not feel for each other or read each other's minds. Nonverbal checking and blocking of communications should also be observed and, when appropriate, pointed out and halted.

The parental subsystem should be protected from intrusion by children, as well as by other adults inside and outside the family. Frequently, in order to strengthen the executive, parental system, sessions that exclude everyone but the parents should be held. Tasks (described below) to build closeness are suggested. Hospitalization may often be necessary with substance abusers and its boundary-marking powers should not be neglected. In general, when boundaries around a system are strengthened, that system functions better.

Assigning Tasks   Tasks may be assigned within the session or as homework (Minuchin, 1974a). As Stanton and Todd point out in this book, it is preferable for a task to be accomplished in the session before homework can be given. Talking clearly to each other is a frequent early task. Asking a central figure to be quiet for five minutes or a quiet member to conduct a monologue are simple in-session tasks that build shifts based initially on briefly maintaining changes. A distanced couple can be asked to explore each other and the space around them for five minutes.

Therapeutic homework assignments permit the therapist and the therapeutic work to "live" with the family until the next session. A father who had neglected his medical and dental care because he was worried about his son's drug abuse was asked to make an appointment with a dentist. Sons who always shop with their mothers have been asked to shop with their fathers or by themselves. Parents are frequently asked to take a vacation or to go out dancing or to dinner together. A husband and wife might be asked to plan a pleasant surprise for each other without telling about it. In response to this task a wife planned remarriage in a church and the husband planned for a new set of wedding rings. Disengaged fathers and sons are asked to do something that brought them close in the past. Fishing, attending sporting events, or even watching television together can help bridge gaps. After there is some common experience, a more intimate assignment such as taking a walk or talking alone for 30 minutes a day can be used.

There are four major purposes of tasks (Haley, 1977):

1. To gather information
2. To intensify the relationship with the therapist and to continue the therapeutic change process outside of the session
3. To enable people to behave differently.
4. To provide a focus and organization to the therapy

There are many *ways to motivate families to perform tasks,* some of which flow from other aspects of the principles of family therapy (Haley, 1977):

1. Join the family first, using family language, rituals, and metaphors to frame the tasks.
2. Choose tasks in the framework of family goals, particularly those that are directed toward correcting the symptoms of the IP.
3. Choose tasks that bring gains to each member of the family, particularly if there is conflict about doing the tasks.
4. Ask what solutions have been tried and failed, in order to enhance therapeutic leverage.
5. Ask what has worked in the past and why it was abandoned, as it may work again.
6. Accept the family's desperation, as it will motivate them to follow the tasks.
7. Have the family accomplish a task in session before they are given one for homework.
8. If family members are improving, use their progress to prescribe further change so they can improve even more.
9. Use your position as an expert to emphasize the need to perform the tasks.
10. Cut off disagreement about doing the tasks and tell the family to "do it anyway."
11. Provide the general framework of the tasks and let the family work with you to develop the specifics.

Haley (1977) has also made a number of suggestions for *how to give tasks properly* so that they will be successfully accomplished. I have also integrated these into my work as rules of thumb with substance-abusing families.

1. Be specific.
2. Give the tasks clearly, concisely, and firmly. Do not tentatively suggest them.
3. Formulate the tasks throughout the session, highlighting important areas, but be certain to emphasize all specific tasks at the end of the session.
4. Be as repetitious as necessary to have the family remember the tasks. Have each family member repeat and/or write down the tasks and his or her role.
5. Involve everyone in the household. One person may perform the task, another help, and another supervise, plan, or check on it.
6. Review how each family member may avoid performing his or her role or prevent completion of the task.
7. Make the task part of contracting at the end of each session.
8. Remember the task, writing it down specifically if this is necessary for full recall.
9. Review the task at the beginning of the next session.
10. Use failures as learning experiences to reveal the dysfunctional aspects of the family or the poor timing of the task. Support the family in what they have learned from not doing the task.
11. Remember that negotiations about the task may be more important than the actual task.
12. Do not let the family off easily, particularly if they forget the task. Explore why they let themselves (not the therapist) down.
13. Build incrementally from easy to more difficult tasks.
14. Use complementarity (e.g., emphasize the interactive need for both to change as well as the mutual benefits to both).
15. Tasks should be used to achieve structural change.
16. Always assign at least one task per session.
17. Avoid assigning more than two or three tasks in a session.

One exception to limiting tasks to two or three per session is taken from Richard Stuart's (1980) caring days technique in which each partner chooses 18 loving tasks and agrees to do 5 a day.

Paradoxical Tasks

In the time elapsed since the first edition of this book, paradoxical techniques first achieved great emphasis and subsequently were placed into a more moderate but utilitarian perspective. I prefer to use, in general, a more directive, structural approach, shifting to paradox mainly when the structural approach is not successful. I find that paradoxical techniques work best with chronically rigid, repetitive, circular, highly resistant family systems, particularly ones that have had many prior therapeutic failures (Papp, 1980). In other situations that seem to call for a paradoxical intervention, I find difficulty using this technique, perhaps because it feels dishonest to me, but in other situations application of a paradox feels much more comfortable and natural.

I will not use paradox when family motivation is high, resistance is low, and the family responds readily to direct interventions (Papp, 1981). I do not use paradox in crisis situations such as violence, suicide, incest, or child abuse; here, the therapist needs to provide structure and control. I avoid paradox with paranoid IPs and in families with widespread mistrust. I *will* use paradox to slow progress so that a family is chafing at the bit to move faster, or I may exaggerate a symptom to emphasize the family's need to extrude it. An example of this is encouraging a family to continue the "glories" of overindulging and infantilizing a substance abuser. A symptom that is an externalized acting-out of family conflicts (stealing, secret drinking) can be prescribed to be performed within the family so that the family can deal with it.

I am very comfortable in adding a paradoxical "twist" to certain interventions, particularly with highly resistant, defiant, oppositional, and/or repetitive family systems. An example would be stating to a family that they should change a behavior but that they are not ready to change it yet because they still need the behavior to serve some function in the family. I do not prescribe an individual's behavior without relating it to its function in the family system. The symptom should *only* be prescribed if its function in the system is understood and if it can be prescribed in a way that changes the functioning of the system. At times, it seems to me that paradox is a way of making a psychodynamic or system interpretation that motivates the family to change behavior in a way that classical interpretations do not (e.g., encouraging an adolescent to continue to act out because his parents need the behavior to argue about in order to avoid intimacy).

The beginning therapist should avoid several pitfalls in applying paradoxical techniques (Kaufman, 1985):

1. Being too pat and not tailoring the intervention to meet a family's specific needs
2. Being too mechanistic and distant and/or overlooking affective cues so that the family feels misunderstood
3. Using paradox to deal with your own frustration with the family's lack of change
4. Not relating the directive to the behavior's function in the family system
5. Giving up when the family doesn't respond immediately

6. Undoing the paradoxical thrust by supporting initial changes with a great degree of enthusiasm
7. Relying exclusively on paradox when direct restructuring is indicated
8. Being disappointed with your therapeutic efforts merely because you are not working paradoxically

Utilizing the Symptom   Paraphrasing a frequently quoted statement of Freud's, Minuchin (1974a) finds that the symptom of the identified patient is "the royal road to family structure." Thus, this symptom is in a very special position and the first goal should be to influence the rest of the family to help the identified patient with it. The symptom is not dealt with directly by the therapist. If the symptom of some other family member is focused on before the IP's symptom is alleviated, the family will frequently resist strongly or leave treatment.

Relabeling or reframing the symptom may be very helpful, as when drug abuse is termed an attempt to bring divorced parents together or to alleviate parental child responsibilities. Relabeling can be used to gradually broaden the focus of treatment.

Manipulating Mood   The family's affect can be taken in as a joining operation and then manipulated or exaggerated to achieve change (Minuchin, 1974a). After several sessions with a family in which the adolescent son had been truant and smoking pot constantly, the father came in furious, depressed, and ready to quit therapy and leave the family. The son and mother were both quite depressed. My cotherapist asked me to play the son's "alter ego" to facilitate communication between the son and the father. I stated that the family's mood had made me feel too depressed to try to communicate, as I felt the son had subtly undermined the therapeutic contract in order to bring his father's anger back upon him and his mother.

I reluctantly agreed to serve as alter ego as a way to shift this apparently stuck family. In doing so I became in touch with the son's anger at having lived up to so much of the contract and not yet receiving any support and "strokes" from his dad. The mother, in her traditional role in the family, tried to cheer me up by pointing out to me and the family all the gains they had made. We were then able to focus on the father and his need to perpetuate his angry state at the unhealthy coalition between his wife and son. The father then shared with us the fact that his anger at his son was similar to his anger at his brother, who had constantly "ripped him off" and had been supported by their mother in doing so. By then I was out of my depression. I gave the family the task of involving the father in the first step of decision making instead of the last step, where he was the bad guy if he refused and felt ripped off if he agreed. When they returned the following week, they reported that father and son were able to communicate in an open way, which was unique for them.

The alter ego is a powerful technique for manipulating mood. In this case, my use of my own "depression" was one way of shifting the family's mood, and the alter ego, still another. A therapist reported to me that he became so depressed in dealing with a disengaged, ungiving family that he began to cry, as he had done with his own similar family. When he shared this experience, the rigid family system opened up.

Support, Education, and Guidance   The support and nurturance that a family offers its members must be understood and encouraged (Kaufman, 1985). Since most addict families do not know how to give these "strokes," they must be taught and enhanced with embers of support kindled like sparks into a fire. The therapist may have to assume executive functions as a model and then step back so the family can assume them. Ex-addicts who have "made it" are very valuable in teaching addicts how to reintegrate in the straight world with straight friends. In MFT, parents teach other parents to "close the back door" and help their children individuate. Families are taught how to recognize when their child is using drugs and how to not support it.

Balancing and Unbalancing

Balancing techniques tend to support a family, and unbalancing techniques tend to stress the family system. Balancing is similar to Minuchin and Fishman's (1981) complementarity. It challenges the family's views of symptoms as part of a linear hierarchy and emphasizes the reciprocal involvement of symptom formation, while supporting the family. Mutual responsibility should be emphasized and tasks that involve change in all parties should be given. The therapist must be aware that an individual's view of his or her responsibility for a symptom may be so skewed that what the therapist feels is balancing may feel very unbalanced and unfair to that person.

Unbalancing involves changing or stressing the existing hierarchy in a family and should only be attempted after the therapist has achieved sufficient power through joining. The therapist unbalances by affiliating with a family member of low power so this person can challenge his or her prescribed family role, or by escalating a crisis. The latter is done by emphasizing differences, blocking typical transactional patterns, developing implicit conflict, and rearranging the hierarchy (Minuchin & Fishman, 1981).

The therapist may also paradoxically unbalance by affiliating with a dominant member in order to elicit a challenging response from those of less power. The therapist's affiliation unbalances the system and interrupts rigid, repetitive cycles. The therapist may alternate affiliations so that the family explores new ways of relating rather than competing for a position.

When a therapist joins in alliance or coalition with a family member or subsystem, it must be motivated by restructuring rather than the likes and dislikes of the therapist. It is also critical that the therapist be able to extricate himself or herself from these alliances when necessary. If support of one member is intolerable for the family, then the therapist may have to retreat to a more balanced approach. Unbalancing may be difficult for some therapists because it feels "unfair."

Creating Intensity   The purpose of creating intensity (Minuchin & Fishman, 1981) is to enable the family to hear and incorporate the messages sent by the therapist. One simple way to be heard is to repeat either the same phrase or different phrases that convey the same concept. Another way of creating intensity, isomorphic transaction, uses many interventions to attack the same underlying dysfunctional pattern. The amount of time a family spends on a transaction can be increased or decreased, as can the proximity of members during an interaction. Intensity can also be created by resisting the family's pull to get the therapist to do what they want.

This concludes the section on structural techniques. These techniques are not used as discrete separate entities, as most interventions simultaneously use two or more change modalities.

Jay Haley has utilized and developed many systems of family therapy that bridge several of the five general categories we have described. He began with important works on communications before he teamed up with Minuchin and SFT. He has evolved his own system of therapy, which includes many behavioral techniques as well. His *Problem Solving Therapy* (Haley, 1977) is highly recommended to the reader, particularly Chapters 1 and 2, which cover the first interview and giving directions. Haley describes four stages of the first interview: a social stage, in which the family is greeted and made comfortable; a problem stage, in which the presenting problem is stated; an interaction stage, in which members talk to each other in a way that actualizes the conflict; and a goal-setting stage, when the family spells out the changes it seeks. These stages are deceptively simple. When employing them, it must be emphasized that no standard approach works with the wide range of problems that families present. With substance abusers, a more authoritative approach is frequently necessary. These stages are a matrix upon which flexibility and spontaneity can be superimposed.

The First Interview as Model of Continued Family Therapy

In the social stage, the therapist functions as a host. The therapist should shake hands with each member, introduce himself or herself individually, and remember everyone's name. Everyone should be made comfortable and should be given a flexible choice of where to sit so that they can have a full range of seating possibilities. Seating choices are a strong initial key to family structure. Social interaction should take place with each family member before the problem is presented. This initial period of socialization is essential in all therapies. It is particularly important with Mexican-American families, where its omission would be considered gross rudeness on the part of the therapist. This phase is characterized by early joining techniques, particularly maintenance and tracking. In subsequent sessions, a brief social interaction should begin the session.

Most families will feel quite defensive, particularly when their being asked to come in implies to them that they are the problem rather than the IP. At this stage, the therapist should gather information but not share it, as this could increase the inevitable defensiveness of the family. The family's mood should be noted and matched. The parent who attaches quickly to the therapist may be trying to involve him or her in a coalition.

The onset of the problem stage is demarcated by a shift in posture and voice tone on the part of the therapist, with responsive shifts by the family. The therapist may state what he or she knows, including his or her position on family therapy, and ask for everyone's ideas about the problem or merely ask what the problem is (Haley, 1977). With recognized substance abusers, the problem of the family's reactivity can be explored by questions such as: "What's it been like to have Johnny in the family and abusing drugs?" or "How do you handle Sheila's drug abuse and requests for money?" or "What are the problems in this family?" The *s* on the end of *problems* gives the family the opportunity to look at problems other than those of the IP.

General and ambiguous questions have the advantage of giving the family members room to display their point of view (Haley, 1977). Haley recommends that "the adult who seems less involved with the problem be spoken to first and the person with the most power to bring the family back be treated with the most concern and respect." It is not a good idea to start with the addict and ask him or her why the family is there, as it may appear as if the therapist is blaming the IP for everyone being there. Some therapists start with the least involved child. I find that this child can frequently provide an objective view of the family but is too passive and reticent to be put in the spotlight at the beginning of the session.

The therapist should attempt to define the problem clearly so that the dysfunctional family sets can be changed by using that problem as a lever (Guerin, 1976). Everyone should have a turn (i.e., "by preventing an over-talkative parent from being the only one who talks, the therapist is actually helping him or her" (Guerin, 1976). Although one can assume that a child's problems are a reflection of marital problems, the therapist should not comment directly on indirect communications such as nonverbal messages at this stage. While focusing on the IP, the family should be led to begin to look at the problem in broader terms.

In subsequent sessions, the problem statement is replaced with a description of the family's participation in the tasks assigned in the prior visit. The interaction or enactment stage has been described earlier in the section on actualization in SFT. Haley adds some important points here, including the idea that when two people are talking, a third should be introduced into the conversation so that ultimately everyone is talking to one another (Haley, 1977). Actions should be fostered, as they reveal more about the family than words. If the father's role is to be controlling and hostile, he can be asked to act that way so the family can respond to him.

In ensuing sessions, the enactment will often focus on an issue that arises out of the family's difficulty with the tasks or builds new growth based on a successful task. Defining desired changes help us to know what everyone in the family, including the IP, wants from the therapy. This leads to the therapeutic contract, which we also described in the section on SFT. "The clearer the contract is, the more organized the therapy will be" (Haley, 1977). The therapist can center the therapy around the presenting problem while achieving other goals that he or she feels are essential for families of substance abusers. The presenting and crucial problem is always the substance abuse of the IP but it must be restated in an interactional form that renders it solvable. Thus rigid problems should be made more ambiguous so there is more room for growth.

An initial goal is frequently to enlist the family's support in initiating detoxification, hospitalization, residential care, or drug maintenance, when necessary. Family support is often essential in helping the IP to stay in treatment as long as necessary. The next goal with the family is to facilitate a drug- and alcohol-free state and/or gradual return to society as a priority. When the substance abuse is not sufficiently severe to intrinsically prevent family therapy from occurring, then therapy can begin without requiring a totally drug-free state as an initial goal.

The first interview should end with setting up the next appointment. Important members of the family system, such as grandparents, housekeepers, siblings, cousins, aunts, and uncles who did not attend, should be invited. Other family members who are actively abusing chemicals present a problem. They should be invited to at least one session to understand their effect on the family and to see how the family deals with them. However, if their substance abuse is too disruptive to the family therapy, then they may be excluded from the treatment until their abuse subsides. Future sessions will also have to deal with the family's efforts to enter that abuser into appropriate treatment. Once that person has achieved a drug-free state (or a level of occasional substance abuse), then the former substance abuser must be included in the treatment, as he or she is invariably crucial to the abuse pattern of the IP. In my experience, two drug-abusing siblings can be treated in the same residence.

The therapist may assign homework (tasks) at the end of the first session, particularly if the family has responded to directives in the session and the therapist has initiated adequate rapport. Tasks in the first and subsequent sessions are made a part of the contract, which enhances the family's commitment to follow through with them.

Communications Therapy

The proponents of this system include Haley (1977), Watzlawick (1974), Satir (1972), and Bateson (1956). However, pointing out and shifting problems in communication is an important aspect of all therapies. In this system the IP's symptom is viewed as a communication to the family and as evidence that more appropriate forms of communication are blocked (Bateson, 1956). Incongruent messages are focused on, particularly when nonverbal communication is at variance with the verbal message (Bateson, 1956). One of the earliest contributions of these therapists was the double bind (Anderson, 1983), which was initially demonstrated in the families of schizophrenics. The four characteristics of the double bind are: (1) two different messages are given simultaneously, frequently one verbal and one nonverbal; (2) the receiver of the message is intimately involved with the sender and so cannot become detached from the message; (3) the messages are mutually exclusive; and (4) the receiver is not permitted to comment on the double bind or express his or her feelings about it.

Double binds are present in all families, and more in the families of substance abusers than in "normal" or "neurotic" ones. However, double binds are of a different quality in the families of substance abusers than those of schizophrenics. In the former, double messages are clearer, more overt, and less confusing. However, the potential drug abuser may find that drugs are the only way he or she can leave the field of communication. The retreat to adolescent drug abuse then interferes with the development of alternative ways of dealing with confusing messages.

The goals of communication-centered therapy are to correct discrepancies in communication. This is achieved by having messages clearly stated, by clarifying meanings and assumptions, and by permitting feedback to clarify unclear messages (Bateson, 1956). The therapist acts as an objective governor of communication who teaches people to speak clearly and directly in a structured, protected experience. This can be facilitated by a simple exercise. One partner speaks for 5 minutes without interruptions, while the other listens with encouragement. The second partner tells what he or she has heard. The first partner then provides helpful feedback.

The following 10 rules of communication are an example of individualized rules that were developed with a 24-year-old cocaine addict and his 22-year-old wife after observing several enactments in the early phases of their couple therapy.

Rules of Communication

1. Finish discussing a subject before you jump to another. Skipping around from one topic to another is poor communication and is usually based on anger and hurt. Thus nothing is resolved and anger escalates.
2. *Don't assume* that you know what the other person means — if you think someone is cutting you down (or complimenting you), check it out before you react.
3. *Listen* to the other person *without interruption*. This goes with number 2 — you won't have a two-way communication unless you really hear what the other person is trying to say.
4. Don't put words in the other person's mouth by answering or talking for them. This makes the other person angry because he or she feels that you have no respect for them or their opinions. They will get particularly angry if you're wrong but being right will also incite your partner.
5. Talk to each other instead of through a third person, particularly either of your parents.
6. Don't bring up past or present relationships with others when you're trying to prove a point about the relationship between you two. This only confuses the issue and changes the subject. Generally avoid the past when dealing with present problems.
7. Don't replay old arguments over and over again — this solves nothing, it just brings up old hurts and resentments. After you have repeated an argument, either of you has the right to call a truce.
8. Don't make promises or threats that you don't really mean, particularly about leaving.
9. Don't use words like *never, always,* or *you should.* Statements like *now, sometimes,* and *could you* are much better ways to communicate. There are always exceptions to *never* and *always.* In addition, they make the other person angry because they are judgmental, critical, pessimistic, and patronizing.
10. Don't call the other person names — hanging a label on someone means that he or she will hear only the name and not the point you are trying to make. It *will* make the other person angry, but it won't help you solve a problem.

Experiential Therapy

Most family therapists who work with substance abusers are experiential in that they deal with the immediate moment of experience between themselves and the family. Whitaker (1976) describes how involving this approach is for the therapist. "It became clear that my personal growing edge must become my central objective in every relationship if experiential therapy was for my experience, then patient modeling could be for real. If I could change, they might try to." Thus the therapist is involved as a real human being with the use of substantial self-disclosure. The therapist is a genuine, involved person who uses common sense skill and in guiding intimate conversation in order to achieve change.

Behavioral Therapy

Once again, much of the change that is achieved by successful family therapists involves the use of behavioral techniques, even when the therapist is not specifically schooled in this theoretical approach. Malout and Alexander (1974) and Stuart (1971) are leading proponents of a purer behavioristic approach. They emphasize that the parents' responses to the child continue his or her undesirable behavior. Thus the parent is taught extinction of these responses and how to give positive reinforcement for desired behavior. Paul Wood (1977) suggests a modified behavioral approach in which the child is never punished because being punished may be seen by the child as an alternative to desired behavior. Wood points out that if parents join together and present a clear message to the child with no alternatives, then behavior can be modified.

Behavioral therapy techniques can be taught to therapists and to patients more easily than many other family approaches. Noel and McCrady (1984) have clearly listed these steps as applied to alcoholic couples, but they can be readily applied to couples with abuse of other drugs.

1. *Functional Analysis.* Couples are taught to understand their interactions that maintain drinking, and the alcoholic is taught to quantify alcohol consumption (three sessions).
2. *Stimulus Control.* The therapist teaches specific techniques to avoid drinking by viewing it "as a habit triggered by certain antecedents and maintained by certain consequences." The client is taught to avoid or change these triggers (two sessions).
3. *Rearranging Contingencies.* The client is taught techniques to provide reinforcement for efforts at achieving sobriety: (a) reviewing the positive consequences of sobriety as contrasted to a list of negative consequences, three to four times daily; (b) self-contracting for goals and specific rewards for achieving these goals; and (c) covert rein-

forcement by rehearsing in fantasy a scene in which the client resists a strong urge to drink (Noel & McCrady, 1984) (three sessions).

4. *Cognitive Restructuring.* Clients are taught to modify self-derogatory, retaliatory, or guilt-related thoughts, which often precipitate drinking. Clients question the logic of these "irrational" thoughts and replace them with more "rational" ideations.

5. *Plan Alternatives to Drinking.* Clients are taught techniques for refusing drinks through role playing and covert reinforcement (one session).

6. *Problem Solving and Assertion.* The client is helped to decide if a situation calls for an assertive response and then, through roleplaying, develops effective assertive techniques. Clients are to perform these techniques twice daily as well as to utilize them in a difficult situation that would have previously triggered the urge to drink.

7. *Maintenance.* The entire course of therapy is reviewed and the new armamentarium of skills is emphasized. Clients are encouraged to practice these skills regularly as well (final session).

In closing this final chapter, Minuchin's (1974a) phrase, "The road is how you walk it," comes to mind. We have provided a variety of techniques from which the therapist can choose those most suitable to his or her needs. However, one should never use a technique that intrinsically runs counter to one's grain. Psychoanalysis was very appealing to me when I was in training, and I was drawn to it largely because of peer pressure. However, I found structural family therapy to be much more suitable to my personal style. Still, psychoanalysis provided a body of knowledge that I have found extremely valuable in every therapeutic contact I have ever made. This is particularly true when the past is not used as a "cop-out," but rather as a facilitator to enable immediate change to occur. Strategic techniques have been more difficult for me to integrate, but I have slowly incorporated this with which I am more comfortable. Many elements determine how we walk the road of family therapy.

I hope that the material in this chapter will stimulate the reader to study the original source material so that these intelligent minds can be experienced more fully. The ideas I have presented are meaningless if one merely reads them. They must be tried and tested before one can decide whether they fit one's personality and approach as a therapist and can be used to change other human beings within the setting of families.

Endnote

1. In the alter ego technique, each therapist sits beside a family member and speaks for that person. It is used to tap underlying feelings or help change behavior.

References

Ackerman, N. W. (1958). *The psychodynamics of family life.* New York: Basic Books.

Anderson, C. (1977). Lecture delivered at Orange County Department of Mental Health, October 6.

Anderson, C. M., & Stewart, S. (1983). *Mastering resistance: A practical guide to family therapy.* New York: Guilford Press.

Bateson, G., Jackson, D. D., Haley, J., & Weakland, J. H. (1956). Towards a theory of schizophrenia. *Behavioral Science, 1,* 251-264.

Boszormenyi-Nagi, I., & Spark, G. (1973). *Invisible loyalties.* New York: Harper & Hazelden.

Bowen, M. (1971). Family therapy and family group therapy. In H. Kaplan & B. Sadock (Eds.), *Comprehensive group psychotherapy.* New York: Williams & Wilkins.

Carter, E., & Orfanides, M. M. (1976). Family therapy with one person and the family therapist's own family. In P. Guerin (Ed.), *Family therapy,* (pp. 193-219). New York: Gardner Press.

Guerin, P. J., & Pendagast, E. G. (1976). Evaluation of family system and genogram. In P. J. Guerin (Ed.), *Family therapy,* (pp. 450-464). New York: Gardner Press.

Haley J. (1977). *Problem solving therapy.* San Francisco: Jossey-Bass.

Kaufman, E. (1985). *Substance abuse and family therapy.* Orlando, Fl: Grune & Stratton.

Malout, R. E., & Alexander, S. F. (1974). Family crisis intervention: A model and technique of training. In R. E. Handy & J. G. Cull (Eds.), *Therapeutic needs of the family* (pp. 47-55). Springfield, IL: Charles C. Thomas.

Minuchin, S. (1974a). *Families and family therapy.* Cambridge, MA: Harvard University Press.

Minuchin, S. (1974b). Structural family therapy. In S. Arieti (Ed.), *American Handbook of Psychiatry* (Vol. II, pp. 178-192). New York: Basic Books.

Minuchin, S., & Fishman, H. C. (1981). *Family therapy techniques.* Cambridge, MA: Harvard University Press.

Noel, N. E., & McCrady, B. S. (1984). Behavioral treatment of an alcohol abuser with the spouse present. In E. Kaufman (Ed.), *Power to change: Family case studies in the treatment of alcoholism.* New York: Gardner Press.

Papp, P. (1980). The Greek chorus and other techniques of paradoxical therapy. *Family Process, 19,* 45-58.

Papp, P. (1981). Paradoxical strategies and countertransference. In A. S. Gurman, (Ed.), *Questions and answers in the practice of family therapy.* New York: Brunner/Mazel.

Paul, N. L., & Paul, B. B. (1975). *A marital puzzle.* New York: Norton.

Satir, V. (1972). *People making.* Palo Alto, CA: Science & Behavior Books.

Stuart, R. B. (1971). Behavioral contracting within the families of delinquents. *Journal of Behavioral Therapy and Experimental Psychiatry, 2,* 1-11.

Stuart, R. B. (1980). *Helping couples change.* New York: Guilford.

Watzlawick, P., Weakland, J. H., & Fisch, R. (1974). *Change: Principles of problem formulation and problem resolution.* New York: Norton.

Whitaker, C. A. (1976). Family is a four-dimensional relationship. In P. J. Guerin (Ed.), *Family Therapy* (pp. 182-192). New York: Gardner Press.

Wood, P., & Schwartz, B. (1977). *How to get your children to do what you want them to do.* Englewood Cliffs, NJ: Prentice Hall.

Zuk, G. H., & Boszormenyi-Nagi, I. (Eds.) (1967). *Family therapy and disturbed families.* Palo Alto, CA: Science & Behavior Books.

Index